Last in Line
An American Destiny Deferred

Jamal T. Mtshali

To David Russell Parker, Esq.
(1950-2014)
May You Rest in Peace

Chicago, Illinois

Front cover illustration by Damon Stanford

First Edition, First Printing

Printed in the United States of America

ISBN #: 0-910030-22-7

ISBN #: 978-0910-030-229

Table of Contents

Preface iv

Introduction ix

1 "Get Over It" 1

2 A Model Myth 21

3 The Injustice System 39

4 Affirmative Inaction 77

5 The Miseducation of the…African American? 95

6 The Plexiglas Ceiling 117

7 Hooked on Ebonics 129

8 Failure to Thrive 143

9 A National Salvation 163

Conclusion 181

Endnotes 185

Preface

It's trite to say, but the confines of this preface do not offer sufficient space to thank my loved ones. Between research, writing, and publication, *Last in Line* has been seven years in the making. I have forged through many late nights, caffeine-induced stupors, and moments of frustration in search of truth. All journeys are born of collaboration; mine would not be possible without the calibration facilitated by numerous inspirations.

I thank my ancestors for inspiring me in many ways. This is a story not only of what so many endure in America today, but also of what you endured in America and the world for generations. Your experiences both defined and confined your lives but did not limit or imprison your humanity. While writing this I have sometimes felt myself going into autopilot, my hand somehow operating by the will of a force outside myself. When this happens, I know your collective spirit possesses me and conveys the sentiments of eras in which I did not live.

I owe thanks to the innumerable authors, researchers, nonprofit organizations, think tanks, and beyond that developed much of the empirical content this work attempts to do justice. *Last in Line* began with an ambitious thesis endeavoring to profile America's racial dynamic in context of both historical and contemporary social systems to enlighten the public and safeguard America's soul. I embarked on this mission with the belief that the sanctity of America's soul is threatened if even one of its components is denigrated. During my first year writing this, I dithered. As I sifted library shelves and combed endless databases, my path became clear. All of your works proved monumental in affirming my direction. That your group is defined by such admirable diversity is fitting of a work devoted to the idea and affirms the truth that the battle against institutional racism cannot be waged on separate black, white, Asian, or Hispanic fronts, but must be waged along the battle lines of a united, harmonious front.

I thank my parents, Dr. Progress Q. T. Mtshali and Marya J. Parker, NP, and my siblings, Marya and Marcus. You unite in a pillar of fortitude and standard of academic excellence from which I will continue to draw inspiration. I am grateful to be part of this family. I thank my late uncle David Parker, Esq., who was the first to read the completed manuscript and offered such sound advice. We love you. May you rest in peace.

I thank both the Richland County, South Carolina Public Library and Montgomery County, Maryland Public Library systems. It was inside the latter where I first outlined the contents of *Last in Line* and between the walls of the former that I finished the original manuscript. Without your facilities and resources, my writing of this book would not have been possible. We must strive so that everyone in America, regardless of age or background, has access to the basic tools that can enable them to articulate their visions and philosophies into works such as this.

I thank Bud Ferillo, director and producer of the documentary exposing South Carolina's neglect of its public school system, *The Corridor of Shame*, for making himself available to me. In my quest to contribute to the salvation of America your work has allowed me to better understand the circumstances necessitating that salvation.

I thank all those loved ones who have assisted in the completion of this book—unbeknownst to them. *Last in Line* has been a top-secret mission; over the past seven years I have unveiled little to anyone. I hope my loved ones will be both delighted and edified when accessing these newly declassified documents. Through personal struggles, abundant amounts of school work, and in spite of imperious deadlines breathing down my neck, I have received solace and strength from you all in myriad ways. I could not have written this book without you.

Lastly, I thank President Obama. I thank him not for his politics or who he is, but because his presence in the White House has taught Americans more about racism than perhaps anything else in recent history. His election is a confirmation of the existence of the American dream that eluded so many for so long; it is also a requiem for those cast in American night terrors that strike with eerie lucidity and recur *ad infinitum*.

Seven years prior to this book's final edit, I exited a cozy station and made my way through joint-stiffening, glacial treatment uncharacteristic of Maryland's temperance. I marched Washington's streets in throngs reminiscent of Roman legions, warming my hands with circles of merriment, singing and dancing an unprecedented episode of American communion. Ours was a 21st century Great March, not comprised of Americans calling for freedom but Americans heralding freedom's arrival.

As I walked the streets and lawns of Capitol Hill, I thought of my ancestors and their bondage beneath Old Glory. President Lincoln's first inauguration was their auspice, the sign of a future in which their chains would be cast off and melted into material with which a new, free America would be cast. Paralyzing chills came not from January's pricks and pierces, but the vision that my ancestors may have regarded Abraham Lincoln the way I on this day regarded Barack Obama.

A silhouette rose from the east; rays shone amid the multitudes along the Western front. "Not in my lifetime." I couldn't help recalling the words I, born a score and seven years following Freedom Summer, often spoke with a tone of practical resignation. My ancestors' words came into my hands a truism and dissipated in inaugural air a platitude. A hurried gust brushed my 18-year-old face, bypassing it to seize and escort the falsehood elsewhere. It was *persona non grata* in presence of the revered utterance, "God bless the United States of America."

A chuckle froze. It turned me. "Man—racism is finished. It is *dead*." He gazed for seconds, a heavy grin complementing eyes radiating limitless optimism. He turned toward the projector in injected stiffness, freeze frame belying motion picture. I tried to mirror his effervescent smirk, but found paralysis—a pensive discomfort unbefitting, perhaps even insulting of, this moment.

For the rest of the afternoon as the world celebrated Barack Obama's ascent to the Oval Office, I mulled that stranger's words. Friends and family,

Last in Line: An American Destiny Deferred

some who witnessed the height of the Civil Rights Movement, marveled at images of the president and first lady greeting the nation. I could not marvel, for I could not help chewing that late twentysomething's verse. It seemed to fly in the face of the dispiriting elements of American scripture I had known. Like the Book of James Byrd. Its ink dried when I was seven years old. What was that—solitary confinement? An outlying emblem of hatred long since banished from America's heart? Given the experiences of my family members, my friends—even myself—I was reluctant to accept his prophecy. It seemed unfulfilled—his belief that race was anywhere near the finish line. I heard praises of victory but no buzzer flatlining us from scorched Earth to Eden's divinity.

I entertained that he was perhaps right. Perhaps I'd glorified myself in some malcontent archetype, covering my eyes and ears as strange, partisan fruit of petulance. This was not James Byrd's day—this was Barack Obama's day. Reformation was upon us. This was America's dawn, the day which would heal the sufferings of the multitudes—every James Byrd. America rejoiced in a new Pontifex Maximus—a man with whom I shared not only blackness but first-generation African descent—yet all I could do was groan. America saluted a black president hoisted by a variegated will, entertaining an era free of the sit-ins, bus boycotts, and freedom rides that convened about an operating table excising cancers threatening our Constitution with a threadbare fate. Many died for our sins, nailed to fiery crosses, mocked by unholy masses, blood-sacrificed unto Sodom's devils. They rose from the dead in schools, neighborhoods, and colleges convoked in Christ's name. The day of reckoning portended in the prophecy of resurrection dawned. I blasphemed. My wanton thoughts were libel, spilling blood upon consecrated soil.

As I walked Washington's streets on inauguration day, disparity accosted me. Its profile was black—and in the neighborhood of a palace where, because of the discriminate acquiescence of mortgage lenders, a black man and his family would soon reside. Middle-aged black men idling on porches, frozen by January, arrested me. Children held me captive; I recoiled at clones made in my image a foot, one hundred pounds, and ten years prior taking baby steps that, with socks, shoes, and bootstraps, would be giant leaps. Young men bearing resemblance to the then-me mean-mugged—their cruel contortions perhaps originating from some intoxicant peddled by a kingpin on a far-away planet. Perhaps not so far.

Truth frisked; I had no right to resist. "These people"—my people— were not stuff of inanimate will, feral sentiment, and Petri dishes. Laziness, violence, pathology—measurements of the dark visage America struck and neglected—stared not with concrete savagery, but a graveled, dispossessed affect. Where men of titles and tailors saw feral children, I saw human sorrow. That sorrow harked to a familiar face—one of hard work, humility, and hope. I looked into those eyes, dark as my own, and saw the sorrow I, as a child, once saw slip from the eyes of my grandfather, a man born and reared in rural Georgia. It was a sorrow somewhat assuaged by his migration to Buffalo, New York, an exodus affording him, his family, and many black Southerners of the Great Migration some semblance of spirit. But no dam could contain such falls. I wondered if, on this day, the souls of black folk would at last be free.

On this day, Americans autopsied sorrow. We tested its vital signs. We placed our frozen fingers over its face, feeling no fumes. We grasped steel; its caged, rocking ribbing ceased. We declared it deceased. On the day of this great coronation, we designated ourselves licensed coroners; our degree of qualification became apparent as we declared racism's death after determining its proper resting place. We dared to dream. Dream we can. But the dream is cruel fantasy. In this dream, there is no justice ruling against minorities and on behalf of injustice. In this dream, there is no euthanasia failing black organs, harvested both from poverty's casualties and Jack and Jill card-carriers. In this dream, there is no birthing room denying admission to two black infants for every one white failing to thrive. In this dream, there is no executive shredding African American opportunity, shouting black credentials to double doors *ex officio*. In this dream, none of these figments permeate into present. Wrapping embalms King's body from substance seeping to spoil the slumber deferring America's awakening.

It is not the vision of which he spoke or the one that made Barack Obama leader of the free world. It is a hallucination we have confused with the waking state we deny breath. It is a recurring night terror, thieving breath and beats for stress and beads. It is hot, flashing withdrawal seizing millions of hearts denied rehabilitation. It is not a lucid, whiteout treatment cast of hosed fleeing, sinking fangs, and hot mobbed pursuit. Its script is not patched with epithets, separate schools, and back doors. It is not stuff of Oscar nominations—bronze handout casts invariably supporting gold and glory of handsome white saviors. No one could write a script for this narrative, for its fantasy is too explicit. It transcends reality, scaling jasper walls to the realm quartering crusaders' coronals—Evers, X, and the dream's purveyor himself. It is a Constitution victim to gladiators—contested in courts, confounded in cases, cut into castes, and covered in Tyrian robes by curious conservationists.

I entered a cozy station. Frostbite yielded to a sweltering wave fostering equilibrium. Its sheltering did not consummate with bodily homeostasis, but with consumption of the sacrament it bore. Spirit's nourishment conceived *Last in Line*; it is sacrament for a greater body. I believed then and believe now, at the end of his presidency, what all Americans knew on that day—that President Obama's election is both a symbol of change and a representation of our country's potential for greatness. Where I, along with many Americans, diverge is in the belief that his election is far from a sign that America has salvaged its damaged soul, crediting its constitutional "master promissory note." American masses have certified Barack Obama's election a sign of long-awaited heaven on Earth. In doing so, these denominations perpetuate the strangely pernicious idea that racism is no more—and that to speak otherwise is to assume the dark mantle of the victim. On January 20, 2009, while American congregations, young and old, black and white, rejoiced in a dream, spirit commanded me to desert.

Last in Line: An American Destiny Deferred

Last in Line is not a denial of the American dream. It is a conveyance of the truth that American destiny is deferred. It is an exegesis of the bootstrap. A profile of the black child who seized me that January morning—roaming cold and barefoot—in search of his. It is an audit of shoemakers—callous, leathered houses of business and government denying him and his loved ones the warmth the Constitution's commandments guarantee them.

Let us dare dream. But let us dare not delude.

That evening, I left warmth—food, family, and the image of our new president and first lady strolling Pennsylvania Avenue—for truth.

Introduction

"God is dead." So the madman of Nietzsche's *Gay Science* proclaimed in 1882. "We have killed him, you and I!"[1] That such perfidy could be spoken upon a continent entrenched in Christian doctrine was unimaginable. Nietzsche's Europe bore soil rendered fertile by the blood of devout, sacrificial crusaders proclaiming unequivocal belief in God and Jesus Christ. Nietzsche was radical to declare God's obsolescence in 19th century Europe. To prophesize the damnation of religion in the European culture contemporaneous with most of his works guaranteed his own. Such was adultery's retribution. His words lied with sin; they did not lie without truth. Although far from being extinct in Industrial Age Europe, religion was coming to be viewed as an institution incongruous and incompatible with an emergent era.

The Industrial Revolution's onset, with the accompanying social, political, technological, and ideological transformations the age entailed—including the rise of capitalism and socialism—fissured the Church from the people of Europe. The Papacy responded to the steam engine's innovation not with benediction, but trepidation and disdain, deeming it an abomination "prejudicial to religion."[2] The Church's excommunication of technology further intensified the rise of the atheistic doctrine that philosophers such as Nietzsche espoused. In a culture in which scientific advances were being made not in ponderous stumbles, but nimble and graceful leaps, and rationality and philosophy opposed rather than legitimized religion, Christian dogma was coming to be viewed as obsolete.

Auguste Comte, the father of sociology, characterized religion as antiquated.[3] Comte and others felt human fervor need not be centered on a supreme deity, but rather humankind.[4] Marx's socialism argued that man need not rely on some figment of the Jungian collective unconscious, but rather himself and his mortal fellow.[5] Leo Strauss' pioneering atheistic ideals germinated the minds of thinkers such as Ludwig Feuerbach, who characterized the scriptures as a compilation of myths, much in the vein of Aesop's Fables (albeit esoteric and perhaps more ostentatious).[6] Religion, they argued, entailed the primitive, the antediluvian, and was well on its way out.

Although these radical philosophies did not supplant the rapture, their failed *coup d'état* inspired a sentimental fixture in 19th century sociopolitical affairs. Among other things, they played a pivotal role in catapulting both communistic and democratic political institutions in the West and toppling its theocratic political institutions. Had these philosophers seized and wielded the papal *ferula*, society's pews would no longer have admitted the primordial and superstitious. In their reality, we would have encountered Nietzsche's atheistic madman heralding utopic emancipation, preaching, "God is dead. God remains dead. And we have killed him."

On November 4, 2008, a moment deemed unfashionably late by some and too early an hour by others arrived. It was the historic election of the first African American as President of the United States of America. Barack Obama's election as the 44th President of the United States was viewed as a milestone for several reasons, of which the most conspicuous was that he would stand as the first elected minority (and furthermore, person of sub-Saharan African descent) to lead the "free world." But the implication of Obama's election far transcended this. Obama's election, according to some enthusiastic Americans,

Last in Line: An American Destiny Deferred

signaled the long-deferred burial of racism. Many insisted that this coronation of a black man—one of mixed parentage—was indeed the final rectification for America's sins of racial injustice, the ultimate cleansing of the tombal residue of a past all too recent. As Americans cast ballots for the charismatic U.S. senator from Illinois, they each felt themselves shoveling bits of dirt, interring remains of the nefarious institution. Engraving a succinct, most befitting epitaph in fine granite, they graffitied, "Racism is dead...and we have killed it!"

As social constructs, religion and race make for an odd comparison. Religion is of the spiritual, race of the physical. Religion is a mechanism for making sense of the world around us; race is an immutable characteristic of that world. The two have often intersected; Christianity furnished understandings of racial inequality as being ordained by a higher power, a matter of Creation, and thus organic. But religion and race are subject to different critical understandings. Religion, particularly in its fundamentalist forms, is often criticized, but race has become anathema. The objectionable concept of race we today term "racism" was, to our forebears, the given truth of a natural, inevitable stratification of the races. Races rose or fell in accordance with their endowment with intellectual, physical, and moral qualities. When at last identifying and recognizing racism for the damaging social ill it is, we conceptualized it as a contemptible product of the combined prejudicial, exploitative, and murderous proclivities of the world's groups that in one way or another achieved and established domination.

Religion and race bear no similarity in countenance, but relation is to be found in their visceral makeup. Religion and race—and, necessarily, racism—are objects converging in the realm of belief; both bodies are constructed of conceptual rather than corporeal elements. These conceptual blocks fashion them both as institutions. Whereas religion is the institution that qualifies human moral value on the basis of adherence to spiritual ideology, race is the institution that differentiates human moral value on the basis of phenotypic and genotypic qualities. The phenomena are not mutually exclusive, but do operate in distinct ways. Religion is a pillar of the society, a vehicle through which the culture shapes and expresses its beliefs, philosophies, perspectives, and character. Race is not objectifiable in the same way; it is more entrenched in the culture's soul, a most rabid manifestation of the ethnocentrism that often seems natural to humankind.

Even though the blasphemous ideas of 19th century philosophers bore undeniable influence, such radical rhetoric failed to turn Europeans away from the Holy Book. Racism has faced no such threat, for its entrenchment requires no revival, no fervent Great Awakening. It requires no Bible, no Church, and no Pope. It proselytizes absent sirens and sermons—sans shouts and soliloquies. It is the silent commandment that curses the other, banishing the ungodly presence from both pulpit and pew, condemning them to an eternal hellfire of exclusion. It is invisible—elemental as air. We cannot perceive it. It is this invisibility, this normality, that most aids racism's cunning. For this reason—its granted normality—the putative Church of Racism has privately secured a greater following than any and all organized religions.

The beliefs of the revolutionary 19th century philosophers—Comte's positivism, Marx's socialism, Feuerbach's concept of religion as mythic— did not take hold with enough fervor to supplant religion's influence, but undeniably took hold of society with enough grip to shape it indelibly. Atheism, a doctrine unspeakable before the ascent of such men, solidified itself as the

x

quintessential anti-religious movement. Marxism brought forth political ideas of communism that would characterize two of the world's largest nation-states, Russia and China, in the coming century. Positivist enclaves took hold in continents far away as South America, presaging the energy and disposition of New Age movements. Although these anthropocentric, godless ideologies did not displace society's religious foundations, they offered a lucid, superterranean alternative to sedimentary material fated to the depth of Hades.

Although Western racism was born with the European's New World encounter with the nonwhite, any idea of innate racial differences was at first amorphous. The early relationship between the races was best characterized as a tenuous hierarchy legitimated by the victors of military conquest and buttressed by their subjection and enslavement of the vanquished. Beyond this, a definitive idea of a natural racial hierarchy had never been conceptualized. But while European philosophers were devising ways to overthrow religion, Charles Darwin was developing in his *Species of Man* liturgical texts that would define his own Church—one that arguably made the white man God.

Scholars continue to debate whether or not Darwin was racist, but it is undisputed that many used his scientific research and theories to advance racist ideas.[7] This "Church of Darwinism," advanced by the denomination of social Darwinists, canonized racism. With business magnates Andrew Carnegie and John D. Rockefeller preaching social Darwinism,[8] many of society's most influential individuals and institutions followed suit, their conversion giving rise to the racist anthropological doctrines of eugenics, racial hygiene, and phrenology among others. Social Darwinism wasn't anything new, per se. It was just a new conceptualization of the racial hierarchy, better explaining why some races fell into obsequious, sullen existence while others ascended to zeniths of power and dominance. It was perfect for an American society resistant to the idea of "Negro equality." By the grace of science, America's long-standing racist sentiments were righteously vindicated.

It was this pervasive belief that nursed the disparity and inequality that thrived in late 19th and early 20th century America. It was taken as a product of biology that blacks and whites had segregated destinies. But in the wake of the civil rights efforts of the 1950s and '60s, venom spread, paralyzing the proverbial Church of Racism.

The Civil Rights Movement was poison to racist doctrine. In an America in which the preceding decades saw theories of eugenics and Nordicism resonate with Americans in the Northeastern United States and structures of racial supremacy remain intact in the Southern caste system,[9] no one foresaw the oncoming destruction of America's system of racial supremacy. In the early 1950s, African Americans in the North and South alike lacked access to equal education, well-paying jobs, and other essentials. In the decade prior, valiant African American servicemen returning from the same battlefields as their paraded white brothers were hung throughout the South in dress uniform,[10] their epaulets glistening amid an inglorious spectacle. Such overtures radioed that blacks could not expect anything, even patriotic valiance, to win the respect of white Americans. The unemployment rate for African Americans staggered above that of white Americans and the many vestiges of slavery,[11] such as sharecropping, left African Americans ensconced in a sordid, unequal system with no hope for progress.

Dawn rose. *Brown v. Board* overturned *Plessy v. Ferguson.* Dr. King proclaimed his dream. The Civil Rights Act of 1964 was signed; the Voting Rights Act supplemented ink one year later. Affirmative action programs arrived

Last in Line: An American Destiny Deferred

under the auspices of Lyndon Johnson's Great Society. And, like magic, racism was no more, wiped from America's visage.

Or so many believe. The idea that the Civil Rights Movement destroyed racism is as absurd as Nietzsche's idea that, between machines and morals, man destroyed the institution of religion in the West. It cannot be forgotten—this was the declaration of a *madman*. It cannot be doubted that just as the agnostic ideological revolutions of the 19th century played a significant role in undermining the influence of religion in society, the Civil Rights Movement played a critical role in eroding the foundations on which institutional racism stood. It is not to be argued that these movements were impotent in the face of the almighty edifices that stood before them. But Nietzsche's "God is dead" proclamation does not even begin to approach gospel. Power systems defy revolution's wrecking balls, rising from ash and rubble to reconstitute as sturdier edifices. In the examples of religion, racism, and even capitalism— which has survived numerous threats of effacement, from the Great Depression to the Great Recession—the proven permanence of established systems belies the conclave's consensus on change's inevitability.

In 2016, around one-third of the world population identified as Christian, a proportion projected to hold through 2050.[12] Over the course of the century during which most of the Industrial Revolution and ensuing Industrial Age transpired, missionaries freight-hopped round the world. By the time of Nietzsche's death in 1900, Christianity already reached about a third of the global population, up from 23 percent a century earlier.[13] Coming in a close second, Muslims made up about one quarter of the world's population in 2016.[14] Atheism's influence has spread, too (a plurality of Norwegians, for example, eschew belief in a god).[15] But despite the madman's insistence, God is nowhere near "dead."[16]

While the Church was condemned by the bite of an apple, the Church of Darwinism was felled by a slingshot trailed by colorless resistance. Although the genius of Nietzsche and other philosophers cannot be denied, they were wrong. Theirs was a specious supposition. Despite philosophers' notions that religion was a dying phenomenon, it remains very much alive. We witness Western nations embroiled in quasi-holy wars, with one former U.S. president proclaiming his military efforts a "crusade,"[17] and observe unyielding opponents proclaiming intent to carry out jihad to obliterate deplorable infidels. Nietzsche may be horrified to find that the very being whose pulse he expected would cease is alive and well. Similarly, our enthusiastic cohorts from the "racism is dead" camp may find truth unsettling.

As Nietzsche did with religion, we have applied to racism the mistaken conjecture that a temporal or moral evolution of society would render its systems and structures incompatible. Before the onset of the West's technological boom, nature was seen as God's dominion, His servants tilling and harvesting in His name. Man's creation—steam engines, steam liners, and eventually "steam radios"—made the phenomena of biblical anecdotes seem obsolete and offered reason to question God's omnipotence. Technological development was Nietzsche's glorious proof, citing man's success in mutating the environment in ways far more extraordinary than illustrated in scripture.[18] Yet somehow scripture possessed mega-screens and mobile apps, rendering technology's purpose subservient to a higher power.

For Americans today, the election of an African American, given that race's unique history of oppression, proves racism's ejection from society.

Introduction

Furthermore, to many Americans Barack Obama's presidency symbolizes not only racism's waning influence on the American soul, but also America's excommunication of *race*. As intuitive, progressive, and compassionate as we think we have become, we are, in Nietzschean fashion, incorrect in presuming racism dead.

Comparing racism to religion demonstrates society's dangerous tendency to view the erasure of ills like racism, religious intolerance, homophobia, and poverty as inevitabilities. The most devout "Nietzsches" of the racism is dead camp believe mainstream society has jettisoned racist philosophies in favor of egalitarian, race-neutral "colorblind" perceptions, ideologies, and policies. Evidence abounds: the civil rights legislation of the 1960s, affirmative action policies (which many decry as embodying "reverse racism"), the increase of African Americans in white-collar professions, the rise of the self-made black sensation (Oprah Winfrey, Bob Johnson, etc.), the success of the "model minority" (many who surpass whites in various measures of success), and of course the election of an African American to the most prestigious and arguably trusted position in the United States. These successes, they maintain, labored together to hammer the final nail in racism's coffin.

If we reflected on the nature of ongoing racial disparity in the United States, we would startle in realization of our remissness and exhume racism for its delayed autopsy. Boasts of Barack Obama's election (which sparked a stark increase in the number of hate groups in the United States)[19] would give way to investigation as to why, for example, rates for housing discrimination in the United States reached an unprecedented high the year of his election,[20] or why implicit bias tests reveal a stunning commonality of racist attitudes among Americans.[21] Forensics would demand answers as to why public funds for education are still allocated unequally and along racial lines throughout America's communities,[22] why young black American men are accosted, tried, and incarcerated at higher rates than white males who commit the exact same crimes,[23] and why patriotic Muslim Americans continue to endure Islamophobic treatment more than a decade following 9/11.[24]

In the process of our autopsy, we sift organs whose warmth is somehow not felt by our touch. Our hands travel the body in whose abdominal realm lie the organs perpetuating the prejudicial policies and practices of the past. An odor lingers—not of rigor, but vigor. At last, we reach a beat—strong, steady, menacing. It strikes us. It thrives, indelible and ever livelier. Eyelids peel and we jump back, stunned nearly to our own deaths. Popping upright, bearing a wicked grin, the corpse greets us, "Hi, I'm racism—and guess what? I ain't dead today and I won't be tomorrow!"

Although I emphasize that racism remains pervasive in America, I do not insinuate that the many historic endeavors and campaigns against racism are short of creditable. The campaigns of 19th century progressive abolitionists, the legislative programs of liberal and assimilationist Republicans of the 1860s and '70s, the magnanimous efforts of progressive Democratic presidents of the 20th century, the sacrifices made by leaders and followers of the Civil Rights Movement in the 1950s and '60s, and the labors of the heirs to these social movements, like Black Lives Matter, to create a just, even-handed society were and are all necessary to fashion a better America. Without the tremendous efforts of these movements and their tremendous successes in ameliorating racism, America's minorities would occupy a much worse position than what they do today.

xiii

Last in Line: An American Destiny Deferred

But that fact cannot supersede a greater truth. It must be understood that these movements are better viewed as effectual palliatives than cures—remedies that soothed our nerves, relaxed our respiration, and made it possible for us to walk, albeit with a stagger, but failed to eradicate the illness ravaging our system.

America's civil rights reforms have yielded positive effect in areas of education, voting, immigration, employment, and beyond. But the yield is meager. In recent times, tides of regression have swept much of progress away, leaving sediment. Statistics show that desegregation peaked in 1988, recalculating for a retrograde destination nearby the divided schoolhouse of pre-civil rights America.[25] A 2005 study conducted by the Civil Rights Project at Harvard University found that the percentage of African Americans at better-funded, predominantly white schools was at "a level lower than in any year since 1968."[26]

Similarly, research has shown that developments brought about by the Voting Rights Act are receding.[27] This recession slid into a crash when, in June 2013, the Supreme Court struck down Section 4 of the Voting Rights Act. Section 4 established a formula which determined that some states and jurisdictions, based on histories of voter discrimination, required federal preclearance before making changes to their voting laws.[28] The abrogation of this provision, which many held to be the heart of the law, paved the way for the passage of voter ID laws in former preclearance states, which many insist have the effect of disproportionately disenfranchising minorities.[29]

African Americans voted in unprecedented numbers in 2008, but just eight years prior had been subjected to extensive voter suppression efforts. Controversy erupted in Florida during the 2000 presidential election when the names of honest, law-abiding African Americans were purged from voter lists.[30] Their crime was that their names resembled, often faintly, those of felons. Data aggregate company ChoicePoint (since acquired by LexisNexis) was found in 2000 to have purged the names of thousands of African Americans from Florida voting lists at the behest of secretary of state Katherine Harris.[31] Even as recently as 2010, under guise of the apocryphal "Black Democratic Trust of Texas,"[32] charlatans launched vigorous campaigns to suppress African American voter turnout. In one scheme, they distributed fliers erroneously insisting that straight-ticket Democratic votes wouldn't be counted.[33] These aren't isolated manifestations of racial prejudice confined to America's "backward" parts. They are persistent, widespread, national problems.

As Americans, we take pride in the traditions we feel distinguish us as a model of democracy. We tout our stable democratic process and robust economic system, among other feats, to the rest of the world. Beyond these concrete and quantifiable measures, we take pride in abstract but equally valuable qualities—our legendary work ethic, our belief in fairness, and our faith that no matter how great the task, we can get the job done. These traits, and many more, qualify our nation alone for the honorific "Leader of the Free World." We hold neither reservations nor qualms of the verity of our greatness. There are neither cracks nor chips tarnishing the marble surface upon which spirit has engraved, "America the beautiful...bastion of life, liberty and the pursuit of happiness." In spite of this, ours is a history laden with contradictions—paradoxes and travesties that might be humorous if they were not so devastating to the lives of so many.

Introduction

America declares a commitment to "life, liberty, and the pursuit of happiness" for all while denying all three unalienable rights to her masses. We insist on the immutable and unassailable fullness and humanity of each and every man and woman while claiming some constitute three-fifths of a person— many thinking even this too liberal a figure. We inscribe beneath the Statue of Liberty, one of our finest national monuments, "Give me your tired, your poor—your huddled masses yearning to breathe free," while depicting the very tired, very poor, and very much short of breath immigrants and their sons and daughters as members of an invading, criminal, parasitic sub-race.

We profess an unwavering hatred of tyranny and oppression, citing our historical opposition to these evils as the driving force behind our existence. We profess never to embody these characteristics. We then turn our backs on Lady Liberty, allowing these traits to harass her. We pledge allegiance to the beast that threatens to devour men marked with the hues and features for which it has a cruel penchant. We insist the beast is exterminated all the while failing to realize *we* are the beast.

It is a legacy of disloyalty to the American spirit, one of contradiction, falsehood, and sacrifice to safe havens of privilege. We grip a legacy that sustains the status quo and discards those cast below. If we look within ourselves in search of truth, we will realize that which distinguishes us is less pleasant and romantic than hoped. When we draw forth a magnifying glass, the lens reveals festering wounds and abscesses that, to ethically calibrated minds, inspire disgust.

We celebrate an African American president's two terms in the White House, congratulating ourselves for having shattered some proverbial glass ceiling which still looms over the head of a young Hispanic American child whose future is threatened because some insist that he is not American. A glass ceiling hovers over the head of the Arab American girl ostracized and alienated by her peers, so confused by the degree of isolation she faces that she truly feels she must suffer some form of leprosy. This glass ceiling, as firm and molecularly bonded as ever, remains fixed over the head of the young African American child living in South Carolina's notorious "Corridor of Shame," bereft of any opportunity resembling that of his or her wealthy, privileged sibling just a few counties over for whom opportunity abounds.

We pat ourselves on the back for the wistful ideals that we feel America embodies while ignoring that there has never been a point in our republican history of more than two centuries in which we have endorsed these ideals of freedom for each and every American. That is the great American paradox. We boast love for equality while having never known equality. That America remains in arrears, having delivered little of what it promised, may call for greater frugality in our pride as a nation.

It is a pride of power rendered tenuous by hypocrisy. It is founded on reverence of noble Founding Fathers who, belying the heroism for which they are honored, held Americans in bondage and deprived them of the unalienable rights they professed to defend in the Constitution. It is a pride in which we reminisce of Manifest Destiny, the great American Gold Rush, the Homestead Act, and other measures credited with opening doors to the vast expanse of the Western frontier—doors slammed shut and latched several times over to those with the wrong phenotypic code.[34]

We adulate over the great wars that established us as a force—the War of 1812, the Civil War, the First and Second World Wars, all the way down to today's Middle Eastern conflicts, in which whites, blacks, Asians,

Last in Line: An American Destiny Deferred

Native Americans, Arab Americans, and beyond have played vital roles on behalf of our national interest. Yet still, in so many cases people of color have been thrust onto front lines, confined to subordinate and servile stations, and denied decoration for their valiance. It is a pride based on a revisionist story in which hard facts are mollified, excused as appropriate "for their time," and adapted to tropes of complex rebel heroes struggling against evils both of their atmosphere and hearts. That odor of nobility permeates to present, burning our lungs and debilitating our senses.

A truth compound is produced from gases of relief and consternation: blacks and other racial minorities do not have a monopoly on suffering. Poverty, hardship, disease, and other visceral pains are strangers to no color, creed, class, gender, nationality, or background. In the wake of the War on Terror deemed by some a modern crusade, religious minorities, particularly Muslims, have found themselves thrust onto the American periphery. Damning aspersions are cast upon both them and their faith—even by those representing them in Congress.[35] Such religious discrimination must be banished. If we are truly the world's greatest nation, then we Americans must endeavor to erase all preventable suffering of *all* members of American society. Racism is but one form, yielding untold devastation. But to highlight the magnitude of racism is not to usurp the voices of those afflicted by other maladies.

This truth does not alter the fact that the difficulty of human circumstance is exacerbated when factors of racial or religious minority status are equated into what may be an already difficult lot. One may wallow in want, but find themselves spared the stigma of racial and ethnic otherness, whether that otherness is "Arabness," "Muslimness," "Asianness," or—God forbid—blackness. They can rest assured that their life condition will not be attributed to any sort of inherent inferiority, ineptitude, or moral flaw grafted to skin or soul. Neither their ability nor their humanity will be questioned; they will be presumed. Their lack is noble, simple, and respectable. To be white and poor is to be poor. The condition bears no epidermal link. But to be black and poor, to be black and downtrodden, to be black and dispossessed— is simply to be black.

Post-racial America doesn't exist. The fantasy bears false comfort; true relief can only be experienced by disabusing ourselves of this illusion. We conflate racism and bigotry, the overt, demonstrative gestures of hate exhibited at Mizzou—students yelling racial epithets, drawing fecal swastikas in dormitory halls, and Yik-Yakking genocidal death threats.[36] This is in the vein of the graying woman who, on seeing the approach of a wild pack, clenches her teeth and picks up her pace; or the stoical, upper middle-aged Southern man adorning himself and everything he owns in recreations of the Confederate flag and proclaiming to any so foolish as to blend to dusk in his parts, "We don't like *yer* kind 'round here." America bears a heavily caricaturized perception of racism. Our concept isolates racism to the fringe, among the unhinged. It is the Klan, it is the neo-Nazis, it is even the Black Panthers. It is Yale frats, it is Mizzou. It isn't Abigail Fisher. It isn't us. Upon reflection, however, we might realize that our moral compasses require calibration.

The Implicit Association Test, pioneered by Harvard University, belies every modern notion we have about racism as a latent, outlying, and frustrating but ultimately atrophying phenomenon. The IAT was devised to detect bias in several forms, among them gender, religion, nationality, weight, disability, and political.[37] The IAT can test almost any bias. The race IAT has yielded results many would find surprising, not excluding those fancying themselves colorblind proponents of inclusion and multiculturalism. If this category includes you, the IAT may beg to differ with that self-description. The IAT has revealed that a staggering 80 percent of whites demonstrate an implicit preference for other whites.[38] This is no simple matter of birds of a feather. Rather, this is ascribed to deviant shepherds treating flocks with vaccines that grip the heart with a disorder suppressing empathy.

The race version of the IAT uses words and images of both white and black people to correspond to words and images considered either pleasant or unpleasant.[39] Available in a computerized form (and accessible at implicit.harvard.edu), the test requires split-second reactions to match one's associations of individuals of particular races with words and images connoting things either pleasant or unpleasant. Eight out of ten white people associate words such as "glorious" and "wonderful" with white faces while associating terms such as "failure" and "evil" with black faces. Participants' reactions are so rapid as to preclude them from making conscious decisions. African Americans too show bias. They show a preference for whites with staggering figures ranging anywhere from 50 to 65 percent.[40] The idea that colorblindness has rescued our spirit proves blind to a harsh, encircling reality.

Last in Line explores the American problem of institutional racism, focusing on its unique affliction of black America. This does not neglect the plight of other minorities, even so-called "model minorities," who are also victimized by American systems. But the role that institutional racism plays in immolating the black community into self-immolation calls for distinct examination. It is important to recognize that the so-called "pathologies" of the black community are potent corollaries of institutionally racist policies that remain extant in the justice, education, health care, and economic systems. Because of this, *Last in Line* profiles African Americans' sufferings at the hands of these power systems, although parallel examinations of other racial groups' sufferings are offered to establish both systemic racism's prevalence and the existence of a concrete, ordered American racial hierarchy.

Although emancipation, the Civil Rights Movement, and other endeavors did not free black America, these events loosened the noose about its neck. Many black Americans are born into circumstances that do not permit them to dream in the ways others do, but it cannot be forgotten that we live in a period of unprecedented opportunity—opportunity we sometimes fail to seize. This thesis may be confused with "respectability" finger wagging and thus seem to contradict premises earlier put forth, but it is consistent with them. African Americans have more opportunity than ever before—but *still* cannot boast of possessing the same level of opportunity as do their more privileged counterparts. Though we have more opportunity we do not have equal opportunity. For African Americans, progress has stagnated, even regressed in certain respects, especially for black males steeped in statistics of low college attendance and graduation rates,[41] un- and underemployment according with meager income and vast poverty,[42] and high levels of crime, violence, and incarceration.[43] Although many argue a neglect of behavioral responsibility is to blame for this "failed seizure," I demonstrate that these phenomena are primarily attributed to the limitations imposed by an unjust society.

A towering, formidable, and controversial man once said, "Power in defense of freedom is greater than power on behalf of tyranny and oppression."[44] He knew little in the world other than abuse. Unlike us, he

Last in Line: An American Destiny Deferred

could not have even attempted to don eyewear enabling perception of a society in which color did not exist. If he were alive today, it is doubtful he would even fathom our idea of a so-called "colorblind" society. To him, race was elemental. It was as tangible and natural as air, water, and fire. The anguish fomented by Ku Klux Klan terrorism—their razing of his boyhood homes, death threats, and fiery commitment to cruel vows—made a burning impression on him as a young boy.

These threats seared his consciousness and branded his person the day his father, a minister and community organizer, was seized by members of a white supremacist terror group, the Black Legion, fastened to steel tracks near his home, and obliterated by a fast-moving street car. We may dispute his militancy and argue the validity of his beliefs, but we cannot deny Malcolm X's wisdom in knowing from direct experiences and struggles with racism the futility of defending it as an institution. Malcolm X preached of that institution maintaining invariable iniquity, disparity, and division. Malcolm X knew that a society founded upon inequality was doomed to perish. He understood that truth spurns the oppressor, lying with the oppressed. *Last in Line* carries the torch hoisted by Malcolm X, Martin Luther King, Jr., and so many others so that the flame of truth illuminates rather than inflames America.

Confusion, misinterpretation, and misunderstanding will arise in response to *Last in Line*. For clarity's sake, I feel it necessary to stress what this book is not meant to be:

This is not a "black book." It is of all colors. *Last in Line* is about black America's unique historical trajectory. Its mission, however, is not to raise African Americans above any other racial group or to empower them for their sole benefit. Its objective is to empower the whole of America. African Americans comprise 44 million individuals, approximately 13 percent of the U.S. population.[45] To have three-quarters of a million African American men behind bars,[46] many more unemployed, and a vast number of single black women unable to sustain their households leaves a huge source of American social, economic, and sheer human potential untapped. That such dormancy jeopardizes not only the state of black America but the future of America as a whole must be understood. This missive is addressed to all Americans.

Last in Line is not only for African Americans, but all Americans. Still, it is a story of the African American struggle in context of the American racial hierarchy. Although the struggles of other ethnicities are treated as ancillary for the purposes of this book, they are not minimized. Native Americans endured some of the most appalling and criminal offenses known in history. Duplicity, biological warfare, economic destruction, and outright genocide ravaged them. The effects of such destruction are evident in their community today. Chinese Americans, Japanese Americans, Hispanic Americans, and other minority groups too know the yoke of American oppression. America's racial hierarchy cannot be understood absent profiles of nonblack minority groups; *Last in Line* constructs this caste system's profile with the objective of inspiring the masses to dismantle it.

This is not a call for reparations. The great failure of emancipation and Reconstruction was that they did not render compensation, however small, to ex-slaves or their descendants. In a country in which the value of hard work is stressed, one of the greatest ironies is that many of its hardest-working people—those who toiled gratis to make America into the bastion of wealth it stands as today—were never remunerated for their labors. Germany's Jews and their descendants received tremendous settlements for the

Introduction

conflagration of the Holocaust; interned Japanese Americans received settlements for the hardships they underwent during their detention in the United States during World War II; the Inuit received compensation for the injustices they bore; and Native Americans were granted fractions of their ancestral lands as well as exclusive rights to ownership in gambling industries in certain places. African Americans have received nothing of the sort.

Indeed, many argue that affirmative action is the remuneration for the efforts expended by the ancestors of African Americans.[47] But those arguing this fail to realize that affirmative action policies are not formulated to mitigate the unique circumstances engendered by the experiences African Americans alone underwent both during and after slavery. Affirmative action is not a policy in the same vein as the aforementioned treatments, but is instead an over-the-counter form of quasi-mitigation ironically benefiting white women more than it does members of any minority group.[48] Regardless, reparations are impractical; the legal complexities entailing qualification, calculation, and payment of slaves' lost wages to their descendants as well as overwhelming and likely dangerous public opposition makes the implementation of reparations in America all but impossible. The subject of reparations continues to generate hot debate; the passage of time does nothing on behalf of its case. The moral wrongness of America having never taken steps to render compensation for slavery is a theme integral both to the African American narrative and *Last in Line*. This theme and the explanations surrounding it should not, however, be misinterpreted as a call for reparations.

This is not an attempt at arousing white guilt. Too often when institutional racism and its children—slavery, Jim Crow, and today colorblindness—are critiqued, those critiquing it are charged with guilt-tripping white Americans. This is not *Last in Line*'s mission. As guilt offers no redress, it lies outside the scope of the direction in which *Last in Line* aims.

No American today ever held anyone in bondage. But as a nation, we continue to benefit from the immense wealth generated by the slave trade. This slave-generated wealth has made the robustness and endurance of our nation's financial, political, and social systems possible. All Americans benefit from the labors of enslaved Americans, but these benefits still allot along stark racial lines without regard to the presence of a direct participant in one's family tree. This truth should arouse outrage, horror, and change. Guilt accomplishes no redress. If anything, guilt is a pass, an apologetic proclamation accompanied with a tearful display meant to suffice in place of actionable rectification. America must resolve to act against its institutionally racist systems and ideologies that are heirs to slavery. Conferring sweat toward that end will prove more effective than tears.

Still, I pull no punches with regard to statistical information and data used to corroborate this book's thesis. When I speak of percentages of specific races being more likely to hold a bias, being disproportionately victimized by a practice or activity, unduly benefiting from a practice or activity, etc., it is not intended to imply that all members of a particular group are either good or evil people. Rather, within context of a racially disparate society, each of these statistics is in some way explicable, such as those concerning implicit bias and the way it emerges in a society in which a preponderance of racial stereotypes serves to shape individuals' unconscious perceptions of certain ethnic groups. That individuals possess or lack such implicit biases doesn't position them somewhere in a good-bad moralist binary. Rather, these phenomena are corollary of society's racially disparate disposition. (And on

the point of statistics, one will find no Pioneer Fund or human biodiversity bunk defacing any page of this book, save inclusion under the profile of bogus research.)
  This is not an anti-American book. It is American. Some will depict this as a work of anti-American proselytization. Nothing could be further from the truth. I love America for the opportunities that she bequeathed on my father—opportunities he would not have had in his South African homeland under apartheid. Although he has not been without experiences of discrimination in the United States, we are grateful for the opportunity America gave him to experiment with social mobility, further his education, and create for himself and his family self-sufficiency which is much harder to achieve elsewhere.

  Although my mother was raised in an America segregated by law, her upbringing in an America also marked by revolution allowed her unprecedented access to opportunities that, until then, were forbidden to most African Americans. Her Northern home state, New York, offered the sort of egalitarian measures that would afford her and all of her siblings college educations, opportunities unavailable to her forebears. Despite the unpleasant realities of American society, I believe that no other nation could have created the opportunity that I experience today. My gratitude for these opportunities is not to be understated.

  Self-examination is the American way. Our democratic process calls for the ability to evaluate our national state of affairs so that we may improve them. Some may look at the partisanship of the Congress and insist that perhaps we take this idea to a corrupted extreme. Although our process may get out of hand, when we observe democratic principles in good faith our government is the world's best. That is what we are meant to be. But the provincial notion that all actions comprising the American way are righteous by virtue of them being American is both insecure and self-defeating. We must not be above criticism. Criticizing our faults as a nation is not tantamount to self-deprecation or self-abasement. It is the only way to save ourselves from the harsh deprecations the world may confer upon us if our iniquitous systems persist. God forbid their criticisms be well-founded.

  Lastly, this is not a racist book. "I Have a Dream" is not only recognized as the most eloquent and riveting of Martin Luther King, Jr.'s speeches—it is heralded as the greatest oratorical piece of the 20th century. It has overshadowed much of his other work, notably his "Letter from Birmingham Jail." A prisoner of war, King, 34, penned the less-celebrated "Letter" while confined in a place that hadn't experienced such searing atmospheric conditions since Sherman razed the South a century earlier. Enlisted in the Southern Christian Leadership Conference's Birmingham campaign, King, with his brothers- and sisters-in-arms, employed not the bombs and bullets used to part the flesh of black and white civil rights activists, but the virtues of civil disobedience—a weapon proving of nuclear proportions yet life-preserving.

  To some Birminghamians, King and his fellow crusaders were causing unnecessary trouble, upsetting the pacific, racially harmonious apple cart. Days after King's incarceration, a group of white Birmingham clergymen made it clear to him and the rest of the city that it was not Alabama's social order that was in need of salvation, but rather the disobedient civilians who appeared hopeless to the truth that "hatred and violence have no sanction in our religious and political traditions."[49] The clergymen went on to commend the efforts of law enforcement officials for the "calm" way in which they handled the demonstrations (with, of course, the amicable assistance of bruising hoses and ravenous dogs). King and the SCLC, they asserted, were the only ones bereft of "law, order, and common sense."[50] Birmingham's healthy race relations were, in their pious eyes, agitated. King's determined political agitation—to them, senseless and arbitrary—was to blame.

The tradition of these clergymen has not crumbled with the oppressive edifices of old. It remains erect, albeit disassembled and reconstructed in a similarly Sodom-inspired kingdom. Here, the antiracists are the racists. Those who speak of the immediate, shocking manifestations of racism (such as the 2014 extra-judicial execution of 12-year-old Cleveland native Tamir Rice) or its abstract, institutional incarnations (such as racial disparities in the Drug War's administration of mandatory minimum sentencing policies) are accused of stirring racial division and hatred. Such ideologies have been encapsulated in the unfortunate platitude that proclaims "antiracist is a code word for anti-white"—a strange statement that could not be true if the utterers did not somehow at a deeper level associate whiteness with inherent racism.

That this book conveys the need to deconstruct racism in the United States should be apparent to those who read it in its entirety with an objective eye. However, long before publication my presentiments tell me at least a few critics will depict this work in much the way Birmingham's clergymen and many other Americans painted the efforts of King and other soldiers of the Civil Rights Movement—as accusatory, subversive, communistic, intent-on-blaming-whitey, and whatever other negative adjectives they can conjure in their dealing of aspersions. Such rhetoric has proven effective in silencing the efforts of those who, in their hearts if not their hands, agitate for racial equality in America.

Broaching the issue of race frightens Americans so much, many of them our very leaders, that they tiptoe around the issue for fear of backlash so strong as to lead their careers down a path of ruin. Silence, however, is no sort of convenience. Silence does not peer into the eyes of injustice with indissoluble determination. It turns away in diffidence. It supports, enables, and motivates racism and the oblique, pervasive political dialogue that gives it life. Silence kills us. Where pride should reside, guilt rests. Where action belongs, complacency sets in. Where courage should prevail, fear paralyzes. We must refuse those who, for reasons of either sheer ignorance or hatred, would try to silence us, the inheritors of the legacy advanced by King, the SCLC, and other agents of the Civil Rights Movement.

Last in Line's mission is too vast to capture in just a few paragraphs—hence its book form. For clarity's sake, I will highlight just a few of the things this book is meant to be:

This is an effort at policy reform. America's ills will not be healed by dialogue. They will not be healed through guilt or remorse, no matter how sincere. Dialogue and understanding are only prerequisites for reform. Conversation only tells us how best to take action to implement reform. Moral objection only motivates exploration; it need not be guilt. Dialogue and ethical grounding are only starting points for the actions Americans must take to bring lasting, effective reforms to our system.

The U.S. government was once the most notorious sponsor of racial discrimination, legislating, legitimating, and legalizing many of the inhumane practices whose effects manifest today in surreptitious forms. In the justice, education, economic, and health care systems, institutional racism manifests in its most rabid and injurious forms, impairing the average American minority's quality of life, especially African Americans. It is government's responsibility to respect the lives of all Americans. Americans must call on their government to review policies that hamper and jeopardize lives and amend them in a just and constitutional fashion. **This is an indictment of American society.** I am grateful to be American. Part of this gratitude is being in tune with the suffering of my American ancestors—the labors, the humiliation, and the outright suffering that they experienced under this flag and with the endorsement of those elected to represent that flag. I sympathize with those of other ethnicities, including those of Hispanic, Chinese, Korean, and even European immigrant ancestry, who bore their own devastating forms of oppression on arrival in the United States, but I indict America's aberrant treatment of African Americans that is as much as a staple of my ancestors' lifetimes as it is my own. I will not capitulate to those who insist we "get over" transgressions that still impair us today. I rather indict these Americans and implore them to stand up to the injustices for which all Americans must be held accountable.

And above all, this is a call to save America. "A kingdom founded on injustice never lasts."[51] From the mouth of Seneca, great Roman thinker and statesman, came these words. Commandeered lands, genocides, forced bondage, social exclusion—these are realities that cannot be refuted, no matter how much many deny them.

America's race problem may yet implode—it has done so before. The Civil War eviscerated our then-young republic and threatened to truncate its history to a period spanning not even a century. America yet again suffered racial implosion a century later as some of the most intense race riots in its history erupted in cities in and between all its corners. The 1960s was the season of assassination, the abundant blood of patriots watering Jefferson's proverbial tree of liberty without the complementary contribution of tyrants. Blacks rose, casting off diffidence and the vulnerability and submission it chaperoned. They took the lesson of the Founding Fathers in asserting freedom with force. Many, black and white alike, saw race war as imminent as America yet again burst at her seams, tearing the sacred fabric of the Star-Spangled Banner.

The saying is at once trite, elusive, and incomprehensible: those who do not learn from history are bound to repeat it. American history is a pattern of neglected injustice followed by revolution—this has characterized us from the beginning. We ourselves, under the yoke of the British Crown, revolted against injustice only to emulate such wrongdoing in our own American fashion. If we do not alter this pattern, it will alter itself unto permanent implosion.

I love America and desire her longevity. As long as she inhabits this universe without propitiating spirit for her sins, she is imperiled. Alongside her virtues, her unpleasant realities are documented in history's annals. They are inerasable. Though inerasable, they are rectifiable. This is a call for Americans to right these wrongs once and for all and ensure national eternity.

We must define ourselves not by words, beliefs, or desires, but actions. By itself, thought is inconsequential; action is the stuff of creation. Although I compel all those who hear my message to meditate, above all I compel them to act.

①
"Get Over It"

"Pound Cake" forever altered Cliff Huxtable's palatable image. Its recipe called for one pungent, heaping tablespoon of indignation. Bill Cosby had not been known for stridence—or any significant political or social commentary, really. Jell-O? Cardigans? Sexual assault? Sure. Each of these things figured in the schema associated with Cosby. (In all fairness, the third only became a synonym for "Cosby" a decade later.) But Cosby's "Pound Cake" speech was a different jingle—less gelatinous yet more appetizing to America's insulin-resistant masses. America devoured. Cosby's criticisms of the black community's gross imperfections and shortcomings were lauded by many, perhaps effusively so by mainstream America.

Cosby arraigned the usual suspects: negligent and absent black fathers; insolent, truant, rambunctious, gang-banging adolescent black males; and irresponsible, ever-pregnant teenage black women. In a harangue of the black "lower" and "lower middle"[52] income brackets that elicited scarce smiles from the stone-cold faces of Middle America, Cosby cast stones in a paternalistic back-in-my-day fashion that left much of the nation nodding (albeit in starkly different ways). Cosby didn't even spare rod-shy single black mothers, inquiring of their orange jumpsuit-donning sons, "Where were you when he was two…twelve…eighteen? Why didn't you know he had a pistol?"

Of course, all this was before Cosby again reintroduced himself to the American public as a prolific dispenser of Quaaludes—and probable rapist, to boot. But few stars are even twice-born and Cosby was one of those stars, spit shining his way to the endearment of a large, right-wing swath of the American public. Cosby came to the NAACP's 50th anniversary celebration of the 1954 *Brown v. Board* ruling equipped with statistics, attesting to the "50 percent [high school] dropout rate" among black students as well as a similarly credible claim of the commonality of black women having babies by "five or six different men." Cosby also bore anecdotal testimony of young black males getting "shot in the head over…pound cake!" by police officers whose lethal judgment we shouldn't dare question. Why? "What the hell was he doing with the pound cake in his hand?" His thoughtful analysis assumed an interestingly xenophobic slant, insisting that in its misguided, ignorant, linguistically inept African American youth, America was breeding its own "ingrown immigrants" who like to "shoot…and do stupid things" for kicks.

Cosby's diatribe continued as he shared the story of another hapless black youth who murders someone over pizza, as well as stories of the myriad women with "eight" or maybe "ten" husbands (forgive him—he didn't make note of this particular statistic) and multimillionaire athletes who "can't read a paragraph" (or playbook, presumably). In spite of such perspicacity, Cosby's remarks were not without detractors. Many in the black community rebuked Cosby for his hyperbolic, extended lamentation, accusing him of spewing fabricated anecdotes in the vein of Ronald Reagan's "welfare queen"[53] fables and neglecting systemic racism's role in engendering many of the ills to which he colorfully alluded. To them, Cosby did nothing productive except add to the black stereotype repertoire—that of the hungry black male who risks his

1

Last in Line: An American Destiny Deferred

life and those of others for to-die-for—literally—cakes and pizzas. Perhaps killing over fruits and salads would, to Mr. Cosby, be a more salubrious, forgivable pathology (not to mention something we could never conceive of Fat Albert doing).

Scholar Michael Eric Dyson issued a pointed rebuttal to Cosby's comments entitled *Is Bill Cosby Right?* Dyson argued that Cosby's deprecations were shortsighted and accused Cosby of shifting the blame too far from the problem of institutional racism, insisting, "All the right behavior in the world won't create better jobs with more pay,"[54] and adding, "...if the rigidly segregated educational system continues to miserably fail poor blacks by failing to prepare their children for the world of work, then admonitions to 'stay in school' may ring hollow."[55] Reverend Al Sharpton's appraisal of Cosby's remarks was reserved; he agreed with most of Cosby's points, but cautioned, "We also must be careful not to relieve the general community of what they've done to our community."[56] Maryland congressman Elijah Cummings added more critically, "It gives a society which may have racist tendencies at times...a pass, an excuse, while so many African Americans are working very, very hard."[57] Contrarily, conservative pundit Bill O'Reilly commended Cosby, stating that he was preaching "self-reliance" and that those in contention with Cosby were making "excuses."[58]

Cosby's cognitive dissonance with regard to racism—a more direct and explicit problem during his youth—is rather stunning. His nostalgia over the seeming cultural coherence of his era is unbridled. He adds that African Americans back in his day, "[Knew it was] important to speak English," at least when not hanging out on the street corner. Cosby evokes shame in lackadaisical and imprudent black youth, reminding them of the stalwart blacks of his day who were showered in "rocks" and "firehoses" for such opportunities which their posterity now squandered. Cosby's statements corroborated what much of America wanted to proclaim but was often afraid to.

Black America's dysfunction is often said to result from its imprudent use of a broken moral compass. This explains the misdirection of irresponsible, marijuana-smoking, baby-making, school-quitting (and, according to Bill, pound cake-stealing) black teenagers, as well as criminal, sex-crazed, malingering adult black men (not to mention the tax dollar-embezzling black women for whom conception is a fiscal matter). Antiracist author Tim Wise cites several statistics corroborating the ubiquity of belief in such stereotypes, one documenting that 70 percent of white Americans admit to believing at least one erroneous stereotype about African Americans.[59] But Cosby's publicized corroboration of such attitudes lent an enlivening air of legitimacy. It's one thing for someone white to proclaim such beliefs. But for a famous, respected black man to qualify sentiments ubiquitous in white America was vindicating. White America sighed, praising Cosby—"Finally, one of them's got it figured out!"

Where does mainstream America's perception of a black America in dire need of calibration come from? Is it procured from nightly newscasts? Reality series on VH1 or Black Entertainment Television? Are Americans confusing the subject matter of fictional television shows and movies with real life? Perhaps there is a sounder, empirical basis. Perhaps researchers are bivouacking in housing projects, recording observations of the rough and wild African American habitat. Clearly, there is *some* sort of intimacy that gives mainstream America license to profess certain and legitimate

2

understanding of just what black America is really like. Whatever the method of research, white America is quite confident in the conclusions it draws from it.

A national survey measuring the prevalence of beliefs in racial stereotypes about African Americans found such attitudes pervasive. The survey asked respondents to assess the degree to which blacks exhibited attributes such as laziness, determination, dependability, work ethic, and discipline. Thirty-one percent of those surveyed agreed with the statement that blacks were lazy, 20 percent concurred that they were irresponsible, 50 percent said they were aggressive, and 60 percent believed that blacks were lacking in discipline.[60] Tim Wise's *Colorblind* cites further statistics attesting to the congruence between Cosby's beliefs and those of Middle America. Believing applicants with black-sounding names (e.g., Shamiqua, Jontavious— Jamal, even) to be less fit for certain jobs, they were less likely to be called back for interviews, qualifications notwithstanding.[61] Additionally, employers were more likely to question the legitimacy of black applicants' qualifications.[62] White homeowners agree with these employers that the presence of impulsive, hell-raising African Americans is undesirable. One in four say that the ideal neighborhood would have none at all.[63]

During the time in which Cosby says black Americans had better-calibrated moral compasses, they underwent some of the most brutal and open forms of racial violence witnessed in history. In 1955, the year Cosby (himself a high school dropout)[64] turned 18, Emmett Till's murderers were infamously acquitted. In the ensuing decade, race riots swept major metropolitan centers all across America, the furious national inferno inspiring burning and bombing in some cities. Governor and perennial presidential candidate George Wallace of Alabama famously declared his intent to eternalize the institution of segregation. Arizona senator Barry Goldwater, the 1964 Republican presidential nominee, decried the Civil Rights Act as an impractical attempt to "legislate morality."[65] All the while, white Americans were unaware anything was wrong in the black community. Despite turbulence and frustration coming to a head in the black community, two-thirds of whites felt blacks were "pushing too hard, too fast"[66] for civil rights.

Gallup polls from 1962 and 1963 indicate that between 66 and 90 percent of whites thought that blacks received equal treatment with regard to opportunities for jobs, schooling, and housing.[67] Needless to say, these sentiments were contradicted by the national conflagration that erupted in response to the question of whether blacks deserved equal rights in America. That such attitudes were pervasive in the early '60s seems preposterous. As for today, we feel we have arrived. We boast of equal opportunity not as an unrealized ideal, but a social norm, and hold any further agitation for rights as unnecessary, perhaps even threatening to the ideal of equality. This time we got it right. Racial prejudice has been erased, a black president has been elected, and Dr. King's dream has at last come to fruition. Racism is a documentary, a history term paper, a museum exhibit. But to speak of racism in a modern context? That's beating a beast slayed long ago.

Except that beast has not been slayed; we know this by our reflection. Racism is not a tired topic—racism is *itself* tired. The ability to grasp this distinction separates Americans like Bill Cosby (and the millions who, in the wake of his sexual assault scandal, retain the message but not the messenger) from Americans who get that race is a neglected blight on America's moral legacy. The sound research conducted by the Cosby crowd has convinced

3

them that racism lives only in imagination, an extinct Easter Bunny poached by a suddenly race-blind America in the 1960s only to be resurrected by a modern, attention-seeking, race-baiting element.

Americans still look forward to the day when racism exhales its last breath, living only in retrospective contexts. Considering institutional racism's capacious respiration, that day seems far off. In the 2016 presidential campaign cycle, ISIS, oil prices, debt-free college, gun control, and other salient issues found no shortage of room in the books, speeches, and debates of candidates. Institutionalized racism garnered more mention than in previous cycles (thanks largely to Black Lives Matter), but the topic remains, at best, an afterthought and, at worst, a sideshow rather than a national priority. Even during the 2008 presidential campaign cycle, the most mention the subject of race received was in regard to President Obama's ties to controversial pastor Reverend Jeremiah Wright. Incendiary barks again seized media headlines in 2016 as Republican presidential nominee Donald Trump eschewed antiquated, Nixon-era dog whistle technology for direct incitement to hatred and violence. Although Obama's path to the White House depended on retreat from fiery rhetoric, Trump's demagoguery may raze that road en route to the rebirth of a nation.

American think tanks, foundations, and NGOs deem conflicts and crises in the Middle East more troubling than the state-sanctioned institutional race war carrying on within our borders, despite the thousands upon thousands of casualties piling up each year. They are not victims of mortar shells, suicide bombings, or the AK-47s of ISIS insurgents, but a negligent health care system, a justice system with no regard for just cause, and a society that is, at best, unmindful of and, at worst, supportive of such disparate trends.

In *The Anatomy of Racial Inequality*, Professor Glenn C. Loury posits why racism receives little acknowledgment from American policymakers. He writes, "A racial group is stigmatized when it can experience an alarming disparity in some social indicators, and yet that disparity occasion no societal reflection upon the extent to which that circumstance signals something having gone awry in *our* structures rather than something having gone wrong in *theirs*."[68] The normality with which society regards black incarceration, indigence, and illness is, to say the least of Loury, evidence of the existence of an intricate, largely unrecognized stigma that afflicts black Americans.

Without a thought, we witness the local newscast starring yet another black criminal and emit a derisive remark and a mere yawn before retiring for the night. While tending to our daily errands, we ride past a line of indigents, speckled white but mostly black, emanating from a downtown soup kitchen, granting a thoughtless glance. Whether viewed on our flat screens, commutes, social media feeds, or even in our imaginations, the black image is the static face of failure. Society has come to regard many of the stereotypes associated with blacks with frightening expectation. Criminality, unemployment, poverty, and mortality form just a few elements of the sociopathological constellation that captures what it means to be black in America today.

"Get Over" What?

Few dispute that chattel slavery was reprehensible. For most, the notion of trafficking humans in the manner of cattle or sheep is unfathomable. Not only do we agree that slavery is objectionable—we regard it as America's greatest sin. President John Adams summed up the sentiments which the provident abolitionists of his day sermoned. Adams said, "Consenting to slavery is a sacrilegious breach of trust, as offensive in the sight of God as it is derogatory from our own honor or interest of happiness."[69] Like Adams, we know beyond a shadow of a doubt that slavery is evil. But it was "back then," part of a shameful past to be remembered, learned from, and never again tolerated upon our soil or anywhere else in the world. This consensus on the evil of America's "peculiar institution" is accompanied by the idea that just as the system is trapped in time—a relic accessible only through diaries and daguerreotypes—so are its symptoms and effects.

Still, somehow a farsightedness exists. Alongside the brutal narratives woven into screenplays for *Django Unchained* and *12 Years A Slave* exists a somehow innocuous, somewhat fanciful *Gone with the Wind* recollection. Sure—slaves were sometimes beaten when they got out of line or when they attempted to steal themselves in fleeing. Of course it was heartbreaking when families were broken up and separated by frugal and calculating masters, never to see their beloved again. But, still—it's hard to look at Butterfly McQueen's smiling visage and imagine that anything could have been *that* bad.

Don't we all endure tragedy of some sort? Slavery perhaps doesn't look so bad in comparison to the sort of want and suffering Scarlett and her family endured in the wake of Dixie's defeat. After all, Sherman's March reduced their station to that not so unlike those they held in bondage not long before. Close enough to equality, right? Slavery was unfortunate. But is it truly of the magnitude that African Americans can't get over it? No one today has a "massa" for whom they must suckle children, fiddle, pick cotton, or suffer any other similar indignities. What is there to complain about?

This is the "get over it" argument in a nutshell. Blacks today aren't slaves. Their parents weren't slaves. Their parents' parents weren't slaves. Their parents' parents' parents weren't, either. So what's the big deal?

Though this argument declares itself the progeny of sincere rationality, its lineage can be traced only to utter lunacy. If America had fulfilled the promises of Reconstruction and the country saw rebirth as the egalitarian society abolitionists and freedmen alike envisioned, a euphonic tune would be in order. Instead, a cacophonous, deafening medley blares. There were certain activists—progressive, radical Republicans of the North—who spearheaded efforts to ensure black equality. In Congress, they passed the Thirteenth, Fourteenth, and Fifteenth amendments, promoted the Freedmen's Bureau, and championed the establishment of educational institutions for blacks of all ages. They agitated for black enfranchisement, ushering 17 African Americans into both houses of the United States Congress between 1868 and 1880.[70] With such efforts came the radical implication that blacks might indeed be *humans*, of character and mettle, among the "men" the U.S. Constitution deemed unalienably equal to one another. This was the original Civil Rights Movement, arriving a century before the one with which we are more familiar.

This movement encountered fierce resistance. Ex-Confederates resumed arms, the companies of Bull Run and Antietam reforming as night-riding squadrons dedicated to eradicating signs of black progress abominable to the old guard's memory.[71] Riding high upon stallions like the relentless Confederate officers who they fought under and as, they tore through Dixie imposing brutal vigilante justice upon uppity, carpetbagging elements who dared to usurp white, patriarchal, Southern authority. The Ku Klux Klan of this day wasn't the fringe, isolated element its modern incarnation is depicted

5

as, but one that raged on behalf of the white collective. They refused to be emasculated by their Northern conquerors and the docile, inane Negroes whom they held in bondage only yesterday.

Contrary to popular belief, white resistance to racial equality was not confined to the postbellum South. Their Northern enemies too squirmed at the idea of social intercourse with blacks. Thoughts of sitting next to blacks in restaurants, schools—in church pews, beside black soon-to-be in-laws—were abhorrent. Crusades of equality in the North were met with resistance as fierce as that displayed by Union troops at Gettysburg. Civil rights freedom fighters responded with retreat; once determined efforts regressed to inertia.

Although 16 African Americans served in Congress during Reconstruction (an additional man, John Willis Menard, was elected to the U.S. House from Louisiana in 1868 but was refused his seat),[72] none of them hailed from the same states as their freedom-fighting, carpetbagging saviors. In Pennsylvania's 1866 gubernatorial election, Democratic candidate Heister Clymer campaigned on a vehement platform of racial revulsion, accusing his opponent John W. Geary's efforts of being solely "for the Negro" in contrast to Clymer's advocacy for "the white man."[73] Though Clymer would lose the election, he garnered a respectable number of votes and parlayed his demagogic appeal into a seat in Congress, serving alongside many of the "Negroes" whom he reviled.

In the White House, Lincoln's Democratic successor Andrew Johnson declared a similarly fervid commitment to upholding white American dominance. President Johnson bitterly warned the "splay-footed, bandy-shanked, hump-backed, thick-lipped, flat-nosed, woolly headed, ebon-colored"[74] Negroes that voting rights and public service were exclusive properties of a white political domain. Johnson opposed slavery, but not with moral objections. For Johnson, if packing slaves into *Amistad*s and transporting them along the routes of the Middle Passage was necessary to save the United States government from destruction, he would not hesitate.[75] Johnson further underlined his sentiments with an unequivocal statement:

> This is a country for white men, and by God, as long as I am President, it shall be a government for white men .... This whole vast continent is destined to fall under the control of the Anglo-Saxon race—the governing and self-governing race.[76]

Though many Northerners made effortful strides toward racial equality in the United States, their pace slowed to capitulation. The 1876 presidential election (which embroiled the nation in a degree of controversy only rivaled in 2000) was the harbinger of the end. Republican Rutherford B. Hayes would succeed the pro-civil rights Ulysses S. Grant, but only after Republicans and Democrats brokered a death-blowing deal spelling out Reconstruction's end. The immediate pullout of Northern troops and dissolution of military districts in the South beckoned a stalemate unbecoming of such a long and bloody battle.[77] The souls of those who shed blood on the flag, from heavy arms—some wielding guns, others garden hoes—cautioned us, crying for yet more. But those cries were ignored. Though a Tilden White House was not to be, his service in interest of the sanctity of white American dominance paid due homage to the previous Democratic president. In the hearts of opponents of change, it likely yielded Tilden a greater legacy than his presence in an Oval Office beholden to a Reconstructionist agenda would have.

6

Chapter 1: "Get Over It"

In the aftermath of the Compromise of 1877, Republicans in the North felt they now had the best of both worlds—a third consecutive term in the White House and an excuse to abandon the fruitless effort to bring about racial equality in the South. The Southern man would not relent. Maybe the idea of Negro equality was absurd, after all. Reconstruction—and its ideal of racial equality—was dead. Jim Crow was born.

Birth of a(n) (unequal) Nation

African Americans would not again see such a determined effort to achieve equality for nearly a century. Even though in the span of just over a decade 17 blacks had been elected to the Reconstruction-era Congress, 89 years passed before the next 17 were elected to Congress. After Reconstruction, an African American was not elected to the U.S. Senate again until 1967, when Republican Edward William Brooke III (ironically conservative and palatably light-skinned) took office in Massachusetts. This decrease in representation correlated with a decrease in black suffrage, a trend seen throughout the South. In 1897, 130,000 African Americans were registered to vote in Louisiana.[78] In the subsequent year, the Louisiana state legislature passed a new constitution that included a triple whammy of grandfather clauses, poll taxes, and literacy tests that curbed the tide of black voter turnout. By 1900, Louisiana's African American voting bloc was reduced to approximately 5,000 persons.[79] The waxing of black progress' tide proved ephemeral as it waned into the state of prostration with which it was all too familiar.

But the loss of political representation was neither the only nor worst devastation. The inability of blacks to establish economic self-sufficiency proved the most damning consequence of Reconstruction's abortion. Throughout the 250-year period of free labor in which African Americans generated an amount of wealth equal to anywhere from $2 trillion to $4 trillion today,[80] America's key industries were germinating, many of their seeds sprouting into verdant markets. The key industries responsible for America's proliferating wealth, like lumber, mining, coal, and steel (not to mention the agrarian sector that continued to enjoy exploitation of black labor postbellum) were restricted to white investment during slavery. Not even free blacks were welcome on capitalistic playgrounds with the future titans of industry. It was not only the condition of servitude, but also the conspicuous stigma of blackness that disqualified black participation in the capitalistic Manifest Destiny that came of age beneath the same roof as its geographic sibling.

Jim Crow America did, however, engineer an industry just for blacks: sharecropping.[81] An insidious, subsistence-based system crafted by Southerners to both enable the continued exploitation of blacks and hamstring black society's attempts at independent enterprise, sharecropping was in effect "slavery by another name." Blacks in the North begged for low-paying factorial jobs, drawing fierce competition from hostile whites[82] willing to resort to violence of the Southern echelon to protect their racial birthright.[83] The 1863 New York City Draft Riots were but one instance of a true "War of Northern Aggression" directed not against Southern white planters but rather Northern black indigents. Many of the rioters were poor Irish immigrants, outraged that America dare ask them to shed blood for the creation of an emancipated class that may then shed theirs on the job market. American industrialization represented the assumption of a new imperial destiny in which, as usual, the only station available to blacks was that at the bottom.

Last in Line: An American Destiny Deferred

Floating the concept of a rising tide lifting all boats wouldn't have gotten one very far in those days. But today, the idea that government can engineer one-size-fits-all policies that work for everyone without consideration to history and circumstance is common among policymakers. It is also shortsighted. Though the tide has risen, it is uneven. It raises some boats—formidable, ironclad supertankers—into the stratosphere, leaving others—old frigates with torn masts, leaking hulls, and bogging impedimenta—just miles above sea level.

In *Black Labor, White Wealth*, Dr. Claud Anderson captures the congruity between the severity of contemporary black poverty and that of blacks in postbellum America:

> One hundred and thirty years after slavery, American society has become more pluralistic and competitive, but blacks' marginal conditions remain relatively unchanged. In some respects, they have worsened. The socioeconomic inequalities that existed between whites and blacks during and shortly after slavery are now structural.

> For example, on the eve of the Civil War, records indicated that more than 50 percent of free blacks were paupers; all *free blacks collectively held less than one-half of one percent of the nation's wealth*, with wealth being defined as a great quantity of money or valuable goods or resources within both the private and public sectors. A century later, in the 1960s, an era considered by many as a "great decade of progress for blacks," more than 55 percent of all the blacks in America were still impoverished and below the poverty line. And, *blacks barely held one percent of the nation's wealth*. (Emphasis added.)[84]

An entire century followed emancipation during which African Americans tried their best to adapt to a society that structured its incompatibility. Despite America at last being home to a free, determined black population, in a century the total amount of wealth held by African Americans increased by just *one-half percent*. Anderson cites further statistics highlighting the similarity between the financial lack of blacks in the late 20th century and those in the era preceding the Civil Rights Movement:

> The [National Urban League's] discomfort index further indicated that black unemployment worsened between 1960 and 1990, while economic conditions for white society improved. Blacks' lack of progress was reflected in the fact that blacks earned 53 percent of what whites earned in 1948. In the 1990s, after nearly 50 years of civil rights activities and affirmative action programs, blacks [earned] 59 percent of what whites [earned].[85]

By some measures, the trend of widening racial wealth disparity is worsening well into the 2010s. The typical American white household in 2016 had anywhere from 13 to 16 times the wealth of the typical black household.[86] Compare that to 2001, when it had just six times as much. A joint study by Brandeis University's Institute on Assets and Social Policy and New York-based think tank Demos corroborated this, showing that the median wealth of a white household in the 2010s was $111,146 compared to $8,348 for Hispanic families and $7,113 for black families. Among other factors, the study cites the relationship between homeownership and wealth returns, showing that blacks and Hispanics both have lower rates of homeownership and lower rates of return from homes when they do own them.

A similar study exploring the dynamics of wealth and race in America found that by 2016, blacks' collective share of national wealth had increased to just 2.6 percent.[87] For all the affirmative action jobs, handouts, and "free stuff" conservatives lament, 50 years of ostensibly post-racial public policies have yielded just a *one and a half* percent increase in black America's total share of national wealth. Even that little bit affords no cause for celebration. Given the growth of the racial wealth gap and the persistent poverty characterizing much of the African American community, it stands to reason that even this small gain has largely been afforded to a sliver of wealthy blacks.

Such information belies the notion of progress that so many argue characterizes the time-lapse between the passage of the 1964 Civil Rights Act and today. Despite the increased presence of African Americans in white-collar professions, the economic fortunes of the black community have improved little since the Civil Rights Movement. Furthermore, the notion that blacks have made tremendous progress in white-collar positions doesn't hold much weight upon scrutiny. Although there are more blacks in white-collar positions than ever before, whites still account for 83 percent of all managerial positions.[88] Though we often speak of a "glass ceiling" that characterizes the discriminatory gender pay gap, there is a "Plexiglas ceiling" (explored in the sixth chapter) characterizing the racial pay gap often neglected in our national dialogue. Such disparities hold even when controlling for education. By one estimate, whites earn 20 percent more than blacks of similar education levels.[89] More than individual wealth, however, the abundance of wealth in major corporate institutions has for decades attested to the tremendous racial disparity seen in America's economic system:

> Whites own nearly 100 percent of all corporate stocks and bonds, which amounts to approximately $13 trillion. In 1986 the 256th largest company of the Fortune 500, a [white-owned] corporation, had sales equal to the $16 billion total combined sales of the nation's 100 largest [b]lack-owned businesses...[90]

Skeptics question claims of racism's role in fomenting these disparities. They maintain that slavery and Jim Crow are things of the past and that today no institutions deny African Americans access to the American dream. They insist that blacks' avoidance of agency is the culprit. The absence of work ethic, education, responsibility, law-abidingness—and fathers—from the black household condemns black America. They argue that the time in which blacks were denied equal opportunity has passed and that blacks are now given a fair shake in society—perhaps too fair. But when such disparities persist even when blacks have degrees and other meritocratic markers and lack criminal records, there can be no rationale other than institutionalized racism. In the story of Tulsa, Oklahoma lies a poignant example refuting the meritocratic myth that ethics and values suffice for progress.

The Tulsa Riot

Tulsa was booming—especially Greenwood. Arriving from the Southern United States just a generation earlier, residents of Tulsa's all-black Greenwood Township shook off the fatigue and disappointment that enclasped their Southern communities during Reconstruction. The North's abandonment and the onset of racial terrorism left them despondent, bereft of any hope that the South might deliver them from destitution and suffering. They hoped that, at the very least, escape from that uncharitable world might give both them and their posterity a chance at peace. They got far more than they could have bargained for.

White Tulsans first derided Greenwood as "Little Africa."[91] But derision gave way; as that name boldened, so did their impulse to blooden. Tulsa began as a singular entity but was demarcated when black Tulsans became self-sustaining and ambitious enough to christen their hemisphere "Greenwood," the namesake of the street that ran through it.[92] O. W. Gurley, a wealthy African American landowner from Arkansas, paved the way for Greenwood's establishment as a financial center for black Oklahomans. Taking advantage of the Indian Appropriations Act signed into law by President Grover Cleveland (and administered under his successor Benjamin Harrison), Gurley staked out his share of nearly 2 million acres of land allocated in the Oklahoma Land Rush of 1889.[93] He made a symbolic purchase[94]—40 acres—with the intention of selling only to fellow African Americans.[95]

One would be wrong to blame Gurley for such explicit "reverse racism." After all, Tulsa's laws prohibited blacks from shopping in white-owned stores or residing in white areas. Blacks were systematically locked out of competition with the 150,000 white settlers who claimed the famed Land Rush's vast expanses.[96] Mob violence, Ku Klux Klan bellicosity, and institutionally racist legislation kept the program a whites-only free-for-all. Still, Gurley somehow got his hands on the proverbial 40 acres (perhaps sans mule) and embarked on a journey to manifest his vision of an affluent black metropolis.

Gurley spearheaded the establishment of many businesses in the town and galvanized Greenwood's burgeoning black population. Led by Gurley with the hope, ingenuity, and work ethic their enslaved ancestors ingrained in them, Greenwood's inhabitants produced a prosperous professional class. Doctors, lawyers, realtors, and white-collar workers of all sorts were present, working to fulfill the needs of community. Among this class were both descendants of slaves and ex-slaves themselves, men and women who not long before lived in bondage, destitution, and constant fear of Ku Klux Klan reprisals. They found paradise, a promised land of biblical proportions upon Earth.

This newfound heaven would soon, however, reduce to rubble and ash, conflagrating black ambition in an inferno of hellish proportions.

Blacks may have been out of sight from white Tulsan society, but they were not out of mind. Tulsa's Ku Klux Klan chapter mimicked Greenwood's unforeseen growth, reminiscent of the marauding bands Greenwood blacks fled decades earlier. Racial tensions reached a fever pitch when rumors circulated of an assault on a white woman named Sarah Page by an African American man named Dick Rowland.[97] Police investigations determined that no such assault had transpired, but this assurance did little to mitigate brewing tensions.

10

Chapter 1: "Get Over It"

Sensationalist headlines went viral, imploring white Tulsans to "nab [the] Negro for attacking [the] girl in an elevator!"[98] Though Rowland was still detained in the courthouse, in typical fashion a lynch mob gathered outside and demanded Rowland be handed over. Armed African Americans, wanting to prevent a repeat of the 1920 lynching of a local resident named Roy Belton,[99] went to the courthouse to offer the Tulsa sheriff their assistance in defending the stronghold. Though the sheriff persuaded them to return to Greenwood, the mere sight of blacks with guns was enough to rouse whites into overrunning the local National Guard Armory in an attempt to arm themselves for an ensuing racial battle.[100] Rebuffed, they returned to the scene of the courthouse. From here, tensions further brewed and soon spilled over with a blood-red hue.

Sporadic gunfights evolved into shootouts. Bullet sparks bore stark contrast with the sky dark as their intended targets. Dawn cracked, the first shot of one of the bloodiest race riots in American history. Volleys and explosions gave chase, fiercely competing for the most destructive impression. Armed, furious, and early rising, whites poured into Greenwood to obliterate the niggers who had forgotten their place. Outgunned and outmanned, African Americans offered futile defense of Greenwood. Stores, shops, and offices shared inferno.

Black men, women, and children lay where they stood. On their backs, they took last breaths of dust and chaos. Their penultimate life sights were those of planes flying overhead—their last of the descent of bombs and bullets of aerial fighters.[101] By noon most of the between $1.5 million and $4 million (1921 value) in damage had been done. Several, black and white alike, lay dead in the streets.[102] Although conservative estimates put the death toll of the Tulsa Riot at 39, as many as 300 may have been killed.[103] Following the riot, no fewer than 37 black men were employed to dig 120 graves in which black victims were interred.[104]

Blacks in postbellum America made the most of what little they had. Throughout the South, they tried to form their own cohesive, self-sufficient communities. When they couldn't do that, like the inhabitants of Greenwood they went some place where they thought they could. At every turn, judicial and political obstruction met these efforts, often enforced through violence.

During this era, the federal government implemented numerous measures for the financial benefit of Americans. Manifest Destiny was in full swing and the government was intent on settling new and soon-to-be integrated lands with red-blooded Americans. These revolutionary government-sponsored programs aided the creation of what would become the American middle class. Furthermore, they provided American citizens with the potential to build capital to invest in businesses and industries that would proliferate in value in the late 19th and early 20th centuries. White Americans reaped the benefits; blacks were excluded.

Although most instances of economic discrimination weren't as bloody as those witnessed in Tulsa, they bore tantamount devastation. The consequences of these economic policies would transcend generations. In 1862, the Homestead Act permitted settlers access to near-free, 160-acre tracts of federal lands.[105] A total of 250 million acres of land were transferred gratis to 1.5 million pioneering white families, courtesy of the United States government.[106] The value of such a huge transfer of wealth is felt even today, as 20 million white Americans boast transgenerational benefit from these early land giveaways.[107] Additionally, more than 50 million living persons, almost all of them white, can boast of status as homesteader descendants.[108] African Americans who dared to place stakes in white-reserved lands were threatened by mob violence and a general refusal of the government to recognize their claims.[109] Although blacks did indeed have a destiny, the federal government refused to play any role in its manifestation.

More such exclusion occurred later in the 20th century, leaving blacks unable to take advantage of the financial growth sweeping America. President Warren Harding signed the Mineral Leasing Act into law in 1920, giving the federal government authorization to lease public land for exploration of oil, gas, and other valuable minerals and resources. Authorizations were granted only to white citizens, preventing blacks from making stakes in these lucrative industries.[110] Technological advancements gave way to a nascent media industry which the government also regulated for white benefit. Signed into law by laconic, *laissez-faire* president Calvin Coolidge, the Radio Act of 1927 authorized the awarding of radio broadcast franchises to private citizens. No licenses were granted to African Americans.[111] Decades later, radio broadcast licenses valued in the billions are still held almost exclusively by whites.[112] The FCC issued the first television broadcast licenses in 1939 under the administration of Franklin Roosevelt.[113] For more than three decades no broadcast licenses were given to blacks.[114] By the 1980s, all television franchises were still white-owned, ranging in value from $5 million to $10 billion.[115] In government contracting, African Americans were similarly kept out of play.[116] From 1941 until 1980, approximately $3 trillion in contract awards were made almost exclusively to white-owned firms.[117]

When one fails to consider the prohibitive circumstances that stood in the way of African American efforts to "catch-up" to their white counterparts, they subscribe to thoughtless theories ascribing these failures to black inadequacy. Blacks have had 150 years to "get it together," they insist. Anyone making such an assertion fails to grasp that although African Americans did indeed realize legislative freedom, they have been denied the economic emancipation that would enable them to thrive and succeed in America. Given that African Americans are still subjected to various forms of economic discrimination, we should understand that the reins of economic enslavement haven't loosened much. When the nation's unemployment rate exceeds 8 percent, we have a crisis on our hands. But when the black unemployment rate remains above 10 percent, American society perceives that as normal. This reflects the normalization of economic race disparity in America and the endurance of age-old biases in America's national consciousness.

Given their four-century subjugation in the United States and the only recent legal mandating of racial equality, the expectation of total black self-realization is nothing less than absurd. The period during which blacks faced *de jure* discrimination in ways both explicit and myriad (from the 17th century until the passage of the Civil Rights Act of 1964) is the period during which white Americans staked claims in crucial economic industries that were the foundation of the American economy. While whites pioneered, invested, and earned, sweeping *de facto* and *de jure* discrimination left blacks disabled. The time and means needed to acquire such resources are great and even now could never be afforded to blacks without great expense. Absent compensatory measures or revolutionary affirmative action initiatives, it would take millennia for blacks to even approach "catch up"—and that's assuming the pace of white development is overtaken by that of African Americans, an onerous prospect in itself. America has failed to go beyond half-century old laws to engineer effectual solutions to race disparity. Perhaps America never truly sought a republic of equality in emancipation's aftermath. Some have always regarded the notion of such equality between white and black as absurd. U.S. senator and fervent Lincoln supporter David Wilmot, a man noted for his anti-slavery views, is alleged to have insisted in spite of his support for emancipation, "Black people are inferior to Caucasians...blacks constitute a totally distinct group; they overshadow the country with the germ...of evil." His philosophy doesn't seem to differ much from that of current U.S. senator Jeff Sessions, who allegedly referred to an African American coworker as "boy," quipped that civil rights groups were "un-American," and expressed an opprobriously ambivalent attitude about the Ku Klux Klan.[118]

That blacks, who yesterday had been slaves, could be rendered human by a pen's strike was a notion contemptible to many whites of that era, Democrat and Republican alike. Certainly, Democrats in Congress—in concord with Lincoln's successor, President Andrew Johnson—did not view it as a moral prerogative or democratic obligation to ensure blacks safe passage from servitude to freedom. They found improbable allies across a rocky aisle. Reconstruction dragged on; the idea of black equality trailed, sullying in soil rendered ruddy by the Civil War's martial aftershocks. As the Republican Reconstruction platform lost its luster in the eyes of Northern voters, conservative Democrats made big gains in Congress. Johnson's rejection of the supplemental Freedmen's Bureau Bill in 1866 swore fealty to this opposition and accorded with sentiments ubiquitous in America.[119] Whatever the reason for this betrayal—whether it was the Southern man's indignation at the black man's seizure of his office or America's obsessive belief in black inferiority—its penalty and price have been the victim's burden.

Legislated Liberation

The 1964 Civil Rights Act was a promise. It pledged to secure black enfranchisement, prohibit public racial discrimination, and outline an education blueprint that would make use of the raw materials manufactured by *Brown v. Board* a decade prior. It vowed demolition of the sturdy social barriers dividing the races. The Civil Rights Act outlawed discrimination in public places partaking in interstate commerce—which, it was argued, was every public place. Hotels, restaurants, theaters, stores, and other places of business found themselves in the curious predicament of accepting everyone's dollars in return for equal accommodation and service. Despite the expected procedural obstructions from members of the Senate's Southern delegation, like Strom Thurmond of South Carolina and Robert Byrd of West Virginia, the bill was passed on June 19. The Civil Rights Act of 1964 wasn't the first law to make such lofty guarantees; part of its promise was that it would refuse accommodation to the past's failures.

The Civil Rights Act obviated the hoary American distinction between black and white. Commerce, education, voting, and housing now afforded equal access. Delivery did not delay. Just three years following the bill's enactment, black voter registration in Mississippi rose from under 30 percent to over 50.[120]

13

Last in Line: An American Destiny Deferred

The Civil Rights Act paved the way for affirmative action policies that would afford pathways previously off-limits to blacks. Affirmative action owed its life to the Equal Employment Opportunity Commission, formed to protect the employment rights of all Americans regardless of race, color, religion, sex, national origin, disability, and age. Its enforcement entailed punitive measures against conspicuous violators of minority employment opportunities. The EEOC's leverage remained evident decades after its founding, taking in $111 million in punitive damages for plaintiffs in 1997.[121] In 2014, the EEOC took in $296.1 million in damages on behalf of Americans claiming to be victims of unlawful discrimination, again proving the persistence of its potency.[122]

The Civil Rights Act ushered in ideals of social intercourse once considered intolerable by Northerner and Southerner alike. Public schools, libraries, universities, pools, and other facilities were no longer *de jure* blank havens guaranteeing security from the American *swart gevaar*. Places of worship, theaters, and stores now had to deduce for themselves what the looming epiphany did not—all money is green. Public water fountains and restrooms now belonged to everybody. Spaces often defaced with urine, feces, and other substances conveying whites' sentiments of blacks would be shared by all. Such gesticulations now seemed imprudent.

The Civil Rights Act provided not only existential equality, but also a measure of spiritual healing. It promised miraculous erasure of slavery and Jim Crow's terrors, indelibly impressed in millions of hearts and minds. It amended the social *modus operandi*, striking the clauses which ruled that the black front door lay in the rear, commanded avoidance of blue gazes, made salutary affairs of sidewalk step-asides, and rendered sunset views strangely unromantic. Its ability to heal the collective African American psyche would instill confidence, enabling black rebel yells echoing unto eternity.

Though the world it promised was belated, the Act's historical significance and unprecedented efficacy cannot be understated. It dared to bring America closer to the mode of equality promulgated in the Constitution. But despite its unfamiliar, upright gait, it inherited one trait from its legislative forebears. More than it did, it did not. Although public consciousness ratifies the 11th commandment—thou shall not speak without exaggeration of the Civil Rights Act's successes—it ultimately failed in its duty to repel institutionalized racism's effects. More than anything else, the Civil Rights Act bestowed an inadvertent curse—the malignant myth of colorblind America.

The modern interpretation of the law's historic impact is seen through rosy, revisionist spectacles, particularly with regard to education. In fuzzy reminiscences, ecstatic African American kids were bused to desegregated schools, rushing into embraces of parents, principals, teachers, and students. No longer were the communities of Little Rock, Montgomery, and elsewhere allied with America's Wallaces and Thurmonds. Lollipops and coloring books greeted black schoolchildren—not rocks, hoses, spit wads, or Orval Faubus. Pleasant dreams do not Molotov cocktails, bricks, and bullets make.

"Come play with us!" White classmates presaged King. Enthusiastic teachers, protective of their roles in rectifying the miscarriages of the past, made acquaintance of bright, beaming bearers of a golden black-and-white future. For these children, enviable report cards, accolades, and graduations loomed. PTAs rivaled in excitement, eager to welcome new colleagues and, with them, horizons. Principals marveled at this inclusive revolution, eager to

14

institute across-the-board faculty and staff integration serving justice unto the values espoused in the Constitution.

Not even in a parallel universe could this narrative be true. The opposite narrative agrees with history. The same unpleasant truth holds for efforts to change the American workplace's racial fabric. In the early decades of affirmative action policy, opponents took their fights off the streets and into the same courtrooms tasked with upholding the Civil Rights Act. Affirmative action cases were perhaps the fiercest fought of civil rights cases. Plaintiffs assumed the noble mission of defending the archetypal hardworking white family man backed against the wall by a government betraying its duty to serve him. He was a brave, competent saver of lives—a steward of both community and nation. The real American hero. The villain? Affirmative action. And the unqualified, incompetent, lazy Negro. It was *too* easy to argue. Wasn't the unfairness plain to see?

Though the stubborn resistance of America's Wallaces, Thurmonds, and Faubuses is well-known, few recall that similarly obdurate sentiments occupied the hearts of Americans in the North. Fervid opposition to integration blighted the progressive, liberal reputation that attracted millions of Southern black migrants northward in the Great Migration. In Boston, the decision to enforce desegregation wasn't met with cheers, but outrage and staunch opposition. In a 1974 case, federal judge Arthur Garrity accused the Boston School Committee of reserving Boston's best-funded and -staffed school for white students.[123] Garrity ordered the committee to enforce busing to reduce blatant levels of segregation. Because of this, schools such as the all-Irish Catholic South Boston High would bear begrudged faculty, opening pristine cafeterias and classrooms to nonwhite contamination.

Rather than acquiesce, they resisted. White parents made the movement a family affair, urging their children to boycott classes. Wielding heavy rocks, explosives, and other projectiles, objecting crowds of unconscientious parents and truant children pelted African American children throughout their round-trip journey from bus to building.[124] Rocks burst through windows; shards scarred skins and minds of those who sought mental sustenance yet found anguish. Abased, they were bused back to their ghettos—the cesspools of government policies where their new colleagues preferred they remain. Violence disregarded bounds of hearth; bullets offered relentless pursuit of black flesh, tearing through brick walls and car windows like parched hellhounds hunting cursed blood.[125]

Bostonians also made use of political channels to advance their agenda of intolerance, forming the anti-integration advocacy group Restore Our Alienated Rights. At a ROAR-sponsored march reminiscent of a Ku Klux Klan night ride, a 5,000-strong legion stampeded downtown Boston in opposition to forced busing policies.[126] Members of the Boston School Committee barged into the *cause célèbre*. When they found themselves on the fight's losing end, Bostonians abandoned their residential strongholds in a mass white flight exodus. They formed new enclaves, establishing whites-only schools under auspices of private and parochial mission statements. Suburbs throughout the North offered similar performance of dramatic resistance and tactical adaptation, adopting a tenor approximate in both pitch and range to that of the Southern *divo*.

Opposition to civil rights law went past state and municipal governments all the way to the executive branch. The Reagan administration initiated a tremendous onslaught against affirmative action programs, placing quotas in their crosshairs. In the mid-1980s, the U.S. Commission on Civil Rights (headed by four Reagan appointees and staffed with four members of Congress) declared that affirmative action programs constituted "unjustified discrimination"[127] and vowed to abrogate them in all forms. Some in the media argued that affirmative action fostered "the idea that different races should be treated differently."[128] To them, the policy was egregious—and unprecedented. When had America ever known of treating races in different ways?

Reagan and company justified their decision with the presumption that racial prejudice had disappeared from American public consciousness, thus obviating the need for affirmative action programs. Luckily, the Civil Rights Commission's advisory nature precluded it from altering civil rights laws and thus enacting dangerously myopic policies. Still, the six Republican yeas to two Democratic nays (both from individuals whom Reagan sought to oust)[129] represented a conservative roar. These toothless, emblematic gestures warned of a coming, brutal bite.

In 1984, the Supreme Court of the United States ruled 6-3 that job seniority plans could not be set aside in favor of affirmative action programs designed on behalf of women and minorities. At center stage in the case was the Memphis Fire Department, which often hired blacks last during hiring cycles. To compensate for their disadvantage in lacking seniority, policies exempted blacks from layoffs and demotions.[130] As if oblivious to the fact that the seniority policy from which they alone benefited (having secured jobs long before blacks were even allowed the opportunity) discriminated against blacks whom they intentionally hired last, a firefighters union accused the MFD's affirmative action policy of discriminating against whites.

As with other such invisible quotas and surreptitious, white-biased forms of affirmative action, the job seniority plan's implicit racial bias went unnoticed. Affirmative action hiring quotas stood as the lone scapegoat. Because of this ruling, minorities and women experienced substantial job loss, ceding to both junior and senior white male colleagues. In no time, talk arose of the Justice Department using the precedent set in the Memphis case to overturn other affirmative action programs across the United States.

Affirmative action was not the sole scapegoat. The Reagan administration also voiced its opposition to state and local governments that tried to reverse practices of exclusively awarding contracting deals to white-owned firms. President Reagan strongly opposed such measures and his Justice Department argued that because there was no proof that black contractors faced discrimination in contract bids, they should be afforded no exclusive rights to contracts. An Urban Institute report showed that even years after Reagan's assertion, vast disparities in the awarding of government contracts persisted. According to the report, "Minority-owned businesses receive far fewer government contract dollars than would be expected based on their availability..." It added, "...minority-owned businesses as a group receive only 57 cents of each dollar they would be expected to receive based on the percentage of all...firms that are minority-owned."[131] Mere decades after the Civil Rights Act was signed into law, American policymakers argued that the colorblind society had already been realized. The only people still seeing color were the people of color themselves.

Reagan and his conservative successors have refused to accept affirmative action's purpose of enforcing that which cannot be enforced by the provisions of the Civil Rights Act alone. Government can legislate and rule on civil rights, but it cannot force employers to shed biases. Without affirmative action measures, employers are given free rein to discriminate on the basis of race and other characteristics. Race, gender, ability, and other traits supplant credentials, becoming key criteria for job qualification. The outcome is that qualified applicants are disqualified from job opportunities.

Even well-meaning employers are capable of assessing applicants through a lens of implicit racial bias; without affirmative action, these deep-seated impulses are left unchecked. The same goes for other modes of discrimination, like seniority-based employment systems in which employers hire whites first and blacks last.[132] Such practices are not explicitly discriminatory, but are employed as a means of exercising racial prejudice with impunity and without detection. These unyielding obstacles necessitate the existence of affirmative action programs that guarantee opportunities to working minorities and their families.

Affirmative action does not send *any* qualified applicant to the back of the line or render opportunities for whites secondary to those of nonwhites. Neither does it endorse the ouster of qualified, competent whites from their jobs. Affirmative action effectively sets aside a modicum of positions for which nonwhites must be considered. Given the statistically proven prevalence of racial bias in hiring, such protective measures are necessary to guarantee minorities even a sliver of access to job opportunity in many higher-earning professions. Furthermore, although they foster opportunity, that affirmative action policies secure only minimal opportunities in these areas means they fail to seriously threaten racial bias' grip on the American workplace.

Enforcing affirmative action policies gave the Civil Rights Act and its demands for equal opportunity teeth; barks would not have moved biased employers claiming to have picked the "best man for the job." A *minimum* of jobs, admissions slots, and other opportunities are subject to affirmative action's enforcement, allocated for the expressed purpose of negating the effects of institutionalized discrimination and hiring bias. This leaves plenty of spaces effectively affirmative action-free, subject to the biased whims of the employer. Still, affirmative action is the shining accomplishment that arguably saved the 1964 Civil Rights Act from reduction to the ineffectual status befalling earlier incarnations. But its longevity is far from a foregone conclusion. Its gradual erosion in the private sector—giving way to the subterfuge of corporate diversity and inclusion programs—and endangerment in the college admissions process threaten to guarantee the Civil Rights Act a plot in the legislative graveyard.

The Civil Rights Act's legislative cousin, the Fair Housing Act of 1968, bore affective resemblance. The Fair Housing Act did not go as far as expected in desegregating America's rigidly homogenized communities. Although the ghetto was said to be the "fundamental structural factor promoting black poverty in the United States,"[133] housing discrimination was questionably acquitted of the charge of confining blacks to ghettos. The onset of integration gave rise to a curious trend of hyper-segregation characterizing blacks in both metropolitan and suburban areas. Many of the so-called "Chocolate Cities" such as Washington, DC, Philadelphia, St. Louis, Baltimore, Detroit, and Los Angeles represented a distinct class of the most segregated cities well into the post-Civil Rights Movement era. Though gentrification is shaking up the dynamic, they remain so today. The passage of the Fair Housing Act compelled once open discriminatory behavior into undercover mode. Before the law, realtors had freedom to turn away black clients or declare racial preference on condition of sale. Such prejudice would persist in spite of legal hazard, but only with the adoption of survival strategies.

Audit studies have proven the prevalence of racial discrimination in real estate. Using pairs of white and black subjects presenting themselves to realtors as prospective homebuyers, researchers compare subjects' experiences:

> Teams of black and white home-seekers are paired and sent to randomly selected realtors to pose as clients seeking a home or apartment. The auditors are trained to present comparable housing needs and family characteristics, and to express similar tastes; they are assigned equivalent social and economic traits by the investigator. After each encounter, the auditors fill out a report of their experiences and the results are tabulated and compared to determine the nature and level of discrimination.

> Studies found that African Americans had a 20 percent chance of experiencing discrimination in the sales market. The percentage more than doubled for the rental market, to 50 percent.[134]

The ongoing prevalence of such discrimination should occasion both dialogue and action. Instead, choruses of pundits and politicians whose lies and misrepresentations stymie true progress drown change's pleas.

When did racism become a vestigial organ in American anatomy? When did the visual systems of courts, schools, workplaces—and America itself—become blind to color? It is a strange question for which no satisfactory answer has been given. The conclusions of equality drawn by policymakers and the American public are pumped from a well of shallow and faulty construction. They have presumed, in spite of contamination by myriad transgressions chronologizing 1865 until today—the gore of lynchings, the mold of disenfranchisement, the decay of education funding disparities, the blood of police shootings, and the altogether grossness of these offenses— that America's *terra firma* is level. But the stations of America's races do not reflect leveling. This desecration of American soil seeps into our wells. The colorblind do not deny this water crisis. They only deny that it has anything to do with past or present edifices of division. The culprit is the flawed spirit of agency that enchains African American destiny.

The Civil Rights Act cannot be credited with creating the colorblind society. Neither can revisionist scriptures of America's history that excise verses unbecoming of America's constitutional legends of glory. And neither can the status quo in which the epiphany of racial equality persists in elusion. Nothing can be credited in the creation myth of the colorblind society except that which lies in the realm of allegory.

Conclusion

"For God's sake, give a man a chance!" Zachariah Walker was accused of killing a white police officer.[135] Though he insisted his innocence, Walker's pleas were accorded no due process, no trial, and no jury. He argued his case skidding the streets of Coatesville, Pennsylvania before a 5,000-strong jury of men, women, and children whose deliberations had concluded long before. They knew the true charge. Walker knew. "Don't give me no crooked death because I'm not white!" Walker's body was hoisted to the sun, a dutiful blood sacrifice in homage to the god of white supremacy. Walker's screams roused the crowd. Insatiable, blue-eyed stares sparked a death inferno disintegrating lithe, sinewy limbs into ash carried off by gusts colder than their hearts. The charitable breeze left amulets, prizes for the ringleaders of this rite of racial hatred. Spectators kicked, screamed, and punched, mocking their way to possession of these fetishes. Through remnants they hoped to commandeer the essence of a man who had, a day before, breathed, loved, lived. Does anyone wonder where Zachariah Walker's body parts are today? Or those of the thousands of other African American lynching victims that were, instead of being honored with burial, stowed away in chests and trunks in America's attics and basements? I wonder what person smiles at the face of the African American man preserved in a jar of formaldehyde (and sold by an antique dealer, shrugging it off saying, "No matter what, there's always a buyer").[136] I wonder the last moment his wife and children saw this face they loved. I wonder his last moments. I don't wonder his face's expression in those last moments. I do wonder what went through the mind of the person who not only rendered a crooked, demented death, but cut off a man's face and stuck it in a jar of formaldehyde as a keepsake.

I wonder about all of these family heirlooms but question only one thing. It is not how some can cherish these talismans, grasping lifeless hearts to their beating chests in joyous retellings of the organ's demise. I question how a consciousness that normalizes such depravity can accommodate the expectation that Americans "get over" this cruel present. That thousands of murders took place in the United States, many with thousands of witnesses and active participants for which not one individual was ever convicted of murder, occasions outrage in the mind of empathy and justice.[137] That so many respond to this phenomenon of impunity, flanked by slavery on one side and the edifices of institutionalized racism on the other, with an impassive demand implies the absence of ideals of empathy and justice in so many American hearts and minds. It threatens that there are many willing to participate in the endeavor to cut away and mount black America's face to laugh at in an eternal ecstasy of hate.

To deny history is to deny self. To deny the unpleasant elements of American history is to deny America. To deny the history of racial discrimination and violence, to deny the geography of that discrimination and violence, and to deny justice to that past is to perform sacrilege unto America. Implicit bias testing proves the verity of this denial, offering evidence of the pervasive belief that black people are less than white people, a claim that contradicts common proclamations of belief in equality. These modern attitudes are identical to those of old, ones that rendered the black man helpless, the black woman defiled, and the black child hapless in service to the American cornucopia denied to them. Even though it was black sweat, black blood, and black soil that begat white wealth, for them exacted labors begat only death.

In 2005, the U.S. Senate apologized for its failure to pass anti-lynching legislation, having ignored repeated demands made during the trend's bloodiest decades.[138] Three years after the Senate's equivocal *mea culpa*, the House of Representatives apologized for aiding and abetting the institution of slavery.[139] A year later, the Senate issued its own apology for slavery. They included a

19

conspicuous annotation, stipulating that the apology could not be used for reparations claims.[140]

Congress took a century and a half to issue a formal apology for America's most sinister institution. Within years, Jews victimized in the Holocaust and their descendants began receiving sums from the German and Austrian governments now totaling billions of dollars.[141] In addition, they received official apologies from Germany, Austria, and numerous nations and governments that were active or passive participants in the Holocaust (including the United States), some of which turned away Jews fleeing the Nazi onslaught. And rightly so. African Americans have been granted no such courtesy. Venom supersedes the veneer of an apology. The mass labor efforts undertaken by blacks and their forebears which established the United States as a bastion are thought unworthy of so much as "thank you."

In certain parts of the world, telling a Jewish person to "get over" the Holocaust brings a jail sentence. Although that person has free speech rights in America, we Americans use that same right to shout that person down. Yet to minimize the tragedies and sufferings of African Americans brings not penalty, but often praise. The advice of closure should go not to the legacy of the victims; it should go to America. America must move past its unwillingness to confront its skeletons, literal and figurative.

America must get over its fears; it must pull gruesome fetishes from its closets. It must honor them with proper burial. We are not the America of the antebellum period, we are not the America of Reconstruction, and we are not the America of today. Those Americas thought—and consequently proved—themselves unprepared to confront racial injustice. But we are prepared, just as we have always been. We are ready to move into the future as the America that the veterans of the American Revolution may not have envisioned, but which was delineated in the Declaration of Independence that they signed in blood, vowing fulfillment. That America is born of sacrifice. That America believes all men and women are created equal.

②
A Model Myth

A myth was born with the Pacific landing of America's first nonwhite immigrant group. Like all labors, its was panged and spasmodic. But no matter contractions that, numerous times, threatened miscarriage, wails would be answered with paternalistic doting. Although small numbers of Chinese immigrants were already present in the Western United States in the early 19th century,[142] large-scale Chinese immigration commenced with the California Gold Rush of 1848.[143] Though numbering in the hundreds at the start of the Gold Rush, the Chinese American population proliferated and by 1852 stood at more than 20,000.[144] Three decades later, nearly 300,000 Chinese Americans comprised a substantial portion of California's population.[145] Though the Chinese endured varying levels of animosity during the Gold Rush, relations with white Californians grew inimical as their numbers further proliferated in coming decades. California's Sinophobic climate boiled over, manifesting in acts of terrorism such as the Chinese Massacre of 1871.[146]

In their own Tulsa-style riot, Chinese Americans were attacked, beaten, stabbed, and lynched for their perceived threat to the dominant status of white Americans. Precipitating the attack was the accidental murder of a white rancher by quarrelling Chinese men. Robert Thompson found himself caught in the crossfire of an intense gunfight among Chinese settlers. On October 24, 500 armed white men responded with swift brutality. They stormed Chinatown, avenging the white death brought by harbingers of the "yellow peril." No fewer than 19 Chinese Americans were killed in the rampage during which Chinese homes and businesses were set ablaze and reduced to ash.[147] Bodies of the dead were hung on posts, grotesque, victorious displays for all to see. The riot portended an increase in anti-Chinese racism that would spill into the halls of Congress, where stringent immigration measures were enacted.

Tensions worsened in the massacre's aftermath. Chinese immigrants experienced mass expulsion from their communities, being displaced to less profitable areas and thus suffering a loss of access to jobs.[148] Despite their pleas for peace, further Sinophobic violence was imminent. The 1877 San Francisco Riot yielded horror reminiscent of the conflagration six years prior.[149] Chinese Americans had little recourse; an 1854 California Supreme Court case quelled cries for justice, ruling that Chinese Americans could not testify against whites in court.[150] America turned its cheek, leaving Chinese American immigrant families defenseless in the face of the violent caprices of inhospitable neighbors.

The savage disposition of 19th century Californians couldn't match the despotic bearing of the United States government. The federal government subverted the rights of Chinese denizens by the tip of the pen more so than by the barrel of the gun. In 1882, Congress passed the Chinese Exclusion Act. Signed into law by President Chester Arthur, it indefinitely halted all Chinese immigration into the United States.[151] The law also stipulated that all Chinese Americans who left the United States were barred from reentry unless they had proper certification (which proved impossible for most to obtain).[152] Labor unions hailed the act, ostensibly because it prevented mining companies from hiring Chinese labor to the exclusion of whites, a practice that reduced both job availability and overall wages for whites.[153] Chinese Americans were split from their families in the homeland and left with the dilemma of choosing between being locked in or out of an oppressive United States. Those who remained submitted to the yoke of oppressive policy that negated both their rights and their humanity.

Today, Chinese Americans are one of the most socioeconomically successful groups in the United States. In measures of education, entrepreneurship, employment, and income, Chinese Americans are among America's leaders.[154] The same goes for other Americans of East Asian descent, like Japanese Americans, who have similar histories of oppression at the hands of the U.S. government. They exceed white Americans in household income among other economic metrics.[155]

Chinese Americans have turned out successful, prospering, self-sufficient generations. They share with African Americans familiarity with extreme racial violence, social ostracism, and government-endorsed forms of institutional racism. But despite the prejudice that they once faced in American society, it seems that both they and other Asian American groups have, with ingenuity, hard work, and a bit of serendipity, overcome institutional racism's roadblocks. In defying the unjust restraints of the American racial hierarchical system, they have made themselves unwitting architects of the mirage that is the colorblind society. If Asian Americans apparently succeed in areas of education and employment without affirmative action and are self-sufficient enough to require less assistance from SNAP and similar welfare programs than other ethnic groups, how could American society be anything but colorblind?[156]

Fair or not, African Americans and Asian Americans are often compared. Taken as wholes, both ethnic groups occupy vastly different stations in American society. The clearest distinction lies in history. The ancestors of African Americans were not immigrants, but subjects of forced migration. Also, unlike Asian immigrants, who have at worst been refugees—a doubtless tragedy—African Americans were slaves. African Americans' forefathers were packed into ships by the dozens and, if they survived the journey, whipped to death upon arrival on American soil. Meanwhile, their foremothers were humiliated en route, being broken in for use as breeders for future generations of chattel labor.

This is in stark contrast to one who chooses America. Sirens and tempests threaten all journeys, but chaperones of community, education, skills—and agency—ward off shipwrecks. Certainly, not all Asian American immigrants enjoy such smooth sailing. Indeed, some arrive with little more than flotsam to their names; some pant, swimming to America's shores as refugees and asylum seekers.[157] But, as a group, Asian American immigrant passage is facilitated by bookings of wealth and education.[158] No matter their travel class, the shining image of the model minority proving the absence of racial barriers and inanity of black excuses has seized American consciousness.

This perceptive racial gradation is not only shored by recent waves of Asian immigration. Although settlers of early Chinese American immigration waves were in some cases relegated to status beneath that of blacks,[159] in some areas—like U.S. labor markets—they found themselves outdoing African Americans.[160] Many employers and policymakers thought the Chinese more intelligent than blacks.[161] Although this inspired fear of Chinese imperial ambition, necessitating immigration restriction, others argued that Chinese intelligence, in addition to traits of industry and frugality, made them useful—some might even say "model"—workers. Even in the South, Chinese Americans were a peg above blacks in the racial hierarchy, granted license to engage in enterprise[162] and in some instances even intermarry with whites.[163] Indeed, early Chinese American communities fixed themselves on the stream to model minority status in part by deliberately distancing themselves from African Americans.[164]

The idea of the model minority has assumed great political significance in recent decades. Proponents argue that the existence of so-called model minorities attests to the realization of colorblind America. It is peculiar that we ignore the plights of some races, their ordeals often ascribed to the past's ever-looming demons, yet laud the accomplishments of races having escaped that haunting. Regardless, the crux of the model minority theory is that success is credited to the exhibition of qualities such as hard work, intelligence, education, and family-orientation, and that any race that embodies these traits reaps fruits of success and status. Thus, minority racial groups undeserving of the title are capable of reaching this distinguished status, so long as they too somehow work within their cultural structures to employ values conducive to the creation of strong, principled societies. The rise and fall of races is a matter of values, not racism.

Evidence does not uphold this theory. For one, although successful immigrant groups in the United States have historical experiences with racism, the extent of their experience does not compare with that of African Americans. Although early immigrants of East Asian descent felt hate's heavy hand, such strikes were not many and varied as those lashed on tarred backs. Their status in the American racial hierarchy was deemed above that of blacks; their social and economic experiences reflected this.[165] Furthermore, the overwhelming majority of Asian Americans today are either immigrants or first-generation descendants of Asians whose emigration was made possible by the Immigration and Nationality Act of 1965, another legislative feat of the Civil Rights Movement. These immigrants arrived after and because of the major civil rights battles for equal public accommodation that African Americans spearheaded. Hence, few were subjected to the deleterious effects of residence within a distinct, legally sanctioned, stratified caste system.

Evidence also shows that these ribboned, adulated model minority groups actually *are* victims of institutional racism. Research shows that despite having both higher earnings and levels of education, Asian American groups are afforded less access to socioeconomic opportunity than white Americans. Tim Wise elucidates the disparate, perhaps expected rift between model minority groups and white America:

> Although median income for Asian Americans is above that of whites, in the aggregate, this is because the Asian American population, on average, has far higher rates of college and post-graduate education than the white population. Because Asian immigration to the United States has been relatively selective, with a disproportionate percentage of Asian immigrants coming with pre-existing educational backgrounds, economic advantages, or the intent to pursue higher education upon arrival, the Asian population as a whole is more highly educated than the white population. As such, they will logically earn more, per capita, than whites with less academic background. But

considering how much more education Asian Americans have, on average, relative to their white counterparts, their earnings advantages are much smaller than should be expected.[166]

The mere fact that Asian Americans and other such "model" groups are, on average, better-educated and higher-earning than whites does not speak to equality. They do so primarily because they overcompensate in terms of what advantages they possess on arrival on American soil. In general, they have advantage in access to family and community units that can serve as sources of capital for business. They also arrive in America either already educated or intent on obtaining it, benefiting from access to communities that can aid them in financing their studies. Just how much they have to leverage those advantages to transcend the discrimination they experience in America is astounding. Asian American immigrants *have* to outdo white Americans. To obtain only the same level of education as their white counterparts would spell out lower levels of income.

Wise cites college graduation rates and their relationship to race and socioeconomic achievement:

Whereas fewer than 16 percent of whites had a college degree in 2000, 22.4 percent of Chinese Americans did, as did 31.3 percent of Japanese Americans, 24.4 percent of Korean Americans and Asian Indians, nearly 31 percent of Filipino Americans and 28 percent of Taiwanese Americans…although Chinese American income is 17 percent higher than white income, they are 40 percent more likely than whites to have a college degree and 2.3 times more likely to have an advanced degree.[167]

Despite being more highly educated than whites, Asian Americans earn proportionally less. It's a compelling refutation of the model myth that pervades American social and political discourse. If Asian Americans' incomes truly "modeled" values a colorblind society would yield, the moniker would be more fitting.

Although floated as flattery, the "model minority" label is condescension. It minimizes the struggles of minority groups both by reducing the plight of the "model" group and dismissing the historical struggle of the "bad role model." The concept presumes that the model group thrives not only because of its remarkable work ethic, but also because there is no monolithic, obstructive edifice of institutionalized racism standing in any group's way. But institutionalized racism is not only a problem for African Americans, who withstand both its past and present forms. Institutionalized racism also proves a tremendous problem when it denies fruit to those groups that are hardworking and already armed with resources and opportunities prior to their arrival in the United States. Systemic racism's widespread effects prove the nonexistence of the myth that purports to disprove systemic racism's own existence.

Color Contrast: The Imperfect Minority

Immigration must be the starting point of any comparative analysis of model minority groups and African Americans. There are innumerable motivations, goals, and driving forces that compel a particular individual or ethnic group to immigrate to the United States. Entrepreneurial ambitions,

Chapter 2: A Model Myth

religious persecution, military conflict, and other phenomena motivate emigration from host countries to America. The expatriate's purpose for immigrating is significant because, depending on the rationale, the group or person immigrating may or may not be equipped with the resources—financial, social, educational, and otherwise—to make for firm establishment in the host nation.

Groups whose members often come to the United States for education, such as Nigerians, tend to have both the means of financing that education and a plan for using it for monetary benefit.[168] They have resources that enable them to reside in the United States, whether through savings, family assistance, grants, or other sources. Similarly, American immigrant business owners either have capital or know how to access capital channels long before arrival, capitalizing on family assistance, grant programs, loans, and other sources.

Family differentiates model minority groups and African Americans. Families are the building blocks of immigrant communities. Immigrants are attracted to host countries for a number of reasons, financial security being the biggest impetus.[169] As pioneers relay stories of a better life, trickles of immigration become Niagara-like falls. Networks emerge as promises of soft and secure familial landing pads assuage fears of uncertainty. It is through these family units that immigrant communities establish social and economic adequacy.

This pattern is not only reflected in today's heralded model minorities, but has been observed since the Puritans landed on Plymouth Rock. Although outcomes vary, virtually all immigrant groups share in this pattern. European immigrants, Hispanic Americans, Asian Americans, South Asians, and, today, African immigrants all situated in America as communities, not individuals. Moreover, these communities came to America on their own volition with the latitude to pursue the educational, social, and political opportunities that enable a freer existence. All America's immigrants, be they English pilgrims or Somali refugees, came here on their own volition, save one group—African Americans.

Slaves arrived in the United States in accord with the will of slave traders and other captors, including West African kings and chiefs who sometimes sold prisoners of war,[170] criminal and vagabond members of their societies,[171] and, most numerously, innocent civilians. Unlike immigrants of all sorts, slaves had *no* agency in their arrival in America and therefore no framework or structure for charting the economic and social trajectories of their individual, familial, or community lives. But even had they had a plan, they would have lacked the agency and resources for its implementation. *They* were the resources, the key ingredient in the recipe for economic prosperity that nourished the maturation of the white American body politic that, as pilgrim posterity, had no such lack of power in charting its destiny. Slaves had only their physical abilities and their trade and professional skills, the fruits of which belonged not to the possessors of those traits but the possessors of those possessors. The same applied to their reproductive abilities, which became industrial processes integral to the slave economy. Slaves had only their souls and eternal torment.

Unlike with immigrant communities, ethnic cohesion was not incipient in the African American process of forced settlement. Enslavement forced the mass amalgamation of numerous African tribes and nations, each with unique languages, customs, appearances, and religions.[172] Such heterogeneity ensured the preclusion of any meaningful cohesion among early African Americans. This was the greatest obstruction to African Americans'

25

Last in Line: An American Destiny Deferred

development of the sort of New World culture that exists in all immigrant groups. Thus, the African American menu lacked the gourmet cultural soups of languages, religions, and customs sautéed in a concoction cooked to order; its recipes did not call for an appropriate stewing of ingredients. Slaves' origins in cultures distant, remote, and sometimes even hostile to each other supported bondage's duty of preventing the emergence of a semblance of a united New World African culture. In sustaining a fractured entity, America's peculiar institution precluded slaves from organizing effective resistance to their captors.

Because slaves brought few cultural objects to America and were purged of what they managed to smuggle through customs, they were left a void of consciousness to be filled by the indoctrination of the master culture. This cultural miseducation would define Africans' humanity in context of an American racial hierarchy that undervalued the totality of their being, circumscribing it to subservience and an inchoate, subprime acculturation to the Western modality. Vestiges of African culture were rarely tolerated in this slave paradigm.[173] Despite fervent pleas in defense of his anatomy, Kunta was resigned to life as Toby. More mind-altering than these superficial inoculations were the baptisms that exorcised the African spirit and possessed in its stead a soul fated to veneration of the omnipotent instrument of Western religion. The triumph of this endeavor is nowhere more apparent than in the existence of African American church.

The Christian church has long and rightly been regarded as a cornerstone of the African American community. The church was the vehicle through which the wills of Africans in America were fashioned into something resembling a unified entity. Although slave masters gave the Word to Africans so as to enable clear transmission of white American destiny's dictation, that Word empowered an otherwise downtrodden, despairing class to cast off their chains. By no means can it be said that Christianity destroyed African American spirit. It offered community leadership in the slave clergy (who sometimes retained African religious practices), who offered guidance that America's democratic systems refused to blacks.[174] The clergy bellowed the people's anger, cried their tears, and held their communities together with charisma and force inspired by God. The church's sacred role as an essential component of African American society remains strong today, as gospels preaching power against poverty, crime, teen pregnancy, drug use, and other perceived social ills pour forth as libations for a verdant future.

Despite Christianity's positive impact on the black community, it was not meant to uplift. The brand of Christianity that masters and missionaries intended for slaves was of a different sort than that intended for whites. This brand of Christianity was manufactured as a mechanism of psychological manipulation to convert free Africans into docile slaves. Sermons stressing war and resistance in the face of injustice were censored. Sermons stressing patience and tolerance were encouraged. These tactics had the effect of convincing slaves that their humble, obedient asceticism would one day be rewarded with a utopic afterlife.

West African religions were radically different, often encompassing beliefs in magic, honoring of ancestor spirits, and polytheistic worship.[175] Open practice of these blasphemous faiths was often halted when slaves arrived in the United States.[176] Some managed discreet worship, risking cruel punishment if masters unveiled such impiety.[177] But the unanimous rejection of African religions by masters did not equate with a universal desire to bring black Africans into the Christian faith. Some masters thought the practice "a

26

piece of foolishness"[178] obviated by the enforcement of "proper discipline."[179] Masters at first eschewed the idea of converting slaves for fear that it would amount to an acknowledgement of slaves' rights to personal sovereignty and, therefore, freedom.[180] When this was made impossible by law,[181] many masters reassessed the benefits of teaching slaves the gospel. The Word proved the tool with which slave owners would transmogrify an abominable, wholly unholy institution into one divine and preordained.

In *The Peculiar Institution*, Kenneth Stampp synopsizes the message the master-missionary sought to impart upon the slave:

> Through religious instruction the bondsmen learned that slavery had divine sanction, that insolence was as much an offense against God as against the temporal master. They received the biblical command that servants should obey their masters, and they heard of the punishments awaiting the disobedient slave in the hereafter. They heard, too, that eternal salvation would be their reward for faithful service, and that on the day of judgment "God would deal impartially with the poor and the rich, the black man and the white." Their Christian preceptors, Fanny Kemble noted, "jump[ed] the present life" and went on "to furnish them with all the requisite conveniences for the next."[182]

A South Carolinian agricultural society concurred that Christianity contributed to slaves' "government and discipline"[183] in no small manner. Slaves, fearing the repercussions of a stringent God, were behooved to obeisance before their masters lest they be cast into pits of fire in the afterlife for insolence. Heaven was the incentive for hard work and submission. Equality resided in the afterlife, the gift for humble resignation to an unequal incarnation.

Masters were careful to censor biblical passages suggesting the impropriety of slaves' bondage. Narratives concerning Moses, for example, and his very pro-civil rights stance in the face of his Egyptian oppressors would confound the intended message of the nobility of subservience. It also interacted with a conscience-soothing soporific available in book form—the Curse of Ham, which interpreted earthbound black hell through a theocratic lens.[184] Their masters lain down to sleep, a Watchful Eye compelled the sons of Ham to, for lack of a better phrase, "suck it up." Beatings, endless workdays, rapes, forced breeding, and other administered sins were hidden behind the Cross. From the tainted pulpit, masters preached sermons explaining the social order sanctioning these acts as right, natural, and in accordance with the law of God. They weren't hellish sufferings, but rather mere inconveniences that blacks were obligated to endure in favor of a divine duty to three masters—one in the Holy Spirit, one in Jesus Christ, and one in the planter.

This policy necessitated a proverbial license requirement; blacks were denied license to impart proverbial scripture in many locales.[185] Even when devout African Americans were allowed to preach to captive brethren and sistren, they did so only under the watchful, suspicious eye of their lords.[186] Thus, *Pulp Fiction*'s hair-raising Jules Winnfield Ezekiel 25:17 sermon was abominably denied its preordained incarnation—this antebellum take casting a sweat-beaded master staring down the antiprop of the white supremacist set, his unwitting defiance of a black script guaranteeing the Lord's promised wrath.

Though some masters may have felt morally compelled to impart Christian ideology upon slaves, the primary impetus for introducing slaves to the gospel was to ensconce them in an immutable, servile, God-endorsed prostration. One Missouri auctioneer offered a striking imploration as to why religiosity appreciated slave value:

> The religious teaching consists in teaching that slave that he must never strike a white man; that God made him for a slave; and that, when whipped, he must not find fault—for the Bible says, "He that knoweth his master's will and doeth it not, shall be beaten with many stripes!"[187]

There was no divine master in the sky orchestrating such suffering, only one incarnate, inheriting immense profit from the scorched prostration of bodies black and chained.

The Splintered Black Family

Religion represented but one defined brush stroke in a dark portrait contrasting with a variegated, more aesthetic picture of the American immigrant experience. The slave master employed other tactics to purge African identity and institute a tailored Western identity fitting only of one subjugated. One such tactic was the deliberate dismantling of the black family. In the absence of the community building blocks that families represented, systems for conveying values of order, leadership, morality, and beyond were nonexistent. This does not mean enslaved Americans or their descendants lacked these traits. They did, however, lack the structures for imparting them for the organized construction and maintenance of a strong black identity. African Americans were deprived of the premium fabric required for weaving the familial unit and instead offered substandard, tattered textile product. Community's material quality is predicated on the grade of the individual familial threads comprising it. As Dr. Amos Wilson professes in *Blueprint*:

> Generally, the power generated by a culture derives from the structured coalescence of interdependent family kinship groups, clans, and tribe [*sic*] for mutual defense against outsiders and other mutually beneficial outcomes.[188]

The cultural barriers that prevented African Americans from group coalescence were supported by the slave master's imperious management of the black family. Although West African homelands were built from strong, structured family units, the expatriates of these lands found it impossible to reconstruct that dynamic in the New World. This was no accident. The stable black family would refuse service to the slave economy; it would only foment insurrection à la Turner, Vesey, or Cato. The same values that constructed the stable black family unit were chemical ingredients of dynamite marked to demolish the peculiar American edifice.

Disarming such weapons of mass destruction necessitated dissolution of the traditional roles assigned to the black father and black mother. The office of the black father was abolished,[189] all duties being assigned to his children's mother—with the exception of that of the child disciplinarian.[190] That went to the slave master.[191] The slave master was a dual head of household, fulfilling the foremost, personal role as head of his white household with that of the impersonal, remunerative vocation as head of the slave household.

Marriage was not omitted from the agenda. "Jumping the broom" was a symbol hollow as the drinking gourd, deprived of legitimating legal substance.[192] Because of this, masters were able to impose matrimonial moral codes upon slaves that were travesties of those they and their belles took. Slave "marriages" often came with obscure expiration dates. Because masters frequently relocated or sold slaves, separations between husbands and wives were common.[193] But it was no joke on them; slaves knew the frivolity of their marriages, often readily moving on to find new partners in the aftermath of their demise.[194]

Other times, such involuntary familial separations met bitter resistance and mourning. The unconsummated marriages that took place between black men and women and the accompanying lack of control over their own "households" took significant psychological tolls on parents.[195] This sometimes even drove them to abuse. Slave mothers sometimes neglected their children, whom masters, for the sake of fiscal expedience, still expected them to nurture. Stampp recounts instances of slave women whose negligence resulted in the deaths of their children:

> An angry Virginian attributed the death of a slave infant to "the unnatural neglect of his infamous mother"; he charged that another infant was "murdered right out by his mother's neglect and barbarous cruelty."[196]

In place of warm, loving, familial relationships, slaves and their biological kin often had detached, aloof relations. In the absence of a unifying manifold, blood similarity proved insufficient for the creation of familial consciousness in enslaved African Americans. Slaves were denied the acquaintance of leisure and its accordant opportunities for bonding and nurturing, thus forgoing the developmental processes of attachment so critical to emotional and psychological well-being.[197] This, coupled with the astounding psychological stress which inhumane laboring conditions tendered (evidenced in mental illnesses which often arose in response),[198] guaranteed the splintering of relations between husband and wife, parent and child, brother and sister.

But slaves were not totally without ability to feel for loved ones. The lamentations and escape efforts of Eliza in *Uncle Tom's Cabin* weren't fictional inventions, but literary reflections of slave reality. Though bonds with spouses were sometimes strong, bonds with children stood better chance of becoming well-developed and difficult to dissolve. Mothers often violently protested separation from their children and even attempted escape to reunite with them.[199] Such acts attested to the fact that, despite the bondage, indignity, and emotional fissuring which often characterized slave families, their humanity and sentience were not eroded.

The dissolution of the black man's role as father had a particularly disruptive impact on the familial legacies from which slaves were torn. African societies were, and still are, predominantly patriarchal.[200] Although the mother is the body, her hands fashioning in children appropriate traits and values, the father is the head of the familial anatomy. In keeping with this metaphor, the slave family was a decapitated entity. In the societies slaves came from, fathers provided for the home and protected the homestead while mothers assumed the mantle of child rearing. Such a dynamic was not to be had in the New World.

Masters saw not mothers and fathers, but broodmares and sperm donors. The slave father's responsibilities often started and ended with impregnation. This is not to say that husbands did not ever feel loyalty or devotion to their wives and children. But the black father could not feel the pride and power emanating from the station of household leadership, for he was no sovereign. He had no powers of decision-making, child-rearing, or provision. Today's fatherless black household is a collateral descendant of this dynamic engineered in the slave economy's interest.

Children of slave families were effectively parentless. After brief childhoods, slave children were forced into labor on behalf of their masters and assigned the responsibility of following masters' every wish in their personal conduct.[201] At this stage, the limited influence a parent may have managed to wield over their children altogether yielded. Slave children may have been familiar with their mothers and fathers, often residing on the same plantation, but affinity was not tantamount to influence. Life lessons, moral codes, and other values—what semblance there was of such things—passed from the parent's mouth to the child's ear in inchoate whispers. African Americans were thus deprived of the moral heirlooms containing, among other things, the blueprints for the construction of the stable family unit. This bears stark contrast with immigrant dynamics in which intact heirlooms are prepackaged with a just-add-conveyance instruction.

Slavery did not permit the possibility of African American group coalescence. The heterogeneity of the incipient slave population prevented the emergence of a black mass that could destroy America's peculiar institution. Amalgamating tens and hundreds of tribes, languages, and nations into one community was unlikely in itself; the stress fractures that the system of slavery impacted on the African American skeletal system made it impossible. Having weathered a lethal tempest in the Middle Passage, these unfamiliar Africans were thrust into a brutal institution that chained them to a miserable existence depriving them of agency over their work, sexuality, faith, minds, and families. The transgenerational effects of slavery continue to loom above the heads of African Americans, guarding their ascension to heights befitting the "model minority" moniker.

The trans-Atlantic slave trade was the most brutal form of human trafficking ever known. Similarly, the American system of slavery was human history's most brutal. The arrival of the first Africans in America in 1619 as involuntary laborers ushered in an unprecedented era in which a dominant race imposed a ruthless, tight-gripping, bondage-based caste system upon a powerless group stripped of its humanity. American slavery was the world's first race-based system of slavery. Humanity's earlier slavery systems were not exclusively or even primarily racial affairs, but were often based on factors of class[202] or military advantage.[203] American slavery defied those precedents, establishing itself as an institution preoccupied with the objective of targeting a single race of people for bondage.

Compare America's system of slavery to that of the Roman Republic that inspired the American model of governance. The Roman elite looked to destitute members of its plebeian class and vanquished adversaries, like the Carthaginians, for slaves.[204] Although Carthage offers the example of an entire nation that, at the end of the Third Punic War, was subjected to mass enslavement, it does not imply that the Roman concept of the slave was associated with the Carthaginian or any specific ethnicity, race, or class. It was not stigmas of identity that placed the Roman slave at the point of the patrician's gladius, but rather characteristics of poverty, criminality, or captivity from warfare.[205] [206]

The stigma of this cruel, peculiar form of slavery damningly contrasts the African American experience with the fates of history's enslaved populations and America's modern immigrant populations. These populations were not without stigmatization, but both those ancients and today's models are without the unique stigma of blackness that emerged from trans-Atlantic slavery and stubbornly persists in American consciousness. Although African Americans eventually achieved emancipation from this system, emancipation by itself did nothing to confer rehabilitative healing that would at last allow the emergence of an African American model minority. Perhaps in a paradigm in which Reconstruction succeeded, that black paragon emerged—weaving elements of struggle, faith, and transcendence into the world's greatest story, that of the true model minority. But this narrative did not unfold in our universe. Jim Crow all too happily stood in for the terminal slave master, guaranteeing black America's eternal wasting.

The Korean Case

Like Chinese Americans, Korean Americans are often tagged with the model minority moniker. The Korean American migration narrative also bears strong contrast with the abrupt, discordant migration of America's first Africans. Korean immigrants arrived in the United States independent and armed with a coherent and effective plan for the creation of a Korean American society. Korean immigrants were scrupulous in orchestrating ways to circumvent the racial stigmatization America guaranteed them. Their most effective tactic was employing the monetary and academic resources accumulated over generations in their homeland toward this goal. Professors Ivan Light and Edna Bonacich profile how this strategy ensured Korean immigrants an American experience quite unlike the chained and destitute one of the first Africans in the United States:

> In the specific case of Koreans in Los Angeles, both ethnic resources and class resources supported the entrepreneurship of group members. That is, Koreans were highly educated in their country of origin, often well-endowed with money upon arrival in the United States, and commonly middle or upper middle class in social origin.[207]

In 2013, the Korean American population stood at about 1.7 million.[208] This number was totaled in three waves of immigration. The first consisted of a relative trickle in the early 20th century; the second happened in response to the Korean War; and the third occurred as a reaction to the lifting of restrictive immigration quotas in the 1960s.[209] The third and largest wave is responsible for today's large Korean American population in major metropolitan centers like New York, Los Angeles, and Washington, DC. The first wave flowed with the gravity of employment opportunities in then-territory Hawaii's burgeoning agricultural industry around the turn of the century.[210] Ironically, the Chinese Exclusion Act paved the way for Korean American immigration to the United States. In the absence of Chinese laborers, farmers first responded by exploiting the Japanese American labor force. When Japanese American laborers boycotted poor working conditions, the Hawaii Sugar Planters Association successfully petitioned the Korean government for a large

31

employment force.[211] [212] In the coming years thousands of Koreans arrived in Hawaii to supplant the striking Japanese workforce. Inevitably, Korean immigration was soon halted as a result of exclusionary immigration reform, but not before the seed of what would become a verdant Korean American community was planted.

In the aftermath of 1960s immigration reform, new Korean immigrants passed through customs dual-wielding arms of education and class. Koreans used these weapons to their advantage in carving out a high position in the American racial hierarchy. In addition to education and prosperity, their possession of cultural capital enabled community cohesion.[213] Unlike earlier waves largely made up of single, male immigrants, this third Korean immigration wave arrived in the United States in the form of self-sufficient, united family groups.[214] But they were not without struggle. Although many of them had been white-collar professionals in the homeland, barriers of social adjustment and institutional racism barred these new Americans from mass entry into professional ranks.[215]

Although America's avenues of financing and employment were closed off to Korean immigrants, resources of community enabled many Korean Americans to undertake successful forays into entrepreneurship. Korean-owned enterprises enabled the economic fortification of the greater community, thus obviating dependence on a hostile and unaccepting labor market. Had Korean American immigrants lacked the relative financial prosperity accrued in the homeland, such prosperous forays would have been impossible and their position in America's racial hierarchy would be precarious. Instead of enjoying the mantle of ownership and the accordant power to themselves discriminate in employment selection, they would have found themselves in competition with poor and lower middle class whites, African Americans, Hispanics, and individuals of other communities for low-paying, often menial jobs. But the cornucopia gifted in the homeland and the relative sanctity of agency they enjoyed on arrival in the United States allowed the construction of the nation-within-a-nation that compensated the prosperity institutional racism denied them.

Still, the most important immigrant resource has not been the dollar, but identity. Immigrant communities are often ethnocentric—Korean Americans are no exception. But this brand of ethnocentrism is necessitated by an American society that casts them onto its periphery. Rather than react to this with desperate attempts at assimilation, Korean Americans ardently held on to their ethnic identity.[216] There is no doubt that the strength of the Korean family unit was paramount to this effort. Group immigration (as opposed to the splintered dynamic of African slaves) ensured the foundation of family units with accordant emphases on transmission of educational and professional values unto posterity. These procedure words are received; 53 percent of Korean Americans have at least a bachelor's degree, nearly twice the national average.[217]

Korean Americans have been lauded for their ability to succeed in spite of the stigma the American beast of xenophobia attaches to their ethnic and racial identity. But without the restraints that institutional racism places on them, their success would likely be greater. America offers model minorities like Korean Americans a disingenuous pat on the back in praise of surviving the very obstacle that America itself so often represents. Even worse is the American tendency to use model minorities as pawns for perpetuating the status quo. Instead of congratulating success in spite of racism, society should itself spite racism. No one should have to overcome racism; everyone must confront the lethargy and denial that enable its survival.

Chapter 2: A Model Myth

The socioeconomic conditions today characterizing Korean Americans and African Americans could not be more glaringly different. In rates of incarceration, drug use, teen pregnancy, school dropouts, levels of personal income, and other sociocultural measures of progress and development, their side-by-side comparison makes for pronounced dissimilarity. But this is expected. These groups' trajectories could not be more dissimilar. How can one group—having undertaken an organized migration made possible by accrued capital and then using those resources toward success in American enterprise—be compared to another, chained to slavery, Jim Crow, and their enduring legacies? The only way such a comparison could be fair and valid is if America's first Africans had arrived voluntarily as a migrant community comprised of family units possessing the values and resources of the homeland, settling into an America affording them some semblance of freedom to chart their own destiny. Or, conversely, if Koreans or other "model minorities" had arrived packed into slave ships, without semblance of family or wealth, donated to a world of Jim Crow and the eternal spirit of racial oppression.

No amount of hard work alone could have brought about the achievements of today's model minorities. To point to such groups as examples for African Americans to follow is not only disingenuous, but also serves to both justify and promote antiblack racial bias. All groups are equally capable of demonstrating model minority status; contrary to common misconceptions, all of them do. But to understand the variance in groups' propensities toward model behavior it is necessary to examine their unique trajectories. Somehow, careful examination gives way to the telling of fairytales featuring diverse casts of heroic characters that leave but one shade for the villain. These propagandist myths lull Americans into neglecting the duty of eliminating their community's problem of institutionalized racism. America promises colorblindness but elects fanatical cognizance of color. It ignores that socioeconomic success and sociopathological malaise alike are inseparable from America's systemic structures. These structures malnourish one segment of America's being in a deplorable, disparate distribution of destiny's fruits.

One group offers a shining indication that, with better circumstances, the same Africans brought to the United States as chattel would have proven an exemplary group. Their example drives the point further home that cultural values are not Chinese, Korean, white, or anything other than simply human. This group's trajectory is like that of stereotypical Asian model minorities, but they look to a different meridian for the land bearing harvests nourishing their value systems. In measures of wealth and income, education, crime, and beyond, their test scores are equal to—if not better than—those of the model minorities with whom the American media carries on an illicit love affair. In fact, these men and women hail from the very same lands from where the captive and enslaved ancestors of African Americans came—countries like Nigeria, Ghana, and Cameroon—as well as regions outside the West African homeland, like Ethiopia. They are America's African immigrants and they are threatening to redefine not only the misleading moniker, but also America's racial hierarchy.

The Black Model

"Black model minority" intuitively registers as a paradox, but the phrase reflects something real. There is indeed a black model minority exemplifying values of education, professional employment, entrepreneurship, ethnic pride, and familial stability. As a disclaimer, it is both unfair and erroneous to suggest that slave-descended African Americans *do not* exhibit these values and have not created, in both theirs and America's interest, an affluent, educated, business- and family-oriented class. That this class exists is both apparent and not wanting of substantiation, except perhaps to those helplessly biased. But for this profile's purposes, "black model minority" refers to immigrant black populations in America hailing chiefly from Africa and countries throughout the black Diaspora.

It is necessary to craft this distinction to emphasize the enormity of impact that America's peculiar form of oppression has had on the African American trajectory—one not always harsher than Caribbean forms of slavery or the colonial regimes that afflicted Africa, but more effacing. Slavery, Jim Crow, and the modern phantom maintaining African American enervation in spite of the endemic colorblind condition are uniquely inhumane institutions. What differentiates these American modes, particularly slavery, is the erasure of identity that occurred via the inculcation of Western cultural values to the end of maintaining bondage not just of black American bodies, but black American minds and souls. Although African Americans and black immigrants both withstand antiblack racial bias, it is African Americans who are "last in line" in all of the wrong categories. This suggests there is something beyond the lone stigma of blackness at play with regard to the problems African Americans today face. That something is likely found in historical and contemporary forms of institutionalized racism which have inflicted continuous trauma that has precluded the emergence of a model African American identity.

The black model minority's journey differs from those of traditional model minorities. Immigration patterns of model minority groups like Chinese and Korean Americans were characterized in part by mass exodus, with significant parts of their homeland populations uprooting for transplantation to the United States. The black model minority dynamic is varied, being characterized by both mass, central migration (e.g., Ethiopian Americans, Nigerian Americans) and small, sometimes individual migration patterns from corners of Africa and the Diaspora. In the latter case, the cohesive communal networks for which traditional model minorities are known are often lacking. Still, blacks in such groups utilize tools to fashion a black model minority group whose unlikely existence challenges the American status quo. Black model minority groups are also people of unique legislative descent, being the legacies of post-1960s immigration reforms like the 1980 Refugee Act and the 1990 Immigration Act, which introduced the Diversity Immigrant Visa.[218]

Still, black model minorities show likeness with stereotypical model minorities in numerous areas. Much like their Asian counterparts, African immigrants tend to be highly educated, often obtaining degrees from the satisfactory universities of their homelands or in European academic institutions prior to arrival in the United States.[219] U.S. Census data reflects their prioritization of education, showing that 41 percent of African immigrants possess college degrees (Nigerians registering a notable figure of 61 percent).[220] In addition to education, they often arrive in the United States with the intact familial units[221] and relative prosperity[222] that mitigate the turbulence of adjusting to a new country. They also share in common with the familiar model minorities the experience of having their skills undervalued. Many Africans educated outside the United States as doctors, lawyers, or engineers suffer underemployment as a result of holding foreign degrees, which carry less value on the U.S. labor market.[223] These Africans also withstand both overt and institutional forms of racism.[224] But given America's evolution into a society of unprecedented—albeit still limited—opportunity, these African model minorities have capitalized on the modern social milieu for a chance at a better life.

Ethiopian Americans

Ethiopian Americans are among the most populous black immigrant groups in the United States. There are approximately 200,000 Ethiopian-born Americans,[225] primarily coalescing in the Washington, DC, Atlanta, and Los Angeles metropolitan areas.[226] Although the first Ethiopians arrived in the United States in 1808,[227] significant migration did not take place until Emperor Haile Selassie's ouster in 1974. The rise of Mengistu Haile Mariam's Derg government stimulated a mass Ethiopian brain drain embodied in a wave of emigration by Ethiopia's educated professionals. Many of these Ethiopians came to the United States as refugees, eschewing the new, Soviet-allied regime for an America that would permit greater altitudes of achievement.[228]

Ethiopian migration was not limited to the elite ranks, as those of lesser means also undertook voyage in pursuit of America's freedom and opportunity. Class dynamics did not prevent the construction of a shared community edifice of entrepreneurial success. Their success is evidenced in their average median household income of $40,977 compared with $38,705 for African Americans in 2010.[229] Ethiopian American prosperity has also been used to the benefit of the homeland in the form of remittances that generate a significant portion of Ethiopia's GDP. In remittances alone, Ethiopian Americans contributed a staggering $1.2 billion to their homeland economy in 2009, approximately 3.5 percent of Ethiopia's GDP.[230] This exceeds the dollar amount the United States provides Ethiopia in economic assistance.[231]

As children of one of the oldest Christian nations in the world, Ethiopians carried their orthodox form of Christianity with them to the United States as a consecrated cornerstone of the Ethiopian American community. Orthodox Christianity is the traditional religion of Ethiopia's dominant ethnic group, the Amhara, and for centuries functioned as Ethiopia's *de facto* state religion. Most of those who came to the United States were steeped in this tradition. A smaller portion of the community identifies as Muslim. Although Ethiopians practice Orthodox Christianity much in the same vein as Greek and Russian Orthodox worshippers, theirs is a culturally distinct form incompatible with other denominations:

> Although there are Russian and Greek Orthodox churches that have strong roots in America there are doctrinal differences that inhibit Ethiopians from attending these churches. What is more, in addition to the doctrinal difference between the Ethiopian and the aforementioned Eastern Orthodox Churches, the Ethiopian Orthodox church is hugely influenced by Judaism and indigenous elements in its practice and dogma. This sets it apart from the rest of the Orthodox churches. Other differences preclude Ethiopians from attending these churches: For Ethiopians, Orthodox Christianity is something that they inherited from their forefathers.[232]

Ethiopians demonstrate an unyielding desire to preserve their identity and the cultural traditions that define it. Though African Americans and Ethiopian Americans both are Christian populations, the religion served distinct functions for these groups. For Ethiopians, Christianity is a millennia-old tradition integral to a rich, glorious history of independence. But for African Americans, Christianity was used as a tool to program them for devotion to their damnation in slavery and only took on a culturally unifying role in the wake of emancipation. For Ethiopians, Christianity is not merely a matter of faith but also devotion to a long-standing ancestral tradition that is the centerpiece of their culture. Though African Americans' brand of Christianity is no less valid, the Ethiopian Orthodox church's representation of the nation's independent history gives it an identity function unlike that of the black American church. Ethiopian Orthodox Christianity is the trademarked pillar of an ancient culture, protecting a cherished legacy from infringement.

This Ethiopian American tendency toward ethnocentricity has caused a somewhat strained relationship with the African American community.[233] Although most Ethiopian Americans self-identify as black, Ethiopians have a genetic and physical makeup that is distinct from both African Americans and immigrant populations from West African nations.[234] Anthropologists believe that this biological distinction is to some degree attributed to intermingling or genetic relation with Caucasoid and Arabic races.[235] Whatever the narrative, the belief in this racial distinction has largely limited the degree of assimilation that Ethiopian Americans have had with African Americans.[236] Coincidentally, Ethiopians partook in their own system of slave trading, dealing chattel both among the denizens of their nation as well as to other nations. Ethiopian slavery was like the American form in that it largely targeted East African populations whose members tended toward Negroid physiognomies.[237] Ethiopian slavery (outlawed under the rule of Haile Selassie[238]), however, was not the brutal and "peculiar" institution that American slavery was, being a more limited and domestic system.

Many immigrant groups fail to comprehend the unique brutality and surviving traumas of the American institution of slavery. It is not entirely their fault; they arrive in America long after the last shots rang on behalf of emancipation, with education from systems that do not include this history in their curricula. But this lack of historical awareness contributes to a dynamic of misunderstanding between African Americans and other ethnic groups, including Ethiopian Americans. That, and the preponderance of stereotyped depictions of African Americans in U.S. and global media, motivates Ethiopians to repudiate black Americans for the sake of safeguarding cultural values on which they place high premiums. This phenomenon itself attests to the influence erroneous concepts like the "model minority" have in sowing seeds of discord among the roots of immigrant communities.

Nigerian Americans

Nigerian Americans also challenge media notions of what the model minority looks like. The United States is home to approximately 376,000 Nigerians.[239] Although first arriving in smaller numbers in the 1960s, en masse Nigerian immigration commenced in the 1980s in response to government instability in the homeland.[240] Nigerian immigrants coalesce in Maryland's Prince George's and Montgomery counties,[241] New York City, and Houston among other metropolitan areas.[242] By at least one estimate, a staggering 64 percent of foreign-born Nigerian Americans above the age of 25 surveyed had bachelor's degrees,[243] supporting a median household income of $57,375.[244] This level of education puts them ahead of *all* groups in the United States.

Nigerian American immigrants even lead Asian migrants in the number of master's and doctoral degrees possessed.[245] But these facts are not necessarily causes for celebration. Like Ethiopia, Nigeria suffered a brain drain of its educated professional class that some posit has inhibited the country's economic and structural development.[246]

Nigeria's development of sizable middle and upper classes was made possible by the country's abundant natural resources. In particular, their lucrative oil industry has served as the foundation of a robust economic structure. Nigeria's gross GDP was $573.652 billion in 2015, placing them 21st internationally and 1st in Africa.[247] Much like Asian immigrants, many Nigerians arrive in the United States equipped with wealth and education.

Although Nigerian culture is stereotyped as corrupt and conning, a supportable depiction of Nigerian culture lies in its extraordinary emphasis on economic development. In spite of high poverty and unemployment rates,[248] Nigeria has enjoyed prodigious growth through the 2000s, averaging 6 percent between 2005 and 2015.[249] Nigeria's economic performance has been strong enough to justify its inclusion on the list of the eleven 3G countries expected to grow substantially through 2050.[250]

Nigeria's native population is split between Christians and Muslims,[251] but the majority of Nigerian Americans are Christian.[252] British colonialism preached the Christian faith to Nigerians who had for centuries practiced Yoruba and other traditionalist religions. Similar to America's slave system, Britain abused Christianity as an agent to format and reprogram African psychology for submissive operations.

Although the partial success of this endeavor is evidenced in Nigeria's large Christian population, Nigerians retained a substantial degree of cultural consciousness which served as the bedrock for Nigerian nationalism and sparked the liberation movement that culminated in Nigeria's independence from Britain in 1960. Christianity could restructure, but not demolish, the cultural constellation of customs, language, history, and ethnicity that Nigerians retained. The Christian element's indelibility to Nigerian American identity is exemplified in institutions like the Redeemed Christian Church of God, which is headquartered in Texas and claims 758 global congregations serving mostly Nigerian worshippers.[253]

Nigerian Americans, unlike Ethiopians, are genetic and ancestral cousins of many African Americans. The Igbo, Nigeria's dominant ethnic group, are heavily represented in the Nigerian American immigrant population. Coincidentally, the Igbo were also heavily represented on the slave ships of the Middle Passage.[254] One state offers a particularly striking example of this contrast. Igbo slaves were most frequently imported to the state of Maryland. Today, Maryland is the U.S. state with the highest population of Nigerian immigrants.[255] This "twin study" yields a fascinating result; that two related ethnic groups could have such different outcomes shows that there is no biological basis for the problems of African Americans. The socioeconomic achievement gap between these cousins is attributed to separate trajectories of nurture. Neither trajectory was without trauma. But, in retaining their culture, Nigerian Americans held on to the pot of gold that slavery stole from the African American spirit.

Ethiopians and Nigerians offer just two examples of black model minorities who disprove notions of black inferiority and, when contrasted with African Americans, demonstrate that history lives in contemporary social dynamics. The history that robbed African Americans of the values essential for the creation of successful societies lives on in the African American minority who, despite four centuries of existence on American soil, finds themselves beat out by the African immigrant before they even step off the boat. The most important fact to reconciling the model minority myth with reality is that, despite the implications of the common model minority stereotype (and perhaps even this analysis), African Americans too are model minorities. In communities like Tulsa, where African Americans outdid whites in demonstration of all necessary values, their attempts at becoming America's original model minority were thwarted at every turn by the same system that chides them for this failure.

Conclusion

America's model minorities—Asians, Africans, and beyond—deserve full credit for seizing the opportunities available to them. But to cite their successes as proof of the existence of a level playing field is to perform an act of duplicity. In elevating model minorities, we lower them. Despite being celebrated, Asian model minorities still face institutionalized racism; black model minorities face yet harsher forms (partly evidenced in their having lower incomes than Asian Americans despite being more highly educated).

America's implied appreciation for the model minority is belied by a social order that hypothesizes no just world, but justifies larceny in allowing the shortchanging of its workers on the basis of race. Nowhere is this evidenced more than in the fact that immigrants endowed with the "epidermal capital"[256] of the lightest skin shades earn, on average, 20 percent more than those with the darkest.[257] That all these immigrants, categorized as one model minority, lag behind whites in areas of income and employment despite their *overqualification* demonstrates the magnitude of injustice and the prevalence of the myth that harasses destiny.

Although they endure these struggles, it must be understood that model minorities dodged the bullet in arriving in the United States both long after and because black America's bloody liberation struggles had been fought. The opportunities that model minorities enjoy were yielded by the blood and struggles of American freedom fighters who waged their own independence war within the borders of the United States. To ignore that history is to insult America's history. These efforts created the social dynamic of greater economic opportunity and less overt, less violent racial discrimination that were necessary conditions for model minority success. America's Tulsas, Rosewoods, and lynch mob agitations gave birth to the Tiger Mom. Without the effects of those brutalities, nothing about her parenting would merit the laudatory dynamic yielding book contracts and talk show appearances. The afterlife promise of heaven made to America's architects has been forsaken for protracted hell. Our maledictions damn them to posthumous service unto an unholy social order.

There are voices—perhaps of those who perished in bondage long ago—that guide us to truth's promised land. But the myth drowns them. It engulfs us in a deluge of duplicity, carrying us upstream, departed from America's destiny. America's destiny will at last emerge—and lay to promised rest its enslaved souls—once America's models and mistakes demand the dominant majority answer why it distributes the deceptions and disparities that amount to a damned social order.

③
The Injustice System

JoAnn Wilson was stabbed to death on July 9, 1980.[258] Police encountered a macabre scene. Wilson had been raped and her home ransacked. Wilson bled; she gasped. "My baby, my baby." Her four-month-old daughter had been home; Wilson did not know if she too suffered some cruel fate. Wilson did know, however, the harbinger of her own. An officer urged Wilson to divulge the truth the Specter of Death coveted as a grave secret. In her last breath, she testified. The statement was slurred, almost indiscernible, but sounded like "Elvin did it."[259] JoAnn did not know an Elvin. She did know an Alvin; the two were close.

Alvin Moore was 20. He worked at the local VA hospital—quiet, unassuming, but not without charm. His gentle bearing belied a past checkered with misdemeanor convictions, fights, and a school expulsion. "He was no angel." On the night of the murder, police tracked down the only person to whom they thought Wilson's deathbed testimony could apply. Moore was found with a single drop of blood on his pants. That drop of blood was later tested and found to be type O—the same as JoAnn Wilson's. Police also found items in Moore's possession that belonged to Wilson, presumably ransacked at the time of the murder. In the back seat of Moore's car, officers found a radio and a jar of pennies which they surmised Moore had absconded with in the slaying's aftermath.[260]

After interrogating Moore, police arrested Arthur Stewart and Dennis Sloan. Both had been with Moore and Wilson on the evening of the murder. When questioned, Stewart and Sloan—undertaking a curious legal enterprise—admitted that they, not Alvin Moore, had stolen the radio and pennies. They had schemed in secret, waiting until Moore and Wilson were out of their sights to carry out the meager heist. Alvin and JoAnn wanted Stewart and Sloan out of their sights, too; theirs were set on each other. They had schemed a bedroom rendezvous. Despite their confession, Stewart and Sloan insisted their plot did not include the stabbing. The men plea-bargained, agreeing to testify against Moore in return for lesser charges.[261]

Stewart and Sloan claimed that when they left Wilson's home at the end of the heist, they heard screams. They saw a knife-wielding Moore emerge from the house, exclaiming, "I stabbed the bitch nine times!" The judge hearing the case found Stewart and Sloan's testimony credible, so much so that Moore's lawyer's request for a continuance was denied. Moore's attorney even later admitted to having felt so little faith in the prospect of the jury buying Moore's innocence that he felt offering a defense statement would have been "silly." The prosecution's allusions to Moore's questionable background joined with Stewart and Sloan's eyewitness testimony to make for an open-and-shut case. Alvin Moore was convicted of murdering JoAnn Wilson. He was sentenced to death.

A few years after Moore's conviction, Stewart and Sloan recanted their testimonies in sworn affidavits. They confessed that Moore never claimed to have stabbed JoAnn Wilson. They also admitted that when they left Wilson's home that evening, Moore was with them and Wilson was alive and well.

Last in Line: An American Destiny Deferred

Their retractions invited retrospective scrutiny of the prosecution's arguments and use of evidence. The murder scene at Wilson's home was so bloody and gruesome that a reasonable person would have expected the killer's clothes to be blood-drenched, not -specked. Also dubious was the argument that the blood's type bore any circumstantial value. Though Moore was not type O, 40 percent of Americans are. Because Moore worked in a hospital, there were thousands of potential explanations for the fateful stain.

Furthermore, the details of Stewart and Sloan's confessions weren't exactly breaking news. The prosecution argued that the murder occurred between 9 and 9:30 p.m., but withheld compelling evidence—a trial testimony from Wilson's husband, Aron—that proved Moore, Stewart, and Sloan left Wilson's home before this time. Aron Wilson, a mechanic, admitted to returning home around 9 p.m. to retrieve a tool. He came and went quickly, seeing his wife alive, well, and alone.

In trial, however, Aron claimed to have arrived and departed much earlier than 9 p.m. Dispatch records showed that JoAnn Wilson did not call police until 9:35 p.m. The prosecution's use of Wilson's apparent deathbed testimony was also questionable. An officer present at the scene admitted he was unsure what Wilson actually said. "Elvin" could just as likely have referred to "elephant" as it did to the defendant, given Wilson's strong Southern drawl. All of these factors exposed the case against Alvin Moore as fragile. Though conviction required proof beyond a reasonable doubt, the best anyone could say for the district attorney's case was that its conviction was, without a doubt, beyond reason.

The apparent fragility of the district attorney's case should have joined with Stewart and Sloan's retractions to exonerate Alvin Moore. It did not. Nearly seven years from that muggy, ill-fated night, Moore sat still and stoical. His countenance reflected an inner storm—resigned but resistant, taciturn yet screaming. A priest offered a presumptive sacrament, suggesting Moore appeal to God for forgiveness; salvation bore hope even for murderers. It was a sour last supper. Pangs twisted Moore's face into a grimace bitterly declaring, "They can kill my body, but they cannot kill my soul." A lever fell. A surge, guilty and gratuitous as JoAnn Wilson's murderer, sent waves of uncertain justice through Moore's body. Fissions quivered skin black. Flesh burned. Pulse ceased. Alvin Moore was 27.

It is still not known if Alvin Moore killed JoAnn Wilson. If he did, the evidence used to convict him gave no such indication. The jury's alacrity in convicting Moore—a black man who just so happened to have committed the social crime of sleeping with a white woman—in spite of the sheer lack of evidence seemed more consistent with the Southern tradition of unbridled white supremacy than with constitutional ideals of justice. That bias rendered this trial a travesty is clear. No matter the evidence, the all-white jury saw themselves fit to exercise their traditional right to kill a black man by any means necessary. Kill they did. It was no novel, unforeseen sin, but the dues of homage being paid unto heritage. Theirs was a burning birthright. In place of the torch of justice, they hoisted the inflamed cross—an emblem of the Southern brand of refusal, whisking and immolating the slightest idea of black humanity.

A year prior to JoAnn Wilson's death, in the same jurisdiction, Alvin Moore's cousin suffered a similarly senseless fate. Three white men kidnapped Virginia Smith.[262] They sought pleasure—and not only from her life. After the men forced Smith into their pickup truck, they raped her. The men then

40

robbed Smith, but not before stabbing her to death. That they had committed the crime was inarguable. The evidence was in their truck, her body, and most conspicuously, their faces—smug and unrepentant. They received life sentences.

America's Pledge of Allegiance proclaims an unwavering commitment to existence as "one nation, under God, with liberty and justice for all." Cases like Alvin Moore's are products of jurisprudential alchemy that poison and mutilate that pledge of loyalty. For certain groups in the United States, there is neither liberty nor justice. That a nation declaring its unequivocal commitment to God sanctions injustice necessitates its plea for the salvation for which the priest thought Moore wanting.

And it is not only to high places that we must look for this performance of salvation. This miscarriage of justice was a performance of judge, attorney, and citizen alike. That the jurors in Moore's *Apologia* all disregarded evidence urging to make him a free man shows that the betrayal of the Pledge of Allegiance is a sin unfamiliar with limits of class. And for these same citizens to acknowledge the incontrovertible evidence in the trial of his murdered cousin, Virginia Smith, and yet give her killers life further underscores the blatant disrespect not only for the sanctity of our Constitution, but for life itself.

Many Americans would argue that we need not look as far as the Jim Crow South or even the execution of Alvin Moore for evidence that the system sanctions black death. On July 13, 2013, George Zimmerman was acquitted of the murder of 17-year-old Trayvon Martin.[263] In what had from its inception been a racially charged media frenzy, many pointed to the actions of Florida's police and justice departments as proof that American legal policies negate the value of black lives. The incipient question in the Zimmerman ordeal did not concern how one should be punished for taking a black life; it concerned if one should be punished at all.

The question began February 26, 2012. Zimmerman patrolled as a vigilante Neighborhood Watch Captain in a gated community in Sanford, Florida. From his pickup truck, he spotted a hoodie-clad Martin walking behind townhomes that, it was later discovered, weren't far from Martin's father's home.[264] Zimmerman called police to report his sighting of Martin. He claimed that Martin was approaching him and appeared to be circling his vehicle.[265] Zimmerman then told the dispatcher that Martin fled.[266] He pursued Martin, undeterred by the dispatcher's dissuasions.[267] Zimmerman later claimed that at some point after the call Martin "jumped out from the bushes," punched him in the face, and began beating his head against a sidewalk. Zimmerman's testimony gives no clear indication of when or why he left his truck. A ground struggle ensued between the two during which, according to Zimmerman, Martin attempted to grab his firearm. Zimmerman fatally shot Trayvon Martin once in the chest.[268]

The media's racially biased portrayals of the individuals throughout the trial's duration outraged many African Americans. Although both Martin and Zimmerman were shown to have blemished histories, many accused media outlets of engaging in a defamation campaign against Martin, who had been suspended from school for fighting, snapped pictures with gold teeth, and was found to have had marijuana in his system at the time of the fracas.[269] The media made much of Martin's questionable past but appeared to turn a blind eye to Zimmerman's history of aggressive incidents, which included being issued a restraining order at the insistence of a battered ex-girlfriend, getting fired from a stint as a security guard after picking up and throwing an intoxicated female partier, and being arrested for "resisting an officer with violence," among other alarming incidents.[270][271] One witness, a female cousin of Zimmerman, claimed that he molested her for a decade and further stated, "I know George...does not like black people."[272]

In contrast, although Martin's history was not clean, he lacked a history of the same egregious magnitude. Martin didn't even have a criminal record. That Zimmerman's checkered past failed to merit even equal scrutiny seemed evident of racial bias in the eyes of many. Although Zimmerman is half Hispanic, many perceived the American right's embrace and defense of Zimmerman as occurring only because of his victim's race. Zimmerman was also shown to have made 46 calls to Sanford Police over an eight-year span for suspicions involving black males.[273] He did not want for support. Many were eager to grant him the benefit of the doubt, presuming that if he killed a black male then he was not without good reason.

Law enforcement's dilatory response to Martin's killing drew the greatest indignation in the ordeal's midst. Zimmerman was not arrested until more than a month after the killing[274] and it was at first unclear that he would even be prosecuted.[275] His defense argued that his actions were justified under Florida's controversial stand-your-ground law. Opponents argued that Zimmerman's pursuit of Martin against dispatch orders showed that if anyone was entitled to a stand-your-ground defense, it would have been Martin. Even if Martin struck Zimmerman, circumstances suggest that he did so in self-defense.

No one but Zimmerman has eyewitness knowledge of what happened that night, but evidence points to the fact that Martin fled from a man whom a friend he had been talking to in the pursuit's midst said he described as "creepy."[276] In spite of evidence that made the defense's stand-your-ground invocation dubious, the jury acquitted George Zimmerman of second-degree murder charges.[277] If not for the presence of a sixth half Hispanic juror, it would have been an all-white jury decision.

What happened to Martin—and Zimmerman—proved consistent with patterns of the American justice system. But black America, perhaps drunk off copious amounts of colorblind Kool-Aid, reacted with shock. Although some speculated that riots would ensue, frustrations did not erupt. No one can be sure just what occurred on the night of February 26 or what Zimmerman's motivations, conscious or unconscious, were. But in the years following the trial, Zimmerman's actions continue to reflect an antisocial disposition.

Since his acquittal, Zimmerman assaulted his (now former) father-in-law,[278] has been accused of domestic abuse by numerous women, and is alleged to have sent an explicit photo to an 11-year-old girl.[279] None of these actions brought prosecution. Zimmerman also attempted to stage a "celebrity boxing match"[280] and cashed in on a painting alluding to his trial to the tune of over $100,000.[281] He has milked such infamy into a Twitter platform with nearly 20,000 followers, trumpeting anti-Obama messages, lambasting black criminals, and taking occasional potshots at Trayvon Martin's corpse. But Zimmerman cannot alone be blamed. He had plenty of assistance from a jury and society much like that which let Emmett Till's murderers walk free in 1955.

The trials surrounding Alvin Moore and Trayvon Martin serve as symbols of the blatant racial bias of America's justice system. At both ends—

that of alleged murderer and that of alleged victim—if the identity is black and male, it is portrayed in such a way as to make the individual seem non-human, both lacking and unworthy of rational and objective standards, and invariably in the wrong. The only just verdict in the Zimmerman ordeal was that of black America's post-trial outrage. But the judgment that the verdict was of a primitive, anachronistic nature was mistaken. Well into the 2010s, names like Jordan Davis, Renisha McBride, Jonathan Ferrell, Eric Garner, Michael Brown, Tamir Rice, Freddie Gray, Alton Sterling, and beyond are inscribed on the stone tablet chronicling the eternal injustice of America's justice system.

A New Bondage

In 2015, the United States prison population totaled over 2.3 million persons, the largest in the world.[282] A list of countries ranked by incarceration rate showed Russia following the United States.[283] It is not until the United Kingdom appears ranked 102nd that another major Western power appears. The United Kingdom leads Western Europe in number of persons imprisoned per 100,000 people at a rate of 143.[284] That pales in comparison to America's generous 698 people per 100,000 individuals.[285] Despite a comparatively minute incarceration figure many American judges would laugh at, Britain has developed a cuff-happy reputation throughout most of Western Europe. The United States also distinguishes itself as the only major Western nation still handing down death sentences.

By itself, a high prison population is not indicative of a flawed justice system. What matters is whether the prison population is commensurate with the prevalence of crime in a society. So long as systems of justice are functioning properly—which requires just performance of its legislative, enforcement, and judicial components—then questions concerning mass incarceration must be directed elsewhere. America's figure represents either a tough, efficient system that doesn't let criminals off the hook or a system in which the processes of legislation and enforcement have broken down, producing a consequent, defective casualty of mass incarceration. A diagnostic assessment of America's justice machine shows it to be in dire need of overhaul, its legislative, enforcement, and judicial parts each showing profound malfunction.

In 1860, 607 Americans were incarcerated per *million*.[286] This translates into a mere 60.7 prisoners incarcerated per 100,000 people. There were exactly 19,086 prisoners incarcerated in the entire country on the eve of the Civil War.[287] Our current prison population number trumps that figure by approximately 12,000 percent. Adding perspective is the fact that in 1860, the United States' population totaled 31,443,321,[288] compared to 322,762,018 persons at the start of 2016.[289] The percentage of increase in our population is a "mere" 926. The increase in the prison population is *not* proportional to the increase in overall population, which necessitates a deeper examination in search of the cause of the disproportionate increase in the incarceration rate. Although one could frame factors like improved efficiency in systems or increased crime rates, a historical investigation of institutionalized racism shows it to be the culprit.

At the end of the Civil War, the South was left with around 4 million newly freed citizens[290] and a caste system on life support. As Union soldiers and couriers carried word of freedom to plantations, many slaves simply put down their shovels, gathered what little they had, and walked away.[291] Thus began Reconstruction. For some, the path up from barren soil was meteoric; stars fell on Washington, cratering consecration. Men born slaves consummated impact, replacing planters in the South's congressional delegation. Ebon hands blended with soil; they'd engineered earthworks. Dixie's caved overnight. The presence of manumitted African Americans, supported by carpetbaggers, Union soldiers, and scalawags, portended the earth of a nation in which, at best, the black man was social equal and, at worst, he was master—bifurcated roots of filth.

Nine Southern states passed vagrancy laws to uproot emancipated destiny.[292] Although not explicitly biased, vagrancy laws were passed with intent to recapture freed African Americans and shackle them to a new slavery.[293] African Americans found not working—for the only people for whom they realistically could work, ex-masters—were subjected to excessive fines. The exorbitant charges, which unemployed, dispossessed ex-slaves could not pay, were levied by contracting the former slaves to private employers.[294] In a dynamic reminiscent of the bondage from which they had just been freed, the fruits of the black man and woman's labor went not to him- or herself, but the ever-looming white master.

Blacks had no effective option but to submit to the effective reinstitution of slavery. For a time, pressure from Unionist governments forced abrogation of the South's vagrancy laws.[295] But the bugle calling Reconstruction's retreat signaled a fiery regrouping of vagabonds. Sheets and stallions were victuals, integrating white and black into their eternal separation. Bands heralded their rout, dressing and parading disaffected tools of white supremacy over peculiar black terrain back into Dixie's state legislatures for the Southern man's second inaugural ball.

In *The New Jim Crow*, scholar and activist Michelle Alexander explains how vagrancy laws engendered slavery's resuscitation:

> Tens of thousands of African Americans were arbitrarily arrested during this period, many of them hit with court costs and fines, which had to be worked off in order to secure their release. With no means to pay off their "debts", prisoners were sold as forced laborers to lumber camps, brickyards, railroads, farms, plantations, and dozens of corporations throughout the South. Death rates were shockingly high, for the private contractors had no interest in the health and well-being of their laborers, unlike the earlier slave-owners who needed their slave, at a minimum, to be healthy enough to survive hard labor. Laborers were subject to almost continual lashing by long horse whips, and those who collapsed due to injuries or exhaustion were often left to die.[296]

In many ways, the new system was harsher than the old. Prison contracting effectively made black bodies state property. In this new quasi-slave system, the state was the master. Whereas private masters may have tempered abuse and neglect, at least for pragmatic purposes, contractors felt no obligation to maintain property they did not own. For masters, slaves had represented investment; for contractors, prisoners represented disposability.

This unsustainable Jim Crow system maintained its clout in the South until the 1930s and '40s, when African American sharecroppers and their families began migrating north.[297] With the arrival of the Civil Rights Movement, vagrancy laws were once again scrutinized and found unreasonably ambiguous; they were repealed in many jurisdictions.[298] But the enactment of vagrancy laws was merely the first in a spate of Jim Crow policies that would combine to reincarnate the Old South's spirit and recall the incumbent Thirteenth, Fourteenth, and Fifteenth amendments bestowing justice on blacks. It would confine the black race to a jail cell, confiscating rights, sovereignty, and humanity and ensconcing a generational standard emblazoned in America's justice system today.

Legislative policies such as vagrancy laws and other "black codes" set the precedent for ambiguous, functionally racist policies that remain prevalent in all aspects of America's justice system. Just as they were during the post-Reconstruction era, African Americans today are arrested, convicted, incarcerated, sentenced, and executed in disproportionate numbers. The figure representing black men behind bars is erroneously ascribed to black criminality. But statistical analyses of crime show that African Americans are no more likely to partake in many of these activities than whites. Furthermore, it has been documented that adolescent blacks abuse drugs *less* than their white peers.[299] In reminiscence of Jim Crow, this modern system strips blacks of rights which most Americans take for granted—like rights to work and vote—and contributes to their descent into an incessant cycle of criminality that corporate policies like job application check boxes, corporate prisons, and government policies like felon disenfranchisement prevent them from breaking out of.

Even at our highest legislative, executive, and judicial levels, we find our government officials reluctant to enforce the civil rights amendments and laws set in place to protect African Americans from age-old biases that manifest in today's systems. Their policies cement the hierarchical American racial system that tears and threatens to altogether shred the social fabric of the United States.

The Colfax Massacre

White Louisianans were outraged by the revolutionary civil rights onslaught thrust upon their social order. Though the Civil War was lost, white Louisianans clung to the Confederacy, fancying themselves citizens of a government that declared an unambiguous intent to keep blacks downtrodden. The CSA's own constitution mandated this commitment: "The institution of Negro slavery, as it now exists in the Confederate States, shall be recognized and protected by Congress."[300] These emancipated Negroes immediately challenged white hegemony throughout the South and in Louisiana. Just seven years following Appomattox, the state saw the ascent of its first African American governor, P. B. S. Pinchback, who succeeded suspended governor Henry Warmouth and served out the remaining 35 days of his term.[301] Equally momentous and trailblazing was Louisiana's election of the United States' first African American congressman, John Willis Menard, in 1868.[302]

The election of African American politicians throughout the South, some of them having been slaves only yesterday, seemed the consummate incarnation of the principles and policies promised by the historic Reconstruction amendments. The election of these 17 African Americans to Congress during Reconstruction paid homage to these nursling amendments, nourishing them with the guarantee to carry out their equalizing specifications and elevate once shackled African Americans to positions of governance and determination over the future of the nation that had always been theirs.

Following Pinchback's term, a gubernatorial crisis erupted in Louisiana. Although both candidates were white, heavy racial tensions characterized the electoral dispute between Republican William P. Kellogg and Democrat John McEnery.[303] Kellogg's most fervent supporters were the African Americans for whom the Republican Party promised a government that would acknowledge and defend their rights.[304] Conversely, McEnery—a former Confederate commander and avowed white supremacist—found his most zealous supporters in the ex-Confederate soldiers, former slaveholders, and large segments of Louisiana's populace that saw the accompaniment of "Negro" and "rights" as a most contemptible juxtaposition. Each man's party fancied their candidate the election's victor and both held inaugural balls. After a lengthy dispute among members of its election board, the majority-Republican legislature certified Kellogg governor.

Like a tyrannical Roman senator, McEnery led a 5,000-strong march on New Orleans in March 1873.[305] Fancying himself a Confederate Gaius Marius, McEnery and his troops fought off police forces and state militias before ousting Kellogg.[306] McEnery made himself governor, receiving a tawdry civic crown from a rump legislature of his intimate Democratic colleagues. Upon learning that federal troops were en route, however, "McEnery's Mules" retreated. The battle continued in Colfax, where armed McEnery supporters laid siege on the courthouse, which Kellogg's black troops had dug trenches around and claimed as a stronghold.

McEnery's troops found an abhorrent sight. Not only were blacks assuming government offices; they were daring white men on battlefields. McEnery's men replied with furious volleys, exacting bloodstained revenge for the silent, black insults hurled at the Southern order. Despite the extensive efforts militia-trained blacks made to defend their base, they were outgunned and outmanned. Hoping for mercy, Kellogg's supporters surrendered and agreed to hand over their weapons.[307] Two hundred of McEnery's fighters employed those weapons to slaughter upwards of 105 blacks who, in their eyes, merited such regard for neglecting their designated role in Louisiana society.[308]

The Colfax Massacre did not set a precedent of mass racial violence against blacks. Nearly a decade earlier in the gratuitous Fort Pillow massacre, around 500 surrendered federal troops, the overwhelming majority of them African American, were mowed down by Confederate soldiers.[309] Confederates were possessed with blinding rage at the sight of Negroes wielding guns and donning uniforms, so much that victory alone could not soothe. Nathan Bedford Forrest, the commanding general, later mocked that a nearby river was "dyed with the blood of the slaughtered" and gloated his success in conveying the idea that "Negro soldiers cannot cope with Southerners."[310]

In an earlier Civil War pogrom, the Saltville Massacre, Union general Stephen Burbridge's army retreated and left several wounded black federal troops for Confederate disposal. They took the blood oath, dispatching of almost 150.[311] Such instances were not incongruent with the pervasive belief in the non-humanity of blacks and the idea that beyond their utility toward white ends, black lives were worthless. Such war crimes would stand as audible calls to civil rights trailblazers that the postbellum South would neither subject itself to notions of Negro equality nor recognize federal civil rights protections.

Chapter 3: The Injustice System

The Civil War's racial massacres were almost impossible to dispute on legal grounds. The Civil War transpired long before the Hague Conventions, international conferences that were fundamental in codifying and punishing war crimes. Despite the conspicuous aberrance of the crimes that occurred during the Civil War, there were almost no judicial mechanisms for recognizing such atrocities as punishable. In any case, it was beyond doubtful that Confederates would be willing to assume any moral accountability for war crimes against even whites—much less reviled blacks. Still, the Colfax Massacre offered an unprecedented opportunity to enforce law in defiance of gross human rights violations. The massacre opened a window for President Ulysses S. Grant and the Supreme Court through which an egalitarian precedent could be set for the full enforcement of federal law against those threatening the human rights of Americans.

President Grant sought action against the Colfax butchers under the Enforcement Act of 1870. In *Inherently Unequal*, author Lawrence Goldstone describes the mechanisms that enabled the Enforcement Act's utilization against actions involving racial violence:

> The 1870 law was one of three enforcement acts (the others were passed in 1866 and 1871) designed to give teeth to the Fourteenth and Fifteenth amendments. They applied criminal penalties to a wide variety of activities that could be seen as interfering with the exercise of civil rights guaranteed both implicitly and explicitly in both amendments. Most significantly, they transferred jurisdiction away from state government to federal court.[312]

The Enforcement Act's powers were so great that they even allowed the government to suspend *habeas corpus* if doing so was necessary to facilitate intervention in cases in which violence was used to violate blacks' civil rights. Most essential to the Enforcement Act was its power to commandeer state governments' powers over such cases and transfer them to the federal judiciary, a move that gave hope for such cases receiving fair trials. Although it was indeed a milestone that such egregious violations could be argued in federal court, in the Colfax case the Enforcement Act would not subject the defendants to the possibility of the death penalty. U.S. attorney J. R. Beckwith charged the defendants with:

> Unlawfully and feloniously [banding] together with the unlawful and felonious intent and purpose to injure, oppress, threaten, and intimidate one Levi Nelson and one Alexander Tillman, being citizens of the United States of African descent, and persons of color, and in the peace of the state and the United States, with the unlawful and felonious intent thereby to hinder and prevent them in their free exercise and enjoyment of their lawful right and privilege to peaceably assemble together with each other and with other citizens of the United States for a peaceable and lawful purpose.[313]

Of the more than 100 men indicted, three were found guilty. Justice Joseph Bradley, a Grant appointee, argued that there was no evidence that the Colfax defendants had massacred the black Louisianans because of their race. Bradley did not consider it substantive enough that an ardent faction of 200 white Louisianans supporting an avowed white supremacist candidate had massacred 105 African Americans. What was obvious to others did not to him yield the slightest measure of inductive insight—at least while in costume. By Justice Bradley's masquerade—a ludicrous evisceration of the Reconstruction amendments and federal civil rights laws—the Colfax butchers would have had to *publicly declare* a racial motivation for carrying out the crimes to be charged under the Enforcement Act.

As fast as the window of opportunity for justice opened, it slammed shut, blocking the defenestration of injustice that the United States Supreme Court had complete power and responsibility to carry out. Instead of setting a precedent that would ensconce the promises of equality offered by the recent revolutionary legislative acts and punish violators to the fullest extent of the law, the Supreme Court set a fatal precedent that lives today. The Court promulgated that unless alleged acts of racial discrimination or violence were underscored by a *declared intent* of racial motivation, they could not be argued under the Enforcement Acts and hence could not be recognized as violations of the Thirteenth, Fourteenth, and Fifteenth amendments.

The Colfax Massacre's motivations were all too evident. But because the Colfax killers never said they murdered their victims because they were black, the prosecution could not argue under federal law that the crime constituted an act of racial discrimination. The butchers were free. Memories of Colfax, Saltville, and Fort Pillow were trampled. The case was closed.

For many today, the Colfax Massacre is another of those "back then" things. We acknowledge its deplorability, regret it ever happened on American soil, and pat ourselves on the back for having evolved from that condition. Compassion and understanding have replaced the unjust, base instincts that somehow bypassed the guards of the Constitutional Convention and entered the American soul. Never today would we allow a Colfax-style ruling that declares the lives of 105 black men without value, their pain not warranting rectification. Our jurisprudential spirit has ascended to heights that make it impossible for us to ever again sanction gross civil rights violations. Better yet, we believe our citizenry today would never render so brutal an action necessitating invocation of the Enforcement Act or any measure that would require America's justice system to lay a heavy hand upon violators of American freedom in ardent defense of American humanity.

Those who believe the spirits of Colfax do not haunt us hallucinate. They would find themselves disabused of false notions of progress if they knew that no case in the history of the United States has ever successfully argued under federal law for an instance of racial discrimination in which the defendant did not demonstrate explicit racist motivation or intent.[314] That is how far we have evolved from the era of Justice Bradley. We've evolved so far that we adhere to the same unsatisfactory standard he and his colleagues on the Court set a century and a half ago. Rather than opt for freedom, justice, and good old-fashioned rationality by bearing a revolutionary ruling that would not only have defined our legal system as just but taken a stand in defense of human rights, Justice Bradley ruled in favor of injustice.

Today, Colfax-style victims abound in America. Twenty-first century courts target them in different but equally brutal ways. The historical scope of injustice has expanded to include men pursued without mercy by a justice system impaired by undue influence of stigma. They abound in our federal, state, and local prisons, confined as a consequence of questionable public policies. They are vagrants by virtue of their socioeconomic status, the neighborhoods in which they live, and, most of all, the color of their skin.

The patrilineal descendant of black code policies, vagrancy laws, and other such mechanisms that served to remove an unwanted "social ill" is the War on Drugs, a campaign that contests its paternity under a long-form guise but is exposed as none other than the naked legacy of American institutionalized racism.

The War on Drugs

President Richard Nixon's christening of the "War on Drugs" was no semantic error. It has indeed been a full-scale operation on the level of any of the United States' greatest military campaigns. Its strategy, which includes the deployment of SWAT units reminiscent of Vietnam platoons and stated missions of freedom and security (not to mention spoils), mirrors that of the U.S. military. It also reports to the same commander—the U.S. government. Waging battles on legislative, judicial, and executive fronts, this drug resistance coalition has demanded nothing less than complete surrender and imprisonment of its opponents. It offers no chance for reformation, no opportunity for remediation, and plenty of room for quarter. But unlike U.S. military conflicts, the Drug War's enemy combatants are Americans themselves.

Despite the overt declaration of their own government, Americans somehow fail to recognize the Drug War as an actual war. To many, it seems more a noble crusade with the mission of protecting American communities from invasions commanded by Pablo Escobar-like warlords from lands afar who equip shady dealers and hopeless addicts with weapons of mass destruction. That common characterization doesn't reflect the reality of the Drug War's policy of fixing its crosshairs not on the major distributors and peddlers of illicit substances—the warlords—but rather the impoverished, destitute, small-operation foot soldiers and civilian addicts, many who are black.

Just as Nixon's wording was no gaffe, the Drug War's targeting of African Americans was not happenstance. One of Nixon's chief tacticians, John Ehrlichman, reminisced in 1994:

> The Nixon campaign in 1968, and the Nixon White House after that, had two enemies: the antiwar left and black people. You understand what I'm saying? We knew we couldn't make it illegal to be either against the war or black, but by getting the public to associate the hippies with marijuana and blacks with heroin, and then criminalizing both heavily, we could disrupt those communities. We could arrest their leaders, raid their homes, break up their meetings, and vilify them night after night on the evening news. Did we know we were lying about the drugs? Of course we did.[315]

In measures of impact, the War on Drugs has been impressive in its ability to one-up the prejudicial political precedents of the past. Even though the United States has a long history of disproportionately imprisoning black men for reasons of bias, the efficacy of Jim Crow policies like black codes pales in comparison to those of the Drug War. In 1980, black men were three times more likely to be enrolled in college than incarcerated.[316] Less than two decades into the Drug War, however, these numbers saw a drastic change with 791,600 black men behind bars compared with only 603,032 enrolled in colleges in the United States.[317] This statistical change is directly related to the advance of the Drug War's brutal campaigns. But statistics can lie. By itself, the considerable increase in the rate of black male incarceration does not imply the unfairness of Drug War policies. Independent of the tricky context of statistical evidence (which entails the outright admission of one of Dick's chief commanders), this correlation indicates nothing of the justness or unjustness of this operation. Many surmise that the substantial increase in black incarceration is not attributed to discrimination, but blacks actually distributing, selling, and using drugs at higher rates than those of other races. If that's true, then the War on Drugs is an impartial and justified campaign.

But is it true?

Research shows it is not. Although African American men have achieved most-everything status on virtually all levels of the judicial and law enforcement systems, from the ankle monitor to the electric chair, research indicating the undue nature of such enforcement would leave many dumbfounded. A 2013 report from the National Institute on Drug Abuse found that among college students, illicit drug use was 25.1 percent for whites compared to 19.7 percent for blacks. Among those 12 or older, illicit use was 9.5 percent for whites compared to 10.5 percent for blacks.[318] In examining the drug proclivities of high school students, surveys conducted by Monitoring the Future found that "African Americans are generally more likely than white students to abstain from substance use, across all grade-levels."[319] The study further indicated that the racial discrepancy gap regarding drug use was smallest for marijuana, suggesting that African American adolescents who did use drugs were likelier to use marijuana to the exclusion of harder drugs.

The Centers for Disease Control and Prevention's 2011 "High School Youth Risk Behavior Survey" showed results similarly incongruent with the reality that America's predominantly black penitentiaries would have us believe. The survey's data showed that black high school students were less likely than both their white and Hispanic classmates to use cocaine, tobacco, alcohol, and most drugs. Furthermore, it showed that although almost 7 percent of white students had tried cocaine at least once, less than 3 percent of African American students had.[320]

Ancillary but significant to the figures regarding drug use are those concerning weapon possession and violence, two factors people often view as going hand in hand with drug use. Incidentally, many believe that African Americans are more likely to partake in these activities. A 2013 CDC study showed that of students surveyed, white males were more likely than black males to have carried a weapon onto school property, gotten into a physical fight, and carried a gun in the last 30 days. White males were also more likely to have driven drunk.[321] An earlier CDC survey showed whites and blacks to be involved in assaults at similar rates (36 percent for blacks and 32 percent for whites).[322]

One would conclude that if these federal statistics were accurate and America's justice policy was fair, the demographic makeup of our prisons would reflect them. But American public policy defies logic. African Americans make up a far greater percentage of the U.S. prison population than government statistics suggest they should. Despite the reality reflected by these drug use and behavioral statistics from the Department of Health and Human Services, African Americans abound in American prisons.

Although 314 African Americans per hundred thousand are arrested for drug offenses, just 175 whites per hundred thousand are arrested for the same offenses.[323] In 2012, 31.2 percent of those arrested in the United States for drug abuse violations were African American.[324] Further bolstering this unsettling fact is that nearly 50 percent of all those detained for drug use are African American—a grossly disproportionate level considering African Americans' lower levels of abuse.[325] As one study confirms, the tactical aggression of American law enforcement is largely to blame:

> Blacks are just 12 percent of the population and 13 percent of the drug users, and despite the fact that traffic stops and similar enforcement yield equal arrest rates for minorities and whites alike, blacks are 38 percent of those arrested for drug offenses and 59 percent of those convicted of drug offenses. Moreover, more frequent stops, and therefore arrests, of minorities will also result in longer average prison terms for minorities because patterns of disproportionate arrests generate more extensive criminal histories for minorities, which in turn influence sentencing outcomes.[326]

Why are African Americans incarcerated for drug offenses at disproportionate rates? Is there a conspiratorial motive? Is it a matter of inconvenient geography, given inner city areas' closer proximity to police departments? Is the influence of bias so strong as to command the consciences of law enforcement agents, prosecutors, and judges?

The answer to each of the above is an equivocal yes. Given John Ehrlichman's testimony, it's not a stretch to argue that there looms over the African American community some surreptitious, Hitlerian campaign targeting African Americans for annihilation. But, although America is no stranger to brutally unjust measures of discrimination (e.g., the Tuskegee experiments), absent whistleblowing or similar high-level admission we cannot be sure this applies today. However, that which has been proven proves just as troubling.

Proponents argue that in addition to black criminality warranting these practices, it is more cost-effective for police departments to target black, inner city areas. It should go without saying, but cost-effectiveness should not be among the factors dictating neighborhood policing. As with all government organizations, police departments operate within the confines of budgets—but they are not businesses. To place a price tag on policing at the cost of freedom is contrary to ideals of justice. Even if we take cost-effectiveness to be a legitimate motivation, we still cannot eliminate institutional racism from the equation given that housing discrimination remains a major culprit in African American inner city segregation. That African Americans' living arrangements are circumscribed to urban ghettos means heavy inner city policing is inherently biased. Additionally, police have other logistical motivations. Police are less inclined to police their own often suburban neighbors and less willing to risk entangling their departments in the legal battles that whites more often can afford to wage. All these facts suggest that the best explanation lies in the pervasive prejudicial attitudes of society from which law enforcement agents and policymakers have no special immunity.

The "criminalblackman" has an enduring legacy in the repertoire of American stereotypes. Long before the dehumanizing archetypes fitted for Asian, Hispanic, and Arab Americans, the idea of black criminality's intrinsic nature was deeply entrenched in American consciousness. Its image holds

51

Last in Line: An American Destiny Deferred

America's consciousness hostage. Harking back to the era of vagrancy laws, the "criminal" label was stamped on the black visage in permanent ink. Thus far, no amount of laser treatment seems able to remove this tarnish from the race's face. The criminalblackman's ubiquity is indeed great. Invading feature films, television programs, and nightly newscasts, the black male—for whom crime is more essential than eating, sleeping, or breathing—can be found armed and casting a wide smile for a Corrections Corporation-sponsored photo shoot. He does not go unnoticed. In fact, he makes a strong impression. Statistics have shown that 54 percent of whites see blacks as more likely to participate in criminal activities.[327] When asked to picture a drug abuser, most individuals picture someone black—even though statistics don't support this presumption.[328] Not even children are spared the influence of the black boogeyman. As one study reports, "Even as children whites view blacks as more aggressive than other whites engaged in the very same behavior."[329]

Many Americans take no issue with the justice system's disposition toward blacks, dismissing black accusations of injustice as emblematic of opportunistic "race card" politics. The rhetoric of political pundits, dinner table snarks, and unsightly comment sections all attest to this minimization. Ironically, these individuals themselves symbolize the malignant race bias that has engendered mass incarceration. Bias is a cancer that metastasized throughout the American anatomy long ago. The debilitated limbs of the justice system and failing organs of the citizenry are all harrowing indicators of the advancement of the condition that clouds American sensibility.

The Process

Criminals are made. The design and function of the American justice system yields a process of criminalization by which Americans are tracked through a machine that seizes law-abiding individuals and reconstitutes them as miscreants. Functioning like a well-oiled, fatally efficient assembly line, the justice system's victims are processed through a machine that betrays its intended purpose of ensuring fair application of the law to service policy's misguided production quotas and satisfy bias' arbitrary demands.

Criticizing criminal activity in and of itself without an accompanying examination of the structural flaws in the system that help to create it, like wealth, health, and education disparities, is disingenuous. Only by indicting the justice system for its role in processing those impacted by those disparities can justice be served. The criminalization process is explicitly geared toward those from marginalized racial and socioeconomic backgrounds. It starts on America's streets in the form of unconstitutional yet legally sanctioned searches and—in the best-case scenario—ends in the stigmatic rebranding of an American citizen, stripped of the rights and livelihood that are their birthright.

Stage One: Search & Arrest

John lives in a predominantly black, inner city neighborhood. You choose where. Make it Compton, Harlem, Brownsville, or Hartford. If you'd like to venture south, make it Atlanta or Birmingham. At 17, John is aged out of youth's protective clemency. He is old enough to be charged as an adult in most jurisdictions.[330] He is both unemployed and a high school dropout. This outcome isn't surprising. John has no examples, either at home or among neighbors—certainly not among his peers—suggesting the possibility of a different path. His peer group offers his only outlet for masculine expression, albeit of a wayward sort. His father's absence renders that milieu's formative impact uncontested. It's uncertain his father's presence would even be of any benefit given his own extensive criminal record. John's teachers have little desire to challenge his circumstance. They regard him much in the same way they do his peers—a hopeless, unwelcome nuisance. A trouble, a disciplinary problem, a sad excuse for a paycheck.

John does not have a criminal record. Whether or not John realizes it, that won't last long. His being young, African American, male, and an inhabitant of a low-income inner city area makes him more likely than anyone else in the United States to be accosted and searched by police. A predominantly white system of law agents, from the beat to the bench, pits itself against John's neighborhood. John is their adversary, an enemy combatant. That most of the police detaining, prosecutors charging, and judges sentencing his friends are white does not necessarily imply disparity. But with the inclusion of data, the checkered portrait of an unsightly legal system is completed.

Although whites comprise approximately 44 percent of New York City's inhabitants, 88 percent of individuals stopped for searches by police in the first three quarters of 2015 were nonwhites.[331] A staggering 54 percent of police stops involved black suspects, with 29 percent involving Hispanics and just 11 percent involving whites. In 2006, 45 percent of black suspects who were accosted were also frisked, compared with just 29 percent of whites.[332] The evidence of racial disparity in the use of stop-and-frisk remains even when controlling for precinct.[333] Under the administration of Mayor Bill de Blasio, incidences of these stop-and-frisk searches declined precipitously.[334] But the disparities have remained. Defenders of stop-and-frisk argue that the policy is crucial for keeping crime rates down. As for the statistical disparities, they argue that they only reflect minority propensities toward possessing illegal weapons, drugs and drug paraphernalia, and other incriminating material. It's simple—disproportionate prevalence of crime necessitates disproportionate incidence of stop-and-frisk searches. Data contradicts this supposition.

White individuals whom police stopped and frisked were 70 percent more likely to have a weapon on them.[335] With regard to recovering drug contraband, officers found such paraphernalia on white suspects 6.4 percent of the time compared with 5.7 percent for African Americans and 5.4 percent for Hispanics.[336] If the frequency of stops is tied to the incidence of crime among ethnic groups, then NYC's whites should be accosted at much higher rates than any other group. After all, according to the data any given white person in New York City is more likely than an African American or Hispanic bystander to be carrying a Smith & Wesson pistol or a vial of heroin. The data reveals the truth: the frequency of stops is strongly tied to the prevalence of bias among law enforcement agents.

In 2013, United States District Court judge Shira Scheindlin ruled the NYPD's stop-and-frisk policy both unconstitutional and illegal due to both its violation of the Fourth Amendment and its racially discriminatory nature.[337] Former mayor Michael Bloomberg criticized Scheindlin's ruling, stepping forth in firm defense of the tactic that was a central component of his administration's law enforcement policy. Claiming in a *New York Post* op-ed that "frisks save lives,"[338] Bloomberg insisted if there was anything flawed about stop-and-frisk, it was that the NYPD "stop[ped] whites too much and stop[ped] minorities too little."[339] Bloomberg's ideological obstinacy in face of statistical truth is a perfect example of how policymakers allow misguided biases to ruin the lives of their constituents.

At an inevitably inopportune moment, police enter John's home and search him. John used to smoke marijuana, but quit when his mother threatened to throw him out. Not so for his neighborhood buddy Michael, who can only be described as a connoisseur of "ganja." He even smokes in John's living room—when John's mom isn't around, of course. One day after a lengthy fumigation, in a daze Michael leaves his "baggie" of marijuana at John's. It was the day of a police "sweep." An officer knocks on John's front door and requests permission to search. The first time this happened, it was annoying—enraging, even. But over time, a sort of diminishing marginal frustration sets in. As far as John knows, he has nothing to hide. He welcomes the officer inside. The officer scans the premises for a few minutes before locating the contraband. John's jaw races his heart to the floor. Languid, John offers a tepid, jumbled explanation that seems to confirm suspicion. Such is John's introduction to the criminal justice system.

Studies suggest that rates of drug use in black communities are equal to, if not lower than, rates of use in white communities. Ironically, black communities are the most heavily policed.[340] But the Constitution gives Americans the right to refuse police searches. Why didn't John just say no? He could have; it doesn't mean the officer would have listened. Even with a refusal, John's mother's home could have been subjected to an invasive dog search for which the officer would need no warrant.[341] But couldn't John just hire a lawyer? Because John comes from a single-parent, low-income household, the option of a private lawyer is off the table. Even if he is miraculously acquitted, John can't afford a civil suit against the police department. And expectedly, he knows of no movers-and-shakers in his community marked by sky-high unemployment who can get him off. John will have to settle for a public defender and, with it, precarious odds of acquittal.

From the time of his arrest, John's likelihood of breaking out of the cycle is low. Unless John somehow wins the legal jackpot of *pro bono* support in the form of the Justice Project or an organization of similar stature, the stigma he's about to incur will alter the course of his life forever.

Stage Two: Jailing & Prosecution

The 'hood makes one hard. Its tragedies of crime and violence form calluses on the soul. But as John is about to find out, no amount of street fights, break-ins, or friends lost to violence could have prepared him for jail. Unable to make bail, John remains incarcerated pending charges. While the prosecutor contemplates his fate, he must tolerate the bellicosity of other inmates—many who are in jail for crimes much less innocuous than marijuana possession. Robbers, murderers, and rapists all share the block with John—not the sorts of neighbors with whom one shares hearth. John is much younger than most of these men who examine his face in search of weakness. If their gazes have not mollified him yet, they soon may.

Whether John faces prison time, probation, or an outright dismissal of charges can boil down to the prosecutor's caprices. Prosecutors have the power to dismiss an investigation for whatever reason they choose; for obvious reasons, they tend to employ this power selectively.[342] If John is in Columbia, South Carolina, as a first time offender charged with possession of an ounce

or more of marijuana he can face between one and five years in prison.[343] His charge may not carry a mandatory minimum sentence, but prosecutors can and often do push for longer sentences. Because of John's testimony, police pick Michael up as well. There's more where that baggie came from. He too is arrested pending charges of possession with intent to distribute. Michael denies having handled the baggie, but his fingerprints betray him. Conflicting testimonies set the tone for a fierce plea bargain battle. For testifying against each other, John or Michael can get the prosecutor to reduce their charges, thereby softening their eventual sentences. John could plea bargain by "admitting" that he purchased the marijuana from Michael, thereby closing the prosecution's case against Michael (and qualifying him for a maximum sentence, to boot). Michael, on the other hand, can testify against John and play along with the prosecution's presumption that he sold him the marijuana, thereby cementing John's likelihood of receiving a maximum sentence. John knows a plea bargain can, at the very least, prevent the worst outcome. But he is innocent; he feels freedom should not depend on lies. He hopes honest testimony will bring freedom. Michael's already in a lie; there's no turning back. He knows what prison is like and would prefer death to a second stint. Michael wins.

John is assigned the proverbial overworked, underpaid public defender. John insists his innocence to an incredulous lawyer; he tells John that refusing a plea bargain would make him as fit for a mental institution as it will a prison cell. But John sticks to his guns, ceding plea bargain privilege to Michael; his case is going to trial. John's faithless defender shows up for hearings and offers counsel, but is more interested in wrapping up what he thinks to be a foregone conclusion than fighting on John's behalf. After all, he can only expect negligible earnings that are not tied to the case's outcome.[344] There is no incentive to commit to lost causes, even less so when victory brings no spoils.

John's prosecutor, on the other hand, is not lacking in zeal. After all, the success of his career is judged by how many convictions he secures—not whether evidence proves the defendant's guilt. He insists that John's account is untrue. His only proof is Michael's testimony, which also featured the spicy detail that John was "thinking about dealing." That's all the prosecutor needs. "Proof beyond a reasonable doubt" lies in Michael's words. In determining charges, all the prosecutor had to do was decide whose narrative better fit his presumptions. The same evidence will be used against John. John is charged with possession with intent to distribute and providing false information.

Stage Three: Trial, Sentencing & Incarceration

If the streets are where the criminalblackman is conceived and the police vehicle is where he is incubated, then the courtroom is where he is born. Juries attend to this birthing room like delivery nurses; judges fulfill the role of obstetrician, supervising labors marking new life's arrival. If police and prosecutors are unfair, we at least expect our justices to do service unto their name. If the police and prosecutors fail to defend justice, judges are expected to defend their name in correcting for impropriety. Part of their "good behavior" is the unrivaled prioritization of fairness and the task of ensuring a fair outcome to trial proceedings. Despite our hopes, this last line

of defense does not exist. Even at the justice system's highest levels, we observe judicial complicity in the systematic scheme of withholding justice from the marginalized. Lawmaker, attorney general, and judge alike are complicit in the act of giving life to unjust policies.

After lingering in jail for two months awaiting trial, John appears before the judge. Though he has lost hope—and weight—he has not lost truth. He continues to insist that Michael left the marijuana at his house and he had no knowledge the contraband was in his living room. The judge spends little more than 10 minutes—a unique interpretation of the Constitution's "speedy trial" promise—hearing the arguments of the prosecution and defense before reaching a predictable decision. John is convicted on both charges. Because the judge thinks John to be a shameless liar, he gives maximum sentences for both. Michael gets a lighter sentence. John can appeal, but desperation will do him no good; his foolish dalliance with false hope is over.

John's prosecution exposes plea bargaining's strained relationship with justice. As explained before, prosecutors almost always use plea deals as bargaining chips for manipulating defendants into pleading guilty—regardless of actual guilt or innocence—to preclude the defendant's possibility of receiving the harshest charges. Prosecutors have a job to do—to prosecute—and like anyone, they seek to do it well. But the performance of prosecutors has been measured by percentage of people convicted, not applying evidence and information fairly toward the standard of proof beyond a reasonable doubt.

Prosecutors share public defenders' love of plea bargains, but for a different reason. For prosecutors, plea bargains amount to convictions. For them, it is better to secure a plea deal than go to trial and risk overcharging and failing to secure a conviction. The catch-22 for the innocent defendant is that although they avoid the harshest penalty, they falsely admit guilt. Innocent defendants who value their integrity might, like John, refuse to plea bargain and opt to fight charges. The odds are overwhelmingly stacked against them, however—especially if they are black. That such dilemmas exist in the judicial system in the first place is inexcusable, as is the fact that courts and legislatures have done little to eliminate them.

The mandatory minimum sentence is a defining characteristic of the Drug War. Federal and state sentencing guidelines stipulate that for certain crimes, judges can render a sentence no less severe than a pre-established minimum penalty. Mandatory minimum sentencing, perhaps more so than any other mechanism, has been generously applied to drug crimes. Virtually all crimes involving drugs beyond a negligible level of possession (including some semblance of evidence of intent to distribute) carry stiff minimum sentences which are immutable. Although mandatory minimum sentencing's use with convicts who actually are guilty has itself been sharply criticized, its use with convicts who have no blood (or drug residue, more aptly) on their hands has even more cuttingly called such policies into question.

During his five-year stint, John will see and experience things he expected to only know through the tales of neighbors. John can't afford "prison coaching." Without any white-collar friends, he isn't even sure what it is. All he has are the stories of friends, loved ones, strangers—perhaps "gangsta" movies. To survive, he will have to abandon his often pacific, reasonable way for a persona that is brutal and ruthless. The desocialization process of prison alters one's psychological disposition, making a new—perhaps more sinister—person out of someone who goes inside. Low quality health care,[345] violent victimization by other inmates,[346] rapes,[347] and other phenomena eviscerate the mental and emotional health of prisoners. Even those convicted of nonviolent crimes come out as angrier, disgruntled individuals whose return on release is likelier because of it.[348] John went to prison a law-abiding, mentally healthy citizen. That he will emerge so is doubtful.

Stage Four: Release & Recidivism

John makes it through. Several outcomes were as likely. John could have been murdered; murdered somebody; been caught peddling drugs; and been entangled in other scenarios that would have extended his stay. Although he's happy to be out, he will never be the same. John's psyche bears unsightly scars attesting to deep cuts of trauma. Fights with inmates. Beatings from guards. Perhaps other tragedies. But he made it out. Michael didn't. He was killed before his early release. That's what snitching gets you.

America's justice system is, among other things, characterized by a high recidivism rate. Studies show that as many as 82 percent of people who walk in and out of prison will return.[349] Some argue that certain individuals' frequent use of this revolving door offers evidence that criminality is dispositional. They cite this as proof that it is not the mechanisms of our systems tracking young African Americans in and out of prisons, but their wayward, stupefied ambulatory habits. A thorough examination of justice policy's impact on inmate recidivism shows this to be false.

Although John is 22, as a felon he finds readjusting to life on the outside impossible. His mother suffered a fatal heart attack during his prison stint. Without any local relatives willing to take him in, John is homeless. He surely could get a job—if someone would hire him. Every job application he submits features tiny, imperious check boxes commanding disclosure of his haunting ordeal. Even though they shout bold promises that YES won't disqualify his candidacy, he knows better. His job search is over before it begins. Without means of income, John cannot afford rent anywhere—not even in his former, low-income housing project. Even if he "hit a lick" for the onerous first, last, security trifecta, John's finesse wouldn't guarantee his penetration of the landlord's defense and conquest of the background check. Could Section 8 afford him a roof? John's felon status disqualifies him from that, too.[350] The same typically goes for SNAP and other assistance programs.[351] John alternates between homeless shelters and friends' couches. The local shelter allows a one-week stay. He can return, but must wait one month. There are too many other Johns.

John is jobless, homeless, and hungry—and there is absolutely nothing he can do about it. John is anathema. His criminal history makes him *persona non grata* to the outside. Jobs, housing, and public assistance all escape his reach. Five years earlier, prison was an unfortunate face. Beside a barren outside, that netherworld now appeared comely. The outside has become the inside. In prison, he escapes homelessness and hunger. He is guaranteed vocation. The work is wageless, but offers indemnity of sanity—identity. It offers a generous benefits package. John's pulsating toothaches grow worse with each day. On the inside, they continue to. On the outside, they are treated. As his prison term neared its end, John found himself seized with inexorable longing for greener grass. He stood in it. Reliving those pastures would require ironic daring.

Last in Line: An American Destiny Deferred

John finds his lowest station. Without refuge of friend or nonprofit, he spends a cold, bitter night on a concrete bed. Pastures. John must cut away vines and brush, invasive species that have become freedom. He holds a gas station attendant at knifepoint. He absconds with night. Signed notes and scant change become objects of manumission. Armed robbery is his herald. It makes a quiet, clamorous plea on behalf of freedom. His persuasive litigant secures his release. It is John's green grass—the pasture he walks among thousands of faces bearing striking resemblance to one expressing a wayward, inverted reality.

John's odds of being force-fed murder,[352] HIV,[353] deadly disease,[354] and other fruits of strange freedom is greater the second time around. Even if John eludes these outcomes for yet another release from prison, his odds of return go up again. John is not a fabrication. He is the representation of thousands of young, law-abiding black citizens criminalized by a system purporting to stop criminality. John has different names, different genders, and many homes throughout the United States. One John was an employed, law-abiding, thirtysomething African American woman residing in Alabama. This John—a mother of three—became so entangled in America's faulty legal machinery that only the maintenance work of a presidential pardon would free her.

Dorothy Gaines: A Drug War Casualty

Dorothy Gaines' trail began in 1958.[355] That May, she was born in Alabama to a mentally ill, abusive, alcoholic mother. By 1970, Dorothy and her two siblings were in the legal custody of their grandparents. Three years later, her grandparents were dead; her absentee father, too. She persisted. Dorothy overcame adolescent familial hardship, finding a career as a nurse technician. As a young woman, Dorothy wed Charles Taylor, by whom she bore a son and daughter to add to the company of her firstborn, Natasha (whom she'd given birth to in her teenage years). Her children would also know the void of loss when Charles died of a heart attack in 1986.

The Gaineses managed an ill-fated lot the best they could. Dorothy set an impeccable standard. She hoped the examples of her ascending career and lack of a criminal record would aid her determined efforts to mold her children into successful citizens. But knowing her past, it seemed inevitable fate's homely head would yet again peer. No matter, the Gaineses resolved to seize every bit of promise and joy that slipped from fate's hoarding hand.

Dorothy met Terrell Hines. When they began dating, Terrell was employed and drug-free. He showered her children with such affection that made Dorothy smile in envy; he was perfect. If her model behavior did not suffice, the tandem completed by a young, upward bound African American man's example would break ground for the foundation of her children's futures. Dorothy's construct was upended. Rather than fulfill the role of architect unto Dorothy's family dream, Terrell played that of demolition man. But Dorothy saw in Terrell the stuff of her own vicissitudes. Tectonic shifts and tempests wobbled foundations; still the edifice stood. This was but an ephemeral quake. In 1990, Dorothy persuaded Terrell to enter drug rehab to kick the habit. So he did. But like a high-rise horror, Terrell collapsed. Soon, he was involved in drug distribution. The devastation wrought would go far beyond his lot.

Dorothy lived in a predominantly black federal housing unit. Those words imply "heavily policed." In August 1993, police swept Dorothy's apartment. They searched like a platoon after the last man. Her bunker uncovered no weapons, no paraphernalia or residue, no signs of suspicious financial activity. In short, no evidence. But it was somewhere. They knew. Police pursued proof of her connection to Dennis Rowe's drug empire. Terrell's way into the world of drug distribution was through Rowe. When Rowe's mighty empire fell and he found himself grasped by the legal gauntlet, he squealed. Dorothy's name somehow translated.

In 1994, federal prosecutors indicted Dorothy on drug conspiracy charges.[356] Rowe's testimony had led state prosecutors to charge Gaines with drug conspiracy in September 1993. But aggressive state prosecutors yielded in the face of scant evidence, dismissing charges. Despite a troubling back injury sustained a few years earlier, Dorothy stood firm as ever. It was but another quake. She sought refuge in her former life, hoping the apparition of doom might bide some brief span. It would grant no such clemency. Goaded by her phantom stalker, federal prosecutors levied the same charge state prosecutors had dismissed. But in the span between the state's dismissal of charges and Dorothy's federal indictment, no new evidence had emerged. No matter the absence of incriminating evidence, the federal government was possessed to desecrate the dead. Why?

Viva voce. They were vindicated. They knew.

A looming, lengthy sentence compelled Rowe to implicate Dorothy with fabricated, unsupported testimony. Through plea bargaining, individuals implicated in Dorothy's case, like Rowe, could expect substantial sentence reductions. Thus, mendacity entertained freedom. Notwithstanding that such word of mouth evidence cannot be proven beyond even a minimal doubt (much less a reasonable one), federal law allows for the use of tenuous testimony in such cases. For kingpins like Dennis Rowe, chants of "Dorothy Gaines" are incantations through which molecular bonds comprising bars and handcuffs are parted. Wizard joined phantom to make Dorothy guilty by association. Mystical, imperceptible, atomic substance was law. Drug law enforcement policies are potent; this form of plea bargaining is one way by which myriad men and women are implicated for drug crimes, regardless of implicating material's presence.

Although Dorothy maintained both that she never knew Rowe and that she was unaware her boyfriend was his distributor, Rowe begged to differ. They were not only familiar, Rowe told prosecutors—they were so tight Gaines once allowed him to store a kilogram of crack cocaine at her house. In other instances, Rowe claimed, he transported crack cocaine to and from Dorothy's house with her awareness and consent. Rowe's affirmative mojo reduced his sentence. Such black magic was impossible absent the systemic grid's power, enabled by a court system in which less-than-corporeal evidence suffices. It was effective work. So effective that he, the grand master, received a far shorter sentence than Dorothy, the alleged low-level mage. Dorothy was encouraged to plea bargain. The prospect was coercively tempting. In forgoing a plea bargain, Dorothy tempted Odyssean fate. A two-decade sentence would far outlast sentences of every other individual implicated in the Rowe ring. Plea bargaining would fix a five-year barrier between Dorothy and her children's embrace. Iphigenia's blood spilled. Dorothy's heart of 1,000 ships set sail to Troy.

Last in Line: An American Destiny Deferred

Truth lost Dorothy 19 years and 7 months. Lies won Dennis Rowe 8. Such is the drunken American justice system's deplorable habit of hoisting cheerful toasts to foulness and hurling hateful tirades, *tides of fury*, unto justice.

Unjust mechanisms constitute the entirety of the American travesty of a justice system. In the vein of the South's legacy of legalizing explicit discrimination, the modern Drug War conceals bold-faced injustice in the lackluster veneer of legal legitimacy. Racial discrimination, past and present, has been empowered when legal frameworks endorse. But, although yesterday's modes were explicit, today's justice system preserves them in implicit forms of policy and jurisprudence that silently abrogate rights enumerated in the Constitution. This amounts to the engineering of an *expansion* of the technological capacities of these destructive legal mechanisms.

Today's legal system employs tools of discrimination against minority Americans with unprecedented efficacy. Upgrading from vagrancy laws, curfews, poll taxes, and other mechanisms are the devices of our current system. Mandatory minimum sentences, stop-and-frisks, plea bargains, and other modern appliances engender state-of-the-art destruction. Their emissions generate a climate change milieu occasioning yet smaller response than that waylaying an Earth erupting in concomitant resistance and resignation. But more devastating than these *Brave New World* systems and applications are their coders. Educated with the advanced—implicit—programming language of bias, they design the interface through which machines already tailored toward effectuating the dichotomized reality of Alphas and Epsilons are rendered user-friendly toward operations of its accentuation.

To those of us not versed in these languages, it is mind-boggling that a law-abiding, self-sufficient mother of three, off whom stereotyping stones cast by the Cosbys, Reagans, and Trumps of America ricochet with duck-necessitating alacrity, can hope neither to be protected *by* nor *from* her country's laws. America's justice system, listing product specifications alleging a design to protect the citizenry by code of law, instead programs functions that arraign citizens identified to be living in the wrong zip codes or around the wrong people. The virus spreads, crashing the systems of those who happen to associate with presumed malefactors, not processing the truth function indicating whether they do or do not have knowledge of the wrongdoing, and in the case of Dorothy, whether they do or do not know the *wrongdoer*.

Rather than programming the function of upholding the standard that presumes innocence until proven guilt, the operation establishes the guilt of the party with the tenuous entry of a drug-dealing kingpin. He knows fully that through a user agreement with flawed plea bargaining software, he will be recruited for a sentence or charge downgrade. Rather than design our software and systems so as to operate toward the computative end of justice, we perform the unspeakable violation of hacking the U.S. Constitution, formatting files that guarantee fair, just, and speedy trials, and place a premium on standards requiring *evidence*, not word of mouth, and installing stratagems whose unzipped Myrmidons threaten America with the fate of Troy.

President Bill Clinton commuted Dorothy's sentence shortly before leaving office. She served just six years. It was six years too long. Unable to handle the loss of his mother to the jaws of injustice, one of Dorothy's sons twice attempted suicide. Before fate's visitation, he had been an honors student. Dorothy's eldest daughter, Natasha, was an honors high school student and a dean's list college student before undertaking social work for orphans—her own siblings. If only the damage wrought upon her household could similarly have been commuted, perhaps the Gaineses might have at last escaped the phantom's unrelenting casualty.

The Erosion of the Fourth Amendment

Police power to search and accost without warrant is a recent legal phenomenon. Before the landmark *Terry v. Ohio* Supreme Court ruling in 1968, neither frisk fever nor search syndrome prevailed in the anatomy of American law enforcement. Warrantless searches and seizures have gone viral largely in response to *Terry*'s incubation of the American legal system with a strain that attacks the singular cell that is the Fourth Amendment. Before *Terry*, law enforcement and courts understood that police-seeking search or seizure were beholden to the Fourth Amendment's stipulation of warrant possession. The Fourth Amendment says that individuals have the right to be "secure…against unreasonable searches and seizures" and, furthermore, that warrants for searches and seizures are only to be procured on probable cause.[357] A suspect could only be subjected to a warrantless search if found engaging in conspicuously identifiable criminal activity. *Terry* was a whirl in the maelstrom engulfing the Constitution in a deluge of disregard, waterboarding thread part from document.

Florida v. Bostick flushed threads parted from parchment into an abyss. On August 28, 1985, a Greyhound bus carrying 28-year-old Terrance Bostick made a routine layover in Fort Lauderdale, Florida. *Terry*'s unruly orphans roamed; they absconded so far as Fort Lauderdale's streets. Ticketless, they rushed buses and trains. They were high off antidrug fervor. That fervor swept unsuspecting targets. Bostick too offended laws; he was at the back of the bus. For this, the gods struck him down, planting powdered ambrosia in fated pockets—a duffel bag harboring a pound of cocaine. *Terry*'s Furies stormed the bus in brief abeyance. They pillaged seats and cargo stows, razing to the dark corner betraying its blend. They posed the "legal,"[358] "May we search your bag?" Two officers towered, their weapons protesting embracement. They menaced. Bostick did the "reasonable." He said yes. He consented to a threadbare, mocking fate.

In *No Equal Justice*, Georgetown University Law Center professor David Cole elaborates on the Florida Supreme Court's use of constitutionally respectful jurisprudence in overturning the drug possession charges fated against Bostick:

> When prosecutors charged Bostick with drug possession, he challenged the police officer's conduct, and the Florida Supreme Court held it unconstitutional. The court reasoned that Bostick had effectively been "seized" when the officers cornered him at the back of the bus, because at that moment he was not free to leave. The Fourth Amendment forbids the police from seizing individuals without some individualized suspicion that they have committed or are committing a crime, and the police admitted they had none for Bostick. The remedy for such a violation—under the Fourth Amendment's "exclusionary rule"—is that the prosecution may not use evidence obtained by the encounter to establish its case. In addition to holding the evidence inadmissible against Bostick, the Florida Supreme Court

broadly condemned "bus sweeps," likening them to methods used by totalitarian states…[359]

The Florida attorney general appealed to the United States Supreme Court, which ruled against Bostick's argument that the evidence used against him in court was obtained in violation of the Constitution. Bostick argued that the Fort Lauderdale Police Department's search was commensurate to an "unreasonable search and seizure"; their effective entrapment of him at the back of the bus constituted an illegal seizure of his person.[360] Bostick also argued that, being entrapped in a dim corner by two officers (one of them visibly armed), the only "reasonable" response was to countenance the search. Bostick pointed out the police's semantic chicanery; the officers' inquiry omitted the sort of clarifying counsel officers are required to furnish during arrests in the form of Miranda rights. Bostick argued that because of this, he had no cognizance of his right to reject such a request. He argued furthermore that the context of entrapment made the "request" a demand that he was in no position to reasonably refuse. The Court insisted otherwise, ruling that a "reasonable" person would have said no.[361] The Court also threw out Bostick's seizure argument, ruling that "seizure" entailed the seizure of Bostick's physical body, which hadn't happened. Being surrounded by police without path for escape fell short of the Court's curious reading of the Fourth Amendment. But even if the Constitution offered from its throne a critical, exonerating letter in support of Bostick, its emissaries failed to deliver from the bench.

One can only wonder how the Constitution's drafters, so often invoked by politicians like blood ancestors, would react to their persons being frisked and subjected to requests underscored with the disagreement of menacing tones. What expressions would they bear when their declinations met yet more menacing barks, snouts sifting away scents of 18th century Philadelphia for 21st century odors escaping rigor mortis. That unsightly corpse—fated by an imprudent decision to forgo hygiene yielded by progress in favor of decay rotted by the retrograde. Bostick's best courtroom Don Corleone was neither pitiful nor embellishing. The police *had* made him an offer he couldn't refuse. Police routinely bypass search refusals, letting the dogs out; canine cross-examinations do not require warrants. How police searches—but not dog searches—require consent is an inquiry perhaps best left to the justices themselves. Or perhaps not. Given their insistence on the Constitution's ignition, they will likely respond by smearing it in yet another coat of low-grade petroleum degraded from crude senselessness.

Calhoun's spirit possesses American law enforcement. It fashions Seseshes impaling the Constitution on bayonets, washing plains in blood; nullifiers fertilize *blood and soil* with Bosticks' whipped sweat to harvest a globally envied cornucopia. The virtually unrestricted power of police to stop and detain suspects with causes of "personal discretion" has served to render the Fourth Amendment's potency too weak to mount a Gettysburg. A living element of the Constitution has become an epitaph unto its own demise, an aphasic word salad unbefitting any tombstone, much less the sarcophagus of a once mighty sovereign. "Reasonable" has been given interpretation from the lexicon of some dead tongue. It has tumbled legal parlance's precipice to a belying depth; reason is without itself. *Any* behavior justifies a search. The drug courier lists used by federal agents in profiling suspects show just how indiscriminate police's feckless discrimination is:

- Arrived late at night
- Arrived early in the morning
- Arrived in afternoon
- One of first to deplane
- One of last to deplane
- Deplaned in the middle
- Purchased ticket at airport
- Made reservation on short notice
- Bought coach ticket
- Bought first-class ticket
- Used one-way ticket
- Used round trip ticket
- Paid for ticket with cash
- Paid for ticket with small denomination currency
- Paid for ticket with large denomination currency
- Made local telephone call after deplaning
- Made long-distance telephone call after deplaning
- Pretended to make phone call
- Traveled alone
- Traveled with companion
- Acted too nervous
- Acted too calm
- Suspect was Hispanic
- Suspect was black female[362]

It's interesting that police don't care whether one travels alone or accompanied, first class or coach. Police find it irrelevant whether one arrives at night, in the morning, or in the afternoon. It doesn't even concern them whether one deplanes first, last, or anywhere between. But when it comes to race, evaluative criteria constrain. Whether one is black or white *does* matter. Except for its questionable exclusion of whites, the list offers a remarkable profile of inclusivity. *Millions* of traveling Americans are reasonable "drug courier" suspects and therefore subject to legally sanctioned yet constitutionally illegal searches and seizures. This is but one example of how agents of the Drug War have negated constitutional law. This dilution of law has wrought severe consequences on American minorities. Where the Constitution's role in law enforcement has receded, that of prejudicial discretion has assumed the void.

The phenomenon of police discarding the Fourth Amendment rights of American citizens is in no way confined to cases like that of Terrance Bostick. Such practices have overtaken the entire institution of American policing, profiling it as uniquely intrusive among law enforcement systems of Western democracies. As with all effects of justice system bias, African American and minority communities find themselves bearing its crushing brunt. African American communities are the most policed of any ethnic group in the United States. Surveilled ghettos are playgrounds of search- and trigger-happy police who play "cops and robbers" with unsuspecting black men, leaving the bullets in. It is a cruel modification of Russian roulette, each click foreboding an ominous guarantee.

Although the Second Amendment wants for personnel to service its crazed fan club, the Fourth Amendment somehow lacks the *oomph* that draws zealous devotees by droves. American politics showers riches for ineloquent, purported defenses of one amendment while denying so much as pennies for Cochranesque defenses of the constitutional amendment subject to blatant abrogation that merit ovation. Like our judges, prosecutors, and cops render between God's children, the citizens discriminate between the Constitution's. Belying the parents' unconditional, unbiased love for the brood, strangers with candy tier favored reward. But it is want for strangers' votes that motivates official disloyalty. The rhetorical market's demand for gratuitous, "tough-on-crime" policy has brought about not only saturation but also devaluation of the heavy argument against contribution's encroachment upon the Constitution truly worth its weight in gold. But the regretful "soft-on-crime" derivative only adds to the bubble that portends collapse. It is a sad day for the United States when protecting constitutional rights is viewed not as advocating that which is honorable, but endorsing criminality. It is perhaps an omen for the end.

The justice system's ever-increasing level of aggression toward some citizens should elicit outrage from *all* citizens. As the nullifiers of liberty seize powers created for the American people for the sole end of advancing tyranny, our freedoms are irretrievably flushed away. Americans must be roused to the defense of brothers and sisters unrighteously castigated as infidels in America's antidrug crusade. If fear, complacency, and support for injustice are allowed to march unopposed to our soul capital, freedom threatened will become freedom mourned.

The Black Death

Alvin Moore and Trayvon Martin are not lonely souls. As the body count of the U.S. justice system war machine multiplies, they are joined by young men and women objectified into representations of the miscarriages and travesties of justice. Humans with hearts, souls, and dreams are gunned into grisly souvenirs to be had by a glacial system, uncompassionate to the lifeless face at which it laughs. In all structures of the justice system, we have observed the presence of extreme racial discrimination and bias—in government legislation, in the treatment of African Americans petitioning the courts, and in every step of prosecution.

But the loudest testament to the justice system's devaluation of black life is exhibited in its administration of the death penalty. Throughout America's entire history, it has always used capital punishment excessively on African Americans.[363] Although corroborative data abounds, American policymakers have done nothing to curtail or extinguish this disturbing practice. America has one murderous habit toward black men of putting them to death on foundations of wrongful convictions. But what goes beyond this, and supplements testimony of the justice system's lethal bias, is its tendency to give convicted black men death where white men in cases of similar natures and circumstances are permitted life.

Outside the context of self-defense or warfare, killing is wrong. This holds for both system and citizen, which often intersect to give life to the death act. Murder should not go unpunished, as the trial system so often allows. Many point to the O. J. Simpson, Casey Anthony, and George Zimmerman cases as examples of the justice system's fallibility, instances in which despite the presence of what appeared to be guilt proven beyond a reasonable doubt, the defendants were acquitted. Such cases are exceptional in salience but by no means in principle. In examining not just travesties of

64

justice but also prejudicial failings of the justice system, it is not to be argued that blacks who commit murder should be left free to walk much in the way Emmett Till's murderers or George Zimmerman did. It is not even necessarily to be argued that their sentences should be lighter or any less harsh than what they are. But it is only fair and justifiable that factors of race be ignored in the administration of the death penalty in the United States. Unless the death penalty can be exercised in an unbiased fashion rather than abused as yet another mechanism for solidifying and perpetuating institutional racism—an unlikely possibility—its use is unjustifiable.

Much of contemporary opposition to the death penalty rests on belief in its draconian, hypocritical nature, but a large part of public disapprobation centers on racial partiality in its use. Those defending the supposed racial bias in the administration of the death penalty assert that African Americans are given the death penalty more often because they both commit and are convicted of murder more often than whites. It may be true that the population of murderers has disproportionate African American representation, which in context of capital punishment would alone justify a disproportionate percentage of African Americans being executed. If they more frequently commit murder, after all, it would stand to reason that in a fair judicial system they would be executed more frequently, regardless of hue. But it is telling—and contrary to the aforementioned assertion—that African Americans are put to death at rates disproportionate to their rates of committing homicide.[364]

Studies show the race of the murder victim to be a more influential criterion in determining whether a murderer gets life or death than the race of the murderer.[365] When a white life is lost, the penalty and punishment is harsher than when a black life is taken. The person most likely to be put to death is a black defendant convicted of murdering a nonblack (and especially white) victim.[366] Conversely, the person *least* likely to receive the death penalty for committing murder is a nonblack victim convicted of murdering a black person. (The 2013 Zimmerman case is a consummate example of this.) Because numerous factors can skew the underlying reasons behind such disparity, studies controlling for factors other than race have accurately determined the prevalence of racial bias in the administration of the death penalty. The landmark Supreme Court case *McClesky v. Kemp* used one such renowned study to argue the death penalty's unconstitutionality on the basis of disparate impact.[367]

McClesky is arguably the closest a case has come to undermining the death penalty's use since its reintroduction at the federal level in 1976 (at the behest of the Court's ruling in *Gregg v. Georgia*). Congress' General Accounting Office (now the Government Accounting Office) conducted a study examining 2,400 Georgia cases controlling for variables other than race and found that defendants whose victims were white were 4.3 times more likely to face the death penalty than those whose victims were black.[368] Thus, disparate impact was conceptualized, maintaining that although rulings in death penalty cases may not have featured explicit indications of racial bias, the likelihood of rulings being motivated by surreptitious elements of antiblack race bias was great enough to call the practice's legitimacy into doubt. The Supreme Court did not reject the validity of the GAO report's research or even disparate impact, but rejected McClesky's argument on grounds that racial discrimination could not be explicitly established as a factor in his case.[369] In *McClesky v. Kemp*, the Supreme Court's dismissal of the defense's accusation of racial discrimination encapsulated the fanciful notion that racial discrimination exists not in real life but only the abstract. The Court shattered

Last in Line: An American Destiny Deferred

hopes that a high-profile ruling in favor of Warren McClesky would once and for all overturn the death penalty and set the precedent for disallowing interjection of racial bias in the courtroom.

At all stages of prosecution, African Americans are condemned, more than any other factor, for the color of their skin. What begins as a seemingly innocuous stop can very well end on an electric chair—a fate that may not unravel at all but for the individual's race. But the problem of racial disparity in the justice system is dualistic. Blacks are not only unduly arraigned by the justice system, but are also denied protection by this same system which presumes their criminality based solely on their phenotypic markers. In effect, the justice system jumps into the antiblack hate fray. Therefore, the justice system reveals not a mere overzealous tendency of punishment, but an outright contempt for the rights of America's black citizens. If the justice system were just, then, assuming like circumstances, the white man who murders an African American would receive the same penalty as the African American man who murders a white man. No such justice exists. The racial hierarchy looms, fierce and unyielding in iniquitousness, concretely demonstrating a tiered valuation of life.

The colorblind would insist such a phenomenon is minimal or nonexistent. But it is veritable to the plagued communities and families of African Americans throughout all echelons of society. Contrary to colorblind presumptions, the practice of letting whites off for murdering blacks did not subside with Jim Crow's demise. Throughout the entire 20th century, only two white people were ever executed for the murder of a black person in the United States.[370] The first, a Kansas man, secured this dubious distinction by murdering a black man in the midst of an armed robbery in 1944. The other was South Carolinian Donald Henry Gaskins (known affectionately as "Pee Wee" for his diminutive stature), a self-avowed racist executed in 1994. Pee Wee's rap sheet featured several murder convictions, his last securing the death penalty after he murdered a black man in prison.[371]

The police, judges, juries, and prosecutors—groups overwhelmingly made up of whites—have rendered a collective verdict finding African Americans guilty of being less than human; they have rendered the accordant sentence denying them American justice. Some have suggested that racially diversifying these groups, particularly police forces, may reduce the prevalence of racial bias in the justice system. Such measures might reduce disparity, but this is doubtful. No matter the cop's race, they are indoctrinated in the same society by the same media that saturates the American psyche with images and stereotypes of African Americans that are held as true-to-life. As the IAT shows, although over 80 percent of whites are biased in favor of fellow whites, well over 50 percent of African Americans are biased in favor of whites as well.[372] This says something for the ability of even black cops to demonstrate and enforce the same prejudicial policing as white cops.

But just as the colors of the victim and defendant do not matter, neither do those of judge and jury. What matters is a broken society and a broken justice system. America's judges, prosecutors, police officers, and citizens have broken that system by failing in their duty to ensure justice. But they have not broken that system irrevocably. America's judges, legislators, executives, and citizens can unite to repair that system by fulfilling their constitutional duties and rebuilding the United States into a global and historic model for justice. By suspending the death penalty, altering our abusive political rhetoric, doing away with mandatory minimum sentencing policies (perhaps even by nullifying drug cases), holding judges and prosecutors accountable for racial bias, and other measures, the disease we observe in the modern justice system can be treated and healed today.

Solutions

Abolish the Death Penalty

The United States Supreme Court ruled capital punishment unconstitutional in the 1972 *Furman v. Georgia* case. Factors of inconsistent application and racial discrimination were central to the Court's decision to issue a moratorium on the practice, which was reintroduced just four years later. Since its resumption, the courts have shown no signs of a move toward justly applying the death penalty by extirpating racial discrimination in its use. When convicted of murder, blacks are much likelier to sit on death row while their white counterparts, if not acquitted outright, can reasonably hope to only linger in a desolate cell for some period of time, especially if their victims are black.

Given the discriminatory way in which it has been employed, capital punishment is a blatant violation of the Equal Protection Clause. Its clear and unequivocal unconstitutionality should alone make the need for its elimination obvious. Additionally, as long as perverse courts treat white deaths as more flagrant and punishable than the deaths of blacks by charging those who murder whites more severely than those who murder blacks, capital punishment will stand as a disgusting manifestation of racism rather than a hard but fair mechanism of justice. Capital punishment is itself controversial, absent the element of racial bias. But its charge of bias should suffice to make it America's last execution. As long as biases are present in capital punishment's application, it can neither legitimately nor righteously be upheld by our government.

Jury Nullification

Jury nullification is the act of a jury voting to acquit a defendant even if they believe the defendant is guilty. As controversial as jury nullification is, its history is extensive. In the past, it has been widely used to exonerate whites whose crimes victimized blacks—Roy Bryant and J. W. Milam, Emmett Till's murderers, were among the more conspicuous beneficiaries. Despite the irrefutable evidence incriminating Bryant and Milam—and witnesses and jurors having had awareness of their roles in the murder—they were acquitted in a little over an hour, with one flippant juror quipping, "If we hadn't stopped to drink pop, it wouldn't have taken that long."[373]

Jury nullification also has a long history of use toward just ends. Georgetown Law professor Paul Butler has argued for the endurance of this tradition, as he did in a 1995 appearance on CBS's *60 Minutes*.[374] During slavery, juries in Northern U.S. states often acquitted those prosecuted under the Fugitive Slave Act. Butler argues that jury nullification offers citizens a constitutional prerogative to check laws that are unfair or applied in a biased fashion. In a system in which reforms of law enforcement and drug sentencing policies are slow to come, jury nullification offers a more immediate mechanism for negating bad policy.

Jury nullification has been widely condemned as a defenestration of justice. Still, some argue that punishing Americans for victimless crimes itself disregards justice. Although a controversial measure (and not necessarily supported by the author), jury nullification can supplant laws perceived as unjust. That there are more Americans incarcerated for nonviolent crimes than for violent crimes is a justice policy factoid worthy of our harshest opprobrium. Above all else, critics of jury nullification argue that it would be racist for African American jurors to counteract biases by favoring African American defendants. They ask pointedly, "Would they do the same for white defendants?" A better question may be—"Would they have to?"

As has been shown, whites already benefit from a clandestine type of "jury nullification" that often keeps them from facing juries. African American jurors shouldn't discriminate against white defendants or treat them any differently from black defendants whom they judge. They do, however, have an obligation to protect their communities and to protect young black men who face lengthy sentences for possessing grams of marijuana while their counterparts stash pounds of cocaine and get off with "slap-on-the-wrist" probationary sentences. But white defendants are not themselves problematic to judicial processes. It is the bias of juries that creates problems in the assertion of justice. Citizens wield judicial power that can be used to either uplift or abuse fellow citizens who are part of marginalized groups.

Contrary to nullifying murderers, lynchers, irreverent neighborhood watchmen, and others who have been exculpated by their peers despite committing heinous acts of violence, modern nullification advocates argue only for its use in victimless, drug-related crimes.

Abolish Mandatory Minimum Sentencing

The introduction of mandatory minimum sentencing has made it impossible for judges to rule in a fair and equitable manner. Although mandatory minimum sentencing was introduced with the objective of deterring certain crimes, it has thus far proven ineffective as a deterrent and has, as reported in one study, resulted in "black and Hispanic offenders…[receiving] noticeably more severe sentences than their white counterparts."[375] With mandatory minimums enforced, even judges and jurors capable of unbiased decision-making are hamstrung both by laws and the whims of the prosecutors who, under the influence of bias, decide which charges to introduce or dismiss.

Some argue mandatory minimum sentencing is not racially discriminatory because racial considerations are not written into the statutes. But, as with all modern racially discriminatory laws, its racism lies in its application. Because African American and Hispanic criminals are more likely to be targeted by police than their white counterparts, they are naturally more often subjected to the draconian and often excessive punishment corollary of mandatory minimum sentencing guidelines. Instead of mitigating crime, these sentences take young men and women charged with victimless crimes away from their communities and perpetuate an endless cycle of social malaise. If whites were prosecuted as much as or even more than statistics say they should be, it'd be interesting to see if the fairness of such policies would then be recognized by America's judges and legislators. Perhaps in their children, nieces, nephews, and neighbors enduring this judicial malpractice, they might empathize with African Americans and cease cesarean evisceration of their community.

Furthermore, that convictions like Dorothy Gaines' can transpire—with harsh mandatory minimums not only piling injustice on top of wrongful conviction but furthermore motivating the use of another unjust system in plea bargaining to incentivize false implication—calls the justness of mandatory minimum sentencing policies into yet greater doubt. That law-abiding individuals such as Gaines end up in our prisons at the behest of the law's supposed protectors should occasion in America outrage and opposition. Abrogating mandatory minimum sentencing policies will be the first critical step in reversing the judiciary's discriminatory trajectory.

In one of the most encouraging decisions from the Justice Department in years, Attorney General Eric Holder announced in August 2013 that his department would no longer seek lengthy mandatory minimum sentences for certain drug crimes and released a memorandum offering federal prosecutors guidance on the new policy.[376] The following year, federal prosecutors pursued mandatory minimums at the lowest level on record.[377] Holder cited the need for a more compassionate approach to sentencing policy, which has been responsible for the transformation of the United States into, far and away, the world's largest prison system and among the more draconian governments with regard to sentencing policy. Holder's Justice Department later lobbied the Senate Judiciary Committee on behalf of an effort to grant clemency to over 10,000 inmates identified as having been subjected to unfair sentences.[378] Holder resigned as U.S. attorney general in April 2015. By December 2015, just 89 inmates in federal prison had been granted clemency by the Obama administration. Although it remains to be seen how comprehensive such changes will prove before President Barack Obama leaves the White House, Holder's directive will hopefully prove to effectuate long-term reform in America's prison system.

Abandon "Tough-on-Crime" Bravado

"Soft-on-crime" adorns a missile hoisted and tossed by those aspiring to olive branches, arrows, and a nuclear football. The slogan, frequently deployed in political campaigns, has been so injurious to those struck with it that it has sunk entire campaigns. The most famous incidence of a "soft-on-crime" barb scuttling a political career came from the Bush camp ahead of the 1988 presidential election. The infamous "Weekend Passes" political ad stingingly accused Massachusetts governor Michael Dukakis of bearing responsibility for African American murder convict Willie Horton's escape from prison. As governor, Dukakis—a self-avowed "card-carrying member"[379] of the American Civil Liberties Union—supported a prison furlough program. After receiving a weekend furlough as part of Dukakis' program, Horton absconded to Maryland where he raped a woman and assaulted a man. "Weekend Passes" obliterated Dukakis' already struggling campaign.

The justice system exists to punish criminals, not to excuse them. It is easy to understand why the public would react with opprobrium to a program that removed the barrier between a murder convict and society. Although this may be an extreme example of treating a criminal too leniently, the policies of Bush, his predecessor Reagan, and other conservative presidents and legislators bear the stark contrast of gratuitous stringency in criminal justice. Such "tough-on-crime" machismo allows the War on Drugs, the aggressive targeting of

Last in Line: An American Destiny Deferred

African American males, and the perpetuation of disparity in the justice system to continue unabated. It has also ushered the passage of unconstitutional stop-and-frisk and lethal stand-your-ground laws, both of which disproportionately victimize and disadvantage minorities.

For fear of going the way of Dukakis, politicians across the political spectrum hesitate to reveal the slightest intimation of wanting to protect the rights of prisoners, even in the interest of racial equality. The recognizance of criminals' civil and human rights is itself considered criminal. This narrow American attitude is encapsulated in the aphorism "a criminal is a criminal." Humanity does not apply. This holds doubly for black convicts, also guilty by virtue of their genetic inheritance. As reprehensible as their crimes sometimes are, prisoners, like all Americans, are entitled to rights that the justice system is not constitutionally permitted to refuse. Their fallibility and imperfection—like that of America's justice system—cannot be denied. But even though such fallibility and imperfection often merit strict punishment, it is possible to overreach in the assessment of penalty; the U.S. justice system proves adroit at this. Tough-on-crime imprisoned Dorothy Gaines and her family's future without a shred of evidence. *This* is not pardonable.

Ideologues espousing incendiary tough-on-crime rhetoric imply victimless crimes, like drug offenses, to be more harmful than they truly are. These policies are unjustified in locking up underprivileged Americans and throwing away the key. Such demagoguery fuels the recidivism rate, prohibiting criminalized Americans from finding employment, housing, food, and personal reformation. Instead of mitigating criminality in America, such rhetoric fosters it. Until those seeking public favor jettison undemocratic, tough-on-crime rhetoric, they will contradict their boasts as purveyors, not squelchers, of America's crime epidemic. Citizens must have the fortitude and humanity to form and devote themselves to movements and organizations committed to protecting the rights of the criminalized. Though we may despise criminals as a class, we must understand that so many men and women incarcerated today are not *criminals* à la Willie Horton, but targeted citizens who have sometimes succumbed to the fallibility of the human condition. Our wayward brothers and sisters are no more fallible—and are far less harmful—than our government. America must grant their deserved chance at redemption.

Hold Judges Accountable

It is considered anathema to even contemplate defrocking judges at any level, especially the federal. Associate Justice Samuel Chase, who served on the nation's highest court from 1796 until 1811, is the only justice in the history of the United States Supreme Court to face impeachment proceedings. President Thomas Jefferson sought his removal for an alleged partisan bias—a standard by which all judges today would be impeachable. Even at the state and local level, however, it is difficult to remove judges on the basis of the perceived unfairness of their rulings. In defense of judges, many argue that individual jurisprudence is sacrosanct and judges cannot properly exercise or protect the law unless they are able to rule without bending to popular political trends or facing political consequences from unsuccessful petitioners or defendants in court.

Had the Supreme Court justices of the Civil Rights Movement era been subjected to elections, it is a wonder whether those ruling in favor of civil rights could have kept their posts, considering the number of white

American voters who opposed *Brown v. Board* and other landmark cases.[380] The same thought arises with the entertained scenario of their impeachment. It would hardly have been reasonable for a president to indict a judge ruling on behalf of allowing minorities access to equal education for defying "good behavior." It is not difficult to understand how a higher punitive bar protects the judiciary from penalization by popular prejudice. But Chase's acquittal arguably set the precedent allowing Supreme Court justices to rule at the behest of rigid ideologies and mercurial, often unjust whims. Although Justice Joseph Bradley's racist rulings may not have been regarded as egregious in the segregated political climate of his time, it is hard to believe that a Justice Bradley sitting on the bench today would not, at the very least, be subjected to impeachment proceedings for exonerating mass murder.

Whether at the federal, state, or local level, each judge has an obligation to, as cited in the federal oath, "administer justice without respect to persons...do equal right to the poor and to the rich...and...faithfully and impartially discharge and perform all the duties incumbent on [them]..."[381] When their rulings demonstrate bias and inclination to rule against African Americans and other minorities, judges defy the message promulgated in this oath. Elections for federal judges could allow for accountability, but such a mechanism can work both ways. It is easy to conceive of a scenario in which partisanship and special interests supplant jurisprudence and extreme tough-on-crime, Drug War veteran, anti-minority candidates cause the judiciary to regress toward, rather than away from, draconian policy ends. There is, however, a potentially effective strategy for solving the problem of racially biased jurisprudence: subjecting judges to impeachment proceedings only after affirming clear patterns of racial bias in their rulings. The mention of judges being able to serve indefinitely in "good behavior" generally refers to their refraining from criminal activity. If it cannot legitimately be argued within our system that racially biased rulings are criminal, then there is even less we can say for our defective justice system.

In his legendary defense of O. J. Simpson, defense attorney Johnnie Cochran confronted Simpson's jury with a poignant inquiry—"Who polices the police?"[382] In speaking to both the societal phenomenon of racial discrimination in policing as well as explicit racism in the O. J. Simpson case, he further implored, "*You* police the police. You police them by your verdict. You send the message." However, it is not only police who answer to no authority, but law enforcement agents at all levels, including—and perhaps most dangerously—judges. We might then ask, "Who judges the judges?" When judges rule without answering to anyone—not even the citizens whom their rulings so often disastrously affect—the result is a flawed, grossly biased system. Forcing judges to answer to the people whom their rulings affect will create a more equitable judiciary—one worthy of being called just. Those who remain steadfast and unyielding in the belief that defrocking judges is ridiculous and unworthy of our entertainment because it limits jurisprudential power should at least apply the same reasoning to the phenomenon of mandatory minimum sentencing, a practice which also takes power away from judges (albeit in a manner disfavoring the people).

Repeal Stop-and-Frisk Laws

Although proponents maintain that stop-and-frisk practices are racially just, this claim fails the test of scrutiny. As was cited earlier in the text, blacks and Hispanics who are accosted are actually less likely than whites to be found carrying drug contraband or weapons. This empirical truth somehow translates into their being stopped and frisked at much higher rates. The law's racial bias is apparent. If the law were true to its supposed fairness, police would frisk whites at much higher rates than they now do and those stops would be more likely to lead to arrest than they currently do. The blatant racial discrimination inextricably linked with stop-and-frisk policing is unjustifiable. Judge Shira Scheindlin's promising jurisprudence in ruling New York's stop-and-frisk policy unconstitutional in August 2013 signaled a step in the right direction, one that must be followed by judges throughout the federal judiciary. Public servants like Judge Scheindlin will continue to play critical roles in checking bad, racially discriminatory legislation for the benefit of the public and the Constitution.

Although supporters of stop-and-frisk laws have claimed that they deter crime, dialogue must center on *how* they have deterred crime. Furthermore, even if the claim is true, public officials who endorse such policies must ask whether crime deterrence should be done at the expense of American freedoms. The law's biggest supporters, like ex-mayor Michael Bloomberg, have bluntly indicated their belief that it is acceptable for police officers to take race into account when stopping and frisking suspects. If politicians such as Bloomberg won't even enforce racial profiling practices in a statistically supportable way, it glaringly signals that such legislation exists only as a mechanism for minority marginalization. Although as mayor Bloomberg made headlines for a passionate rhetorical defense of stop-and-frisk in the wake of Scheindlin's ruling, the reluctance of the media to take him to task for suggesting that blacks and Hispanics are not frisked *enough*, in spite of proof of their disproportionate subjection, is disconcerting. In the ideal city, one committed to racial and social justice, such a statement would lead to impeachment proceedings. It is up to Americans to speak out against such laws and "stop and frisk" their public servants, in an arguably fair use of the practice, to ensure that the laws affecting everyday Americans of all colors are constitutional.

Repeal Stand-Your-Ground Laws

George Zimmerman's trial offered America just one example of the wide and disturbing use of stand-your-ground laws to justify homicide against blacks in the United States. An August 2013 report from the Urban Institute showed that whites who invoked stand-your-ground defenses in killings of blacks were more likely to be found justified in their homicidal actions. In fact, such cases are 281 percent more likely to be found justified than white-on-white homicides.[383] It also explored the Zimmerman case, examining these dynamics: 1) he and Martin were strangers, 2) it was a one-on-one ordeal, 3) neither was a law enforcement agent, 4) a handgun was involved in the killing, 5) Zimmerman was nonblack and Martin was black, and 6) Zimmerman was older. In instances in which such factors combine and the homicide victim is black, the act is six times more likely to be ruled justified.[384] There are two key problems at hand with stand-your-ground laws: 1) they effectively legalize murders of African Americans and 2) they sanction discrimination on the basis of the victim's race, thus denying African Americans the legitimacy and immunity of self-defense rights that the laws ironically necessitate.

That states such as Florida—where a stand-your-ground statute nearly enabled George Zimmerman to avoid prosecution—are led by governors who stand beside laws that license racist killing is beyond regrettable. Because stand-your-ground laws reside in the domain of state law, it is up to state legislators and executives to repeal such laws. It is up to citizens of such states to express outrage when their elected officials support laws that can and do permit racist murders to take place in the United States, leaving voiceless victims, devastated families, and broken communities in their wake. The lives of Americans are too precious to allow senseless laws to deprive us of their spirits and permit the vampires of deprivation privileges of bloodthirsted freedom.

Restitution for the Wrongly Incarcerated

Although no legal system is perfect, to merely characterize America's legal system as imperfect would be too charitable. The flaws of the justice system go beyond the inadvertent, robbing innocent people of color of all that freedom entails—family and loved ones, employment, property, the right to their person, and stability. Victims of these "accidents" are afforded little recourse. In 24 states, no compensation is awarded for wrongly incarcerated individuals.[385] These individuals may receive the usual bus ticket and a few dollars, but can never regain employment, loved ones, and time lost. These states neglect to even offer inmates avenues through which they can readjust to society in the form of employment agencies, education, counseling, and other forms of assistance. Even in most states that offer assistance, government often fails to compensate wrongfully incarcerated individuals for the legal costs they may have incurred.

When government botches a criminal case, government must pay. "Oops" and a bus ticket are not enough. Some states, such as Alabama, offer a minimum of $50,000 for each year of wrongful incarceration (with approval of the state legislature).[386]

Florida offers up to $50,000 annually (with a lifetime cap of $2,000,000) only if the wrongfully convicted individual has no prior felonies. Although it is laudable that these states at least have restitution laws, they prove that even where such laws exist, unnecessary caveats can prevent wrongfully convicted persons from receiving the compensation they deserve. Despite (or perhaps as a result of) its less than stellar reputation in justness, Texas has perhaps the nation's most generous restitution program. The state offers the wrongfully convicted $80,000 annually with neither a lifetime cap nor a time limit, provides restitution for child support payments, and sponsors full tuition for up to 120 hours at an accredited postsecondary institution—all without caveats or restrictions. The federal government offers $50,000 a year, doubling it for those on death row.

Although one cannot place a price tag on time lost "on the outside," government can at least offer redress to enable victims of its poor polices to make up for time lost. Budget offices and bondholders may oppose such restitution policies for fear of how such expenditures may affect debt servicing, but concern for the sanctity of credit ratings should instead motivate the implementation of policies that preserve the sanctity of justice. Here—as seems to be the case everywhere—where moral need lies, practical convenience snuggles up alongside in nonconsensual fashion. Because over half of U.S. states lack such redress statutes, it will likely be up to the federal government to in some way mandate laws requiring states to offer a minimum standard of restitution by means of both monetary and service compensation. Additionally, prosecutors found to have handled such cases in ways that are dishonest, injurious, or blatantly irresponsible (such as in the case of Dorothy Gaines, who was federally prosecuted even after state charges against her were justly dropped) must face penalties, up to and including incarceration.

Conclusion

Americans must overturn the system of gross discrimination that whisks opportunity from young African Americans and other minorities and denies them chances at remediation. The courts themselves are in dire need of remediation. Certain measures can be introduced to detect gross instances of biased jurisprudence and allow the legislative branches of government to take punitive action against judges behind biased rulings. However, in instances in which evidence of biased jurisprudence seems present but not overwhelming it will be more difficult and less prudent to exercise this power. Given that negligible disparity cannot, beyond a reasonable doubt, be attributed to any internal bias or discriminatory actions in a judge, arguing a judge's true intentions based on scant evidence will prove precarious.

Although slight instances of disparity may be dismissed as corollaries of chance, jurisprudential bias provable beyond a reasonable doubt must be checked. Judgeships at the federal level can potentially be rendered discrimination-proof if the U.S. Senate is required to review the records of candidates for federal posts—including the Supreme Court—to determine if, in their careers as judges, prosecutors, etc., they demonstrated statistically significant trends of racial bias. Those showing patterns of bias against members of certain protected groups will be prevented by vote from securing judicial posts. After being reviewed by either a bureaucratic organization or Congress, those judges already occupying posts will, by vote, be subjected to impeachment proceedings.

Such a revolutionary change in the judicial system would require no less than a constitutional amendment at the federal level. It would be much more practical and perhaps even effective to implement such a practice of legislative review of judges at the local and state court levels. Although the lengths the government and the people will have to go through to enact such measures are indeed great, we must decide if it is acceptable to allow black and Hispanic men to languish on death row for crimes from which white men walk free. We must also decide if we are willing to callously ignore the moral turpitude of the executions of the Alvin Moores and Troy Davises of America who go to their deaths at the hands of a sanguinary justice system that denies its own standard of proof beyond a reasonable doubt.

America must decide if it thinks it fair to target black adolescents as drug users and heavily police, search, and kill them because of police officers' unfounded notions and despite the fact that their white counterparts abuse such substances at least as frequently as they do. America must decide—and decide now—whether it is willing to tolerate malignant injustice in its sad excuse for a "justice system" and continue to neglect the rights of the people. Just as all law-abiding men and women must be treated equally, all those convicted of crimes must hold equal accountability based only on their actions.

It is also essential that black adolescents are treated as innocent until proven guilty. If our judges fail to enforce equality in the judicial system, then they must be removed in favor of judges whose jurisprudence and evaluation of criminal cases will prove just and equitable.

Where there is improvement, we must offer measured acknowledgment. It isn't imaginable that a case concerning an event like the Colfax Massacre could go before the modern Supreme Court and turn out in favor of racist, unapologetic mass murderers. But things have not improved nearly enough. The judicial system no longer sanctions Colfax. It does, however, continue to sanction Colfax's crime of racially motivated murder. This is witnessed in the flagrant, undue rate of African Americans put to death based on wrongful conviction, the high number of African American murderers put to death relative to whites who commit the same crimes, and the gross number of African Americans obliquely executed at the hands of the state via its remunerative contract-killer system that rewards men like George Zimmerman with spoils of glory and breath their savage tandem seizes from bloodied black bodies. No other attribution can be established for these judicial phenomena other than racial bias, whether implicit or explicit. America doesn't deserve a pat on the back for the fact that African Americans today are sometimes, rather than never, defended by the justice system. It must *always* defend blood, breath, and justice.

Although we may insist on American children pledging this daily, in "post-racial" America the idea of "liberty and justice for all" is at best comical. Liberty and justice are bought by those who can afford it, accessed by those educationally privileged enough to know their rights, and monopolized by ones with the right skin color. African Americans and other minorities tend to fall outside these strata, finding themselves warded from justice's realm. They are neither defended with justice when victims nor treated with justice when defendants. If America insists on maintaining such disparate policies, we must advise America to revise "liberty and justice for all" to "liberty and justice for some."

When Francis Bellamy penned the Pledge of Allegiance, he may not have had African Americans in mind. Many Americans reciting the pledge didn't. But no matter this truth, this pledge is not rendered a useless, parochial relic. It can be appropriated, its meaning extended to encompass African Americans, Hispanics, Asians, and others who are, to varying levels, dismissed by today's justice system. Perhaps then we will cross our hearts while gazing on stars and stripes reciting, "I pledge allegiance…," with understanding that the stated allegiance of all is true because America has at last guaranteed her allegiance to all her denizens.

Affirmative Inaction

Affirmative action is a catchphrase for revolution. It portends cracks of Lexington and Concord; firings of Fort Sumter; bellows of King. Dutiful ammunition *IN DEFENS* against American infamy. It threatens demise of her organs. Her plantations, Gold Rushes, Homesteads, G.I. Bills. Nephroses induced by treacherous plasma. It is marrow. Cell and soldier join to dispense invader in a perennial Freedom Summer. Roberts, Scalia, and Fisher are the Triumvirate marching citizen armies on Washington. Volleys disrupt discourse. They demand preservation of the Patrician birthright. Command executes the bodies of Antebellum America and Jim Crow; it pardons the invalid, Post-racial America. The conventions of modern warfare.

They betray claimed humanity. The Hague consecrated a memorial unto souls transmigrated in autoimmune rapacity. From Carthage. Normandy. Colfax. It convalesced; it nursed them to be reincarnated in unison with humanity's birth. But physicians did not perform Hippocrates' due homage. They played Kevorkian. They forced abortion—one embryo immaculate, one of insemination. The gavel. The scalpel. The Common Core app. Birthing instruments deployed as weapons of mass destruction. Treason unto humanist doctrine declared loyalty unto jagged immortality.

Affirmative action is the death of America. So insist surgeons convening around a Situation Room for a scalpel's invasion. Their operating theatre foreshadows Cannae. Their ignorance of the Oath goads their education on human anatomy. The tumor is a heart. But spears excise breath. And with it body.

How Americans, policymaker and citizen alike, persist in both war crime and medical malpractice would be puzzling if not for guidance tendered by tattered treaties and blood-inked medical records documenting the nation's historical propensity for infamy. As Janell Ross noted, Justice Antonin Scalia channeled Justice Henry Billings Brown, author of *Plessy*'s 1896 majority opinion, in 2015:

> I'm just not impressed by the fact that—that the University of Texas may have fewer [minority students]. Maybe it ought to have fewer. And maybe some—you know, when you take more, the number of blacks, really competent blacks admitted to lesser schools turns out to be less. And I don't think—it—stands to reason that it's a good thing for the University of Texas to admit as many blacks as possible.[387]

Scalia echoed Brown's Gilded Age jurisprudence, which counseled, "Legislation is powerless to eradicate racial instincts or to abolish distinctions based upon physical differences."[388] In a breath, Scalia stripped ill-fitted cardigans embroidered with threads spelling "class not race" and undergarments interlaced from textile of torn Dixie flags, crying "reverse racism." A ruling in favor of indecent exposure. Scalia breathed EMT into Justice. He resuscitated. He let favor slip—a love for the species threatened with extinction, unadapted to the colorblind climate. His preservationist partisanship blemished his purist face, but did not conflict his interest. In any case, bad Behavior made him Good Samaritan.

Scalia is an augur interpreting organs. Where a corpse lies prostrate, tossing and turning in vigorous resistance to sicknesses of natural and probable cause, Scalia sees embers. He and the public heeding his omen. How do they perceive death in breath—air without space? What renders rod and cone a tandem of unholy sleight? Where is their sight? It is in the negation of reality. To them, Jim Crow's death is life. His life is their death.

Jim Crow must die. Jim is the depth of their America. He was once an indispensable ally to that realm's endurance, rewarded in stock of legislative lifeblood. But the market crashed. That necessitated his dispense. It summoned securities. A bond. With nascent charm; grace, firmness—and naïveté—to resist imminent maturation. And ruthless daring. Ruthless enough to *strangle* affirmative action, Jim's junk bastard. Jim hated that kid. Jim *despised* that hue. Jim was born to. But America? Its Step-Mom who once shared in the high-yield ecstasy of torturing that damned, dusky *thing*? She *used* him. He *refuses* to die.

Jim exhales noxious fumes to Post-racial America, the erroneous substance whose enchanting scent bewitches enough of the American public to make Scalian jurisprudence seem anything but a historically convincing defense of draconian drug laws. But Aeneas' son sits atop a Trojan horse. Fire! The sleight is on us. For Scalia knows Jim Crow is only *playing* dead. A faker. Jim's fine. *He's taken care of.* Jim gets his shipments, alleviating burning thirst imbibing blood victuals, frying pristine, hot beach sand with stains, while Tupac and Elvis present oral arguments concerning the justness of the method of the product's procurement. Far too black and bloody, even for a G. All rise! The Late Antonin Scalia! He presides. He knows the post-racial *inkatha* is the object, inanimate save for circulating essence imparted by pale *Impi* hurling hot spears at once burning and stabbing hated encroachment. At once breathing life into Jim. At once fashioning rapprochement.

These revolutionaries assert that affirmative action programs are destructive weaponry utilized to wreak vengeance upon whites for past transgressions—transgressions they say lie in wake, but which reconnaissance shows lie in wait. In the place of Jim. To these triumviratees, affirmative action denies life to innocent, hardworking civilians napalmed by teletemporal, telekenetic necroburns. It wasn't them—it was Jim! They should not be executed for third-degree charges of excess incurred by him. That they are ferments hot, white, warring wine. Berserker drunkenness is justified by the experience of a violation of humanity and being unprecedented on American soil. Why, now, are *they* discriminated against? And their grievances wax altruistic. Their Code encapsulates hatred of affirmative action's tyrannical devaluation of the accomplisments of hardworking people of color. Its beneficiaries are perceived as usurping the right man's stead by right of skin color and the desert island-exiled plight of their forebears. Why, *now*, are *they* discriminated against?

They swear on pain of death that affirmative action is lethal to minority spirit because it paralyzes their capacity for individual achievement; they get twice as far working half as hard. But those retreating from Scalia's advance, flanked by Roberts and Fisher, to fire from the safety of the laager, *shoot, duck, peek, shoot* that it is not so much a device of vindication as it is a mechanism for mitigating the deleterious effects of the lingering, hard-to-kill forms of institutional racism. Jim's island-ordered hits target *them.* They assert the shield is necessary to deflect the effects of ongoing forms of institutional racism that whizz their way out of limitless magazines and threaten to deprive members of minority groups of life and breath. Furthermore, they *shoot* that it is necessary to *duck* the impecuniousness and deprivation caused by institutionally racist programs of the past which prevented minorities from accruing the spoils of wealth, power, and privilege that whites marched with from the field.

Spoiling for spoils spoils; one side *lebensraum,* the other mere breath. But space and air go hand in hand. While conservatives have campaigned to conquer and dispatch affirmative action programs, livestreaming revolutions as crimes against civil rights conventions, liberals have persisted in their mission to clad affirmative action's armor upon all bodies of opportunity—hiring, college admissions, contracting, etc. Although affirmative action has not been deployed successfully in all theaters of this 21st century American Civil War, its arms are invariably supplied to areas of heavy engagement, like the Siege on Education.

Liberals have largely prevailed in the war despite intermittent impasse yielded by intrepid conservative counteroffensives. But that offered in cases like *Fisher v. Texas* threaten campaign scuttles Viet Cong-strong. Affirmative action's foundation is not found. Despite its warriors' noble efforts, inspection of its bricks and wall frames shows it to be out of code but not *yet* condemnable. The base is without base. Although affirmative action was dedicated with a cornerstone fashioned of material concretizing equal opportunity between the races in itself, in the structure it supported, and in salted *terra firma* into which its barracked soldiers sowed operations of freedom, the stronghold has deteriorated into a run-down, abandonable if not for the Stonewall standing of the men it housed into mortarmen. Fisher may need not spear, missile, drone, but mere *huff, puff, blow* to bring the house down.

For all of the fierce mortars firing ceaselessly upon Fort Affirmative Action, U.S., one would never guess that it is not retreating African Americans, Hispanics, or other protected minorities most enjoying affirmative action freedoms. It is *whites* overwhelmingly *womanning* the stronghold.[389] Since the introduction of affirmative action programs—arms presented to mitigate racial disparity—white women gained the greatest spoils from its victories in the form of professional school admissions,[390] employment,[391] income,[392] and other measures of socioeconomic progress. By 1997, Department of Labor statistics showed that 6 million more women workers—most of them white—were in higher occupational classifications than would be without affirmative action policies.[393]

Statistical tribunals showed drastic increases of women in certain professions, the number of women lawyers jumping from 4 percent to 23,[394] the share of women chemists going from 10 to 30 percent,[395] and the percent of women architects going from 3 to 19.[396] These ranks all generally require professional degrees. Considering that a majority of women college graduates are white,[397] it stands to reason that it is white women who are reaping the lion's share of opportunity to become lawyers, chemists, architects, doctors, etc. Given triumph's sacrifice, it's a wonder they don't lend riveting war effort support à la Rosie. In a 2006 Michigan referendum on a constitutional amendment banning affirmative action in education and public sector hiring, 59 percent of white women voted in favor.[398] (The amendment was overturned in 2011 and later upheld by the Scalia Company of the United States in 2014.)[399] 2010s data shows that in spite of ostensible opposition to the affirmative action war effort, white women continue to enjoy affirmative action's spoils, seeing their representation in leadership positions eclipse minority appointments to such commands.[400]

If it is actually white women who derive the greatest benefit from affirmative action programs, why does the propaganda war machine depict African Americans as the boogeymen? It's a simple construction: the insurgency against affirmative action is an annexation of the bias edifice. Despite the bombproof ceiling pinning down women from earning as much as male captors, women's empowerment—in these walls, white women—authorizes negligence, unlike threats of minority expanse that embolden assault. When affirmative action affords a man's wife or daughter a job, it's no skin off his back. But when it offers a man's off-color the same, that is to be flayed.

There is nothing wrong with white women benefiting from affirmative action programs. What's wrong with affirmative action is not that it "gives" to minorities; it is that it manifests as yet another fissure in the pattern of whites benefiting disproportionately from opportunities for economic empowerment. Like the invisible technological mechanisms of the justice system that, by themselves, know no color, affirmative action policies are employed as blackness is to them a hated, inescapable obsession. But what betrays affirmative action is that its design specifications don't claim race neutrality. Rather, they claim to *advantage* underprivileged subscribers with bandwidth access. Affirmative action professes infrastructure mitigating racial disparity; its action affirms the status quo.

Furthermore, the unmarked affirmative action armory fitting out whites crouches camouflaged from an assault of black artillery exploding in sacrifice. It rests safe and sound in *KwaJim*, gorging alongside. It lives in college admissions, employment searches, and beyond. Red berserkers defend abundant provisions: college admissions point policies that favor applicants with residence in rich, white neighborhoods,[401] alumni parents or grandparents,[402] and parents on faculty or staff.[403] When volleys sprint from Fisher's Legion to fall lines of bias, they drill only those vertical and dark. They render horizontal rigs which aim tall trajectories of fortune that exist if but for their drilling. If they don't fire high, they won't.

The first shots of the affirmative action war were not fired either against or in defense of the modern "preferential" programs to which many politicians and judges, like Scalia, Roberts, and Anthony Kennedy, guarantee the promise of no quarter. As it turns out, affirmative action was once like Jim Crow with regard to allying with the Patrician League. Affirmative action has existed since the United States' founding, dealing prenuclear loyalty to an objective contrary to its purported Atomic Age mission of minority liberation. But this prewar state is distinct from Jim Crow, as it is from slavery. Like its present form, it then resided in social programs sponsored by the federal government. But these programs were tailored to confer wealth upon *whites*. That didn't go beyond the pale—not like today. In a reading, that is right. Without condition of destruction, they enacted a Marshall Plan rationing economic advantage upon those fixed in auspicious crosshairs. They too inhabit the island—from the postbellum Homestead Act, to Franklin Roosevelt's prewar New Deal programs, to the postwar G.I. Bill. Spoils of shots fired on many fronts.

Modern Affirmative Action

In 1961, President John F. Kennedy issued Executive Order 10925 commanding organizations to "take affirmative action to ensure that applicants are employed, and that employees are treated during employment, without regard to their race, color, religion, sex or national origin."[404] President Lyndon B. Johnson would utilize the same language when issuing Executive Order 11246 in 1965.[405] It may seem ironic that affirmative action originally directed government agencies to hire *without* regard to applicant race, religion, or national origin. It did not bestow "points" on minorities for being minorities or as compensation for their plight. It simply held that they should not have points deducted as a result of their stigmatic status. In 1967, gender was included in affirmative action criteria to extend coverage to those discriminated against on the basis of sex.[406]

The orders were toothless. Without mechanisms to ensure minority hiring, employment bias simply retreated beneath an implicit veneer. As long as an employer did not declare "blacks need not apply," they could not be proved to be employing racially discriminatory hiring practices. These same discriminatory practices persist in hiring today, with African American applicants as qualified as or more qualified than their white counterparts being much less likely to be hired. Quotas—the controversial aspect at the center of myriad lawsuits against affirmative action programs—were introduced to force employers, college admissions officers, and other gatekeepers to make room for minorities. Though its use has been repulsed on other fronts, quota ammunition has remained critical for combating bias' role in shaping demographic dynamics at American colleges and universities.[407] In the absence of such measures, it was apparent that institutions weren't going to follow the harmony of affirmative action's Pied Piper; *Dixie* would ring through all America, in fore- and hinterland. Regardless of this oversight and the hypocrisy of benefiting from access to virtual 100 percent quotas for generations, vehement opposition wailed in equalizing programs' neonatal unit.

Affirmative action as we know it has had a brief yet tumultuous history. First implemented as part of Johnson's Great Society programs in the mid-1960s, affirmative action's intent was to mitigate residual effects of historical discrimination in education and employment adversely affecting African Americans and other minorities. Since the inception of its programs, which are now standard in the admissions processes of most public universities and in the hiring practices of many companies, conservatives have vehemently argued that affirmative action programs are ineffectual in mitigating discrimination; they turn whites into sacrificial lambs unto black privilege. Some argue that this only intensifies antiblack resentment. Conservatives maintain that affirmative action programs are unnecessary, unjust, minimize the importance of individual merit, and in effect serve as an exercise in reverse racism. Academic and pundit alike (the latter in preponderance) concur wholeheartedly that affirmative action is discrimination incarnate, repackaging the very sort of racism its authors and proponents intend for it to eradicate and hoisting it on a commercial drone for a signature strike on white America's re-urbanized step.

Last in Line: An American Destiny Deferred

Such was Abigail Fisher's impassioned defense of home that may as well have quartered the Third Amendment. In October 2012, *Fisher v. University of Texas* went before the U.S. Supreme Court. Fisher, a young white woman denied admission to the University of Texas at Austin, argued that admissions policies factoring in race disadvantaged her and other whites. Instead of moving to strike down the constitutionality of race-based admissions, in June 2013 the Court ruled 7-1 that while admissions policies factoring in race were appropriate for the sake of maintaining diversity, strict scrutiny must be used to determine whether workable alternatives to race-conscious policies were also available toward ensuring diversity.[408] Fisher reargued the case in front of the Supreme Court in December 2015. In June 2016, the Court voted 4-3 that the university's use of race in its admissions policy was constitutional.[409] For now, the Triumvirate's legions have been repulsed. But the campaign to marshal a change of course as retrograde as those charted at *McClesky* and *Bostick* marches on.

Conservatives assert that the same legislation tailored to fight discrimination is now abused against white Americans.[410] They have rebelled, taking hostage the Reconstruction amendments and the Civil Rights Act of 1964, laws designed to extirpate racial discrimination in public places, poking and prodding them at gunpoint to inequality's preservation. They negate the fruits of the Civil Rights Act, represented in affirmative action policies, *using* the Civil Rights Act. The Civil Rights Act precludes affirmative action both *for* and *because* of its causes *and* effects. Affirmative action's parents spurn an ostensibly exclusive, spoiled formation to beget a most evil twin, identical in likeness but adversarial in demeanor. In executing racial equality for the racial equality impostor, conservatives are performing a by now yawnful sleight of hand that yet again argues the impotence of law to perform just sorcery absent operators programmed only for that function. The tactics of Fisher and her cohort are gross perversions of civil rights law; she violates the rules of engagement. Yet that speculation yields no boast. It pays in reposition, open in a promised land of immunity from justice. Bradley, Brown, Scalia guarantees it—no money back.

Their argument computes errors of logic; the code is bad on multiple lines. Anti-discrimination law's fitness in fighting discrimination independent of enforcement mechanisms had already once proved dubious given the failure of the more pugnacious 1875 Civil Rights Act. The 1964 Civil Rights Act was, by itself, similarly impotent. These laws could not perform the thaumaturgy of landscaping valleys into flatlands; the lethal successes of the original affirmative action programs of which white Americans were beneficiaries would not crater at the behest of incantation. These laws could not rectify centuries of discrimination that replaced African American destiny with a shoddy, inauspicious substitute. Though our supposed logicians claim the incidence of a '45 revolution that claimed crown jewels for a mere pretender, the historiographic examination reveals a crevassed, inglorious context to *high-* and *lowlander*. It proscribes the offense of retrospection contrary to the necessity and justification of the war. This is not Iraqi Freedom. This is not immunity. This *is* warrant.

Following their Revolution, white Americans assumed a monopolistic stake in industry. This possessed near-indomitable control over the affairs of the nation—political, social, spiritual. The idea that passage of legislation commanding the dissolution of discriminatory habits in the country could somehow on its own convert denominations of society in fealty to white advantage to accommodate blacks in their pews warrants exorcism. This might desecrate the void with salvage; the oversight of unsustainability made by the 1960s authors of civil rights laws condemned parchment, praying ink to landfills. Scripture harbored intelligent design's proof.

There were heretics. The agnosticism expressed by some at the creation of the Civil Rights Act that a universe so complex could manifest absent a bang proved prescient. It did not question that creation was a *myth*— it merely reasoned the exclusion of evolutionary mechanisms would result in the exclusion of evolutionary mechanisms. This much damns hypothesis, flesh transmigrating into truth. It is not to be cursed that the commandments did not tender holy breath for a garden. But as a standalone entity, the Civil Rights Act has proven faithless in eradicating fallen angels of racism that don in vestments and oaths. We need a shepherd to *ensure* devotion—to shepherd the brother's keeping. Anything else ignites primordial soup into hellfire. The destination of heretics.

Skeptics do not observe idols that curse lands 6,000 years old. It was not President Johnson who consecrated the first affirmative action policies on American soil before the erection of Lady Liberty. Affirmative action didn't start with the modern college admissions process or benedictions imploring departments to hire, not fire, African American fighters. It started with the primordial soup; it started with the creation of Eden, where civil liberties and civil rights wed in a small, two-person ceremony. With officiant present, they were gifted an immaculate fruit basket—first of its kind. Snakeskins engendered chemical reaction. They scorched eternal hellfire. Excavations show this beginning to extend far beyond the presidencies of Johnson and Kennedy—all the way to the beginning.

The Original Affirmative Action

Homestead Act

The United States government's first extensive social program was enacted little over a century prior to the affirmative action and welfare policies put forth in the 1960s. Long before President Johnson signed modern affirmative action legislation into law, there was the Homestead Act. In keeping with the relatively liberal stances of his presidency, Abraham Lincoln permitted that emancipated blacks be entitled to the right to apply for a share of the over 250 million acres of Western land up for grabs.[411] Of the law, Lincoln said, "I think it worthy of consideration…that the wild lands of the country should be distributed so that every man should have the means and opportunity of benefiting his condition."[412] But the initiative which Lincoln suggested was not tainted by racism was born directly from it, its land grants made possible by the displacement of Native American tribes who had all since either been displaced or exterminated.

Last in Line: An American Destiny Deferred

Lincoln's famed Civil War general William Sherman said of the courageous men who consecrated that ground, "The more [Native Americans] we can kill this year, the less will have to be killed the next war, for the more I see of these Indians, the more convinced I am that they all have to be killed..."[413] Clearly they were not one of the "every men" whom Lincoln sheltered beneath his umbrella. In a slightly more progressive vein, President Rutherford B. Hayes later declared of Native Americans whose exclusion made the Act possible, "I see no reason why Indians who can give satisfactory proof of having by their own labor supported their families for a number of years, and who are willing to detach themselves from their tribal relations, should not be admitted to the benefit of the Homestead Act and the privileges of citizenship...."[414] Such lofty declarations never translated into actual policy, however, and the Homestead Act would prove both a symbol of Native American annihilation and a gift bestowed for the benefit of 19th century white America and its posterity.

One should look no further than the Homestead Act for a model of socialistic policy. It bequeathed upon white America prosperity rivaling that which the peculiar institution of slavery itself endowed without burdening masters with the hotbox's bureaucracy. The fecund, vast expanse of the Great Plains was some handout. America's own *lebensraum* was fertile, cheap, unoccupied—prime for the picking. Although federal law promised African Americans access to rich terrain, white settlers and agents of the law had other ideas.

Nearly a million and a half white families found themselves exclusively entitled to the privileges provided by the Homestead Act,[415] which remained in effect into the 20th century. Four million claims were made, with just over a million and a half of them being approved.[416] It is difficult to find accurate data indicating how many black families applied for homesteader status—likely because there were so few. Although thousands more sought for themselves a piece of the proverbial pie, many blacks seeking land acquisitions were threatened with racial violence for daring to capitalize on what conservative principles would today deem a massive "welfare program." For myriad black families, many recently emancipated and in search of propitious beginnings, milk and honey were not to be had.

Realizing the rampant racial discrimination gripping the West's winning, Congress drafted the 1866 Homestead Act in an equitable attempt at allocating lands throughout the states of Alabama, Arkansas, Florida, Louisiana, and Mississippi.[417] Forty-six million acres were up for grabs in the region where the majority of African Americans resided, and many sprinted toward settlement.[418] Despite the attempts of many more, just 4,000 African American families were granted entries under the Southern Homestead Act.[419] Acts of racial violence and obstruction halted even these swift black paces.[420] Terrorism resulted in many of the 4,000 losing their claims.

Blacks would continue for decades to attempt claims on the commandeered ancestral homelands of Native Americans, but it became apparent to legislators that guaranteeing blacks access to the hallowed grounds would prove onerous. True to form, Southern whites responded with ardency perhaps greater than that of their Midwestern compatriots. Just a decade after its passage and in coincidence with the end of Reconstruction, a resigned Congress abrogated the Southern Homestead Act.[421] But the original Homestead Act is not the most revered, racially restricted government welfare program in American history. For it, one must look to the post-World War II era.

Chapter 4: Affirmative Inaction

G.I. Bill

In 1994, President Bill Clinton waxed romantic about the G.I. Bill—"the best deal ever made by Uncle Sam"[422]—and its multitudes. Speaking in Warm Springs, Georgia—air hallowed by Franklin Roosevelt's last breath—President Clinton spoke glowingly of the G.I. Bill's impact. Commenting on the bill's act of revolutionizing postwar American society, Clinton stated that the G.I. Bill, "Raised the entire nation to a plateau of social well-being never before experienced in U.S. history."[423] Clinton did not stretch—the G.I. Bill revolutionized in almost every sense. It stands as perhaps the largest, most effective social program in the history of the federal government. As for Clinton's purported narrative of equability, however, the revolution entailed determined resistance on that front.

Signed into law by President Franklin Delano Roosevelt just days after the June 1944 D-Day invasion, the G.I. Bill (formally known as the Serviceman's Readjustment Act) was enacted to facilitate World War II veterans' postwar transitions to civilian society. To claim that the G.I. Bill merely aided in the establishment of the American middle class as we know it today would be a gross understatement. The G.I. Bill *made* the American middle class. The G.I. Bill enabled millions of its beneficiaries and their families to purchase homes in wealthier, long-inaccessible suburban areas,[424] seize out-of-reach educational opportunities,[425] and establish business enterprises that together contributed widely to America's burgeoning postwar economy.[426] By the end of its first decade, the G.I. Bill smoothed postwar readjustment for half of WWII's American soldiers—8 million veterans.[427] By 1971, federal spending for the G.I. Bill totaled over $95 billion,[428] a staggering 15 percent of the U.S. federal budget going to its programs.[429] In 1944, the G.I. Bill not only paid full tuition for veterans wishing to continue their education, but also provided a monthly stipend of $75—much more generous than today's (when adjusted for inflation and consumer price index).[430]

The G.I. Bill was—and is—a welfare program. It has all of the attributes—subsidization for education, homeownership, farms, businesses, and beyond. It was more far-reaching, costly, and socialistic than any government social program before or since—certainly more so than modern "food stamp" programs. The G.I. Bill was essentially—to field the lobbed-about pejorative—a big fat "handout." Some would vehemently challenge this assertion as not only simplistic but insulting to the memory of the brutal sacrifices American soldiers made on Eastern, Western, and Pacific war fronts. But the facts do not waver. The true insult lies in the dishonorable truth that the blood sacrifices America's black veterans made on many fronts were discharged together with the program's national duty. Because the bulk of the G.I. Bill's beneficiaries were not of color, thus keeping the transfer of wealth and opportunity within racial lines, it occasioned no opposition from mainstream America. Some will argue that the G.I. Bill was not discriminatory, as its machinery purported to help veterans no matter their race. The G.I. Bill was not itself discriminatory. But its programmers *did* discriminate, coding their machines to lock out African Americans from even remote access to its caches and leaving the product keys for their white brothers-in-arms.

Black soldiers returning from the war hoped to benefit from unprecedented opportunities to chase education, business ventures, and suburban nestle through the G.I. Bill. Much like the New Deal's programs managed some benefit for African Americans, the G.I. Bill tendered a measure of opportunity for African American veterans. Black colleges saw double-digit percent increases in enrollment in the postwar period[431] and, with that, increased enrollment in integrated undergraduate, graduate, and trade schools.[432] But many administrative agencies mounted ardent offensives to cut off black lines of advance, thus allowing white veterans to capture the lion's share. African Americans returning from war found difficulty in obtaining home loans and other benefits promised under the legislation.[433] Instead of appealing to the federal government, African Americans relied on banks for loan requests, most of which were unwilling to lend to prospective black borrowers, effectively closing the gates of America's suburbs.[434]

Written chiefly by Mississippi representative John Rankin, chair of the U.S. House Committee on War Legislation, the G.I. Bill's provisions were crafted in such a way that much of the power and responsibility for implementation was delegated to the states.[435] This deliberate and disingenuous design permitted racially retrograde states to inject color prejudice into what was intended to be a colorblind bill. In the Jim Crow South, from which most African American servicemen hailed,[436] the decentralization of G.I. Bill programs enabled state-level lawmakers to ensure G.I. Bill benefits did *not* go to blacks, no matter how valiant their service on behalf of country. Thus, the South's enduring hostility toward African Americans was demonstrated not only in the brutal lynchings and other grotesque crimes it committed against valiant black soldiers returning from fulfillment of their patriotic duties. It was also demonstrated by its state legislatures and governor's mansions whose obdurate, prejudiced policies obstructed the uplifting of black Southerners.

In Southern states, approximately 28,000 veterans received G.I. Bill on-the-farm training, but only 11 percent of these beneficiaries were African American.[437] They represented just 1 percent of African Americans drafted into the war from agrarian communities.[438] Furthermore, the bill's United States Employment Service filled 86 percent of skilled positions with white veterans,[439] conversely saving unskilled, low-paying jobs for African American veterans.[440] Even in the North, quotas at educational institutions prevented the African American community from utilizing G.I. Bill funds to increase their overall enrollment in colleges and universities.[441] Quotas restricted the number of blacks who could attend institutions of higher learning, and in the Northern United States just 5,000 were enrolled in colleges and universities under the program.[442] Four decades following the enactment of the original G.I. Bill, just 36 percent of black veterans were able to claim college benefits under its auspices.[443] In stark contrast, over 60 percent of white veterans could boast of a G.I. Bill-sponsored education.[444]

The G.I. Bill is a fine example of what a social program should be. It typifies exactly how much outreach and expenditure it takes to uplift members of lower socioeconomic groups into society's better-off echelons. The G.I. Bill bred a massive professional class, evidenced in the approximately 400,000 engineers,[445] 200,000 teachers,[446] 90,000 scientists,[447] 60,000 doctors,[448] and 22,000 dentists[449] who traced their education and training directly to its patronage. That it enabled myriad Americans to pursue vocational professions such as carpentry, plumbing, and blacksmithing is also laudable.[450] But it was essentially a whites-only social program. In this, it is an ugly reminder of the invariably racist disposition of public policy in the United States, no matter how revolutionary.

The G.I. Bill's mode of implementation was in keeping with government practices, which made it a priority to neglect the innumerable struggles and needs it engendered in black Americans. It is unimaginable that such a massive transfer of opportunity could have ever taken place, either then or now, had the racial composition of the beneficiaries been anything other than what it was. Affirmative action and welfare policies are heavily criticized today, despite the fact that they don't even remotely begin to approach the magnitude observed in an act so influential as the G.I. Bill—and despite the fact that they benefit whites disproportionately. During the bill's nascent period, at the height of the popularity and ubiquity of anti-communist and anti-socialist rhetoric promulgated by such demagogues as Senator Joseph McCarthy, not a word of criticism or disapproval was voiced at America's most socialistic—and arguably discriminatory—program ever, the G.I. Bill.

"Welfare Queens" and Other Assorted Social Parasites

The patron saint of the Republican Party positioned himself as a particularly zealous champion of anti-welfare policies. Ronald Reagan seared perhaps the most potent anti-welfare sermon known, the protagonist of his parable being a deplorable figure emblematic of a tremendous social ill. During his 1976 presidential campaign, one crowd-favorite anecdote referred to this living, breathing parasite:

> She has eighty names, thirty addresses, twelve Social Security cards and is collecting veteran's benefits on four non-existing deceased husbands. And she is collecting Social Security on her cards. She's got Medicaid, is getting food stamps, and she is collecting welfare under each of her names. Her tax-free cash income alone is over $150,000.[451]

Speechwriters jotted on napkins—Laquisha, Kashawnda, Shaniqua, Latrina. Reagan went with "welfare queen." Listeners had 75 other names from which to choose. Reagan's apparition is the most poignant, misleading, irresponsible, and racist ever. This is exactly why conservatives devoured. The Great Communicator did not overtly profess that the "welfare queen" was African American. Just as he declined to name her, he neglected to assign her a race. But there is no denying that the evocation of this social vampire brought to mind images of African Americans, who by this time had already been widely stereotyped as "takers" mooching off government social programs.

Franklin Gilliam conducted a study assessing the association of race with welfare, finding that when participants viewed separate news clips—one story involving a black female welfare recipient and the other a white female welfare recipient—they more easily recalled the details from the news clip involving the black welfare recipient.[452] Ronald Reagan did not *have* to assign a name or a race to the welfare queen. Reagan knew the stereotype was so firmly ensconced in the political collective unconscious that many would, without aid of implication, neatly color a dark shade between the lines.

There is perhaps no stereotype in the political sphere more linked to blackness than welfare parasitism. It is the supposed unwillingness of blacks to join hardworking, mainstream American society, being content to instead lounge and malinger, leeching money hard-earned by taxpayer sweat and blood. Much like Reagan's "Welfare Queen" legend, these conceptions of government welfare programs are mythical—yet they breathe. Although such negative stereotypes about African Americans precede the existence of welfare programs, psychological studies have demonstrated that many of the archetypal black traits of irresponsibility and laziness are subliminally associated with welfare programs.[453][454]

If the common stereotypes regarding welfare breathed, statistics wouldn't show that during the existence of the Aid to Families with Dependent Children program, whites represented 56 percent of first-time clients compared to just 36 percent for African Americans.[455][456] Likewise with SNAP benefits—data on food stamp recipients shows that 36 percent belong to America's majority racial group.[457] Considering these statistics, does it stand to reason that whites may also benefit overwhelmingly from Social Security and Medicaid, programs which aren't typically regarded as forms of welfare but are classified as such by the federal government?

Critics point out that given that African Americans comprise just 13 percent of the nation's population,[458] they should comprise neither 36 percent of AFDC clients nor 22 percent of food stamp beneficiaries.[459] Such statistics are pursuant to common stereotypes—blacks *do* benefit disproportionately from welfare programs. But that assertion is parochial, truant to three things—the lack of job availability for African Americans due to continued job discrimination, the relative exclusion of African Americans from such programs due to the justice system's discriminatory impact, and a disproportionate share of the black labor force being engaged in low wage labor which necessitates the supplementation of public assistance.

African Americans' economic struggle both creates and necessitates their vast dependence on government assistance. Initiatives like the Drug War further underscore the intersectional magnitude of racial discrimination as stigma guards livelihood from the tall, dark Johns of America. A company of barriers even stands at the 38th parallel, guarding qualification from the harvest that malnourishes freedom with steel bars. Not only are these African Americans with scarlet letters of "F" embroidered in their backs unable to qualify for public assistance, but they are also often unable to find employment precisely because of their status as felons. But ostensible black dependence is relative independence—for in dependence lies self-determination. African Americans don the tattered Goodwill hand-me-downs reading "dependence"; the Declaration's fruits are yielded to the takers.

Conscious Admissions

Race-conscious college admissions policies have stolen the spotlight in the debate surrounding affirmative action. Though yesterday the Dark Age shadowed nonwhites, for whom race burdened and darkened futures, today the shadow casts elsewhere. Cursed is the New Black. It is the have nots, the voided heads, who have—stealing the light and promise of the world. Bakke. Gratz. Fisher. It will be a law firm unto their perpetuity. Once you get out of their seat. Yours is electric. Loaf if you will; you will get there, guaranteed.

In a case decided by the United States Supreme Court in 2003, a white student applying to the University of Michigan's school of law argued that because lesser qualified minority students were admitted while she was rejected, she was a victim of discrimination.[460] Her legal team argued that the Court established a precedent prohibiting the use of college admissions quotas in an earlier case, *Regents of the University of California v. Bakke*, which Michigan Law's admissions policy violated.[461] Although Michigan Law did not employ an explicit quota system, the plaintiff, Barbara Grutter, argued that the school's race-conscious admissions policy constituted an effective quota system. In *Grutter v. Bollinger*, the Supreme Court ruled 5-4 that the University of Michigan Law School's inclusion of race in its admissions policy was legitimate and necessary to tailor the student body to the school's aim of creating a diverse and inclusive environment.[462]

The deciding vote belonged to Justice Sandra Day O'Connor, who said that the precedent set by the Supreme Court earlier did not "prohibit the law school's narrowly tailored use of race in admissions decisions to further a compelling interest in obtaining the educational benefits that flow from a diverse student body."[463] However, O'Connor offered a critical temporal caveat, adding, "We expect that 25 years from now, the use of racial preferences will no longer be necessary to further the interest approved today."[464]

George W. Bush, a president never abashed in his opposition to affirmative action, said of the Michigan case, "[While I] strongly support diversity of all kinds, including racial diversity in higher education…the method used by the University of Michigan to achieve this important goal is fundamentally flawed."[465] The Bush White House had filed an *amicus curiae* brief on behalf of the plaintiff, citing President Bush's belief in the unconstitutionality of affirmative action programs.[466] Although this show of support did not result in victory for Grutter, the concurrent case *Gratz v. Bollinger* offered consolation; the legality of affirmative action in undergraduate admissions at the University of Michigan was struck down. Chief Justice William Rehnquist said on behalf of the Court that the university's undergraduate program, "Ensures that the diversity contributions of applicants cannot be individually assessed," and was therefore unconstitutional.[467]

Since the landmark 2003 cases, federal courts have served as battlegrounds for litigation teams arguing either for or against the merits of race-conscious college admissions. In 2011, a federal appeals court moved to overturn the state of Michigan's own 2006 mandated ban on affirmative action which affected both government hiring and admissions policies for public colleges and universities. That appeal was itself overturned in 2014,[468] thus reverting to a default of inequitable race policy more devastating than Detroit's 2008 auto industry crash. Although Abigail Fisher lost her case in 2016, her movement portends emergence from a luminous Dark Age into Dark Age luminosity.

In *White Like Me*, Tim Wise uses an especially fitting metaphor to describe the college-ready mindset of the Grutters and Fishers of America:

> This would be like me going to the mall, looking for a parking space, not finding one, seeing lots of unused spaces for persons with disabilities, or pregnant moms, and then getting pissed at disabled folks or pregnant women as if *they* had somehow kept me from getting a slot.[469]

One could read this as saying that people opposed to affirmative action hold legitimate views but should direct their ire at courts, legislators, and the administrative officials of universities rather than the beneficiaries for allowing such policies to stand. But the metaphor's point is much greater. Jennifer Gratz thought it necessary to attack the "lesser qualified" black applicants accepted over her while not attacking the numerous "lesser qualified" white applicants also accepted over her.[470] Would Gratz not also have a case against those undeserving applicants, dark as her, who had lower SATs and GPAs?

What many fail to realize is that race-conscious admissions policies don't send all whites to the back of the line. They effectively set aside *limited* space for students from minority groups—African Americans, Hispanics, Asians (although the exclusion of Asians from affirmative action programs at many colleges has generated controversy), and other nonwhite ethnic groups. The rest of the "parking lot" is effectively reserved for whites. Lifting those arms of entry and erasing those white lines is not a matter of valeting nonwhites first, leaving neglected, deprived whites curbside. Nor has this ever been the case. It's a matter of making sure nonwhites are attended to, even if it is through the back gate.

Despite President Bush's ardent opposition to affirmative action, he declared democratically, "Our Constitution makes it clear that people of all races must be treated equally under the law."[471] This is precisely what race-conscious college admissions policies do. They serve as the necessary equalizer for the tremendous socioeconomic disadvantages faced by young black students in their pursuit of quality primary, secondary, and ultimately postsecondary education.

From the first day of kindergarten until the moment they walk across the stage to receive their coveted high school diplomas—if they somehow manage to make it—African Americans are, in all ways and at all levels, voided. Because many African Americans come from unstable, single-parent, or parentless homes, they often lack the benefits of a home environment conducive to educational development. African American children often start school lacking the most basic literacy and mathematical skills,[472] partly because of a lack of parental motivation and tutoring. For those lucky enough to have two parents, many lack folks with high school educations—much less postsecondary ones.[473] Education *is* a material good. To be deprived of it tenders wages to generational poverty; they cannot appraise education. But the most profound issues pertain not to those of hearth, but classrooms and hallways incubating nurslings.

A stroll through any given predominantly black public school and its white demographic mirror affords delirium. One is puzzled to know that they are in the same country—that both are under the same government. As will be explored in the following chapter, schools such as those in South Carolina's "Corridor of Shame" are severely underfunded,[474] poorly staffed,[475] and lacking in up-to-date and appropriate resources.[476] Even when African American students attend better-funded schools, they experience pervasive racial discrimination on the part of instructors, administrators, and even fellow students.[477] The disparity daemon is their chaperone.

Black students are more likely to be tracked into hospice of remedial and special education programs, ability notwithstanding, and are less likely to be tracked into advanced and gifted programs, even when qualified for placement in such programs.[478] It has also been found that African Americans are victims of gratuitous, aggressive disciplinary policies and are more likely to be suspended and expelled than white students who are equally unruly and disobedient.[479] For many incarcerated African Americans, their downward spirals begin with draconian, discriminatory school discipline policy—the journey through the school-to-prison pipeline. It has been found that black students are even graded more harshly—and not because they have the wrong answers. Instructors dock points for flawed dermatology.[480]

Research has affirmed biases in other areas, such as the SAT and other standardized tests[481] and in AP and honors program tracking[482] (not to mention the unavailability of such programs at predominantly black public schools).[483] Like African Americans, white students might also deal with the disadvantages of background that render their likelihood of acquiring an excellent education lower than their more privileged peers. But they do not have to deal with the scarlet letter of blackness skewing the impression that instructors should have of them as capable, honest, good human beings deserving of respect and opportunity.

Absent race-conscious college admissions policies, no rectifier would exist for these institutional manifestations of racial prejudice. As much as mainstream America lambastes black America for its supposed lassitude, freeloading, and criminality, one would think it rational for such ardent critics to *support* college admissions treatments as a means of conferring health of opportunity upon African Americans. It would seem sensible that such programs which enable African Americans to pursue higher education, well-paying careers, financial stability, and other such qualities of respectability that many complain so much of blacks lacking would be welcomed.

Sadly, myopic critics will continue to criticize the alleged malaise of African Americans, all the while denying them access to the very tools and programs that enable their ascent from that malaise to fix their children's destinies onto righteous paths, galvanize their communities, and keep their people out of handcuffs and from behind bars. Until the visionless—and one can say too, unhesitatingly, heartless—realize and acknowledge that the only way to ensure that America "stops discriminating on the basis of race" is to enact policies that will negate the pervasive and pernicious practices of anti-minority racial discrimination in America's systems, the battle between those who merely favor equal opportunity in proclamation and those who truly favor equal opportunity in practice will rage atop black soil yielding blood diamonds.

Conclusion

When the intent of affirmative action is not to dispense pure advantages but relative equalities on groups with histories of extreme disadvantage, one cannot reasonably argue such a policy is ineffectual, useless, or racist. The intent of affirmative action is not to promote preference for blacks and other minority groups; it is to negate the built-in, inextirpable systems and policies of preferential treatment that made for a bastion. Although it should aim to do so, affirmative action doesn't even approach offsetting racial bias on a mass scale. That the justices of our Supreme Court criticize affirmative action that's purported to favor blacks while dismissing and disregarding the clandestine, more potent forms of affirmative action favoring whites shows profound, tortuous systemic malpractice.

Even if affirmative action programs did disproportionately benefit African Americans, they'd be hard-pressed to displace the establishment's firm economic presence. White American households, by some measures, possess on average as much as 16 times the wealth of black households.[484] It's hard to imagine what it would take to remedy such spasticity, a result of both the crushing, 100 percent quotas of the past as well as the continuing inequitable, disproportionate riches accrued at the expense of black lungs.

It is troubling that Supreme Court justices think it necessary to prescribe timetables for affirmative action's removal while proscribing timetables for institutional racism's eradication. Justice O'Connor's belief is one shared even by affirmative action's most ardent proponents—that it is a bandage covering a festering wound that, in time, will heal. But we cannot remove the bandage prematurely; the wound must be properly treated. The necessary ointments, poultices, topical antibiotics, and other salves must be applied. The wound must be washed and cleansed, properly and periodically, to remove dirt and bacteria in which cultures fester. To travel the arterial ways, marching on Rome. Invest in infrastructure. That's what the interstate system is for.

Only with tourniquet does flesh cloak in skin; splotch gives way to melanocyte. We bear a sad state of gratitude that Justice O'Connor begrudges its necessity. But the view held by she and many liberals is that we will do without affordable care. We ward the pain of insurance, setting our own timer, our own bandage, our own bondage, our own recovery. We must remove by "use by," even if producing a festering invasion that grips the heart. It is disgusting—no more so than to go without insurance.

Proponents of affordable care repeal neglect the reality of the residual disease of systemic and institutional racism that leaves blacks invalid, dependent to the tune of barely 2 percent of the domestic dime. That's gross. That's singular. America's history is a 400-year health care program. Low premiums, generous subsidies. Universal. In one universe. That is not incendiary, not contestable—like America's history. A Medicare and Medicaid of chains, handcuffs, and admonitions for impeachment.

The economic rights to jobs, businesses, land, *the franchise*, are not ephemeral, confined to a single generation; they accrue and afford opportunities for posterity to not only inherit the health of ancestors, but also clear access to yet more veins through which yet more blood nourishes. An estimated 80 percent of lifetime wealth is derived from assets passed from parent to child.[485] Genetic health—you have it or you don't—can easily influence the other 20. Therefore, it's all in the blood. Pioneer blood. This is why Fund in America remains largely in the hands of racial nepotism, hoarding objects of hiring, contracting, loaning, selling, buying, denying—every object, in two hands. It's equal, between hands.

Those who vote and rule against affordable care argue that the law must be dismantled because it opens an epidemic for American business. But the epidemic that will yield is one of bad shape. The only thing that matters is that this health care is necessary for the preservation of the American *soul*. To accuse modern affirmative action programs of being injurious to race relations is tantamount to an anti-abolitionist arguing that emancipation was contemptible on grounds that it was harmful to "race relations," or a segregationist arguing that the passage of the 1964 Civil Rights Act and dismantling of structures of overt racial discrimination in the South and other regions of the United States was deplorable on grounds that they too would harm "race relations." In the vein of the discussion, there is much circulation entailing the putative want to protect the sacrosanct state of race relations. If those germs caused sickness in the American soul, then it needs *insurance* against insurance. It needs a ruling *against* affordable care. It must hide the veto pen.

What "race relations" are we insuring? The sort of "race relations" that enable unemployment in the black community to hover incurably at abysmal levels while occasioning no idea of inappropriateness from the same status quo that inoculates it? The sort of "race relations" that allow the health care system to neglect the health and well-being of African Americans, thus directly resulting in their higher mortality rates, especially among infants? The sort of "race relations" that allow an accumulation of KIAs and POWs not seen since *nausea, heartburn, indigestion, upset stomach, diarrhea* jingoed out of Civil War prison camps? If these are the sort of race relations that we defend, they are entirely worth our infection. That is the promise of our affection.

It speaks to malignance that convalescence inspires malignance. Terminality inspires remission. Doctors did not recommend the Civil Rights Movement. It was bound to damage race relations. Side effects be damned. African Americans and other minorities were certainly damaged by those relations; it is apparent that this unilateral evaluation of race relations didn't provide a comprehensive plan based on public opinion polls. The empirical impression of cryoablation. Blacks were jobless, disenfranchised, without motor skills, save political or economic medication; yet the movement was deemed pernicious to "race relations."

Do we ever consult the medical association? Asking why it is only satisfied with race relations when the condition is one of sickness in the soul? Our innards ordered unjustly, having bedridden us to ill-repute? It is dumbfounding that such strong opposition to affirmative action programs survives in spite of the fact that they disproportionately benefit *white Americans*, failing to fulfill the stereotype in which these crushing opponents cast them. This protrudes the mere *spur* of the fair and equitable transfer of opportunity that fractures those who detest affirmative action rather than the uninsurance rate. If we want to stop the inequitable virus enduring in our blood from destroying amino acids, we must carry on our suit against the pharmaceutical malpractice of dispensing transfer-of-opportunity treatment that leaves ethnic groups without breath for desperate respiratory efforts.

We have to terminate treatment, but not of the counsel of the Birmingham medical board that denied King's residency and transferred him to a hospital for the criminally fit. They misdiagnosed him. Their degrees, licenses, and research are lifeless, bloodletting unauthorized practices. Death to credentials. Credentials were the Angel of Death assuming life over that Doctor. Credentials called him to death. But credentials were mistaken, for only death calls to death. As it will find out.

"One Nation, Under God" is death. The fervency of King's hope is death. The death of euthanasia; ordainment's requirement. King failed his boards. Ordinance did not fail King. Euthanasia will not fail King's dream.

⑤
The Miseducation of
the...African American?

It's time to turn in. Ordinance calls them. They must cast away soporific chains securing them from the sea of freedom. Night whitened by Pharos—darkness with end. The siren cries. *Get up.* That is a sentence into minimum security.

They scurry from cells into cell. *Brush, soap, deodorant.* They scurry from cell to cell. *Juice, bread, cold cut.* They scurry from cell to cells. *Vroom, bump, crash. Attention! Forward, march.* They spill into minimum security.

They traverse yard and concrete, detecting no divide. Metal detectors don't snitch on handcuffs. Cellmates gather round for today's lessons. First period, the physics of dice; second period, the economics of tobacco. The bell rings. Commissary extends the lesson. Soap? Juice? Cold cuts? Rituals of satiation. *Up.* Shoot! Miss. Rec exposes an incapacity for recollection that alarms *you. Attention!* If only you could shoot, you wouldn't be here. You'd be in the big leagues. You're barred, continuing education.

Dunk. That's the blackboard crashing. Chalk screeches a sentence. Cover your ears! Cover your eyes. Don't watch your back. Focus on road, not rearview; your cellmates' snouts, antennae, and cottonmouths. Back of the class. Allergen-inducing puree of a journey amnesia seized but moments ago. Repression failed; venom induced dry mouth. *Gulp.* Snack time. *Juice.* Not like Pac. That's nap time.

Chains secure body, not soul. *Attention!* A soporific commands projection. Look. No, look down. *Now.* This land about you sown with salt. All industry, all willpower, all denizens. Uprooted. It escorted you on the bus to this corridor of shame. *Remember?* Next page; U.S. History, 1944 edition. Here lies George Stinney, Jr. He who waited 80 years for vacation. He got the electricity denied to the schoolhouse but not the bond secured to its holder. Your vacation awaits. Damned by the bell.

America's XL Pipeline conveys black substance, but not that of mercurial value. Not that inspiring industry in lobbying and research and boring through rock to China and conservation and air travel and consumer satisfaction polling. But it inspires industry. Guns, guards, development, Fox News. Education. Curricula entail suspension. Cumulative material expels. Graduation matriculates into incarceration.

The South Carolina Penitentiary was not demolished on December 8, 2005. It stands, albeit with a centenarian hunch. It was born in 1866, just in time for a fluorescent black future. It has cell blocks of water moccasins and rattlesnakes slithering hallways. A few rats, too. Its ceilings cave, walls wave—bidding repair a tearful farewell. This preserves history. But that doesn't make for anachronism, for it is of our time. It is today and it is Deep South and it is Dillon County, South Carolina and it is accredited with the South Carolina State Board of Education.

The Corridor of Shame is a shining example of the worst of American education.[486] As of the mid-2000s, its students were still reading Stinney-era

95

textbooks loftily asserting, "One day, man will land on the moon."[487] This is but one of several sad attributes through which the Corridor's prison-schools profess the magnitude of disparity in education—curricula of substandard government policies.

Although the 2005 documentary *The Corridor of Shame* drew a measure of national attention to the area's blight, the Corridor's real infamy was highlighted in President Obama's 2007 campaign stop at J. V. Martin Middle School in Dillon, South Carolina.[488] Barack Obama selected an effective backdrop underscoring his exclamation of "hope and change." He chose a set where dilapidated homes and soiled paths don't juxtapose with idyllic dreams just down a stone road—they own the road. Obama stood in the center, daring handle-barred and starred decals with a horse-drawn billboard of hope and change. Stage management commanded that staff, hoisted betwixt Iwo Jima and the left-hand side. Chiefly spirit mobilized forces—students, parents, and educators—laying and cementing gold eggs toward pavestone riches. But, although decals might be dodged, their shrill whistle calls forth fangs tearing aurum from alloy. And so, yolks dislodged by will's torque. But in the Corridor's taped perimeter, Obama honored substance, producing a cornerstone dedicated to a dream fostering equanimity in South Carolina and America.

Obama assumed abandoned powers, condemning shanty projects deserted by Bush administration mismanagement. Speaking at Dillon High School, then-senator Obama railed against Washington's flawed spending habits, insisting, "If we can spend $9 billion a month in Iraq, we can spend a few million dollars…for J. V. Martin…so our children can succeed."[489] Obama's decision to take his message not just to houses on the hill but also those collapsing under construction was celebrated nationally and endeared him to South Carolina voters who selected him over Hillary Clinton in the state's 2008 Democratic presidential primary.

As of 2016, little had changed in the Corridor. Its schools still cannot compete with those in South Carolina's more affluent districts. Low teacher salaries make it difficult to retain talented and passionate educators and administrative obstinacy makes it difficult for schools in poorer districts in counties like Dillon, Jasper, and Hampton to obtain necessary funding for improvements. In 2011, South Carolina's then-superintendent of education, Mick Zais, turned away the opportunity to collect $144 million in federal grants[490]—money desperately needed by districts such as Dillon School District 2 to create and sustain teaching jobs. The Education Jobs Fund, created as part of Obama's stimulus package, provided federal funding for 49 states. South Carolina was the only one to opt out.[491] Even similarly red and academically struggling states like Mississippi and Alabama accepted federal stimulus funding.

Zais argued that taking federal money would have been irresponsible[492]—a stance he failed to elucidate clearly to the parents and students of Dillon County and other educationally dysfunctional districts in the state. Zais erroneously argued that participating in the Education Jobs Fund would be impossible for the state due to the legislature failing to meet the prerequisite funding allocation for education.[493] He also failed to inform students—who study in infested, leaking, one-computer classrooms—why, if this was the case, he failed to lobby the state legislature for sufficient funding. Mick Zais encapsulated his narrow-minded sentiments in stating, "South Carolina can meet our educational challenges without micromanagement by the federal government."[494]

South Carolina ranks at the bottom in measures of educational standards and student performance. Although for years South Carolina hovered at 48th [495] or 49th [496] in education metric surveys, the conservative American Legislative Exchange Council ranked the red state dead last in student performance in its 2010 *Report Card*.[497] The study measures not only student performance, but also the efficacy of education policies and reform efforts. South Carolina's class rank left much room for improvement, but Zais' policies only served to solidify the state's dubious distinction. Prior to rejecting the Education Jobs Fund grants, Zais rejected the chance to obtain $50 million in federal funding from the Race to the Top program despite South Carolina's eligibility.[498] South Carolina's education system suffers from extreme dysfunction, something which is apparent to the rest of the country but clearly not all of the state's education officials. The Corridor is only the worst of it. Numerous South Carolina counties suffer similar problems. Superintendents such as Zais have placed narrow-minded principles over the mission of educating the state's future generations. Zais' term as education superintendent ended in 2015. That year, ALEC's *Report Card* again ranked South Carolina 51st (the rankings include Washington, DC).[499]

Bud Ferillo, director and producer of *Corridor of Shame*, is the former program director at the Initiative for South Carolina's Future and as of 2016 was coordinator at the South Carolina Collaborative for Racial Reconciliation.[500] Ferillo provided *pro bono* public relations services to school districts that joined in suing the state of South Carolina over funding disparities.[501] The lawsuit sat in the docket of the South Carolina Supreme Court for 23 years before being decided in 2014. Before Ferillo's intervention, the case of these underprivileged school districts was almost unknown. Although few knew of the case being tried in a remote Clarendon County courthouse—also the site of arguments in the *Briggs v. Elliot* case which became part of *Brown v. Board*—Ferillo's efforts transformed the neglected issue into salient. In 2004, he organized a 50th anniversary *Brown v. Board* commemorative march, drawing over 6,000 people to downtown Columbia in a monumental effort that courted the attention of South Carolina's citizens and legislators.[502]

Almost seven years later Ferillo said of the case, "There has been little if any change in most of the schools since [*Corridor of Shame*] was completed."[503] In Jasper County (another county featured in *Corridor*), new schools were built only when those on their last legs were condemned by the state as unfit for human occupation. Ferillo said of the state government's responsibility to ameliorate the Corridor's abysmal conditions, "The State of South Carolina...has done nothing, absolutely nothing, to address the immediate or systemic problems in these schools."[504] Dillon's School District 2 flew over the head of the state government to, with help from the Obama administration, secure $23.5 million in low-interest financing that would enable them to replace the ramshackle, turn of the century J. V. Martin Middle School.[505] The Obama administration also extended grants and low-interest loans to other schools in Dillon County.[506] Meanwhile, South Carolina did little to improve "curricula in the critical coursework of math, science and foreign language,"[507] seeing the replacement of textbooks stamped with copyright dates closer to *Plessy* than *Brown* as unimportant or perhaps altogether unnecessary.

Last in Line: An American Destiny Deferred

The performance evaluation of South Carolina education policy bears description much more critical than stagnancy's red ink. Ferillo maintains that in light of his efforts to expose the Corridor of Shame, South Carolina's General Assembly has moved away from, rather than toward, enacting egalitarian educational policies. He cites the state's adoption of a tax code that bases funding largely in business and industry rather than homeowner property. This has only alleviated tax burdens for those in affluent coastal communities rather than mitigate education dysfunction affecting children in South Carolina's poorest counties. Beyond fiscal and curricular policy problems, Ferillo remarks on the "minimally adequate" standard of education set by the South Carolina Supreme Court in 1998:

> The [pending] case rests on whether or not the state is maintaining "a minimally adequate education system,"…producing graduates of our K-12 system who can read, write, do math, be employable and be good citizens. The ultimate solution is to raise that constitutional standard by inserting the words "high quality education" in the education section of the state constitution. That's what Maryland, Virginia and Florida did a generation ago…If we had "high quality education" mandated by our state constitution, legislators and governors would be obligated to fund our education system accordingly. A minimally adequate education is wholly insufficient for academic success or economic development in the 21st century.[508]

Virtually every state in America has educational standards requiring something beyond "minimally adequate." Yet South Carolina's leaders think that the inheritors of their realm are worthy only of minimal effort. Ferillo recognizes that Superintendent Zais feels no differently from these feckless leaders, saying of him:

> [He] has shown no interest in addressing these poor school districts in any meaningful way. In fact, by refusing to apply for available federal funding, he has deliberately passed on much needed federal assistance in the name of avoiding "federal dictatorship" of our school system.[509]

The school districts featured in *Corridor of Shame* and other languishing districts of South Carolina all have one thing in common—they are overwhelmingly black. "Race has a lot to do with it," Ferillo says. The 138,000 students in plaintiff districts are almost unanimously black.[510] Further compounding the race issue is the widespread problem of school "white flight." White families in these indigent counties opt to send their children to private and parochial schools, ceding the cesspools of South Carolina education to black and minority students. Rather than push to improve the condition of public schools, government leaders and citizens evade, leaving monumental odes to an old order to crumble and entrap the futures of South Carolina's black children.

Those entrusted with the duty of ensuring a bright future for all the state's children instead put them on a fast track to the Stone Age. The train might even bypass its retrograde destination, taking South Carolina's children on a field trip to witness the primordial soup in which it resolves to submerge them. In 2014, the South Carolina Supreme Court ruled in the districts' favor, requiring the state legislature to submit a plan for judicial review that was still forthcoming at midyear 2016.[511] Whether the plan proves beyond "minimally adequate" will be evaluated by South Carolina public school students into the 2020s and beyond.

Although the inanity of South Carolina's education policy seems visible everywhere but the State House, South Carolina's lawmakers have company. Few Americans are inclined to acknowledge the way such education policy contributes to the perpetuation of racial disparity on a national level. It is not just districts in Dillon and Jasper counties, the state of South Carolina as a whole, or Mick Zais that stand as icons of America's education dysfunction. This dysfunction stretches beyond the Gulf Coast and Appalachian, traversing a fogged America from sea to murky sea.

No matter how trite or empty the saying seems to become with each iteration, it holds eternally—"knowledge is power." The best way to keep a social group ensconced in deprivation is to dispossess them of knowledge, the means through which emancipation is born. African Americans have experienced a long history of denial of access to education: an outright proscription during slavery, varying forms of inadequate educational infrastructure since emancipation, and, today, government policies that segregate schools and neglect to ensure that black children, like many of their white counterparts, have access to quality education.

That African Americans were, at least prior the Civil Rights Movement, denied equal access to education is universally accepted. What's not universally accepted is that such disparity endures—and that the current education predicament of the African American community is not a product of intrinsic incapability. Conservative pundits and social scientists alike have argued that black students' lower test scores, higher dropout rates, and higher rates of disciplinary violations indicate that African Americans' problems are individual and cultural. It is a combination of the belief that government need play no significant role in improving education and the belief in intrinsic black intellectual inferiority that causes lawmakers' negligence on the issue of education reform. The former point is perhaps best demonstrated by recent decisions of the United States Supreme Court, which have thwarted *Brown v. Board*'s destiny to beacon a new era of equal justice. Since *Brown*, the Supreme Court has all but done an about-face on education. The noble rule of *Brown*, which to many once represented the death knell for segregation in the United States, has fled in face of a *coup* reinstating segregative tyranny of an old order.

Desegregation...or Resegregation?

Plessy v. Ferguson was the landmark case that established the government's right to maintain separate but equal facilities for Americans on the basis of race. Although the Reconstruction Congresses envisioned the Civil Rights Act of 1875 as facilitating the integration of African Americans into mainstream America, the law proved too progressive for postbellum America.[512] [513] *Plessy v. Ferguson* vindicated the political petulance of white America and enabled the continuation of *de jure* racial discrimination in the post-emancipation United States, especially in the South. The legendary 1954 *Brown v. Board* Supreme Court ruling struck down the myth of separate but equal public facilities and demanded transition to integrated destiny. Although this opened water fountains, parks, beaches, and other public areas no longer divisible by race, *Brown*'s most significant victory was won on the education front.

The magic wand notion of a racially blended, equitable, colorblind American society extends to education. We recall *Brown v. Board*, Governor George Wallace blocking young black children from entering destiny's doors, Selma and Washington, and historicize the modern phenomenon of racism through such seeming distance. Once again, we render institutional racism a "back then" thing. The 1960s, '50s, and prior are when things were bad and unequal. Today, we have achieved our egalitarian America. Integration has been effected and black children are now as resourced, facilitated, and supported as white children. Nothing could be more false.

Desegregation was not realized overnight; the slam of Chief Justice Warren's gavel did not effectuate an instantaneous integration of schools. The Court largely allowed states and school districts to set their own paces on integration. Some schools made swift changes, particularly in areas where racial segregation was not as imbued in the social fabric; in others, change was glacial. But, although the guardian of change sought its enrollment, *Brown*'s promise never matriculated. Although *Brown* is widely considered the single most influential ruling regarding inclusion in education, several subsequent Supreme Court rulings have reversed the vision of educational parity that the *Brown* ruling sought to effect.

School districts across the nation have resisted busing and other programs begotten by the Civil Rights Movement to eradicate educational inequality, successfully pushing several landmark cases before the Supreme Court. Observers have endlessly praised *Brown* for progressing America's education system toward racial equality, but the unraveling of its provisions by various rulings such as *Board of Education of Oklahoma City Public Schools v. Dowell, Milliken v. Bradley, Parents Involved in Community Schools v. Seattle School District 1*, and *Meredith v. Jefferson County Board of Education* confers torrent on an unwarranted parade. Such critical rulings are reversing the trends of integration *Brown*'s ambitions set forth.

Milliken v. Bradley was the first thread unwound from *Brown*'s fabric. Ruled in 1974, the Supreme Court's 5-4 decision held that busing across district lines in the city of Detroit was impermissible unless the school districts for which the plans were suggested had histories of *de jure* segregation.[514] Under this ruling, busing could be used to integrate areas where laws enforcing segregation had been in place, but not where *de facto* segregation had existed. The Court argued that there could only have been evidence of segregation if prior laws had explicitly promoted segregation. The proven existence of *de facto* segregation without any accompanying explicit laws was taken as coincidental. Because Detroit did not have segregation policies on the books (despite being, in reality, thoroughly segregated), the city was not required to take action in fostering equitable education. Strangely enough, the Court argued that desegregating effectively did not require "any particular racial balance in each school, grade or classroom,"[515] a rubric which left equivocal parameters for grading degrees of integration.

Board of Education of Oklahoma City Public Schools v. Dowell came down in 1991, 17 years after the *Milliken* ruling dimmed the brilliant light *Brown* shone. This decision cracked the bulb. In *Can We Talk About Race*, Spelman College president Beverly Daniel Tatum summarizes the case's background:

Chapter 5: The Miseducation of the...African American?

The Oklahoma case began in 1961 as the result of a lawsuit to integrate the schools, which had been desegregated by order of the state constitution ever since Oklahoma achieved statehood in 1907. In 1963 the federal judge Luther Bohanon ruled that the "dual" system of education be ended. The school board adopted a "neighborhood zoning" plan in response, but because of residential segregation (the end result of racially restrictive real-estate covenants supported by state and local law), the neighborhood zoning plan was ineffective. Finally, in 1972, because little progress had been made, Judge Bohanon ordered a busing plan designed to achieve racial balance. Five years later, in 1977, the Board of Education of Oklahoma City asked Judge Bohanon to close the case and he did, expressing his confidence that the board would continue to comply with constitutional desegregation requirements.[516]

Judge Bohanon's wishes were unfulfilled, however, and just eight years later Oklahoma City's board reversed course and reinstituted discriminatory neighborhood zoning plans. The case was reopened:

In 1989 the Tenth Circuit Court of Appeals ruled in [favor of Robert Dowell and other original plaintiffs], instructing the Oklahoma City school board to design a new plan to integrate the Oklahoma City schools. The school board appealed and the case went before the Supreme Court. The Court sent the case back to Judge Bohanon to decide whether the state had satisfied the original desegregation order. In the end, Judge Bohanon ruled in the state's favor and closed the case.[517]

Either Judge Bohanon was mistaken in believing Oklahoma City schools to be sufficiently racially integrated or he did not desire that outcome's realization. By 2000, the reversal toward segregation in Oklahoma City Schools had become glaringly evident. More than 50 percent of Oklahoma City's black children attended majority-black schools, with the same holding true for white children and schools in which they constituted the majority.[518] This premature move toward dismantling Oklahoma's still-segregated schools set the precedent for school districts throughout the nation regressing their schooling policies.[519] Because prevalent housing discrimination practices segregate neighborhoods, neighborhood zoning policies have the effect of segregating schools. Short of monitoring and reducing the prevalence of housing discrimination, the only way to circumvent geographically enabled segregation is to allow interdistrict busing. But the colorblind citizens who mysteriously move against these solutions are not solely to blame. The similarly colorblind legislators and judges who enact and support policies that, absent verbal declarations, make their racist intent evident are equally complicit in perpetuating racial discrimination in American education.

The universal abrogation of integrative policies has transcended deep into the current century, evidenced in the Supreme Court's rulings in *Parents Involved in Community Schools v. Seattle School District 1* and *Meredith v. Jefferson County Board of Education*. These cases, jointly decided by the Supreme Court in the summer of 2007, perhaps altogether shattered *Brown's* once luminous bulb. The Seattle School District, which allowed rising high school freshmen to apply to any school in the district rather than only those in established zones, sought a solution to the problem of oversubscription burdening some high schools. Eligibility criteria advantaged certain students in competition for spots. For the sake of maintaining diversity, race was a featured criterion of this methodology. In a 4-1-4 ruling, the Court decided, "The Constitution does not impose a duty to desegregate upon districts,"[520] and that such attempts were therefore unjustified. The majority ruled that the admissions policy violated the Equal Protection Clause of the Fourteenth Amendment. Chief Justice John Roberts stated in the plurality opinion, "The way to stop discrimination on the basis of race is to stop discriminating on the basis of race."[521]

Such a statement can only be described as obtuse. It's even more alarming coming from a man who graduated *summa cum laude* from Harvard in three years and completed Harvard Law School with a distinguished record by the time he was 23 years old. But it also proves that academic achievement has nothing to do with the progressiveness or regressiveness of Supreme Court jurisprudence and everything to do with the prejudices and political biases of our judges. Justice Roberts and his colleagues, like other purportedly colorblind Americans, fail to recognize that the absence of such measures allows for racial discrimination's perpetuation. Discrimination on the basis of race cannot be stopped or reduced unless measures are put in place to guarantee equal opportunity. Implicitly and otherwise, the very much color-seeing individuals of America still commit acts of racial discrimination that transcend the scope of existing civil rights laws. It is apparent in the education system, in which trends migrate toward the inequitable past thanks to the Supreme Court's betrayal of *Brown v. Board*'s monumental promise. It is a testament to the blindness and misdirection of America's leaders that they choose to stand against, rather than in defense of, racial progress.

In the case of *Meredith v. Jefferson County*, five African American students in Jefferson County, Kentucky sued the school district after being denied admittance to a magnet school.[522] Jefferson County Public Schools outlined provisions for racial integration which stipulated that a school could be neither more than 50 percent nor less than 15 percent black.[523] The plaintiffs, whose admittance would have pushed the magnet school beyond the 50 percent threshold, argued that the district's admissions policy ambiguously constituted a quota system, violating the Equal Protection Clause. The Court agreed that the district's admissions policy was unconstitutional. As with *Parents v. Seattle*, the Court ruled in this case that equalizing measures violated applicants' equal protection rights and that the school was not compelled to accept any applicants—including the plaintiffs—in the interest of arbitrary demographic standards.

It is disturbing that civil rights laws designed to enable the realization of racial equality are instead employed to perpetuate racial discrimination. In *Parents Involved v. Seattle School District 1*, the nonprofit Parents Involved argued that the school district's inclusion of race in its selections criteria violated not only the Equal Protection Clause but also the Civil Rights Act of 1964.[524] It is problematic that the Court argues that these laws unequivocally prohibit discrimination on the basis of race—even when such "discrimination" is enacted to combat the tacit, unspoken forms of discrimination ubiquitous in America today. The Civil Rights Act of 1964 states in its title its intent to "provide...relief against discrimination in public accommodations."[525] Certainly, busing and other equalizing practices are in the spirit of the law. But until judges commit themselves to fulfilling the objectives of civil rights laws rather than parochial, political principles, we cannot hope to see such laws practiced and respected in their intended spirit.

Circuit Short

Long before the series of retrograde Supreme Court rulings extending through present, the Court's jurisprudence showed promise toward fulfilling *Brown's* ideals. One of the first and most pivotal examples of integration took place in Charlotte, North Carolina. Throughout the 1960s, integration advanced at a snail's pace in much of America. One of the main reasons, education departments argued, was that because whites and blacks were geographically separated and existing schools were already located within either predominantly white or black communities, carrying out integration was impractical. But, to the chagrin of segregationists, busing was suggested as a means of circumventing this problem. Much like it is today, busing was then met with stiff resistance throughout much of the United States.[526] Although Charlotte was more progressive than other cities, it proved no exception. With those favoring the promise of a new era clashing with those defending yesterday's unjustness, Charlotte's streets became battlegrounds in the fight for education equity.

In a ruling almost as crucial for integration as *Brown*, in *Swann v. Charlotte-Mecklenburg* the Supreme Court ruled busing to be a legitimate means of ensuring racial integration. Before the changes demanded by the ruling, Charlotte was no paragon of integration. Fourteen thousand black children attended schools that were at least 99 percent black.[527] The Court ruled unanimously in favor of James Swann and other plaintiffs, deciding that wholly or predominantly black schools were indicators of segregation's continued existence and that busing was a legitimate tool school districts could employ for integration.[528] For the next several years after the 1971 ruling, Charlotte's citizens and administrators resisted the push. Still, Charlotte would soon fulfill its destiny in consummating integration's teased possibility.

When President Reagan spoke in Charlotte during his 1984 reelection campaign, an otherwise enthusiastic crowd fell silent when he voiced opposition to busing.[529] It seemed that the citizens of Charlotte had viscerally come to value their reputation as America's quintessential integrative model. However, by the 1990s, following suit with citizens in Oklahoma City, Seattle, and Jefferson County, Kentucky, a trend emerged which saw Charlotte renege on its commitment to racial equality. Much like in other parts of the United States, citizens moved to utilize the same courts that had previously handed down pro-integration rulings to reverse decisions on busing and in turn resegregate Charlotte's schools.

Eric Smith came to the Charlotte-Mecklenburg school district with great anticipation of building on its famed reputation. Arriving from Virginia as the district's new superintendent in 1996, Smith was surprised that instead of finding thoroughly integrated schools in which black and white children had equal access to effective facilities, resources, and teachers, he discovered unanimously white AP classes (despite the school district being 40 percent black[530])[531] and a disturbing pattern of increasing segregation in Charlotte schools:

> In some areas…[there appeared to be] a pattern of inequity that seemed to be getting worse during an era of gradual desegregation. By 1996

there were more than two dozen racially identifiable schools in the system, most of them black, and the number was growing. It would have been unthinkable even ten years before, and the worst part was the black schools clearly were being shortchanged. They tended to be in the oldest school buildings, operating with teachers who had less experience than those in the teaching pool system wide. The results were apparent in student test scores. According to one study, the more time spent in a predominantly black elementary school, the worse a child was likely to do on standardized tests—and in high school courses taken later on.[532]

The Southern model of racial integration that Eric Smith—and much of America—envisioned had disappeared. As the racial composition of Charlotte changed (mostly due to a large influx of Hispanic immigrants), the conservative-dominated Charlotte-Mecklenburg County Commission began to make significant budget cuts allowing for the neglect of schools in predominantly minority areas.[533] Smith immediately commenced efforts to salvage Charlotte's school system. Under Smith's stewardship, the Committee of 33 was formed to unite Charlotte's citizens in an effort to reverse the public education system's trend of rapid decay.[534] Despite head-bumping between advocates of busing and those favoring "neighborhood schools," the task force committed itself to the outcome of diversity in Charlotte schools. The Committee issued a report in August 1998 detailing its assessment of the problems of Charlotte-Mecklenburg's education system and offering appropriate solutions.[535] But one disgruntled parent wasn't so keen on preserving Charlotte's crumbling, fledgling tradition of diversity. His angst would unravel the 1971 *Swann* ruling that made Charlotte into a bastion of educational equality.

William Capacchione's daughter, Cristina, was rejected twice from a Charlotte magnet school.[536] The magnet school to which his daughter (who is half white and half Hispanic) applied reserved 40 percent of its spaces for African American students, reflecting the district's African American population. Capacchione argued that this quota system had prevented Cristina from obtaining a seat in the program (despite her being too far down the program's "lottery list" to have a realistic chance at admittance). The school board had agreed to commit itself to maintaining the quotas, but Robert D. Potter, a municipal judge, ruled that the mandate of a "unitary" standard envisioned by *Swann* had been met and ordered the district to abandon its busing policies, effectively ending its quota programs.[537] The ruling was upheld at the appellate level and the Supreme Court declined to hear the case. Once again, neighborhood zoning reared its ugly head and *de facto* segregation gripped the Charlotte-Mecklenburg school district—a seizure which persists. Charlotte had once stood as a model for desegregation that school systems in the country sought to emulate. But the once educationally progressive city today emulates the retrograde policies displayed in many parts of the country by eschewing racial equality in its public school system.

To many Americans, the election of an African American president signified the crowning achievement of a racially progressive society. This, along with the media reign of Oprah Winfrey and the ubiquity of African American stars in movies, music, and television represents the change President Obama evoked to galvanize the nation in 2008 and its ancestral dream preached by Dr. King. But if this American dream is realized, why are modern educational policies in many ways less progressive than those of the late 1950s and early '60s, when lynchings were still transpiring in the South and blacks had yet to obtain universal suffrage? Is it perhaps that our colorblindness has duped us into seeing egalitarianism that is nothing more than an apparition? Is it that this fake egalitarianism serves as a convenient enabler for those who desire a reversion to the old days? Or is there genuine confusion on the part of citizens who believe that the imaginary creation of "unitary" education systems obviates the necessity of busing and other measures?

Let us not for a second fool ourselves into thinking that the policymakers reverting school districts to the clime of pre-Civil Rights America do not know what they do. Busing's purpose—to integrate schools that would otherwise be as segregated as America's neighborhoods—is apparent. Considering that incidences of housing discrimination have not declined in recent decades, it is clear that supplanting busing policies with neighborhood zoning policies will only lead to the resegregation of our public schools. We continue to pat ourselves on the back for the *Brown* decision. But as a nation, we have not only neglected *Brown* but abraded its promise, thanks to *Board of Education of Oklahoma City Public Schools v. Dowell, Milliken v. Bradley, Parents Involved v. Seattle, Meredith v. Jefferson Country Board of Education*, and the overturning of *Swann v. Charlotte-Mecklenburg*.

Although the judiciary handed down rulings forcing school districts in the United States to integrate, it did little to enforce these rulings. Their rulings only tentatively addressed issues of establishing standards for integration, failing to demand that assiduous measures be taken to monitor and ensure integration's realization. In the abovementioned rulings, we see justices insufficiently establish that a "unitary" standard must be achieved, or that racially homogenous schools should, rather than must, be monitored, and, like with regard to affirmative action, that exploding timetables should be set for integrative policies.

What sense does it make to institute a policy for a specific result—especially when the policy is the only viable means of bringing about and maintaining that intended result—only to rescind that policy to allow for a reversal toward the preceding and undesirable circumstance? One constructs a dam to halt the flow of water in a specific direction. Is it rational or reasonable for one to proclaim, "Now, remove the dam; the water is miraculously able to withhold itself from flowing in the protected direction without the dam's assistance"? If the proper estuaries, dikes, and canals are formed to obviate the dam's purpose, perhaps *then* the dam can be removed. If the alternate channels sufficiently divert the water's path, it stands to reason that the dam is nothing more than an unnecessary object. But if no such diversions exist, that dam is still very much necessary to prevent the water from flowing in the direction from which it must be kept.

When Judge Bohanon ruled that "unitary" standards had been met and that busing was no longer necessary in spite of evidence contradicting this supposition, he removed the precious dam that *Swann* erected decades earlier. Hope flew away as flowed the water. Despite the fact that no alternate avenues were ever carved to divert the water (housing discrimination failed to improve even minimally) and despite the continued presence of rushing, ominous waters (racial segregation still inundated Oklahoma Schools), it was somehow reasoned that the dam was obviated. Already seeping and punctured, holed by poor construction, once removed the waters gushed.

Last in Line: An American Destiny Deferred

It was a testament either to the shortsightedness of the Court's justices or their desire to refrain from "pushing too hard" for integration, but its rulings failed to *require* that such policies be enforced until actual, legitimate equalizing mechanisms (such as legislative and executive measures combating housing discrimination) existed to obviate their necessity. Instead, the rulings conferred power upon states and individual school districts, allowing them to craft their own rules on what constituted "unitary" and what did not. America has seen school districts—with the blessing of recent Supreme Court rulings—abuse this power, sending her schools up the creek without a paddle to the destination of total segregation. In the integration battle, the federal government failed to transcend the improvidence and ignorance of its judicial branch. With education systems largely left in state hands (despite the establishment of the Department of Education in the late 1970s), the federal government was unable to enforce the proper, salutary execution integration policies required.

America may seem more integrated today. In the 1950s, racial stratification was much more evident. Today, blacks are present in media, public facilities, white-collar professions, and other areas that seem to indicate integration's victory. Still, that same media depicts African Americans with undue negativity, those same public facilities deny African Americans who seek employment and service in them, and (contrary to the misguided belief that they open their doors to blacks before anyone else) those white-collar professions commonly reject qualified African Americans on the basis on race. Just as it is with these supposed measures of social progress, America's idea of an achieved racially progressive education system is bogus. For once, we must remove our shattered spectacles to analyze what's really going on around us. America is in dire need of a national epiphany—that of the reflection of betrayal which is none other than our own face. Only this will compel us to reaffirm sacred vows of freedom.

Integration is necessary not only for the sake of ensuring that black, Hispanic, and other minority children have access to quality educational resources, but also for its power to teach children of different races the importance of racial diversity as well as the humanity and equality of students who come from different racial backgrounds. We cannot kid ourselves about our kids—racist attitudes are often born in parenting. Media and society undoubtedly foster the development of racist attitudes, but there is no better classroom for instruction on racism than the home environment. When children who grow up in such environments come to school to learn with no one different from them, bad home training simmers.

Mommy and Daddy's offhand remark about black people's stupidity is one thing. But if the child has no belying examples to prove *their* stupidity, Mommy and Daddy's racist opinion will implant deeply into their consciousness. These formed prejudices will prove hard to shake—even when children encounter "exceptional" blacks. When students learn in racially isolated environments and are kept from each other's presence, they are unable to form personal understandings of members of other races and ethnic groups. The stereotypes that they are taught at home, while watching television, or through limited interactions with people of other colors have a profound impact on their psyches and become especially potent when they lack prolonged, frequent interaction with members of other races. Without integration, mutual ignorance will persist between the races, fueling racial prejudice.

Chapter 5: The Miseducation of the...African American?

Beyond fostering understanding, racial integration must be relentlessly promoted and protected for its power to combat institutional racism. This statement—that desegregation would effectively undermine the phenomenon responsible for resegregation—may merit an arched eyebrow. But it is not self-evident; it asserts in clear and concise fashion that true and harmonious racial integration in schools will serve to combat institutional racism in society as a whole. The solution is twofold. On one hand, if schools are successfully integrated—not just demographically, but also with regard to the equitable treatment of students regardless of race—then young African Americans allowed to fall by the wayside in the modern biased education system will be recognized as the promising young talents that they are. They will endeavor to fulfill the expectations held of them. On the other hand, if white children and teenagers attend schools in which they are not—by no fault of their own—pedestaled on the backs of black and Hispanic classmates sentenced to detention and lower-level class, they will equate them as true brothers and sisters rather than computing that there are, at best, occasional positive outliers from an otherwise negative set. It should not be doubted that being reared in a system in which whites appear to perform at a higher level than blacks results in the adoption of racist attitudes which are carried outside the school double doors and beyond the graduation stage, into life where blacks are thought to characterize everything backward and wrong about humanity.

The Achievement Gap

Resegregation and funding disparities are products of misguided public policy. But what about the performance gap between African American and white students? Is this really directly attributable to the persistence of institutionally racist policies, or is it a cultural flaw that we should simply expect black students and families to "get over" (both literally and metaphorically)? Think tanks such as the Heritage Foundation have published dubious studies arguing the nonexistence of the relationship between the availability of funding for public schools and student achievement.[538] But could it really be the case that minority children learning in schools lacking in proper upkeep, competent teachers, strong curricula, and appropriate resources are themselves fully responsible for their substandard academic performance?

The education achievement gap is notoriously present at every level. African Americans fall behind in virtually every category—GPAs,[539] high school graduation rates,[540] SAT scores,[541] matriculation to colleges and universities,[542] and beyond. Statistics even show that poor whites outperform wealthy blacks on the SAT.[543] What's not agreed upon is the cause for such statistical disparities. Some, in the spirit of *The Bell Curve*, attribute agency to African Americans for their supposedly intrinsic dispositions toward misbehavior,[544] academic negligence,[545] and intellectual ineptitude.[546] Others attribute the problems that African American students face in the classroom to systemic issues—poorer funding,[547] less educational resources,[548] and influences of racial discrimination in the classroom. When one observes schools such as those in South Carolina's Corridor of Shame or the Charlotte-Mecklenburg school district today, it is easy to understand how funding and resources can play roles in perpetuating the education gap. But the idea that the achievement gap is carved out by racial discrimination is neither universally understood nor collectively agreed with. What's at the bottom of this seemingly inexplicable void between black and white students?

Last in Line: An American Destiny Deferred

In *The Black-White Achievement Gap*, former U.S. secretary of education Rod Paige and former Norfolk State University dean Elaine Witty establish the case for the existence of the education gap and document its potential causes. The achievement gap is documented in classes at all levels of K-12 education.[549] The gap begins as a narrow space and expands faster than light, practically turning into a supermassive black hole as black and white students approach college age.[550] In statistical analyses of reading and writing aptitude, black and white children are nearly equal at the point of school entry.[551] In mathematics the gap is slightly larger, but still almost negligible. But by the time white and black students reach the fifth grade, achievement gaps have expanded substantially. By the end of middle school, the gap becomes astronomical.

On a scale of 0 to 500 measured over the course of a decade, it was found that white eighth-graders' mean reading scores stood at 272 points while those of their black counterparts stood at an average of just 245 points.[552] Considering this vast expanse, it's no wonder that African American high school students fall behind in performance on standardized college-entrance tests such as the SAT. This pattern is noticeable from the inception of black and white children's academic careers and endures all the way through high school. It culminates in the vast disparity between white and black adults earning college degrees, with just 19 percent of African Americans between the ages of 25 and 29 possessing one[553] compared to approximately 36 percent of whites.[554] One has to go to 1971 to find the last year the white degree rate was less than the African American degree rate in 2007.[555] Not surprisingly, in that year just over 5 percent of African Americans held college degrees.[556]

These facts in and of themselves do nothing to establish specific causes for the existence of the vast achievement gap. Sure—black kids lag behind white kids all throughout their educational careers. But by itself, the gap doesn't say anything for the existence of racial discrimination in education. The achievement gap could very well be the result of a pervasive attitude of disregard for education in the black community, a theory central to the conservative sociopathological argument. If parents aren't teaching their kids academic basics before school entry, encouraging good study habits, and often aren't even around, and if peers discourage and scorn ideas and instances of educational achievement, deriding such accomplishments as "acting white," then shouldn't we expect such a gap to exist? Furthermore, given the statistical analyses of books such as *The Bell Curve*, it stands to reason that such an achievement gap is, at least to some extent, natural—right?

The education achievement gap is part of a constellation of inequality—accompanied by justice, employment, and other dwarves—that has never ceased to exist in the United States. Few would seek to refute the pre-*Brown* existence of an achievement gap. Also, few would argue that such an achievement gap, given the gross and conspicuous inequity of the time, was either fair or exclusively attributable to flaws of the African American community. But today—in our colorblind society—we cross out racism in red ink, convincing ourselves that other factors are responsible for classroom disparity. The authors of *The Black-White Achievement Gap* possess some grasp of the magnitude of racial disparity in education, but, like many Americans, fail to understand the role that explicit racial prejudice plays in lowering the ceilings of African American and other minority children.

Paige and Witty analyze "socioeconomic disparity,"[557] "sociopathological culture,"[558] "genetics,"[559] "black identity,"[560] and "educational deprivation"[561] as causes of the disparities between the races. But they either fail or neglect to adequately mention outright racial prejudice as a significant factor in the achievement gap. As was mentioned earlier in the chapter, there are several studies documenting the phenomenon of educational racism against America's black students. In terms of disciplining, grading, tracking for both AP/Honors courses and remedial and special education, and other measures, it has been found that even when white children and black children are characteristically similar, black children are much likelier to find themselves on the short end of the stick while their white peers are placed into situations conducive to success.

As provincial as their argument is, Paige and Witty's claims should not be dismissed out of hand. They cogently touch on the strong correlation between not just race and educational achievement, but also between class and educational achievement. The persisting socioeconomic inequities of American society certainly seem to influence student achievement. Students who come from less-educated households will be both less likely to afford and less likely to value tutors, prep courses, and other achievement aids that more affluent families both value and afford. The authors seem somewhat partial toward the sociopathological argument wildly popular among conservatives, but "refute [it] as a comprehensive explanation for the black-white achievement gap."[562]

Paige and Witty summarize the crux of this conservative argument, which says, "African Americans should stop whining and complaining and pull themselves up by their own bootstraps."[563] Rejecting this, they mention studies demonstrating "that teacher expectations have powerful influence on student learning"[564] while also pointing to the rare stars shooting from a dark milieu as proof that gases of pathology may be holding back a bigger bang. Paige and Witty dismiss the genetics argument (a view staunchly supported by the authors of *The Bell Curve*). The authors support the idea that a prevailing element of black culture adopts an "oppositional" identity that repudiates traits of success, associating them with whiteness.[565] Finally, they cite the "educational deprivation" argument, which holds that the education system fails to put forth sufficient efforts to target and address the problems of low-income, predominantly black communities.

Save for the genetics argument (which both authors disagree with), the arguments that Secretary Paige and Dean Witty discuss bear critical insights and are, in some ways, legitimate. The problem is that these arguments each fail to grasp the magnitude of institutional racism in contemporary education. Beyond neglecting the role of widespread personal (and therefore altogether systemic) prejudices in perpetuating the achievement gap, they fail to realize that all of these aforementioned factors are *themselves* to a tremendous extent fueled by institutional racism. Socioeconomic disparity is generated by, among other things, job discrimination, which precludes even qualified African Americans from obtaining the sort of employment better enabling them to foster home environments conducive to their children's success.

The sociopathological culture that conservatives so often speak of is born from a system in which, among other things, black families are deprived of constituent parents and children, both of whom the justice system deem unworthy of equitable judgment. Certainly, the fact that African Americans are in so many ways blocked from adopting the traits, identifiers, and possessions erroneously associated with whiteness contributes to the creation of this oppositional, backward, sociopathological black identity (the subject of a later chapter). And when we observe the gross inequality of schools in predominantly black neighborhoods versus those in whiter areas, we can look at the phenomenon of resegregation happening today as precipitously as ever and annotate our notes with a cynical "DUH."

It is relieving that Secretary Paige and Dean Witty recognize that policy plays a role in creating the educational gap and can therefore effectuate solutions. This is more than can be said for colorblind Americans who presume that America's school system serves as a consummate example of the efficiency of integration policies and that, incidentally, the goals set forth by *Brown* have been achieved. But, like many policymakers, Paige and Witty are looking in the wrong places. Each of the dilemmas contained in the arguments enumerated in *The Black-White Achievement Gap* is largely a product of institutional racism. It says a lot for the invisibility of institutional racism in American society that we overlook not only its role in the perpetuation of the educational achievement gap, but also its role in the perpetuation of the rationales that we establish as causes for this universal void. Until we can address institutional racism head-on both in society at large and inside America's classrooms and school halls, the racial educational achievement gap will live on in an infamy attributed to its victims.

Though Paige and Witty dismiss its merits, the argument of a genetic role in the achievement gap is not to be overlooked. Opponents of educational equity point to the fact that poor whites outscore rich blacks on the SAT as undeniable proof that the achievement gap's blueprint lies in kinky strands. College Board data does indeed show that in 2008, white test takers with family incomes between $20 and $40 thousand outscored black test takers with family incomes above $200,000.[566] The details seem damning. They are—for arguments holding race prejudice as anything but a predominant factor in engendering disparity. The trappings of elite status—posh prep or affluent public schools, tutors, and test prep courses—open doors for white students, but for all their might *still* fail to unfasten the Gordian knot racial bias ties around the double door handles at the detection of black footsteps.

It has been established that black students get suspended and expelled at disproportionate rates, often for offenses that merit mediation or even medication for white students.[567] What may seem more surprising is that schools in affluent areas suspend and expel black students at the *highest* rates.[568] A study from Penn State University assessed over 60,000 schools in 6,000 districts and found that school districts in socioeconomically advantaged locales tended to favor policies that gave schools greater latitude over their own discipline policies. In disadvantaged areas, school boards tend to hold the power, typically setting uniform policies that are followed across schools with varying demographic constitutions.

The study found that race bias in discipline was far more prevalent in advantaged areas, in which school administrators were empowered to suspend or expel students at their own discretion. In these schools, the same offenses schools felt merited mental health treatment for white students were met with suspensions and expulsions for black students. We have to remember that gratuitous suspensions and expulsions are the *extremes* of racial abuse in school discipline. If wealthy black students' money can't purchase manumission from the extremes, what toils do black students experience in grading, social experience, and, most importantly, *learning*? The horrors are untold yet ringing. Unlike dusky, despised dirt barred from commencement, segregated destiny matriculates into fine mortar ground from vast endowments.

Chapter 5: The Miseducation of the...African American?

Studies find that whites raised in mires of poverty are much less likely to wind up incarcerated than blacks suffering a soiled strain of "affluenza."[569] Although one would never have guessed it, class-not-race liberals and their *Bell Curve*-thumping, human biodiversity-touting far-right adversaries have one thing in common: the expectation that money *should* enable African Americans to catapult ostensible barriers of racial discrimination. That very ideology—which ignores the fact that wealthy black students are subjected to substandard treatment that not even the poorest whites experience—reinforces those barriers, scaling them ever higher with each iteration. Class correlation with black academic performance holds mostly as an in-group phenomenon. And rightly so, as antiblack racial bias knows no class bounds. African American students and families—and their DNA—are not at fault. Rampant biases of teachers and administrators—who don't require copies of students' parents' 1040 forms to make destructive, life-altering decisions—are.

But the penchant for falsification persists. In recent decades, notoriously inaccurate and skewed scientific research has been produced arguing that African Americans' problems are rooted in inferior DNA. The purveyors and faithful consumers of this research argue that phenomena of familial dysfunction, unemployment, and sociopathological black identity all stem from African Americans being innately less intelligent and mannered than other races. Although a majority of today's scientists have moved to reject such studies, enough still embrace the data to make such claims influential in modern public policy.

Black Incapability

The idea that blacks are intellectually deficient long precedes the publication of recent scientific studies that purport to corroborate the existence of an intellectually defined racial hierarchy. Within the United States, slaves imported from Africa were stereotyped as dumb and docile, somehow lacking the intellectual abilities whites and other races possessed. These stereotypes persisted despite the reality that many slaves were selected for skills in metalsmithing,[570] agriculture,[571] and other trades. President Lincoln himself—the great emancipator of America's slaves and salvager of the Union—did not consider the constitutional phrase mentioning the equality of all men to indicate that all races were intellectual equals. Lincoln said, "[The Founding Fathers] did not mean to say all men were equal in color, size, *intellect*, moral development or social capacity." (Emphasis added.)[572]

It is paradoxical that laws had to be enacted to force blacks to abstain from the educational activities they were incapable of undertaking.[573] South Carolina's contemporarily retrograde education policy (which is perhaps a matter of "heritage not hate") is one example of the endurance of an ardent pre-colonial tradition of proscribing African American education. On September 9, 1739, an allegedly Congolese-born slave named Cato led 20 armed and furious slaves in the infamous Stono Rebellion.[574] The rebel party swelled and before the carnage ceased 25 whites lay dead. The act required no small degree of organization—and, in turn, no mere semblance of intelligence—to carry out. In reaction to this—and the fact that Cato was better able to coordinate his revolt because of his literacy and multilingual abilities—slaves in South Carolina were prohibited from writing.[575]

111

But, of course, some may argue that Cato and his volunteers were intellectual outliers. Black intellectual inferiority was taken for granted by pre-Civil Rights America, but post-racial America has allegedly produced supporting evidence by way of a policy experiment. The policies on our law books no longer proscribe blacks from reading and writing. Some would even argue that African Americans today are unfairly advantaged in such pursuits (e.g., Abigail Fisher). But for some reason, African Americans are stereotyped as not possessing the zeal for education that people of other ethnicities often have. Throughout the 20th century, researchers argued the case of intrinsic black intellectual ineptitude through ideas of eugenics,[576] craniometry,[577] and other scientifically racist disciplines.[578] Although such arguments pervaded much of early 20th century social and academic discourse, it was not until the 1990s that a most notorious research piece purported to forever close the book on black biological inferiority.

The groundbreaking study solidifying the inferiority of the black mind—*The Bell Curve*—was published in 1994. Richard Herrnstein and Charles Murray provided the basis for the reincarnation of scientific racism in turn of the millennium America. In it, Herrnstein and Murray assert that the evolution of different peoples in different geographic environments resulted not only in the development of idiosyncratic phenotypic traits, but also in vast genotypic separations between groups. This genotypic divergence entailed intellectual dimorphism, black Africans being the jestered, weaker hemisphere. Thus, differences in intelligence were attributable to this evolutionary genotypic differentiation.[579] *The Bell Curve* sparked significant controversy from day one of its publication, evidenced in the ensuing deluge of books published defending, qualifying, and refuting its arguments and the studies and research cited therein.

Interestingly, Herrnstein and Murray advocate for the elimination of welfare and affirmative action programs[580] and call for a drastic reduction in the size of immigration quotas.[581] In the vein of Margaret Sanger, the eugenicist founder of Planned Parenthood, Herrnstein and Murray assert that lower IQ populations ought to be discouraged and even prevented from reproducing.[582] Rather than encouraging poor, disadvantaged, underprivileged women—who, for the most part, happen to be black and Hispanic—to reproduce in such high numbers, the authors argue that wealthier, advantaged, privileged women—who, coincidentally, are almost exclusively white—should instead be actively encouraged by government policies to reproduce in abundance.

Strangely, Herrnstein and Murray seem oblivious to the fact that government policies actually allow for high black mortality. Contrary to their unsubstantiated claims, there are no conspiratorial government policies advocating the proliferation of black and Hispanic peoples in the United States. Rather, by sustaining high mortality rates among minority groups, government policies have stymied the populations of these ethnic groups that would otherwise be more robust.

A year following the publication of *The Bell Curve*, J. Philippe Rushton published the as dubious *Race, Evolution, and Behavior*. Rushton took the arguments of race and IQ in *The Bell Curve* a step further, arguing that the alleged intellectual incapacity of African Americans (evidenced in their supposedly smaller brain sizes[583]) correlates with their being both more aggressive[584] and highly sexed (both in terms of libido and "endowment").[585] Rushton also differentiated the races on the basis of factors of "reproductive potency,"[586] "complex social organization,"[587] "family stability,"[588] and "rule-following."[589] Conveniently, East Asians represent the advanced end of the spectrum, being more sexually reserved, better behaved, less inclined toward criminality, and more intelligent.

Blacks represent the converse end, displaying natural and unbridled lechery, rambunctiousness, criminal behavior, and, of course, a total absence of intellectual aptitude. Conveniently, white people were Goldilocks' middling bowl of porridge—"just right"—moderately intelligent, moderately aggressive, and moderately sexual. Rushton maintained that commendable traits such as industriousness and rule-following are also severely lacking in African Americans as a result of their DNA. Such phrenology-like pseudoscience would likely make Adolf Hitler grin with approval. Could it be this simple? Was it *this* scientifically convenient that one entire race of people sat at one genetic extreme, another at the other, and a third so snugly between?

Rushton's work was assailed from all sides upon publication. Outside his small circle of Pioneer Fund-linked colleagues, virtually no scientists found any merit or legitimacy to his research. For one, Rushton collected and aggregated hundreds of studies, many of them dated, without examining the quality of the data.[590] More critically, however, Rushton failed to control for socioeconomic variables in his examination of data,[591] meaning that had such data strictly examined classes rather than races, the statistical disparities would have been much less contrasting if not nonexistent. In many ways, Rushton's work seemed more like a ploy to advance conservative social and economic policies than a sincere, objective effort to contribute to scientific discourse.

Notably, Rushton mailed several tens of thousands of abridged copies of his book—unsolicited—to sociologists, educators, and scientists, many who (perhaps reassuringly) reacted with great revulsion.[592] Arthur Jensen, a colleague of Rushton's, attempted to reproduce his argument, but in his research "could not logically separate out a direct genetic cause for intelligence...from an indirect genetic cause."[593] Rushton furthermore failed to contemplate the existence of the African model minority in the United States—genetically "blacker" than African Americans and both better-educated and higher-earning than both African Americans *and* white Americans—despite the fact that these more "racially pure" African immigrants should, by his methodology, have lower IQs than their racially mixed American cousins.[594]

Following the publication of *The Bell Curve*, both the American Psychological Association and the American Anthropological Association issued statements of opposition. The AAA issued its "Statement on 'Race' and 'Intelligence'," moving to unambiguously reject *The Bell Curve*'s pseudoscience:

> The American Anthropological Association is deeply concerned by recent public discussions, which imply that intelligence is biologically determined by race. Repeatedly challenged by scientists, nevertheless these ideas continue to be advanced. Such discussions distract public and scholarly attention from and diminish support for the collective challenge to ensure equal opportunities for all people, regardless of ethnicity or phenotypic variation...
> The AAA...resolves:
> WHEREAS, all human beings are members of one species, *Homo sapiens,* and
> WHEREAS, differentiating species into biologically defined "races" has proven meaningless and unscientific as a way of explaining variations (whether in intelligence or other traits),

Last in Line: An American Destiny Deferred

THEREFORE, the American Anthropological Association urges the academy, our political leaders, and our communities to affirm without distraction by mistaken claims of racially determined intelligence, the common stake in assuring equal opportunity, in respecting diversity and in securing a harmonious equality of life for all people.[595]

Although it was a gesture both powerful and warranted, the AAA's statement did not dissuade all scientists and social leaders from embracing the 1990s pseudoscientific revival. In 2007, Nobel Prize-winning scientist James D. Watson attested to this, opining of Africa, "I am inherently gloomy about the prospect of Africa...all our social policies are based on the fact that their intelligence is the same as ours...whereas all the testing says not really."[596] Although forced to resign as Chancellor of Cold Spring Harbor Laboratory, Watson's remark once again illustrated the prevalence of such beliefs among the intellectual elite. Watson himself is one of the co-discoverers of DNA. It is terribly ironic that he fails to understand the essence of the very genome which he helped to uncover. But we must keep in mind that discovery is not tantamount to invention.

Much of the research in *The Bell Curve* and *Race, Evolution, and Behavior* was supported and financed by the Pioneer Fund, an organization that openly proclaims its commitment to promoting and advancing scientifically racist causes. One of the Fund's founding members, Wickliffe Preston Draper, declared his intent behind helping to establish the group as wanting to "prove simply that Negroes [are] inferior."[597] Draper both ardently supported segregation in the United States and remained a zealous supporter of Nazi-style eugenics policies years after the Holocaust and World War II ended.[598] Interestingly, another Pioneer Fund founder—also its first president—has an indirect link to James D. Watson. Harry H. Laughlin, an ardent racist and eugenicist,[599] headed the Cold Spring Harbor Laboratory's Eugenics Record Office until a few years before his death in 1943.[600] The Southern Poverty Law Center has listed the Pioneer Fund as a hate group[601]—and rightly so, in light of the preceding information. None of this has stopped the Pioneer Fund-funded *Bell Curve* from becoming a bestseller or being heralded by modern scientists as a necessary treatise documenting the hereditary differences between the races.

Conclusion

While American scientists continue to support scientifically racist agendas, African American and minority children remain ignored in the nation's classrooms, treated not as victims of failed social policies but a scourge by virtue of their genetic kismet. These flawed beliefs continue to influence social policies in the United States and withhold equitable access to education from minority children. It is not merely the idea of black intellectual inferiority that cuts deep welts of corporal punishment into young black backs—it is the ardent hope that so many sick hearts have in the possibility of its *truth*. It is a hope so strong that while America robs millions from emaciated, black inner city and rural education coffers, millions are thrown behind shoddily researched books which distort and misconstrue data to achieve the foregone yet false conclusion that change is not possible. This false hope keeps the dangerous

114

virus of pseudoscience circulating in America's bloodstream, threatening the lives of promising young African Americans and commandeering America's destiny.

⑥
The Plexiglas Ceiling

The "glass ceiling" is perhaps the most discussed material of discrimination in modern American public discourse. This firm, staffed by molecular bonds specializing in corporate defense, shields high rises. It swats bricks of crimson revolution baked-in with memos demanding women's equal qualification merit an equal pay stub. That payment persists in prejudice in spite of women scaling both that high rise and the ivory tower is cause for outcry. Such disparity draws pickets from both women's and civil rights groups. The glass ceiling bears indelible graffiti. The eraser was destined to be the great equalizer for those of different genders and races, but statistics show that in every window of educational attainment—from the high school diploma to the doctorate—low-grade paint discounts human worth, defacing graduation with degrees of unsaturation.

Data from a 2009 study showed that a man with less than a 9th grade education earned $26,789 a year[602] compared to his woman companion who took home about 77 percent of that—just $20,499 a year.[603] At the doctorate level a man earned, on average, $125,393 a year[604] while his opposite-sex colleague earned just $91,733 annually,[605] a staggering 27 percent less. Such data indicates that the glass ceiling doesn't even disappear with one's escalation through higher floors of educational attainment—it rises *high*.

The "glass ceiling" moniker originates from the supposed invisibility of gender pay disparity. The name is fitting in this regard. But it is also appropriate because it signals that the ceiling can be broken. If legislators had the wherewithal to hurl a nicely sized brick through the proverbial ceiling, the income gap between men and women would disappear. Nonetheless, opponents argue that it is neither the right nor responsibility of government to dictate what salaries business enterprises in the private sector offer. They vociferously argue that it is up to the private sector to adopt responsible, gender-equitable policies.

When the sociological concept of the glass ceiling was first documented and explored in earnest in the 1970s, it was viewed through the lens of gender discrimination. Realizing the shortsightedness of this focus, social scientists expanded the scope to include the income plight of minorities. Regardless, minorities have remained on the periphery of income disparity discourse in the United States. This effective exclusion of minorities from the discussion of America's problematic and persisting glass ceiling has necessitated the conceptualization of a different yet congruent phenomenon—one we can perhaps christen a "Plexiglas ceiling."

This too is an apt moniker. Unlike glass, Plexiglas is difficult to break. A simple brick would not suffice for its destruction. Should you choose to hurl a brick at a panel of Plexiglas be certain to duck, as it might mount a vengeful deflection. Plexiglas is strong. Plexiglas is so composed, as a matter of fact, that the most effective way to rattle it is with an electrical saw.

The income gap between men and women in the workplace is indeed large, but the wealth gap between minorities and whites is vaster. That whites control over 90 percent of America's wealth is mind-boggling.[606] It is shocking that only 10 percent of America's wealth circulates among blacks, Asians, Hispanics, and other, less populous ethnic groups in the United States, despite comprising nearly 40 percent of the country. Within the African American community, the panes are worse—shot-out and shattered in dereliction's spirit.

Some of the factors characterizing modern racial income inequality in the United States have already been discussed in this book. Among other things, the topic of job discrimination (and incidentally high unemployment rates) has been discussed in some detail. The problem's sheer magnitude has been demonstrated by research showing that black men are twice as likely as white men to be out of work and that white families possess as much as 16 times the wealth of black families. Income inequality's history was expounded upon in considerable detail in earlier chapters, disparity which was at its worst when blacks were income for white Americans. But one of the most persisting and troubling phenomena of the racial hierarchy in the United States today pertains to the expanding wealth gap between whites and African Americans, a gap that continues to widen despite America's alleged progress.

The Ever-expanding Wealth Gap

It was major cause for concern that during a stubborn and unyielding recession, American CEOs collected higher bonuses than ever before,[607] using added wealth for pocket alterations rather than tailoring tattered fabric of jobs and public welfare. It was the American public's frustration with such mindless displays of indulgence that gave birth to Occupy Wall Street in 2011. Few outside the 1 percent would argue that Occupy is completely unwarranted, somehow not justified in spite of the increasingly desperate economic conditions of the United States. But, although the Occupy movement rendered emaciated rage in 99 percenters railing against the 1 percent's widening waistline, little was said of the enduring wealth gap between white and black Americans. Occupy ignored race, shifting class to center stage. In this, the anti-establishment Occupy proved its commitment to a brand of left-wing American politics that holds dear an exclusionary mantra of "class not race," later echoed by the far-left presidential campaign of self-avowed socialist Bernie Sanders in 2016.

African Americans were hit harder than anyone else by the 2008 subprime mortgage crisis, being disproportionately targeted by predatory lenders and, therefore, being disproportionate victims of foreclosures.[608] African Americans are also hit the hardest when job scarcity strikes. Although the national unemployment rate was at 5 percent at the end of 2015,[609] the black unemployment rate remained almost double that figure. With a rate of 15.8 percent in December 2011,[610] black unemployment hadn't been so high since Ronald Reagan's presidency.[611] Even when the economy creates jobs, African Americans often fail to see windfalls. In December 2011 alone, the economy created over 200,000 jobs.[612] African Americans did not see a single gain in measures of net employment.

The Occupy Wall Street movement was, for many Americans, a rare breath of cool, clean, unpolluted air. Unlike anything else in recent history, the movement galvanized young people to demand justice and change from the powers that be. That so many young people realize the criticality of closing the ever-widening income gap should be reassuring. But Occupy has thus far been both too big and small. Occupy's masses lacked the framework of organization and transcendent, raw materials of intersectionality. It is telling that the continued economic weakness of the black community occasions nothing remotely close to the scale of Occupy from the American left. Given the continued indigence and economic deprivation of the African American community, such a movement would only be warranted in light of Occupy. Perhaps like much of America, proponents of Occupy regard the black community's economic condition as a normal product of black sociopathology. Like much of America, perhaps some Occupy protesters fail to even realize that a racial wealth gap exists. In keeping with the traditions of contemporary colorblind American society, Americans across the political spectrum rage in debate over class, leaving race by the wayside and, with that, the opportunity for African American and minority communities to emerge from their states of economic enervation.

If America were truly progressing toward a state of racial equity, then a decreasing income gap would be expected. With the increased presence of African Americans in white-collar professions[613] (and, more specifically, a higher percentage[614]), it stands to reason that gaps between white and black structures are closing. But statistics do not portend a merger. Rather than shrinking, the expanse of the alley dividing white and African American lifestyles has quadrupled since the 1980s.[615] This despite the increase in the number of African American doctors, professors, engineers, etc., all who take home larger salaries than those earned in the menial and factorial jobs to which blacks were once confined.[616] How could this be?

In *Created Unequal: The Crisis in American Pay*, James K. Galbraith, a professor at both the University of Texas at Austin's Lyndon B. Johnson School of Public Affairs and its Department of Government, explains why the wealth gap continues to expand despite the increased presence of African Americans in white-collar positions:

> The average wage of African Americans can still fall relative to that of the white population even while black representation in higher professions improves. This can happen because rising inequality generally drives down the relative wage of the majority of African American workers, who remain in occupations for whom affirmative action provides no meaningful relief or in industries that are losing ground on domestic and international markets...

> The major changes in the manufacturing wages structure since 1970 have been catastrophic for high school-educated male workers, a category covering a large part of the African American labor force. The decline in the relative wages of this large-group and its black members swamped the effect of increasing average education in the African American population.[617]

As was mentioned in chapter 4, affirmative action programs have thus far failed to help African Americans, as a group, achieve sufficient improvement in terms of pay. High unemployment, as well as regressive fiscal policies that have lowered the minimum wage (when adjusted for inflation and worker productivity),[618] allow for income disparity to persist. By 1986, the average wage had 14 percent less purchasing power than it did in 1973.[619]

119

Last in Line: An American Destiny Deferred

The polarization of wages coincided with this, with those in the basement making even less than before and those peering from high places accruing monetary benefit from that altitude. As Professor Galbraith writes, affirmative action policies aren't expansive enough to effectively mitigate problems like falling wages. Although affirmative action hiring practices are common with regard to white-collar professions and government jobs, in smaller-earning occupations in which job discrimination has been less marked, affirmative action policies were not seen as a necessary security system for minorities.[620]

Now that such jobs, which a high percentage of the black workforce filled, are being outsourced[621] and erased[622] on a vast scale and wages for the remainder are declining sharply, we are seeing a corresponding steep increase in the white-to-black income ratio. An example of this phenomenon took place in the Great Lakes cities in the early 1980s, when over a fifth of African American men in the durable goods industry lost their jobs due to restructuring and deindustrialization.[623] Even those who realize the importance of affirmative action programs may fail to realize that their efficacy is limited if we fail to install measures that will secure and ensure jobs and increases in earnings for African Americans occupying non-white-collar jobs not afforded affirmative action security. Additionally, without policies that retain these jobs in communities where African Americans can benefit from them, the Plexiglas ceiling will remain unbroken, even unscathed.

None of this is to say that affirmative action has not benefited African Americans. Without it, we would see much worse than a mere quadrupling of the white-black income gap. But affirmative action programs, as they exist now, cannot by themselves close the expanse. Furthermore, the displacement of non-white-collar, medium-wage jobs not only contributes to the expansion of the income gap between whites and blacks—it brings about stratification of African American socioeconomic classes. The unilaterality of affirmative action policies allows for the creation of a small but rich black elite standing above a populous, black field of poverty.

Stratification necessitates the enactment of measures that will safeguard the economic interests of lower-earning black classes. Civil rights policies are naked gold; the absence of securing alloy has compromised the safety of classes wielding the pick yet not the yield of the pan. Their pains and labors have honored Spartan tradition, forgoing pangs and thirst to strike blood sacrifice. Helot duty will yield Spartan or Athenian fate; it is up to Occupy to mobilize on behalf of toils and ensure a share of victory's spoils.

Although Occupy lacks an outline for getting us to conquest's finish line, it provides the right starting point for confronting the white-black income gap. The racial income gap is best understood if we first evaluate the general income gap and its origins. Tracing it to turn of the century America reveals a country transformed by the Industrial Revolution. Magnates like the Scottish-born Andrew Carnegie and native son John D. Rockefeller (often considered the richest man in human history[624]) represented extreme wealth while the millions conscripted to drudge for almost nothing represented the spectrum's indigent end. We are taught to believe that it was in this era, and only this era, that extreme wealth inequality existed in America. As we know today, nothing could be further from the truth.

Chapter 6: The Plexiglas Ceiling

In 1915, the "1 percent" possessed anywhere between 15 to 18 percent of income generated in the United States.[625] This sort of data had never existed prior to the publication of Willford I. King's unprecedented economic treatise *The Wealth and Income of the People of the United States*. King's research revealed the gross income disparity that resulted from the Industrial Revolution's economic boom and demonstrated the necessity of instituting measures to combat its widening. Both the income tax as we know it today[626] and the estate tax[627] (signed into law by President Theodore Roosevelt) were introduced as measures to combat the unbridled growth of the wealth gap during this era. Such measures largely stabilized the wealth gap's growth. Although the gap was at its worst during the Great Depression, following WWII income disparity both declined and stabilized thanks in part to the assistance of the G.I. Bill and other far-reaching government social programs. But beginning in the 1970s, progress halted and the gap expanded once again.[628]

A century following the publication of King's groundbreaking work, income disparity is steeper than ever. The 1 percent take home a staggering 24 percent of the nation's income today.[629] That's *one percent* of Americans taking home *a quarter* of wealth generated nationally. America's GDP increased from $1.038 trillion[630] to $17.426 trillion[631] between 1970 and 2014. But proportionally, those outside the 1 percent benefited minimally from that increase.[632] Between 1980 and 2005, around four-fifths of the nation's income increase went to one-hundredth of the country.[633] Such numbers demonstrate just how bad the gap is for everyone, regardless of race. Still, this general income gap contrasts with the less salient white-black income gap, especially when examining statistics pertaining to the relationship between race and social mobility.

The stark differences in the degrees of social mobility afforded to blacks and whites illustrates the industrial-strength quality of the Plexiglas ceiling. Social mobility is supposed to be the chief and distinguishing characteristic of America. It is the trait directly born of our democratic tradition, one that separated us from stratified, feudalist Europe as well as the rest of the known world and which compelled so many to hail from those realms. It should be obvious that social mobility, even as an idea, has applied only to white people for most of America's history. But in colorblind America, most of us take it for granted that the concept applies to all. Even from a "mainstream" standpoint, American upward mobility has today been on a downward slope, with the United States falling behind virtually all of Europe[634] as well as much of Latin America in its measures.[635]

Despite all of this, Americans still attest strong faith in the idea of social mobility. In a survey of nationals of several countries, Americans were the most likely to affirm the statement that people with skill and intelligence are fairly rewarded.[636] Although it should go without saying that such a statement was not applicable to African Americans in the 19th and early-to-mid 20th centuries, our colorblind affliction renders us unable to realize that today the social immobility of African Americans is as rigid as ever. Seventy-five percent of African American families experience transgenerational poverty, compared to just 44 percent of white families.[637] On the other end of the spectrum, the statistical disparity is just as wide, with 55 percent of whites

121

born wealthy maintaining that status as adults compared with just 37 percent of blacks.[638] It's a harrowing reality. Not only are blacks less likely to be upwardly mobile—they are more likely to be *downwardly* mobile than their white American counterparts. It's a sort of social mobility, but not what we had in mind.

After first becoming aware of such information, many of the colorblind manage only head scratches and expressions of puzzlement. Quizzical reactions are quickly assuaged by reassuring reminders of black sociopathology and other delusional minimizations. But not everyone dismisses the reality of racial discrimination. Social scientists, to some extent, do acknowledge racism's role. Given the prevalence of predatory lending practices during the subprime mortgage crisis in which African Americans were targeted for bad and unsustainable mortgages, it is hard to dismiss. But pervasive minimization is a component of the incredible, durable, opaque ceiling. If we were to reach out, however, we would discover its tangibility. It is in front of us, apparent in the everyday lives of African Americans who can't hope for same promotion that their coworkers realistically aspire to, the black family that must foreclose on their home because their skin marked them docile and vulnerable targets, and the young African American male who can't even peer into the job market because a misdemeanor conviction for possession of a minute amount of marijuana occupies the pane of his destiny.

The Wealth Gap's Descent

It is alleged that 40 acres and a mule were promised to American slaves upon their emancipation. Some dismiss this anecdote as legend, but its historicity is not to be doubted. General William Tecumseh Sherman issued his Special Field Orders, No. 15 which delineated a plan for the transfer of seized Confederate lands to former slaves. Forty acres, the size of a typical family plot—and a mule—were considered a sufficient start enabling slaves to generate their own sustenance and wealth.[639] Although it is often said that African Americans have yet to receive their proverbial "40 acres," many African Americans in Georgia and South Carolina did actually come to occupy some of over 400,000 acres of lands formerly belonging to wealthy Confederate planters.[640] However, Lincoln's successor, President Andrew Johnson—a noted Southerner sympathizer—quickly moved to repeal Sherman's order, leaving former slaves once again unpropertied.[641]

It should go without saying that a racial wealth gap existed in the immediate aftermath of the Civil War. The former assets of whites had no assets to their names, and even their freeborn counterparts possessed little in the way of business, land, and capital. Although the Freedmen's Bureau was established to facilitate the adjustment of slaves to emancipated life,[642] little was done to assist African Americans in setting themselves afoot economically.[643] Soon, sharecropping—"slavery by another name"—emerged, severely restricting occupational opportunities for blacks in the South.[644] Elsewhere in the United States, African Americans found themselves in fierce competition with virulently racist Polish, Irish, Italian, and other European immigrants who had appropriated the American doctrine of antiblack prejudice to facilitate their climb up the American ethnic social ladder.[645]

This phenomenon of opportunity and property deprivation has permeated through eras of American history to present, where blacks are still obstructed by business and government from obtaining their modern equivalent of 40 acres and a mule, afforded in the cornerstone of an often more modest, sometimes as rustic expanse—homeownership.

Predatory Mortgage Lending

Homeownership is the quintessential component of the American dream; it is also burrowed beneath vast barriers to entry. Owning a home requires decent credit, a well-paying job, and the fulfillment of other measures of social and economic sufficiency. Although black homeownership has increased substantially since the end of the Civil Rights Movement, it still significantly lags behind that of whites.[646] Income disparity between whites and blacks gives one example of why this is the case. But beyond the African American community's lack of purchasing power, is there perhaps a deeper cause for low homeownership rates that pertains to the practices of banks, realtors, and the other agents bonding the gates denying black dreams entry? The Plexiglas ceiling doesn't limit its obstruction to the efforts of blacks to take home cash earnings equal to whites. It precludes them from being able to take *home*. A vigilante detail guards the safe holding property and assets representative of wealth, the key example being the key itself. During the era in which many white Americans staked claims in middle class residential areas once off-limits to nonwhites, African Americans strived to craft out an existence in better neighborhoods and living spaces. Government proved the vigilante, stalking and dispatching black destiny and crushing its counterfeit key.

The Federal Housing Administration, established under President Franklin Roosevelt's New Deal, endeavored to make housing and mortgages more affordable for Americans.[647] FDR's New Deal also established the Home Owners' Loan Corporation to assist struggling homeowners in restructuring mortgage plans to prevent defaults and foreclosures.[648] Although much larger initial payments (if not lump sums) were traditionally required from buyers to purchase homes, "The FHA ushered in the modern mortgage system that enabled people to buy homes on small down payments and at reasonable interest rates, with lengthy repayment periods and full loan amortization."[649]

Where the FHA sought to make homeowners of Americans, HOLC endeavored to help those who had already achieved homeowner status retain their keys.[650] HOLC's explicitly racist policies prevented African Americans from seeing the tremendous benefits that many whites enjoyed.[651] The eligibility of communities to benefit from HOLC was illustrated in a race-based color coding system.[652] White skin was a green light, as communities sheltering such epidermal exclusivity were deemed to have great "useful or productive life of housing."[653] Conversely, epidermally dilapidated areas—racially mixed or predominantly black—were placed in the lowest category, and therefore largely ineligible for federal assistance.

The FHA promoted housing segregation, believing that a merger of black and white Americas would devalue the housing market. The federal agency declared in its *Underwriting Manual*, "If a neighborhood is to retain stability, it is necessary that properties shall continue to be occupied by the same social and racial classes."[654] It also advocated and enforced the use of restrictive covenants to prevent African Americans from moving into white neighborhoods.[655] Although policies were eventually put in place to abrogate bureaucratically endorsed segregation,[656][657] the "suburban rush" had largely

Last in Line: An American Destiny Deferred

passed by the time these policies came into play, leaving the serene, ideal neighborhoods staked for white Americans. While federal policies were catapulting whites from lower social classes into the economic stratosphere, blacks who attempted the jump bumped their heads against the Plexiglas ceiling, bruising crowns and hopes in the process.

Withered Dreams

Broadway played host to perhaps the first theatrical demonstration of housing discrimination's cruelty. *A Raisin in the Sun* was critically acclaimed upon its debut, hailed as the best play of 1959 by the New York Drama Critics' Circle.[658] Not only was its portrayal of Civil Rights era black family life unprecedented, but the production and direction of a play on Broadway by two African Americans, Lorraine Hansberry and Lloyd Richards, was also a momentous first.

After collecting $10,000 on the insurance policy of their deceased patriarch, the Younger family argues over how to spend it.[659] Although younger members of the family such as get-rich-quick scheming Walter have less frugal and more frivolous plans, Lena Younger—"Big Mama"—proves her financial savvy in wanting to invest a down payment in a home in Clybourne Park, an all-white neighborhood. Despite warnings that a black family's home had recently been bombed when they too forayed into a Clybourne Park-style neighborhood, Big Mama's intrepid will refuses acquiescence. With unwelcoming, glacial intent, her future neighbors in the Clybourne Park Improvement Association appoint Mr. Linder as their community emissary. Mr. Linder, aided by a handsome financial offer, attempts to dissuade the Youngers from tainting what he and the homeowners' association consider their pristine neighborhood. Big Mama rejects the offer. The Youngers realize their dream of obtaining a Clybourne Park home, conquering the neighborhood's homegrown racism.

For many today, *A Raisin in the Sun* is fitting "for its time." It gave voice to a conspicuous and important issue in 1950s America—housing discrimination's endurance and the recalcitrance of white communities to relinquish opportunity to black buyers. All money is green—but realtors were more concerned with the hue of buyers' hands than that of what was in them. *A Raisin in the Sun* has appeared on Broadway several times since its debut and is treated as a sanctified relic reminding us of the horrors of a time supposedly far different from today. America today is supposedly not the America of *A Raisin in the Sun*, whose predominantly white opening audiences[660] were largely housed in their own pre-Younger Clybourne Parks. If the signing and dotting of the 1964 Civil Rights Act was the rite that destroyed institutional racism, the showing of *A Raisin in the Sun* was perhaps the more specific remedy to the evils of housing discrimination. It was a botched demolition—Congress and other government organs have grossly neglected continued housing discrimination witnessed through the parts of realtors, banks, and communities cast in a 2010s-style, Off-Broadway *Raisin in the Sun* production.

Former U.S. representative Joseph P. Kennedy II of Massachusetts can be thanked for pulling the white sheets off discriminatory lenders in the modern era. Following the establishment of the Department of Housing and Urban Development as part of President Lyndon B. Johnson's Great Society, large scale efforts were undertaken to provide housing to low-income families,

124

many which were African American. Though HUD had minor success, in typical fashion the program became a mechanism for the perpetuation of institutionalized racism. During the reign of the unashamedly corrupt Nixon administration, it was discovered that real estate agents, lawyers, and HUD employees concocted a scheme in which—quite similar to the subprime mortgage blaxploitation leading up to the Great Recession—African Americans were shafted with overpriced, low-value properties they could not afford.[661] The scandal shook up the White House, but was soon overtaken by the infamous indignity of Watergate. In response to racially discriminatory practices like those carried out under the Nixon administration, Kennedy felt it necessary to introduce legislation that would require banks to reveal their lending practices toward prospective buyers in low-income areas.[662] As a result of such legislation, banks would be required to reveal lending refusals by race, gender, and income so that discriminatory practices could be better pinpointed and banks participating in such actions could be penalized.[663]

As a result of this legislation, in 1991 the Federal Reserve conducted a study of 6.4 million mortgage applications.[664] The study revealed that major banks denied the mortgage applications of black applicants twice as often as they did whites. Studies further revealed that whites in the lowest income bracket were more likely to be approved for mortgages than blacks in the highest ones.[665] But the impropriety of banks and mortgagers was not limited to denying deals to qualified African Americans; approved African Americans typically got the rawest deals. Despite the transparency brought about by Kennedy's legislative efforts, little was done to mitigate or check redlining practices in the housing market. All of this indicated that Hansberry's raisin still shriveled in a horrid sun, as withered and desiccated as ever.

The style of predatory lending practiced on Nixon's watch visited African American households all the way through the housing bubble's burst in 2007-08. Although lenders targeted Americans of all colors, African Americans were again marked as the most exploitable pawns. Financial giant Bank of America is but one of many institutions which had a hand in predatory lending practices. The Countrywide Financial Corporation (purchased by Bank of America in 2008) exploited African American and Hispanic borrowers and doled out subprime mortgages in their communities like cavities on Halloween.[666] Prime loans were largely reserved for white clients, even when they had credit profiles similar to those of minority borrowers.[667] A study from the Center for Responsible Lending discovered that "blacks were a third more likely to get a high-interest loan than white borrowers with the same credit profile."[668] Collective African American fiscal irresponsibility might necessitate a trend of higher interest rates. But when credit profiles are *identical* in such situations, institutional racism is the lone culprit.

Adjustable-rate mortgages—deals that at first appear affordable to borrowers until the lender capriciously raises interest rates—also horribly affected minority borrowers, who were disproportionately targeted for bad deals.[669] Adjustable-rate mortgages, which are more likely to end in foreclosure,[670] were instrumental in the construction of predatory lending schemes that demolished black neighborhoods. Home foreclosures have a domino effect. One neighborhood foreclosure depreciates surrounding property values, toppling into more foreclosures, and an initially gradual decline in no time becomes precipitous.[671] Countrywide raised a staggering $674 billion during the peak of their discriminatory lending capital campaign from 2004 to 2007.[672]

Last in Line: An American Destiny Deferred

As a result of Countrywide's racially discriminatory lending practices, in December 2011 Bank of America was required to pay a drop-in-the-bucket settlement of $355 million[673]—hardly waterboarded punishment given the exorbitant spoils they procured from violating the rules of engagement. In July 2011, the Justice Department also initiated a probe into Wells Fargo in response to circulating allegations of predatory lending practices[674] and a year later ordered the bank to pay a $175 million settlement to over 30,000 minority borrowers.[675] In response to a separate lawsuit filed by the city of Baltimore, Maryland in which Wells Fargo was accused of steering potential prime borrowers toward subprime loans, the bank agreed to pay an $85 million civil penalty.[676] Lawsuits were also filed against numerous other financial institutions found to have promoted or engaged in discriminatory lending during the subprime mortgage crisis.[677] [678] [679]

It's shocking that proper government oversight and regulation of such abusive lending practices is absent. Housing discrimination is a violation under Title VIII of the 1968 Civil Rights Act, widely known as the Fair Housing Act.[680] Because the law prohibits such actions of discriminatory and predatory mortgaging which have been carried out in public and private spheres, the courts have power to stop housing discrimination in its tracks once and for all. But without sinews of desire and effort, justice will never stand. All we have to show for is the occasional headline, lawsuit, and settlement that is nothing more than chump change to banks that reap unbelievable gains by suckering honest, hardworking African American and Hispanic borrowers into disadvantage. A corporation that brings in billions in profits annually and is ranked as one of the largest companies in the world[681] will not be deterred by occasional slap-on-the-wrist settlements that make imperceptible dents in the profits generated by racist subterfuge. If destroying the dreams of African American and Latino families is necessary for the top rank, they will incur limitless lawsuits en route to that dubious yet profitable distinction.

African Americans trying to "pull themselves up by their bootstraps" and fulfill hopes for a better life by moving up to the hill are, despite their qualifications, frequently denied this journey. Even when homeownership's front doors are open to African Americans, rather than being welcomed into balconies for the recline of their families and communities, they are hosted toward base, exploitative cauldrons of banks and lenders. This is part of the dehumanization of the African American, the universal blindness to the reality that beneath epidermis and behind physiognomy is a human wanting only to care for family, community, and individual well-being. Much like their enslaved ancestors, blacks today are too often viewed as objects, dollar signs, and commodities existing only for purposes of piking and procuring rusted riches.

Conclusion

A platitude proclaims, "Money isn't everything." In our hyper-avaricious, money-obsessed society, it is important to sometimes remind ourselves of this adage's truth. Money really isn't everything. But it is a lot. As long as African Americans hammer unheeded pangs on the doors of financial opportunity in income, business, homeownership, and other asset-value areas, finding their knuckles sore and souls resigned to concrete without security of thatch or even blanket, they will continue to experience stalked, brutal outcomes in many neighborhoods. Unable to afford the golden thatch with which ebon hands build the village necessary to raise the child, they will languish in the statistical slums of economic regress.

The success of African Americans in sport and entertainment has enabled the emergence of a super-rich class never before seen in American history. We commonly cite the Oprah Winfreys, Tiger Woodses, Michael Jordans, Lebron Jameses, Tyler Perrys, Jay-Zs, and Beyoncés of America as evidence that economic discrimination no longer exists. After all, with Oprah having a net worth of $3 billion in 2016[682]—putting her not just in the 1 percent but perhaps the hyperbolic .00000000001 percent—it seems apparent that there can be no such thing as economic racism today. But the "Oprah argument" is predicated on exceptionality. Those like Oprah are wildly rich outliers, not at all representative of the African American masses. The black exceptionality argument only proves the rule of mass black economic deprivation. For every Bob Johnson, there are millions of unemployed African Americans, millions more African Americans confined to menial professions, and still thousands who may, if they were white, reasonably hope one day to achieve the status of America's multimillionaires—or at least a secure standard of living—but are unable to because institutional racism so obstinately obstructs this vision.

Oprah Winfrey's tremendous story of overcoming poverty to become one of the wealthiest Americans is inspiring to Americans of all colors. But African Americans can more easily relate to the younger Oprah Winfrey—who lived in such acute indigence that she wore sewn-together potato sacks as dresses[683]—than the Oprah who jets the globe, stays at the most expensive of hotels, purchases brand new cars for her audiences, and despite her riches was notably turned away from Hermes in 2005 in a blatant act of racial discrimination.[684] Oprah's story is simply a statistical proof—everyone has a *chance* at making it. But when one can't get an equitable education, a chance at a fair mortgage, a decent-paying job that will promote one when worthy and won't fire one unfairly, or a fair shake by the justice system, one's chance is a lot slimmer.

Couple that bounded reality with the picture of America's social immobilization and we have the recipe for the creation of a socioeconomic underclass—African Americans. But we ignore all of these factors while ranting and raving that because *two* black billionaires exist in comparison to over *five hundred* white billionaires in the United States,[685] racism must somehow be extinct. Rather than opt for reality, we choose exceptionality. In this, we opt for delusion. The exceptionality argument is informed by a false empiricism corollary of a condition of comorbid colorblindness and astigmatism. This ailment narrows our focus to a *few* outliers, ignoring the *masses* so strenuously bearing the weight of institutional racism upon breaking backs.

In the nearly 900-page *Blueprint for Black Power*, late activist Dr. Amos Wilson cites a definition of power as "the ability to be, do, and prevail."[686] In America and the world, the dollar is the key determinant of destiny. It—more than anything else—bequeaths or withholds one's ability to be, do, and prevail. Money is power. It makes all the difference between whether one lives well or lives poorly, whether one lives in satiation or lives in hunger, and whether one lives or doesn't live at all. It determines the level of education one will get or fail to get, the sort of home one will live in, and even the dietary habits that one has in life. Money affects us in all ways and although the wistful rhetoric of cultural axioms may fool us into devaluing money (or, perhaps more generously, disabuse us of belief in its absolute power), the

Last in Line: An American Destiny Deferred

truth is that money is the lifeblood of the world in which we live and without enough of it circulating within our communities we—plainly and simply—die. The African American community is in dire need of a blood transfusion because its circulatory system is dangerously deprived.

The Plexiglas ceiling not only obstructs the efforts of the modern African American generation; it fosters a cyclical pattern of deprivation and social immobility ominously hovering over the heads of those not yet conceived. The inability of African Americans to rise to higher echelons as a result of the barrier means that future generations may be even less able to free themselves from the chains of disempowerment—chains bonding all the way to slavery. Delivering the dream of homeownership to blacks today will foster the milieu for perpetuating transgenerational wealth that will enable the black community to at last transcend the state of attenuation from which emancipation should have catapulted them. And if African Americans are able to take home salaries equal to those of their white counterparts, they too will be able to nurture hearth's children. They will be members of the village of prestigious prep schools, elite colleges, and well-funded public schools and universities that grant power in the plaudit that is a college degree along with the skills and knowledge necessary to thrive in a competitive world market.

Although adherents of the bootstrap theory refuse to entertain any idea to the contrary, their lacing doesn't hold up. Loose strings and worn soles are more apparent today than ever before. The famed rags-to-riches story for which America is known is rendered more a quixotic fable than a realistic ideal. In 1900, 39 percent of America's wealthiest were born into the upper social class.[687] In 1950, 68 percent of America's richest had been born into wealth.[688] By 1970, 82 percent of the richest were born into opulent backgrounds.[689] This "patricianization" flies in the face of everything that we are taught to believe about opportunity in America. Such statistics belie the bootstrap idea which ushers Americans into an allegory in which, through work ethic and intelligence, *anyone* can become wealthy. It burrows a reality of tormented souls for whom the extent of knowledge is blankness. Steel shoestrings tie legs in threads of privilege, nepotism, and advantage that forfeit the race. Everyone has a chance in this metaphorical foot race. But it is those spared the cavern's darkness by privilege of education and networks of escape who have the leg up.

Neither income inequality nor racial inequality is sustainable. Throughout history we find time and time again that inequitable states destabilize, collapsing under the weight of bias edifices. When disparity is so great that those in the middle and bottom are deprived of fruits of their labors, fury and public unrest arise and often lead to ouster. We do not need to channel Marie Antoinette to know this. The Occupy protests are only the tip of the proverbial sword. Just because the United States has never had a *coup d'état* and has thus far stood as a paragon of political stability doesn't mean that we are destined always to remain so. The longer we permit race, gender, and general wealth gaps to expand, the more we flirt with lacerated fate. The Plexiglas ceiling is the most obdurate, unyielding of today's bias edifices; patent ignorance and neglect only harden it. American policymakers have allowed it to occupy the pane of opportunity that African Americans and other minorities were destined to leap through in joy and hope. American complacency imperils American fate, etching into that cool, not yet cracked window ominous graffiti spelling "let them eat cake."

⑦
Hooked on Ebonics

What is a race card?

The race card gets more mention in some academic and political circles than do race disparities in justice, education, economic, and health care systems of America. In fact, "race card" is the standard, plastic payment tendered toward mention of any of those issues. It's strange technology. Where one obtains or how one creates a race card—or what one may even redeem it for—is a mystery. But its invocation is often accompanied by admonitions of "cry me a river!" conducting melancholy whines of violins and cellos, underscored by clashing, sorrowful cries of robust divas and rotund baritones. Compassionate, conservative crocodile tears wash away conservationist hopes for a green earth, one Kleenex box at a time. The race card is welfare queens, takers, unqualified applicants, race baiters, thugs, and food stamp presidents all wrapped into a single unsightly, pathetic—dark—package.

It takes many other forms, too. The race card is protesters challenging police violence; the race card is remembering slavery and Jim Crow; the race card is insisting in confidence that African Americans are as capable, competent, and qualified for any job or school that anyone else of any other race is; the race card is remembering Dr. King and Malcolm X; the race card is writing a research report, speech, or book that tears down the pillars of institutionalized racism weighing on America's soul and implores the nation to do better. The race card is—as all of these actions do—making "truth to power" something more than a corpse of a catchphrase. The race card is challenging the idea of the race card that seeks to nullify and obfuscate the realities of persistent, unyielding, damning racial inequity in the United States today. The race card is a stone-cold look in the eye and a firm—"We won't get over it. We, as a *nation*, will get through it."

Race card rhetoric boils down to the centermost tenet of colorblind ideology—that black people's problems are of black people's making. *Last in Line* has thus far almost exclusively examined institutional racism's role in the perpetuation of the black community's many struggles. But it has said little of the African American community's role in the perpetuation of its own struggles. In accordance with its thesis, *Last in Line* cites abundant research firmly establishing that institutionalized racism plays a much bigger role in black America's enervation than any ostensibly pathological habits or characteristics of the African American community. After all, it is hard to see how even the most responsible, hardworking, and abstemious black families and individuals can overcome the monolith of systemic racism that does not stop to judge whether a black teenager standing in court is a "good one," if the hardworking father of three is uncharacteristically "decent," or if the recent college graduate is indeed "qualified."

Analyses have proven that behavior, class, and qualification have limited bearing on social outcomes for African Americans. There is little discrimination within the paradigm of antiblack racial discrimination; pathology applies to all. *Pathology* is somehow always the suspect picked out of the lineup, the sole culprit in the African American community's struggle. This stringent conservative perspective holds that most everything negative that impacts the African American collective is ascribable to the bacteria that are black households and neighborhoods. It holds that racism—if it even exists—bears negligible influence, reduced to fringe, isolated incidents like the 1998 lynching of James Byrd or the 2015 Charleston church shooting.

The case for institutionalized racism's role and magnitude has been made. But is it fair to dismiss the idea that African Americans bear some responsibility for the poverty, crime, dropout rates, and other maladies afflicting their communities? Could it be true that institutional racism's role is overstated and blacks bear greater responsibility for their plight than this book's thesis and arguments suggest?

William Julius Wilson's 1978 book *The Declining Significance of Race* supports this perspective. Wilson holds, among other things, that because education is becoming increasingly available to African Americans, institutional racism is fossilizing into a vestige.[690] If Wilson's premise was correct, then his argument could be sound. But it is false. Wilson argues that as the relevance of race decreases, African Americans are increasingly able to advance in the world so long as they are equipped with skills and education. He neglects that the availability of education and, beyond this, the availability of quality education has not improved significantly for African Americans. This is precisely *because* of their race.

One having read this far knows by now that even when African Americans and other minorities possess skills in excess, they often reap less benefit than their white American counterparts. *The Declining Significance of Race* is more an exercise in wishful thinking than an accurate sociological examination of institutional racism's impact on minority communities. To be fair, at the time of *The Declining Significance of Race*'s publication race relations seemed a bit more promising, with the Supreme Court's jurisprudence on education, for example, having not yet backpedaled. But even in 1978, education disparity in the United States was rampant. Desegregation only reached its peak in 1988, an entire decade after Wilson sounded the bell of holy freedom. Contrary to the quixotic title of Wilson's book, it is all too apparent that race remains highly significant in America nearly four decades after its publication.

The theories posited in works such as Wilson's are quintessentially colorblind. They presume the nobility of society's institutions and operators and presuppose that symbolic civil rights advances inspire people to abandon racist ideas and forgo racist acts. Those of us not in denial know that this has not been the case. But this belief in the existence of an equal opportunity society, coupled with belief in the idea of black sociopathology, has motivated the habit of minimizing those who cite the magnitude of institutional racism as petulant, peevish *victims*.

Victim. Along with "race card," "victim" is among the most frequently invoked terms in the language of minimization that coarse-tongued pundits and politicians have a knack at switching to and from. Theirs is a curious usage. As the dictionary definition indicates, the term *victim* implies the existence of some influential transgressing agent outside the self. A glance at the definitions of "oppression," "subjugation," and "slavery"—and a look back over at that of "victim"—suggests that those subjected to those sorts of acts are, by virtue of that subjection, victims. All of this begs the question: given conservative implorations that African Americans and other marginalized

130

groups get over their victimization, how precisely *does* one "get over it"? Is there some magical, ethereal way to time travel and revisit these eras to stop acts of oppression, subjugation, and slavery from ever happening in the first place?

It would be an onerous task to travel to the start of the trans-Atlantic slave trade and persuade each and every ship captain to return men, women, and children to their homelands, cancelling the journey lest the scourge of eternal victimhood plague American destiny. Maybe we would afford ourselves a better shot by shortening our time distance to postbellum America. Here we can stop the black codes, vagrancy laws, and emergent sharecropping systems and ensure that ex-slaves get their 40 acres and a mule. We can guarantee that the White House, Congress, and Supreme Court all protect and enforce the Reconstruction amendments, the Civil Rights Act of 1875, and the Enforcement Acts. If that trip is not logistically feasible, we could even travel to the Great Depression to persuade Roosevelt's bureaucrats to do away with their laws and policies which minimized African American benefit from the New Deal. Any of these things would prevent the planting of the seeds of victimhood that allegedly paralyze African American individuality and drain government coffers. If only time travel were possible.

Fantasizing about time travel is absurd—as is the idea that a victim is not a victim. Still, the idea of time travel makes more sense. Traveling to the past is the only conceivable way to prevent the malignancy of victimhood from emerging. Victimhood is causal. Precluding the antecedent of black victimhood—slavery, Jim Crow, etc.—would logically preclude the state of black victimhood. Short of some miraculous technological breakthrough, there is no way to "get over" this victimhood. The victimhood argument is not a rational perspective, but an illogical artifice. When politicians, policymakers, and pundits scorn ideas of victimization, they are not actually admitting to the realities of the past and insisting victims get over them. They are minimizing the magnitude of the devastation wrought by that past. The idea that the oppression and subjugation that African Americans have and continue to face in the United States do not victimize only further attests to the scale of racial prejudice in the country.

The victimhood argument is also flawed because it surmises victims' powerlessness. Those employing the argument insist that it is the "victims" who falsely believe themselves to be powerless, but those employing the argument imply that it is *they* who believe in the powerlessness of victims. They assume power of dictation and command over the will of victims, hurling harangues clad in shoddy, thrift shop-quality garments of encouragement. African Americans are not powerless in the face of institutional racism. Dictators neutralized that power, bearing no will or intent toward beseeching African Americans to "rise" out of the plight which they engendered. The man with the foot upon his neck has a right to himself, not to the man strangling him, to defend his life. The man engaged in the strangulation has no right to dictate to the asphyxiating man what he must do to save his life when everything he does is set against the end.

America doesn't need a 12-step program to admit that the plights of African Americans and other minorities fit the dictionary definition of victimization. The black community does not need to explore its "pathologies." For the United States to at last have racial equity, it is necessary to jettison all ideas ascribing black pathology to qualities innate to the African American community. Why? These assertions are tantamount to eugenic arguments put forth both throughout the 20th century and today. The eugenics and pathology arguments differ only on the surface, but in essence both point to some ostensible flaw within black people.

This is not a sweeping assertion, but rather a candid observation of the similarity between the bases of both arguments. Eugenics arguments attribute the attenuated state of the black community to biological flaws, but "pathology" arguments point indirectly to *some* inexplicable phenomenon of backwardness in the black community. It's a prevaricating, wishy-washy metonym for eugenics logic. Eugenicists explicitly and unabashedly point to black DNA as the problem. However, the quasi-eugenicists merely point to some unspecified, enigmatic quality within African Americans that causes their high unemployment, criminality, prevalence of STDs, and a host of other indicators of a pathological milieu.

Peddling the idea that blacks both merit and inherit their status as causative agents for the circumstances of their communities won't in the slightest ameliorate the black community's struggles. This spurious notion evades the problem. To better understand the links between the potent effects of institutional racism and the circumstances of the black community, it is necessary to understand in detail how the phenomena misidentified as pathologies relate to past and current edifices of institutionalized racism. Language captures this in a unique way. Ebonics speaks as loudly to 1619 as it does to present day. It speaks to poverty, education, and justice in one breath. And it speaks, louder than perhaps anything else, to the caricaturizations and mockeries made of African Americans in the world over. Ebonics is, in a sense, the perfect illustration of black America's gross dysfunction.

Hooked on Ebonics?

Part of what defines an ethnic group are its unique, exclusive cultural identifiers. Language is arguably the strongest component of ethnic identity. Even among groups that share language and geographic proximity, separate and unique dialects evolve that differentiate one group from the next. In the United States, African Americans have long upheld their identity through their distinct linguistic expression—the quasi-language, African American Vernacular English, colloquially referred to as Ebonics. Ebonics is not a language per se, but in 1996 Oakland, California's school board passed a resolution that sought to enshrine it among the world's tongues.[691]

The board moved to recognize Ebonics as the "primary language of African American children."[692] This measure was met with uproar from African Americans and mainstream liberals, both who interpreted the act as racist and myopic.[693] To many, this initiative by the Oakland Unified School District appeared a poorly executed attempt on the part of a racist America at yet again questioning black intelligence. The school board's action was perceived as insinuating that African American children were incapable of learning and understanding English. Black activists such as Jesse Jackson and prominent political figures including U.S. secretary of education William Bennett, Connecticut senator Joseph Lieberman, and New York governor Andrew Cuomo all came out of the proverbial woodwork, fiercely criticizing the initiative.[694]

America teaches that there are two basic forms of English—good and bad. However vague that seems, we're generally taught to model the mechanics, grammar, and usage consistent with the good form. What's "good" is generally left up to institutions like the British Council, dictionaries like Merriam-Webster, and textbooks that schools adopt for English instruction. "Bad English" is simply the violation of the established rules of English. Deviation from dictionary or textbook English is not the domain of any specific ethnic group. From the American South, to New York City, to England itself, there exist "vulgar," grammatically improper forms of English spoken among all races, particularly among socioeconomically disadvantaged groups.[695] But when stereotypes entailing bad English are invoked, it is often in reference to the Ebonics dialect some think requiring of its own language classification.

Ebonics is the alpha star in a dim constellation of homely physical features,[696] buffoonery, licentiousness,[697] and intellectual ineptitude.[698] The perverse forms of English spoken among black Americans, both pre- and post-emancipation, came to symbolize innate intellectual inferiority. But to others, it has less to do with mental capacity and more to do with the ineptitude of black character, a result of laziness and complacency toward education. In this view, Ebonics is viewed as one of the most offensive and boisterous gestures blacks make in opposition to assimilation into mainstream American culture. It is part of the greater pathology of the African American community, in line with criminality, unemployment, and other degeneracy markers.

Ebonics' origins date to the beginnings of slavery in the United States. Slaves hailing from innumerable African ethnic enclaves, each with unique languages and dialects, were faced both with challenges of communicating with those speaking different languages and learning a new and unique language immediately upon arrival in the New World. This dynamic produced the numerous New World pidgin dialects that, together with English, comprise Ebonics' family tree:

> African languages survived in the New World for a time…Although many of the slaves may not have had to relinquish their African languages immediately, they all found themselves in a situation in which they had to learn an auxiliary language in a hurry in order to establish communication in the heterogeneous groups into which they were thrown. This mixing of speakers of a large number of languages, with no one language predominant, is the perfect condition for the spread of pidgin language, which is in a sense the ultimate in auxiliary languages. In the colonies which became the early United States, Pidgin English served the purpose of a *lingua franca*…[699]

The word's origin is as interesting as the dialect's. In 1973, African American psychologist Robert Williams coined the term "Ebonics" out of pragmatism. In place of the laborious, syllable-laden "African American Vernacular English," Williams simply drew "ebony" and "phonetics" from the dictionary, spliced them, and created the succinct, colorful portmanteau.[700] Williams explored Ebonics not as a perverted form of English, but rather as its own derivative language. In 1975, he published *Ebonics: The True Language of Black Folks*, the first scholastic treatise seriously examining the dialect.[701] What was until then predominantly viewed as a symptom of black intellectual underdevelopment was more charitably interpreted by Williams as a natural result of blacks not having access to proper models of English. Williams' book aroused extensive commentary about Ebonics, some opposing the idea that Ebonics should be recognized as a language and others concurring that Ebonics was its own tongue, an understandable and perhaps laudable improvisation given African Americans' lack of access to environments in which proper English could be learned.[702] This debate spilled into Oakland, which played host to perhaps the most politically significant battle over language classification in American history. The Oakland School Board fired the first shots by asserting that Ebonics *was* indeed its own language.

In the debate, various questions regarding the nature of the dialect arose. They entertained whether Ebonics reveals the presence of idiosyncratic qualities in the black psyche, whether it is a product of blacks resisting instruction and communication in proper English, and whether other theories could explain its prevalence. Class examinations also affirmed Ebonics' ethnic uniqueness, as even underprivileged whites in most parts of the country seem capable of articulating themselves well enough in English. Still, blacks who are seen as better adjusted in terms of education, income, and other measures of socioeconomic status generally seem to deviate from use of Ebonics, showing that it is by no means black America's *de facto* official language. What explains its mainstay status with the mass, abandoned segment of the black community? Is Ebonics perhaps an idiosyncratic manifestation of a culture long oppressed and subjugated, an inextirpable vestige remaining from the days of American slavery? And if it is able to convey clear, communicable messages as languages do and possesses its own linguistic and syntactical trademarks, why is it not worthy of its own dictionary or textbook?

The controversy surrounding Ebonics highlights an exemplar of a pathology born of racially discriminatory policies being construed as an intrinsic African American flaw. Though scholars and education policymakers turn away from the past, it is necessary to look to the seas of the Middle Passage to comprehend Ebonics. Africans were brought to the United States and forced to learn a language altogether unlike the Niger-Congo dialects they, their ancestors, and their neighbors spoke. Beyond pedagogic barriers were those perilous. The same sons and daughters of ivoried privilege who fashion poached inheritance into structures of Babel, pontificating the legitimacy of black language, minimize that, after the Flood their Father cursed them with, African Americans were hardly permitted to count beyond the number of fingers *he* hadn't yet had cut off,[703] much less speak "good English." Considering that a slave generally could not obtain formal education in the English language without the help of a white person,[704] for a slave to demonstrate even a marginally decent grasp of English would signal a surreptitious instruction that could carry a death sentence.

These language instructors insist it is irrelevant that, even in postbellum times, many African American children had no schools to attend.[705] They ignore that even today, so many predominantly black schools lack sufficient resources[706] and competent educators. From conservative areas like South Carolina's Corridor of Shame to progressive states such as California,[707] the issue of racial disparity in the allotment of resources for education persists. Still, those biasing inquiries of Ebonics in the framework of black pathology ignore the fact that no matter what may be done to minimize its use, the dialect is so firmly ensconced in the mouths of African Americans that the prospect of suddenly jettisoning it is absurd. That Ebonics—a linguistic form existing primarily because of the historical situational inability of blacks to properly learn English—arouses in mainstream America such confusion and disapprobation is indicative of the sort of prejudice that has led to the characterization of African Americans as a natural underclass.

Ebonics: Cool, or Nah?

It is not to be implied that the use of Ebonics among African Americans is not at all problematic. In many ways, it is. The forms of English many black children speak at home are often carried into the classroom, where language standards are radically different.[708] This can obviously create a hotbed of problems with classroom instruction, interaction, and academic performance. It is for this reason, among others, that Ebonics should never be considered a separate language of instruction for African American students. Language instruction for African American children must not differ from that which all American children receive, just as access to education funding, resources, teaching, and fair discipline policies should not differ. All of these things, when unequal, create milieus of miseducation for African American children that complicate the process of learning all subjects, including language. The American reality is that proper English is the language of professionalism, erudition, and power. Depriving African American children of opportunities to learn proper English deprives them of opportunities at survival in America.

The key question in the Ebonics debate asks how mainstream America can criticize Ebonics so vehemently when its systems of institutional racism gave birth to it. Perhaps we should revisit our metaphorical time machine and program it to transport us to the days of slavery. There we can plead with the colonial and antebellum legislatures to do away with the prohibition of slave education. We can one-up the cotton gin's innovative impression, scrolling through rave reviews for the Hooked on Phonics mobile app, pleading its utility in rearing menial slaves into orators. If that's temporally inconvenient, we could go to the post-Reconstruction era, where meager funding for African American schools in the South altogether dematerialized. Perhaps our peaceable, reasoned demonstrations to Klansmen burning Freedmen's Bureau schools would at last convey the importance of nurturing an environment conducive to the education of black Americans.

On second thought, perhaps we don't have to go anywhere. We could just plead to the state legislatures and education superintendents in states like South Carolina that offer beyond sufficient funding for certain, coincidentally white areas, yet only pocket change to areas heavily populated by African Americans and Hispanics. Perhaps they will listen. But, considering the numerous tombstones decorating the petitioners' graveyard, they likely won't.

Ebonics discourse is tricky. On one hand, its use inhibits the ability of African Americans to learn the proper, professional form of English that is essential to success both in school and in employment. On the other hand, Ebonics has evolved into an inextirpable trait of black America—one that is, in many regards, cherished and beloved. Ebonics is as inseparable from African American culture as bread is from butter. Its tradition is apparent in black churches, movies and entertainment, music (and not just America's Fetty Waps), and in the daily interlocutions of African Americans. A black Southerner's pronunciation of "ask" ("axe") is no less indicative of sophistication or intelligence than a white Bostonian's pronunciation of "car" ("cah"). Although many view the use of Ebonics as signaling a lack of education, many African Americans have shown the ability to "code-switch" from the traditional vernacular in relaxed, informal settings to "Standard American English" in professional environments.[709]

President Obama is a consummate example of someone who teeters between employing the Queen's English and opting for somewhat Ebonic-influenced vernacular in relaxed settings.[710] He was even controversially commended for this by Democratic Senate Minority Leader Harry Reid, who said Obama was electable because of his being palatably "light-skinned" and "[having] no Negro dialect, unless he wanted to have one."[711] Although educated African Americans know to use proper English in professional or formal settings, when in less serious environments their use of Ebonics emerges as an innocuous adherence to tradition. In any case, this behavior doesn't differ from that of other ethnic groups whose members don't always employ impeccable English in recreational or relaxed settings. No matter one's opinion on the issue, the fact is that Ebonics has been with African Americans for so long and has become so ensconced in black American identity that deleting it would be tantamount to deleting a significant part of African American identity.

Some may argue that African Americans should *want* to wipe out Ebonics, not only as an obstacle to education but also as a linguistic representation of slavery's horrors. So many aspects of black identity in the United States are also tied to the dreads of slavery, such as our powerful Christian tradition, delicacies, musical traditions, and beyond. If it's supposedly benefiting to do away with Ebonics, then in principle we would be obligated to do away with the aforementioned qualities and traits that are also inextricably linked to black, and furthermore, American identity. Furthermore, it must not be ignored that African Americans are not the only ethnic group with a unique, grammatically imperfect dialect of English. Asian Americans,[712] Hispanic Americans,[713] and white Americans[714] all use idiosyncratic renditions of the English language without being subjected to the sort of derision or ridicule that blacks are. The most obvious argument against abandoning Ebonics, however, is that of futility; African Americans are and will likely continue to be subjected to racial bias whether they talk like Barack Obama or Flava Flav.

There may be no definitive answer to the question of how Ebonics should be regarded. Few prove capable of fairly assessing its situation without minimizing its valued historicity or significance to African American culture. If the education system can somehow compromise between teaching African Americans proficient use of mainstream English, the language of erudition and professionalism, while permitting African Americans to maintain their linguistic talisman for use in impersonal and informal interactions, a reconciliation can be achieved between black needs to sustain identity and adopt traits beneficial to their success in the mainstream corridors of America.

Ebonics is just one racially profiled, ostensibly pathological African American trait. It is part of a manifold perhaps most clearly illustrated in—arguably the root of all black pathologies—the dysfunctional black American family.

Black Values

Former U.S. education secretary Rod Paige and former Norfolk State University dean Elaine Witty (whose book *The Black-White Achievement Gap* was profiled in chapter 5) list the commonly cited sociopathological traits of African American culture:

- Unstable families
- Poor parenting skills
- Lack of drive and ambition
- Negative peer pressure
- Poor choice of role models
- High levels of teen pregnancies, drugs, and crime
- Lower parental involvement in children's education[715]

None of these cultural ascriptions is exaggerated, misconstrued, or unfounded. Although it would be foolish to characterize all or even most black families with such descriptions, it is true that they hold as trends for the black community. Despite the prevalence of disciples of the black pathology school of thought, many in mainstream America will concede that such characteristic dysfunction descends, at least in part, from institutionally racist practices of the past in slavery and Jim Crow. But the contemporary argument concerns whether African Americans or modern social structures bear the onus of accountability for the black community's condition.

The dysfunctional black family has been deemed, above all other factors, the chief culprit in the black community's struggle. Paige and Witty mention the empirically confirmed fact that "a child's achievement in school appears to be closely tied to the extent to which the child's family is able to create a home environment that encourages learning, communicates high expectations for their children's achievement and future careers, and involves itself in the child's education at school and in the community."[716]

In the midst of the Civil Rights Movement in which black leaders were pushing for a society conducive to the stability of black family units, Washington policymakers on both sides of the aisle misplaced the origins of black pathologies inside the souls of black folk themselves. In 1965, U.S. assistant secretary of labor Daniel Moynihan issued his well-known *The Negro Family: The Case for National Action*. Better known as *The Moynihan Report*, his sociological study examined the origins of the systemic problems afflicting the black community.[717] Serving under both the Kennedy and Johnson administrations, Moynihan was tasked with the duty of conducting what one could term "policy reconnaissance" for Johnson's famed "War on Poverty" (which proved as abysmal a failure as America's Vietnam quagmire).[718] Moynihan's central assertion was that the extreme poverty of black communities had been misattributed to problems such as employment discrimination, segregation, and disenfranchisement. He argued that black America's pathology was the legacy of slavery.[719]

From its publication, the *Moynihan Report* was criticized as encapsulating everything the Civil Rights Movement stood against. Moynihan's views seemed congruent with those of many white Americans who felt the Civil Rights Movement was "pushing for too much" and that African Americans needed to look to themselves, not government, for uplift. Many thought it absurd that Moynihan would dare argue in the midst of arguably the biggest human rights push in modern world history that it wasn't institutional racism that was to blame for the black community's woes, but rather the black community's inability to long jump over vestiges of slavery. *Blaming the Victim*, a cogent rebuttal to Moynihan's *Report*, was published in 1971. In *Blaming the Victim*, sociologist William Ryan touched on how Moynihan's view of the "crumbling" Negro family represented a convenient alteration of the longstanding idea of innate black inferiority:[720]

> In taking a look at the phenomenon of poverty, the old concept of unfitness or idleness or laziness is replaced by the newfangled theory of the culture of poverty. In race relations, plain Negro inferiority—which was good enough for old-fashioned conservatives—is pushed aside by fancy conceits about the crumbling Negro family. With regard to illegitimacy, we are not so crass as to concern ourselves with immorality and vice, as in the old days; we settle benignly on the explanation of the "lower-class pattern of sexual behavior," which no one condemns as evil, but which is, in fact, simply a variation of the old explanatory idea.[721]

Moynihan's *Report* attributes every problem of the black community to something *other* than the political and social institutions of the United States which, in 1965, still explicitly engaged in institutionally racist practices. Ryan summarizes the assaults on the black community by Moynihan and others, adding synoptically, "In each case, of course, we are persuaded to ignore the obvious: the continued blatant discrimination against the Negro..."[722] Not all of Moynihan's ideas were retrogressive. He advocated greater employment of African American teachers to serve as surrogate figures for fatherless black boys (in the same vein, dismissing the importance of integration). But even where his suggestions were beneficial, his motivating ideology understood black pathology as a symptom of time and helplessness, not diseased American social systems.

Despite—or likely because of—its gross misunderstanding of the issues facing black America, the *Report* won the adulation of libertarian black economist Walter E. Williams, who sang its praises saying, "The solutions to the major problems that confront many black people won't be found in the political arena, especially not in Washington or state capitols."[723] Even the most diehard of conservatives crossed the aisle to embrace Moynihan's work, undeterred by the scarlet "D" next to his name. The *National Review* wrote, "Conservatives of all stripes routinely praise Daniel Patrick Moynihan's prescience for warning in 1965 that the breakdown of the black family threatened the achievement of racial equality. They rightly blast those liberals who denounced Moynihan's report."[724]

Such myopic sociology not only misunderstands the reality of racial inequality in America, but also obstructs efforts toward effectuating racial equality in America. It is counterintuitive to civil rights efforts to assert that the roles of Washington and the nation's state capitols need be limited and that pushing for measures of progress in the franchise, jobs, and education are wastes of time. Moynihan's suggestion to increase the number of black male teachers is reasonable but pointless without measures addressing the rampant biases among teachers, administrators, principals, and other educational agents in areas of instruction and discipline. The latter is inarguably more important. More black male teachers won't offset widespread effects of institutional racism, but getting teachers of all colors to recognize the talents and abilities of young black students will.

Even more important to education is the issue of funding, of which Moynihan said, "The millions coming from Federal aid-to-education programs and other sources should mainly be going into upgrading the academic level of segregated schools."[725] Moynihan was right in saying that badly underfunded inner city schools need greater resources. But history shows that banking on the efficacy and equitability of separate but equal education, as Moynihan essentially suggested, doesn't work. As long as we have *de facto* segregation, we have biased policymakers and administrators formulating education-funding policies that bequeath the cornucopia of education resources on predominantly white schools while tossing scant pocket change pork-barreled with lint to predominantly black ones. Moynihan was wrong in minimizing the necessity of integration, as it is only through complete integration—demographically and institutionally—that we can ever hope to overcome racial disparities apparent in school funding.

With regard to the curious black male absence from the home and workplace, Moynihan would have been prudent to set his sights on the justice system. Thomas Meehan summed up Moynihan's faulty explanation for black male absence in 1966:

> All in all...Moynihan sees the predicament of the American Negro male as a vicious circle. He is born either illegitimate or into a home where his mother has been deserted or divorced by his father; he later, in consequence, does poorly in school and ultimately drops out; and when he reaches young manhood he then joins the vast army of Negro unemployed. And, being unemployed, he can't afford to support a family, and thus he, too, fathers illegitimate children or, after a try at marriage, either deserts or divorces his wife, leaving behind sons to grow up as wretchedly as he grew up. As Moynihan sees it, the only way to break this circle is (a) to create new Federal, state and local government jobs for Negro males and (b) to make it financially advantageous, rather than disadvantageous, for the Negro man to remain with his family.[726]

Moynihan's point about creating jobs (which contradicts his claim that unemployment isn't a big factor in black family dysfunction) is well taken and is indeed recognized as an effective suggestion. But Moynihan's contrived scenario of cyclical male familial abandonment is shortsighted. It fails to comprehend the causes for black men's conspicuous absence from the black household. Before, during, and after the initial implementation of War on Poverty policies, black males bore the justice system's pigmentary penalization much as they do today.[727] How black men are supposed to achieve the metaphysically improbable reality of bipresence—being at once in the home and in the jail cell—Moynihan failed to outline. But if Mr. Moynihan misunderstood the magnitude of institutionalized racism in the United States, we hope he at least realized that blacks aren't Magical Negroes capable of multipresence.

Incarceration and execution statistics underscore the fact that when black men are so aggressively pursued by the justice system not only for crimes people of all races commit but for the compounding offense of being black, they are causally rendered unable to man their households and communities. The problem isn't limited to situational or logistical dilemmas. It also encompasses the restraints that a criminal record places on the possibilities of black ex-convicts succeeding in life after release. One brief period of incarceration can ruin a black adolescent's chances of graduating from high school. One charge of marijuana possession can preclude a black man or woman's chance at a college education, a job, and even military service. Though justice system disparities are real and central to the black community's problems both then and now, Moynihan neglected to conduct a fair examination of their role.

Although President Johnson's Great Society declared lofty intent to forever reinvent the socioeconomic fabric of the United States of America, it failed to significantly reduce the nation's poverty.[728] That Johnson's War on Poverty failed is no surprise given that generals such as Moynihan were at the helm, leaders who identified black freedom's enemies not as the American institutions commanding air assaults but rather the bombarded civilians. Moynihan concluded his work in saying, "The policy of the United States is to bring the Negro American to full and equal sharing in the responsibilities and rewards of citizenship. To this end, the programs of the Federal government bearing on this objective shall be designed to have the effect, directly or indirectly, of enhancing the stability and resources of the Negro American family."[729] Given his motivational rhetoric, it is a wonder Moynihan never felt motivated to explore America's social systems and their operators, the true generators of poverty in the black community. A charitable, one-sentence sum-up of the 86-page *Moynihan Report* must read: never mind that employers don't want to hire you, never mind that teachers don't want to educate you, never mind that policymakers don't want you to vote, and never mind that banks don't want to mortgage a home for you—your plight is *your* fault.

If Daniel Moynihan were living today, one wonders what he would say to Bank of America, Wells Fargo, and other banks that have discriminated against black homebuyers and, in the midst of their subterfuges, mortgaged homes fitted with dynamite, demolishing hopes, dreams, and futures with a blow. Seeing as even he refrained from chiding the Clybourne Parks of his day, we can surmise he'd say little. Whether or not today's policymakers realize it, until the monoliths of institutional racism are themselves fitted with explosives and obliterated, we will continue to see the dysfunctions of the black family unit characterize and cancel out both modern and future generations.

Conclusion

To some extent, those shuffling the deck to draw the race card theory are right on the point of agency. No one forces a young black male to murder the brother with whom he shares great promise. No one forces a young African American woman to give birth to a child in adolescence. No one forces African American men to abandon their families. No one ever forces anyone to partake in the dysfunctional activities that have taken an assegai to the black community's core. Individuals who commit crimes *should* be held accountable. Individuals who have children out of wedlock and before gainfully positioning themselves to provide for a family do bear responsibility. Individual responsibility is real and true—nothing in *Last in Line* contradicts this. But as a theory, sociopathology manipulates reality to render the context of agency opaque, thereby obfuscating the chain of causality that has such great bearing on pathological action.

"Sociopathology" is one-part social engineering, one-part fantasy. The inadequacy and discriminatory inaccessibility of America's social systems create the first part; an American cultural consciousness informed by an ethos of bias forms the second. Pathology is an element of *human*—not black—

biology. The blackened concept is a cover for the sort of behavior that manifests in all cultures given the wrong circumstances. America's contrived principles of sociopathology also apply outside the black community. White drug use rates—which are equal to and in some cases higher than those of blacks—are evidence of this. The difference is that the justice system's policies hide the white community's existing pathologies while working tirelessly to expose the black community's every flaw and weakness.

Black American "pathology" is a product of pathological American public policy. It is policy that casts an impenetrable Plexiglas ceiling above the black community's head, blocking their ascent to equality. Contrary to media narrative, blackness has no bearing on this bruising. If Asians or whites were subjected to the same burdens of institutional racism, the circumstances of their communities would be no different. American society fosters and allows black community pathology to develop and spread like a metastasizing cancer. Without the potent and debilitating effects of institutional racism, such ever-spreading pathology would not exceed the levels of social deviance manifest in other cultures and ethnic groups.

Worst of all, the myriad wonk wars and policy punitions assailing the black community from all fronts have inspired the black community's autoimmune insurgency. It is red blood cell versus blue, exchanging projectiles ravaging walls and channels of the body. Hand signals convey orders for bloodletting, piling black bodies on black, soaked streets as mothers' tears wash away tormenting crimson hues. Black-on-black crime, perhaps the greatest pathology of all, is frequently traced through bloodstreams to the dark hearts of young black men. This is a dark misdiagnosis.

Given the media's penchant for racially biased reporting, some have argued that the phenomenon of black-on-black crime is exaggerated or perhaps even mythical.[730] Statistics, however, seem to suggest otherwise. Black men are victimized by homicide at much higher rates than men of other races and their killers are most often black.[731][732] What's often ignored in discussions of black-on-black crime, however, is that homicides and other crimes are overwhelmingly intraracial for *all* groups. "Black-on-black" serves to white-out the backdrop of structural violence that in fact engenders the dusky phenomenon. Although black homicide rates are higher, as with other modes of black pathology this is not a cultural phenomenon but rather one that results from society denying blacks' humanity. We cannot ignore the burdens that society places on the heads of young African American men who, despite their promise, ambition, and brilliance, are granted no clemency. Society plays a pivotal role in engendering and often encouraging crime and violence when productive avenues are closed. It is not just African Americans who have a duty toward saving their communities and future generations from destruction—it is a national responsibility.

What can we do? For one, we must not respond with diffidence and dejection, but outrage and tireless intent to push for change in America's social structures. That statement doesn't just go for black people—it goes for *all* Americans. A weakened black America is a weakened America. The United States is no land of islands or gated communities in which the struggles and pains of one's brothers and sisters can be ignored. The Great Recession proved this; it was a crisis that would not have been so acute had America been more racially and socioeconomically egalitarian. Black families must also continue to emphasize the importance of pursuing education, fostering stable family units, eschewing drugs, and committing wholly to uplifting the community. This is not a matter of finger wagging toward the black community, but emphasizing the sanctity of this particular expression of spirit.

The public policy arena must host the most valiant spectacles of combat against America's institutional Goliath. Changes must be made in justice system, like ending the police "Occupation" of America's predominantly black neighborhoods. Changes must be made in the education system that will get America back on a path toward integration and halt the dangerous slide to an oppressive past and that will reform draconian discipline policies and plug the XL-sized school-to-prison pipeline. Changes must be made in the hearts and minds of America's teachers, of whom nine out of ten are white,[733] that will enable the promise of young black girls and boys to spring forth like green grass and flowers and plants in the well-watered earth. Changes must be made in the philosophies and considerations of our policymakers that recognize the humanity of black men and women who are no more criminal, no more deviant, no less hopeful, and no less American than they.

⑧
Failure to Thrive

Why?

Examining discrimination as a phenomenon that has characterized humanity—through all eras, in all corners of the globe, and in all cultures and civilizations—often yields this single question. It should. This question may seem naïve, even laughable, to those familiar with institutionalized racism's scythe. But it represents hope. When the once colorblind apply this inquiry to the American edifice of institutionalized racism, it means they have accepted its reality and have thus healed the colorblind condition. It is an act of healing not only unto their souls but unto the soul of America.

That question not only represents transformation, but also yields an expansion of consciousness accompanied by an array of sentiments which may include guilt. Guilt is powerless—it has no rightful place in the process. The most powerful way to honor the memories of yesterday's victims of systemic racism is to change America for the sake of those who suffer its burdens today. Expanding one's consciousness to accept the existence and magnitude of institutionalized racism in the United States is the first and most critical step in moving to deconstruct it. Any American and any human who makes that giant leap should be duly commended.

But that question of "why" is significant even for those of us who think we've got it all figured out, for it leads to other substantive inquiries. What is the origin of prejudice and how did it become racial? Why are blacks on the bottom, seemingly helpless in the face of the imperious beast that is institutionalized American racism? What will the final solution to the race question be—an end of brutality inspired by the horrors of humanity's past, or hope for an unprecedented future of global racial equality shepherded by an American standard?

Sociologists have advanced numerous theories in response to these age-old questions. Some speculate that racial prejudice originates from a human instinct to guard one's community or territory from unfamiliar and unrelated strangers.[734] Others assert that there is no specific instinctual component to prejudice, arguing that it is an organic development arising when one race arbitrarily comes to possess greater power and wealth than others, adopting defensive and oppressive attitudes toward those others to protect that accrued wealth and power.[735]

As for the Western mode of racism characterizing the United States and Europe, some argue that although Europeans did not at first view Africans as racially inferior, the trans-Atlantic slave trade and consequent mass presence of blacks in Western stations of servitude promoted the idea that blacks were inherently servile.[736] Arguments are too myriad to fill the confines of this book. But whatever racism's root, it has proved a substantial bane of human existence that has come to deeply characterize the spirit of America. More than perhaps any other race in the United States, it has tortured the souls of African Americans.

Have Americans really left ideas of racial superiority and inferiority in the past? Today, we honor Dr. King with both a federal holiday and a national

Last in Line: An American Destiny Deferred

monument and revere him as a titanic icon of the moral potential that lies within the souls of all men and women. We reach cross the Atlantic, beholding Nelson Mandela as a beacon of justice, a holy representation of the potential lying within the heart of each child to affect their Mother Earth. America remains in amorous awe of timeless black entertainment legends—Nat King Cole, Sidney Poitier, Aretha Franklin, and their present-day successors in Denzel Washington, Kerry Washington, and, in the sporting arena, LeBron James, beholding their talents as divine gifts and symbols of the vast human capacity for expression. No American would deny the greatness of these men and women or insinuate that their race bears even slight impact on the validity of that truth. But the success of these figures in a society marked by prevailing attitudes of racial bias raises the question of whether these figures are in fact respected *in spite* of their blackness.

Studies have shown that when whites view pictures of positive and influential black role models, they momentarily abandon negative stereotypical views of African Americans.[737] Thus, for many Americans only images of the Dr. Kings of the world—so few as they are—can serve to even ephemerally disabuse them of deep-seated prejudicial opinion. They fail to offset the overwhelming abundance of stereotyped images mass media markets in music, movies, and television which construct an unartful black portrait jeered by mainstream America. It is that preponderance of stereotyped images that casts the typical African American in a much less flattering light. It sometimes casts them in no light at all, instead shrouding them in cloaks of darkness or outright invisibility.

Studies conducted at the University of Toronto examined the reactions that white students had to videos of people drinking water.[738] Researchers recorded participants' brain wave activities as they watched videos of subjects of different races drinking water. As participants viewed videos of white subjects drinking water, corresponding brain waves in the area controlling eating and drinking showed up, thus demonstrating their psychological identification with the experience. This identification indicates the firing of mirror neurons, which enable us to relate to others' physical experiences—running, jumping, swimming, or even being kicked in the shin. When these students watched videos of African Americans drinking water, hardly any brain waves were detected.

The researchers, Jennifer N. Gutsell and Michael Inzlicht, were not quick to point to racial prejudice as the underlying cause of the absence of brain waves. Although they controlled for factors of age, looks, amiability, etc., they remained cautious in definitively inferring whether or not racial prejudice had any discernible influence on brain wave activity. To determine the racial prejudice of the viewers, researchers tested and measured each of them on the Symbolic Racism Scale. Unsurprisingly, the most racially prejudiced students showed the least brain wave reaction when viewing videos of black subjects. It would be one thing, perhaps, if the video showed people of different races carrying out carjackings or robberies, and the image of the black person triggered a *schema*, a preconceived prejudicial reaction. But for a black person doing something as harmless and mundane as drinking a glass of water to register such a callous reaction speaks volumes as to how deeply racism penetrates the American soul.

144

Chapter 8: Failure to Thrive

Such a study makes Kanye West's extemporaneous criticism of President George W. Bush in Hurricane Katrina's aftermath in 2005 seem reasonable. During an NBC-televised benefit for Katrina victims, West ignored teleprompted script and infamously uttered this controversial statement:

> I hate the way they portray us in the media. You see a black family, it says, "They're looting." You see a white family, it says, "They're looking for food." And, you know, it's been five days [waiting for federal help] because most of the people are black. And even for me to complain about it, I would be a hypocrite because I've tried to turn away from the TV because it's too hard to watch. I've even been shopping before even giving a donation, so now I'm calling my business manager right now to see what is the biggest amount I can give, and just to imagine if I was down there, and those are my people down there. So anybody out there that wants to do anything that we can help—with the way America is set up to help the poor, the black people, the less well-off, as slow as possible. I mean, the Red Cross is doing everything they can. We already realize a lot of people that could help are at war right now, fighting another way— and they've given them permission to go down and shoot us! [...] George Bush doesn't care about black people.[739]

West's statement may or may not be a fair assessment of Bush, but the University of Toronto study suggests his conclusion isn't far-fetched. FEMA's slow response to Katrina (which inauspiciously hit the lower, predominantly black wards of New Orleans), coupled with blatantly racist television news coverage that depicted blacks as "looters" and whites engaging in the same actions as desperate "survivors," roused the ire of West and many black Americans—and rightly so.[740] The actions of blacks, even when no different from those of whites, are invariably pictured through a callous, distrusting lens which devalues the image and essence of the object.

Last in Line has tirelessly exposed the wrongs of America's justice, education, and economic systems and the overarching policy edifice that powers them. It has also assiduously assessed these systems within ideological and historical frameworks. The prejudices of America's various social systems equate to one conclusion: black lives matter less. This extends to America's health care system, in which the refusal to embrace the value of black life is disturbingly apparent. More so than even the justice system, it has served as an unwanted matchmaker, pushing black life's flirtation with death into morbid marriage. This unholy matrimony serves as the greatest indicator of racial inequality in America today.

Although no race can have a moribund monopoly on death, African Americans dominate the mortality market. African American mortality rates are phenomenal.[741] It is not just a result of black-on-black crime, state execution, or police violence. The health care system's outsized influence on this figure can only be described as egregious. Even this adjective is perhaps insufficient to characterize the system that allows 100,000 black lives to slip through the cracks, a statistic reached when one controls for the black-white disparities in infant mortality in the United States.[742] The babies of black women are at least twice as likely as white infants to die in infancy.[743] Even more disturbing (and controversial) are statistics that claim to demonstrate abortion's devastating effect on African American population numbers.[744] From the cradle to the rocking chair—if they manage to survive so long—African American lives are deemed less than valuable by our country's physicians and health care administrators. But it is not only doctors who are to blame. It is the stethoscope of racial bias itself that presses the chests of African Americans, spurning its oath to rhythm by seeping electrical signals into palpitation and, finally, arrested silence.

Black America: Aborted

It should go without saying that slaves did not have access to America's best available health care. Working slaves to premature death was often cheaper than expending resources toward ensuring their health and longevity.[745] In slavery, African Americans had life spans rarely exceeding four decades.[746] One of the Freedmen's Bureau's missions was to ensure newly emancipated African Americans access to the best health care available, no less in quality than that afforded to their former captors.[747] Although the Bureau treated over a million ex-slaves, its medical program was terminated after January 1, 1869. Black mortality rates, even discounting mass lynchings and other genocidal onslaughts, would remain high through the turn of the century.[748]

High black mortality caused by societal negligence is one thing; high black mortality caused by calculated attempts is entirely another. Planned Parenthood was founded in 1916 by Margaret Sanger. Sanger, a daughter of Irish immigrants, was a trailblazer for reproductive rights in the United States. In a time in which American public policy had little respect for women's right to vote, much less choose, Sanger rang the radical principle that women should have freedom to their bodies. Sanger's reverberating platform included the radical notion that blacks should be included in radical movements.

Sanger courted the attentions of black priests and preachers, persuading them to swallow and regurgitate to African American congregations her pleas to regulate the sizes of their households.[749] Blessed by W. E. B. DuBois,[750] Sanger even opened a successful birth control clinic in Harlem, entirely staffed by black workers and supervised by an all-black, 15-member advisory board.[751] King conferred praise upon Sanger for her beneficent influence on the black community and,[752] in her presence, gladly received a plaudit named in her honor, the 1966 Margaret Sanger Award.[753] Outwardly, Sanger's birth control advocacy appeared benevolent and particularly useful to the black community. She was praised as a job creator, a stabilizer of the black household, and a friend to the black community.

Sanger never publicly professed her intentions, but in a private letter spelled in bloodied script:

> We do not want word to get out that we want to exterminate the Negro population...the [black] minister is the man who can straighten out that idea if it ever occurs to any of their more rebellious members.[754]

Sanger's unambiguous language unveils the true impetus behind her charade of goodwill. She is heralded as a sort of Joan of Arc by many reproductive rights activists today, but the fruits of her labors were poison for the black community. Although normally the more rational wing of American politics, the American left displays the awareness of the Flat Earth (or perhaps John Birch) Society when Sanger's racism is invoked. That Sanger preached "racial betterment,"[755] advocated elimination of the "unfit,"[756] and addressed a women's branch of the Ku Klux Klan in a secluded barn in 1926 (retold in her autobiography)[757] occasions from liberals not suspicion of Sanger's intentions, but outrage at those who parse her legacy. Such intolerance is ironic. The right has also distorted Sanger's legacy, perhaps unnecessarily, creating false quotations of more explicit racist and eugenicist voice. Sanger has erroneously been tagged with a quotation from the April 1933 issue of the *Birth Control Review* referring to "Slavs, Latin, and Hebrew immigrants" as "human weeds."[758] Although that quote and its credit are fabrications, Sanger's rhetoric was not alien to colorful, agrarian metaphor. She said in a 1924 address:

> The only real wealth of our country lies in the men and women of the next generation. A farmer would rather produce a thousand thoroughbreds than a million runts.
>
> How are we to breed a race of human thoroughbreds unless we follow the same plan? We must make this country into a garden of children instead of a disorderly back lot overrun with human weeds.[759]

Truth is nonpartisan. The peddled misquote attributed to Sanger never appeared in the *Birth Control Review*, but much of Sanger's writing did. The magazine's articles spurn explicit antiblack rhetoric for dog whistle advocacy; its bylines read like a "Who's Who" of the eugenics movement. Figures such as Harry H. Laughlin,[760] Paul Popenoe,[761] Havelock Ellis[762]—even Nazi official Ernst Rüdin[763] (who, in the midst of the Holocaust, preached the "value of eliminating young children of clearly inferior quality"[764])—grace disgraceful pages. It even waxes poetic with such odes as *Superman Arises*, which incites a nude, white inset toward, "Slaying…monsters of discord and darkness."[765] The *Birth Control Review* makes *The Bell Curve* seem "severely" liberal. The magazine's founder? Margaret Sanger.[766] Sanger served as editor-in-chief until 1928 before ceding editorship to another of her engineered offspring, the American Birth Control League, which later became Planned Parenthood. It is ironic that Planned Parenthood, an organization hailed by liberals today as an enabler of women's freedoms, started out as an organization akin to Nazi Germany's *Lebensborn* clinics.

Does that comparison seem strident?

It's difficult to see how it could be as strident as the *Birth Control Review* or its diametric fringe. Family planning and oral contraception were her chosen ones, but Sanger's birth control advocacy also begat an outcast—abortion. Although Sanger did not preach support for abortion,[767] her maternity cannot be denied. Hers was an immaculate conception; it was this pregnancy, unplanned, that ushered an American deliverance from wombed darkness to earthen divinity. Still, many Americans view the sanctification of abortion not as a divine shepherding of America to women's rights promised land, but a sodomite termination of sacrificial lambs. Such is blackgenocide.org's sermon.

Upon entering blackgenocide.org, one finds an ominous black background headlined by a more portentous quotation from "Civil Rights Leader and Social Worker" Erma Clardy Craven:

> Several years ago, when 17,000 aborted babies were found in a dumpster outside a pathology laboratory in Los, Angeles, California,[*sic*] some 12-15,000 were observed to be black.[768]

Details corroborating the information in Craven's quote are scant. The site's citations of InfoWars and its railing against homosexuality come across as unhinged, to boot. But evidence corroborating the mass abortion of black fetuses is not dubious. A 2010 study from the Guttmacher Institute, a pro-choice reproductive rights nonprofit, found that in 2008, black women accounted for 30 percent of abortions in the United States despite representing just 13 percent of women in America.[769] A separate study showed that in 2004, 37 percent of pregnancies for black women ended in abortion compared to just 12 percent for white women.[770] Such high numbers of abortion suggest that black population growth has taken a substantial hit. Although the debate over the point of conception persists, an aborted fetus is, if nothing else, one potential human being cast into oblivion. With such immense numbers of black women's fetuses being aborted, it is apparent that if fetuses count as human beings, then an extraordinarily large number of black human beings are dying before they see the light of day.

Such statistics will occasion from one an impassive yawn and from another a wide gape of horror. Whatever one's reaction, the website's use of the word "genocide" cannot escape notice. "Genocide" is as loaded a term as any. When one thinks of genocide, the first thing that usually comes to mind is the Nazi-sponsored conflagration of Jewish, Roma, Slavic, and other minority groups of Europe. The Holocaust is recognized as a great horror of the 20th century, undoubtedly one of the greater horrors to ever transpire in the history of humankind. Likewise with genocides in the Belgian Congo, German Namibia, Rwanda, Armenia, and beyond. It's no light matter to draw an explicit parallel between abortion, something commonly recognized as a quintessential human right, and the mass, frightening orgy of carnage that entails genocide. What exactly would compel someone to draw such an outrageous, perhaps even offensive parallel?

The website doesn't bend "genocide's" meaning. Like the dictionary, the website takes "genocide" to reference the great loss of life by members of a particular racial or ethnic group at the hands of some deliberative agent or orchestrator. It argues that if a human fetus is not merely an organism, but a person, and America's social policies purposefully engineer social conditions that engender mass abortion among black women, then the ostensible loss of life that results from this is a kind of genocide. However, the term "genocide" implies *deliberate* action on the part of some agent to extirpate the "other"— usually a marginalized racial, ethnic, or religious group. By this definition, that mass abortion is enabled by reproductive rights policy does not in any way qualify it as genocidal. Blacks in modern America are certainly marginalized, but, contrary to fringe narrative, they are not targeted for abortions.[771] More importantly, African American women are just as sentient and mature as white women, and thus able to decide if an abortive procedure is right for them. Whatever their reasons, although American black women are more likely to have abortions, this is their right.

If mass abortion results from black women's personal choices, how does it make any sense to compare it to the flagrance of genocide? The comparison could only be valid if black women's reproductive rights were being either seized or compelled toward an end of diminishing their reproduction. If public policies collude to create conditions of deprivation that make women of a specific racial or ethnic group more likely to choose abortion because of that deprivation, thus diminishing their reproduction and suppressing group population numbers, it can be argued that the production

148

function is similar. But it is necessary to parse policy from practice. Although reproductive rights policies can be seized and compelled toward nefarious practices, the policies themselves are not nefarious. For promoting reproductive rights, in part, to stymie the black population, Margaret Sanger can fairly be deemed genocidal. She did, after all, privately declare her intent to "exterminate" the black population of the United States. But that doesn't make *reproductive rights* genocidal.

This distinction is critical. As critical is the fact that Sanger's ignominy does nothing to diminish the integrity of Planned Parenthood and all who fight for women's rights in the 21st century. Although Sanger is the most important reproductive rights activist of the 20th century, she is a villainous outlier unrepresentative of the cadre of pro-choice activists who bravely defend women's freedoms. Though the legacy of Sanger's depravity may confound the essence of an unalienable right, abortion is not murder; mass black abortion is not genocide. But if government policies necessitate higher incidences of abortion among African Americans—and do so deliberately—that may constitute something just as egregious.

Population control bears intent as sinister as that of genocide. Forced sterilization procedures, mandated by many U.S. states throughout much of the 20th century, offer a harrowing example of population control policies authorized by the U.S. federal government with explicit racial motivations. With intentions as wicked and demented as those of Sanger, America's forced sterilization advocates utilized the power of government to carry out baleful human rights violations approaching the scale of ethnic cleansing. The survivors of such blatantly racist policies bear indelible scars upon skin, psyche, and soul.

The documentary *Maafa21* recounts numerous incidences of forced sterilization carried out under U.S. government auspices.[772] Sterilization and abortion are not commensurate, but are comparable. Although one is a violation and the other is a right, they achieve the same end—preventing birth. Sanger would have considered mass sterilization a pipe dream; in fact, her magazine featured numerous pieces in support of forced sterilization legislation. Although she herself did not proclaim unequivocal support, Sanger touted sterilization's virtues in stymieing "dysgenic" populations.[773]

"They justified…that my [children] would be feeble-minded…," said Elaine Riddick of North Carolina who, after having been kidnapped and raped, bore a son.[774] For her horrid experience, social workers with the North Carolina Eugenics Board classified then-14-year-old Riddick as "promiscuous" and "feeble-minded" before sterilizing her. Riddick's son, Tony, went on to become the president of his own semi-conductor company, the owner of a construction company, and the owner of his own real estate company. Tony said of the Eugenics Board that condemned him to a pathetic existence, "[Their work] was not far from the thinking of Hitler."[775] Elaine Riddick was but one of innumerable young black women subjected to the Nazi-like sterilization policies of North Carolina, which had sterilization-enforcing statutes on the books as late as 2003.[776] Thousands of North Carolinians, many of them black, were subjected to the same fate as Riddick, their posterity forever lost to sinister syringes.

Stories like Elaine's may seem to be isolated incidents, unworthy of comparison to the massive, intergovernmental logistical efforts of Nazi Germany to annihilate *untermenschen*, but America's population control practices were anything but isolated. At the peak of the eugenics movement in the United States, over 32 states had eugenics laws targeting poor, disabled, criminalized, and, most numerously, black Americans.[777][778] Speculative estimates hold that over 70,000 Americans were forcibly sterilized, but it's impossible to know how many were victimized at the unsterile hands of human rights-aborting governments. Although birth control and forced sterilization are not identical, both were tools in the eugenics arsenal of American health policy for numerous decades. But, although Margaret Sanger's Harlem clinic could reasonably be fitted as a holocaust museum dedicated to those lost who were never with us at all, those wicked machinations no longer bear upon pro-choice policy. America is without those "negricidal" clinics and, similarly, sterilization laws are now off the books.

Although Planned Parenthood and reproductive rights nonprofits today have nothing to do with Sanger's devious population control *practices*, the intimation concerns whether abortion as a reproductive rights *policy* fulfills a population control function. The legislators following Madison Grant's trail in sowing oats of barrenness across America wed population control practice and reproductive rights policy in a eugenic marriage somehow bearing dysgenic progeny. But no matter that the population control practices advanced by the eugenics movement once perverted reproductive rights policy, reproductive rights policies like abortion are today divorced from those practices. If this is the case, how could reproductive rights still serve the end of population control?

Sterilization policy in America was designed toward the explicit practice of population control—chiefly racial. Reproductive rights policy's machinery *can* be *employed* toward such ends, as Margaret Sanger displayed in her birth control activism, but the key distinction is that the policy is not *designed* toward the function of violating black women's individual agency. Its design specification is quite the opposite, as its practice is to elevate every woman's right to choose. Sterilization policies violated the human rights of Elaine Riddick and untold numbers of African American women. Because of their blackness, they were deprived of agency of destiny. But, that a benign policy like abortion can be corrupted toward nefarious ends means that it can still fulfill a population control function. It too can seize the agency of destiny.

Why are black women more likely than white women to choose abortion? Above all, there's the fact that abortion seems to work as a logical preventative to poverty. This goes for women of all ethnicities, but is particularly relevant for black women given their community's critical economic condition. There are practical reasons for impoverished women—many who are black—to opt for abortions. Those who justify this assert that poverty makes it necessary for African Americans to relieve the strain that overpopulation can place on attenuated black neighborhoods. Sanger tanned such reasoning into sheepskin, donning it to promote her "Negro Project" in black neighborhoods.[779] Black families who can barely make ends meet may already be burdened with childcare costs for one or more children. They may also be deprived of the proper health insurance to care for newborns, and eventually children, in sickness. These realities suggest that black women are often better advised to opt for abortions.

But this revelation adds to a troubling pattern. As with "pathologies" of welfare dependence, unemployment, mass incarceration, and other symptoms of the virus of institutional racism afflicting the black community, we notice yet again a phenomenon that is neither isolated nor organic, but corollary of a systemically oppressive manifold. Abortion policy gives black women choice, but socioeconomic circumstances confound that choice.

Socioeconomic marginalization atomizes the chain of causality, reassembling bonds in rusted, low-grade alloys that snap with the yank of a fierce-faced whitecoat bearing arms of race hate. Sterilization laws are off the books; but with chains like this, who needs cords? There is no Nazi-inspired network of eugenicists scheming to wipe out the black population of America, poking and prodding abortion policy down the plank with an unsterilized needle. Black women get more abortions because the institutionally racist patterns of American society *necessitate* that they do.

Blackgenocide.org cites information (allegedly from the Centers for Disease Control, although no specific reports are cited) claiming that 13 million black fetuses have been aborted since *Roe v. Wade* and that America's black population would have numbered 52 million in 2007, compared to 40 million, if not for mass abortion. Although little can be made of this projection, it stands to reason that if not for the economic disadvantages resulting from institutional racism, black America could likely sustain the much larger numbers who may exist if not for mass abortion. There is no black American "Holocaust." There is no Adolf Hitler, barking vitriolic sermons of a "black question" and swearing to answer in the form of a "final solution"—at least not today. But when the *Gestapo* of flawed public policies converges on human rights, seizing and negating unalienable agency, those bearing such sympathies need no *Führer*.

America doesn't need *any* policy changes to abortion law. *Roe v. Wade* is one of the monumental Supreme Court decisions of the 20th century, one that we can luckily say has so far remained faithfully untouched and respected by the Supreme Court. If anything, we must strengthen our resolve in the fight to maintain every woman's right to choose. If black women opt for abortions on their own volition, these acts are entirely consistent with rights that should be neither denounced nor denied. But as long as institutional racism continues to deprive African Americans of the means to care for black children—effectively stealing from black women full agency over their right to choose—the extraordinary black abortion rate will remain a consequence of our protective mechanism for women's choice.

Sanger's fanaticism gave birth to sensationalism. It also begat silence. Her spirit lives, but sermons elsewhere—in places where her pleas resound subliminally. Eerie cries enter the consciousness of those sworn unto gods to preserve the sanctity of health, healing, and human life.

Universal Health Scare

Birth control and sterilization clinics stood as the health care system's most menacing agents of institutional racism toward African Americans in the early-to-mid 20th century, but in the 21st century America's doctor's offices stand in their stead. There are a number of mind-boggling statistics regarding the health care system's contribution to the black mortality rate. As with many issues of disparity, sociologists often ascribe systemic inequities to issues of class on impulse. But, just as is the case with practically all other disparities, race proves more relevant than class with regard to health disparities. Among other places, proof lies in degrees of separation: graduate and professionally educated black women have been found to have higher rates of infant mortality than even white women who *never entered* high school.[780]

Last in Line: An American Destiny Deferred

The problem of infant mortality that Dr. King raised in the same breath as his "Dream" persists. Despite this category of black women having higher earnings and better access to health care, their babies were more likely to die than even those white women who come from backgrounds of the greatest disadvantage.[781] Even among black women who receive early prenatal care, infant mortality rates are nearly double those of white women who receive *no* care at all, pre- or postnatal.[782] High-income, educated black women's statistically established conscientiousness and active utilization of health care scuttles the slightest echo of their agency being the cause.

None of the abovementioned facts alone proves racism's influence. After all, even if black women take advantage of health care they could still fail to take care of their health. If they eat poorly and exercise less, such habits can contribute to poor health outcomes including infant mortality. It's a fact; African Americans are, on average, less healthy than their white counterparts.[783] This results in part from poor nutrition[784] and a lack of exercise.[785] [786] Still, African American women are not so significantly unhealthy as to justify this vast a disparity in infant mortality rates.[787] Even if poor states of health were implicated, they would still necessarily be partly ascribed to other factors. Poor diet and inactivity are two factors that contribute to malnourishment and obesity among black women—but what is it that causes some black women to have such awful diets and such poor exercise habits in the first place? It harks to black "pathology"—the root of which we know is institutionalized racism.

African Americans certainly don't have the most salubrious diets in America. Such dietary disregard has roots in the traditions of American slavery. African Americans weren't afforded the choicest cuts of the beasts that many of them raised for planters. Southern delicacies like chitterlings, pig feet, ox tails, and even pork brains originate from this era in which blacks, in accordance with their status as chattel, were treated to the expendable, unwanted, and less nutritious scraps and fragments of slaughtered livestock.[788] Such traditions endured, becoming proud cultural conventions for African Americans. These dietary fixtures also brought poor health outcomes.

Studies have shown that African Americans consume higher levels of saturated fats[789] and consume fewer minerals than dietary guidelines recommend.[790] Blacks also consume less whole grains than white Americans.[791] Further contributing to blacks' poor state of health is their eschewal of fruits[792] and other natural, unprocessed foods. These abysmal dietary habits contribute to African Americans having significantly higher chances of developing Type 2 diabetes.[793] Higher incidences of high blood pressure, stroke, heart attack, and prostate cancer among black people also result, in part, from traditionally poor dietary habits.[794]

But tradition can only partly explain the unhealthy habits which impair the health of African Americans today. During the Great Recession, African Americans were forced to opt for even unhealthier diets in response to increased financial burdens.[795] High-end grocery stores boasting cornucopias of healthy options, like Whole Foods, are notoriously expensive and often unaffordable for the average black family.[796] If healthier, more natural alternative foodstuffs are cost prohibitive, to where does one turn? Fast food seems to be the answer.

Fast food is cheap, satiating, scrumptious, and, in copious amounts, unkind to one's health.[797] It's also convenient. No one is shoving that Big Mac or 64-ounce soda down any black man or woman's esophagus, but the option of a McDonald's on the corner makes a low-income individual significantly more likely to consume fast food. Some have speculated that fast food chains target black communities, taking advantage of their poverty and incognizance of the significant dangers of fast food.[798] Are those two golden arches really symbols of institutional racism, or are they just representative of a business enterprise that feeds communities on the cheap? There is no decree stipulating that blacks patronize fast food chains, even if they are tantalizingly placed on street corners. Does black consumer demand both warrant and welcome the occupation of their neighborhoods by McDonald's, Wendy's, Kentucky Fried Chicken, and Burger King franchises that seem to operate more like bases of conquering armies than mere restaurants?

There is no doubt that the fiscal activity of African Americans invites fast food chain presence. But it is arguable that this would not be the case if African Americans weren't inescapably ensconced in social echelons that prevent them from taking home the type of earnings that make the purchase of an organic whole chicken from a posh, pricey natural foods store—or even Wal-Mart—an action unworthy of a second thought. Nonetheless, fast food chains aren't vulnerable, powerless entities sucked into minority communities against their will. They are as aggressive in their conquest of black neighborhoods as Roman *centuriae* tearing through barbarous Britannia. The triumph through desolate, low-income communities doesn't offer a street view of low-cost, healthy selections. It shows fast food franchises.

Fast food consumption may be a matter of necessity, in that such restaurants are often the only ones affordable to the residents of such communities. But no matter the cause of their presence, fast food chains are turning the black community into a corpulent mass. Such massiveness is evidenced in the 51 percent increased incidence of obesity among blacks when compared to whites.[799] More specifically, it is illustrated in the 24.8 percent of black girls between the ages of 12 and 19 who are obese compared to just 14 percent of white girls in the same age group, and the 23 percent of black adolescent males suffering from obesity compared to just 17 percent of white males.[800]

Calorie-laden, heavily processed fast food isn't the only option for low-income Americans. But it is an incredibly convenient one, especially for those who work multiple jobs to support households and cannot afford the time cost of preparing cheap vegetables and other healthier, affordable foodstuffs. Even if one is unemployed and therefore unable to excuse their fast food gorging as a matter of temporal convenience, dietary limitation still looms. Grocery store shelves host items that heartily compete with KFC buckets and Wendy's quarter-ponders for the title "worst food in the world." These unwholesome items are often as cheap as, and are sometimes cheaper than, fast food. The common rejoinder that grocery food is invariably healthier than fast food is spurious, as many grocery store inventories are stacked to the ceiling with ready-to-eat, fast food-like product lines.[801] It doesn't matter if blacks turn to fast food joints or to junk food-filled grocery store shelves— economic deprivation effectively limits their food selections and contributes to poorer health outcomes.

It has been established that African Americans have poorer health outcomes, but does this have any bearing on their disproportionate infant mortality rates? African American women may have higher rates of obesity and fall behind in other health measures compared to white women, but these factors cannot alone scientifically explain why the black infant mortality rate is more than double that of white Americans. Furthermore, the fact that affluent, highly educated, healthy black women *still* have higher rates of infant mortality than white women without even a 9th grade education shows that other factors are at play.

Dr. Death

Statistical suggestions of racial discrimination in the health care system are not limited to analyses of infant mortality. Figures for adult mortality don't fare much better, with black adults being 1.5 times more likely to die than their white counterparts.[802] Studies have suggested that the same factors partly responsible for the high black infant mortality rate may also be culpable in promoting the high black adult mortality rate. In response to a congressional request, the Institute of Medicine conducted a study released in 2002 to assess "racial and ethnic differences in health care."[803] Their studies determined that despite their needs for medical procedures, "minorities…[were] less likely to receive routine medical procedures [from physicians] than [were] whites."[804] Why physicians neglect to recommend medical procedures for African Americans in the same way they do for whites remains mysterious.

Access is not implicated at all, as the study focuses on African Americans who are adequately insured.[805] Despite the health concerns and definite health insurance of these black patients, physicians (of whom three out of four in America are white[806]) seem less compelled to engage in certain evaluative medical practices for the benefit of their health and well-being. This does not only apply to routine check-ups or ear-eye-throat examinations—the IOM study examines coronary artery bypass surgery and kidney dialysis among other serious procedures, operations which often narrowly separate life from death.[807] The study found that doctors are less likely to refer black women for angioplasty and coronary artery bypass surgery.[808] The study also examined race disparity in infant mortality, showing that non-smoking black women have higher infant mortality rates than even white women who smoke throughout the entire duration of their pregnancies.[809]

A joint study conducted by the Harvard School of Public Health and Brigham and Women's Hospital, Boston found other details exposing some of our nation's doctors as agents of institutional racism. It found that African Americans were much likelier to be readmitted to hospitals following hospitalizations for serious medical problems.[810] After analyzing Medicare data, the study found that blacks hospitalized for heart attack, congestive heart failure, and pneumonia, among other ailments, were 13 percent more likely to be readmitted following their initial hospitalizations. The study also found that hospitals in predominantly minority demographics were burdened, their patients being 22 percent likelier to be readmitted. Conversely, whites in non-minority serving areas had the lowest chances of being readmitted to hospitals following the original incidence of their medical emergencies. Even when controlling for factors of socioeconomic status, income, and education, the disparities found by the studies in both readmission rates and the avoidance of life-saving procedures remain wide and clear.

But not only does research confirm the presence and prevalence of race disparities in procedure recommendation and readmission—it also shows clear, incontrovertible evidence of racial bias in prescription drug treatment. A 2012 University of Washington study showed that pediatricians show race

154

bias in recommending pain medication, being more likely to offer pain medication for whites' medical conditions and, at that, offering more effective pain medication for their ailments.[811] Another study examined the nature of communication between patients and doctors and nurses, assessing interactions to discern whether or not communications with patients differed on the basis of racial or ethnic background.[812]

The study determined what, if any, advice doctors gave patients in the form of suggested lifestyle changes, recommended health care regimens, and beyond. The study found a substantial difference between the ways white doctors and nurses interacted with white patients and the ways they interacted with black patients, the latter being given a much lower and less intimate standard of interaction. A later study further corroborated this, but extended trends of bias beyond white health care providers. Asian and Hispanic doctors and nurses were also discovered to show negative implicit bias in their interactions with black patients. The study showed that only black doctors showed no biases, implicit or otherwise.

Despite myriad studies proving racial bias' influence in the health care system, little is said of it. Is America oblivious?

Knowledge of the health care system's disparities has not been beyond the awareness of our members of Congress. Former Senate Majority Leader Bill Frist vowed to reduce the health care system's rampant racial disparity. At the commencement of the 108th Congress in January 2003, Leader Frist placed himself in an unusual position with the Republican Party, which is dismissive of the health care pleas of minorities and generally trusts the health care system as beyond reproach. Laudably, Frist said, "For reasons we don't fully understand, but we've got to face and we've got to elevate, we know that African Americans today do not live as long."[813]

Frist, a trained physician, continued his humanitarian declaration, stating intently, "[African Americans] don't have the same access, and the doctor-patient relationship in some way is colored by the medical training. And that's something I began to address a long time ago and will continue to address."[814]

How exactly Frist had previously moved to address such disparities was not explained; neither was the legislative plan for how he and his colleagues would treat such inequality. Still, Frist insisted upon his unequivocal devotion, stating further:

> Health care disparities, minority versus nonminority populations, is something I feel strongly about…you'll see that elevated. So when we say Medicare, prescription drugs, which is what everybody thinks about, let's not forget that there are many health care challenges, which I would call crises, out there today.[815]

Rambling notwithstanding, Frist's stated devotion to minority health care was refreshing, especially considering his membership in a party widely considered insensitive to minority issues. But this treacle, conservative change of heart interestingly transpired in the aftermath of Mississippi senator Trent Lott's questionable praise of former hard-line segregationist Strom Thurmond. Lott—himself a former majority leader and naturally close confidant of Frist—praised Thurmond's legacy at the South Carolina senator's centennial birthday celebration, toasting to his failed 1948 White House bid:

Last in Line: An American Destiny Deferred

When Strom Thurmond ran for president, we voted for him. We're proud of it. And if the rest of the country had followed our lead, we wouldn't have had all these problems over the years, either.[816]

The fallout from Lott's December 2002 remarks was tremendous. It is unclear what "problems" Senator Lott referenced, but given Strom Thurmond's virulently racist background we can rest assured that inadequate minority health care was not among them. Frist's remarks were met with healthy skepticism, widely derided as an empty promise administered as party damage control treatment. Such cynical reaction was further justified when Republicans rolled out their key legislative objectives for the congressional session in January 2003, among them:

- Passing George W. Bush's tax cut proposal
- Improving domestic and national security
- Adopting prescription drug coverage for the elderly
- Financing No Child Left Behind
- Promoting oil drilling in Alaska[817]

Nowhere was there any mention of Frist's lofty promise to "elevate" the issue of health care disparity affecting African Americans. Former senator Rick Santorum justified the vacillation, saying, "When you're in a recession...[and] you're at war...you have to focus on, No.1, winning the war, and No. 2, trying to get this economy up and going."[818] In the eyes of Santorum, Frist, and their senatorial colleagues, black babies perishing so untimely and adult African Americans being diagnosed with terminal hypochondria—treated with boots and doors to their backsides—meant nothing.

Could health care race disparities not have at least warranted a third place ranking on Santorum's metric? Hopefully no African Americans held their breath in anticipation of the passage of Frist's phantom legislation. (If by chance they did, we at least have some explanation for any marginal spikes in the black adult mortality rate circa 2003.) During this session of Congress, no legislation geared toward reducing the health care system's race disparity was passed. To his credit, Senator Frist did introduce the Minority Health Improvement and Health Disparity Elimination Act in 2006.[819] The Senate never voted on it.[820]

The ostensible Republican concern for minority health care proved a charade. Since Frist's departure from the Senate in 2007, his Republican colleagues have shown no desire to rescue his bill from bottom of the legislative heap for much-needed, Red Cross-style CPR. In fact, many of Frist's former colleagues, such as current Senate Majority Leader Mitch McConnell, have placed atop their legislative agenda the goal of abrogating the Patient Protection and Affordable Care Act,[821] better known as Obamacare, the only legislation in recent history that has even remotely offered some means of mitigating racial disparity in the health care system.

At the sight of black patients, some of America's doctors put away stethoscopes, store away scalpels, and tuck away prescription-writing pens. They confront their black patients with blank countenances, dismissing dire, fatal health concerns as a drapetomania epidemic. What's scariest is that it is

156

so often done unwittingly. In the places we turn to in search of humble public servants, we instead find some who first altogether ignore critical issues and then perform a 180-degree gyration, feigning compassion and concern to tranquilize. That doctors recommend that their black patients not consternate about heart palpitations or other potentially deadly symptoms when they would, if the same patient were white, make haste to solve the health crisis reflects black invisibility and a profundity of institutional racism which cannot enough be emphasized. They betray their oath to thousands of black men, women, children, and elderly, denying them the care fate ordains.

It is not even these outward, reprehensible realities that most contribute to the vast African American death toll. It is instead one visceral, systemically distressing the African American, killing them softly with an insidious toll exacted upon body and soul.

Killing Them Softly

"This racism is *killing* me inside!"

The *Chappelle's Show*'s "Niggar Family" skit is one of the more memorable showings from the legendary 2000s Comedy Central series. The character jigging this line—a black milkman serving a white family bearing the decidedly awkward surname "Niggar"—is *kidding*. But, in reality, many African Americans can directly apply these words to actual deterioration of their mental and physical well-being resulting from the unwavering, seemingly inescapable stresses of institutional and interpersonal racism.

Could racism really have psychosomatic influences on the health of African Americans? Being called a racial epithet or explicitly discriminated against in some other way can arouse pain and anger in those on the receiving end of such abuse. But we generally presume the extent of impact is a brief frustration that quickly subsides. Unfortunately, the extent of such abuse goes beyond the ephemeral. Medical research has established an important link between mental and physical health; many hardworking Americans can testify to the negative effects that stress has on the immune, cardiovascular, and other anatomical systems. But, although we may easily see how institutional racism structurally suffocates the black community, can we really go so far as to assert that it suffocates the black individual?

In a speech detailing the health care system's racial disparities, author Tim Wise offered the following:

> The accumulation of trauma and stress on peoples of color subjected to discrimination over many years can, independent of economic...occupational...income...and [other such] factors, affect the health.[822]

Once again excluding the overstated class diagnosis, we see *race* by itself ravaging minority immune systems. A number of studies documenting the relationship between experiences of racial prejudice and stress confirm Wise's hypothesis. Surprisingly, it's not even the overt, open forms of racism that most contribute to the stress that creates and exacerbates minority health problems. It's the little things. Acts of microaggressive racism are even more damaging than many of the horrific, terroristic acts of racism that garner widespread media attention; they cause much greater loss of life. It defies reason that terroristic acts—everything from spray painting racial epithets, to hanging nooses, to mass shootings—*do not* represent the most emotionally devastating doings of racial hostility. As it turns out, it's the vague and uncertain gestures of racism which cause the greatest psychological torment and, in turn, physical injury.

Whereas with direct expressions of racial hostility the recipient is able to clearly identify the event, establish its meaning, and formulate a solution, the more equivocal expressions of racism leave the recipient stuck in the stage of identification, engendering confusion and a persistent, nagging consternation. A sole black diner in a restaurant may wonder if glances are hostile, if a long wait is deliberate, or if generally poor service is indicative of racial inhospitality. It's easy to write off such concerns as overreactions, but when one experiences these events repeatedly, the resulting mental confusion causes a sustained increase in stress hormones. When these perceptions of racial microaggressions—stares, suggestive comments, second-rate service—become a daily or even weekly occurrence, they result in excess levels of adrenaline, cortisol, and other stress hormones circulating in the body. These hormones are healthy in moderation and when released in certain, isolated situations of distress. But when their levels are sustained over long durations, significant damage is caused to endocrine and other anatomical systems.[823]

It is not just African American adults who are affected by racism's faint whispers; not even their unborn are spared. Studies assessed the effects racial microaggressions had on the allostatic loads of African American women.[824] Allostatic load measures the physiological effects of piqued, overreactive endocrine systems that are triggered into overdrive as a result of repeated psychological stressors.[825] These studies found that black women had increased allostatic loads, which inhibited the placenta's ability to attach to the uterine wall, thus increasing the likelihood of miscarriage, low birth weight, and infant mortality.[826] Interestingly, even poor white women were found to have low allostatic loads compared to wealthy black women.

Black children fall victim to the effects of institutional racism long before their first whiff of polluted air or their first frisk at police hands. It hits black infants before they experience hostile gazes, low-quality service, and the ever-looming black, precipitating cloud of doubt hovering overhead. It paralyzes them long before they feel the pain and confusion their mothers and fathers internalize from existence in a rejecting society. Perhaps these unborn black babies possess some strange, disheartening clairvoyance that allows them to foresee the grim, debased future that lies ahead. Perhaps they see the stigma and disposability their skin will guarantee them. Perhaps they see themselves come to term, wallowing through a life in which they are dead long before the heart runs out. Perhaps they actively terminate, sparing themselves the terminal condition.

An Unrealized Fate

Place your feet in the shoes of a 69-year-old African American man. Your health is frail, your days numbered. You reflect on a long, hard road. Unlike many African Americans, poverty does not nag you. You are relatively successful—college-educated and comfortably middle class. It's remarkable that you achieved the average lifespan of a black male in the United States, considering the masses of black men who die before they reach even their

Chapter 8: Failure to Thrive

60th birthday. You grew up in the Jim Crow South at its tail end, thus enabling you to witness America's transition from explicit to implicit modes of racism. You overcame both, going on to receive a college education at a respected, unanimously white Northeastern university. You endure a long four years of exclusion and discrimination, but receive a fine education.

It's not quite like the "nigger"-laden abuses you were accustomed to in the South, but it's somehow as painful. Whether conveyed in the form of seemingly harmless comments regarding your race or intellectual inability, you tolerate constant reminders of otherness. You surmount. Congratulations— you graduate *magna cum laude*, just in time to seize the first fruits of affirmative action policies. You are offered a position at a previously all-white corporation. You eagerly accept the well-paying, white-collar job—and the honor of chucking that proverbial "Whites Only" sign into oblivion. But from day one, snide remarks, curt glances, and interrogations of your background and qualifications abound. Your boss greets you on the first day, saying without flippancy, "It's amazing you graduated *magna cum laude*...it's nice we're *giving* these kinds of things to blacks these days."

You witness white colleagues pass you up for promotions and special assignments—even those junior to you. You continue to work hard and operate punctually, even going for a master's in your field at night. You are working "twice as hard," adhering to the advice your parents conveyed emphatically, but getting only half as far. A white coworker is routinely found sleeping on the job, startling to slaps on the wrist. A black coworker found dozing off once is threatened with immediate termination. After five years, you confront your boss about that elusive promotion. Puffing, he grins, "See...we love having you around here. You really add an element of diversity...it's really valuable. I really like affirmative action...your people need a little help from us in getting ahead. But I can't promote you just because you're black, you know..."

Not only do you endure cold colleagues and a negligent, cigar-aficionado boss—you also have trouble situating your new family. After trying 20 different complexes in an attempt to rent an apartment in proximity to work, you finally find one. It's seedy and overpriced, but it's something—a layover. After a few years, your fiancée is ready to move on. "I'm sick of the rats, roaches, and mildew...you make all that money and you can't do better?" You skip lunch breaks, calling realtor after realtor, trying to find a home near your job. The housing market is booming. Everything is "sold," "no longer available," and "purchased...a few minutes ago." At long last, you find a home. Far away from work, low-income, ramshackle. But, who knows? If you're lucky, rats and roaches won't greet you at the door.

Fast forward a few years. You're a father of two, ages four and five. Thanks to newly instituted busing policies, your kids attend the same well-funded schools as white children. You hope they'll be spared the racism to which you've grown inured. But that's futility. You come home from work each evening hoping tomorrow will bring that next, deserved promotion (after 10 years and lots of similar complaints from other black employees you were reluctantly granted one). One day you come home to a surprise. "Daddy— what's a nigger?" You're certain that wasn't in the day's vocabulary lesson, but you know you have no recourse. Storming into the classroom will convey the lesson of an "angry black man," making things harder for your kids. They'll have to learn the way you did.

Last in Line: An American Destiny Deferred

You finally find a home in an affluent white neighborhood and waste no time making a down payment. The house across the street has moving trucks too—only theirs are taking items from, not to, their house. As you unload items you notice an elderly man peering from across the street. He says nothing, but blue, piercing eyes speak volumes. Six months pass. You, your wife, and your kids are rich in empty gazes and dispossessed of "hellos." You notice a new family moving in the house across from you that was vacated by that fierce countenance. Their wealth accrues differently.

Following 20 years of commitment, you request a third promotion. Your boss' grin collapses. He blows, exclaiming, "You people always want a handout!" You're fired. "Pick up your severance pay, quick, and go ahead and apply for welfare, half of you are on it anyway." You heed his advice—it's not like you have a choice. Despite the unemployment benefits, severance pay, and some of your accrued income, you fall behind on your mortgage. In desperation, you plead with your real estate agent to help you refinance your mortgage deal. She coolly replies, "Gee, I'm sorry about that." You call the bank directly, with an ultimately unmoving supplication for your family's salvation. You lower yourself, begging aloof neighbors to lend you money—to just chip in and help you and your kids continue to have a place to stay. They did so with a family up the street who approached foreclosure's precipice; maybe they have hearts, after all. After getting brushed off by everyone who has "an appointment in five minutes" or who "has to go," one of them responds with some semblance of candor saying, "Sorry...we all have jobs and we all work hard to live here. We don't take handouts, why should you get one?"

You foreclose. Barred from reentry, the bank has a moving company put your belongings in the street. Neighbors watch in silence. Your wife can't take it any longer. You've done nothing wrong; she just can't go on this way. It's over. She takes the children, which you agree may be for the best. Divorced, dispossessed, back you go into that old, seedy apartment you started out in seemingly not so long ago. Aged and poorly referenced, you're reduced to blue-collar humility. It's a tough pill to swallow. But when you recall that, unlike most black men you were born with, you aren't dead, incarcerated, or unemployed, it takes a little easier. This is as good as it gets. You get on with life. Until that day you hit that unlikely age, replaying it all.

You're never really sure just how much any of this is attributed to racism. You spend your nights ruminating, wondering where you went wrong. Yes, *you*. Maybe you didn't study hard enough. Maybe you weren't friendly enough. Maybe you weren't a good enough husband and father. Maybe you just aren't good enough. After all, who's right—one man who happens to be black? Or the many who insist that he didn't measure up?

Does this scenario not sound like the sort that can place continuous mental and emotional strain on a human being? Does this scenario not sound like the type that can contribute to a restless allostatic load, saturating one's system with hormones that drive blood pressure through the roof? Does this scenario *not* sound like the type that can inter a man or a woman long before his or her physical death? And this is the example of a "successful" black man—a statistical outlier. How much worse is it for the many lacking this sort of "privilege"?

We could chalk this representative's experiences up to bad luck—"just life." We could go further and grant that his circumstances are a result of racial discrimination. But few of us will grant that his health could, in such a deep way, be tied to racism. Given the research on allostatic load, those who think that such events do not to contribute to health problems should be disabused of that idea. *Last in Line* has argued that the poor dietary and exercise habits of African Americans are tied to institutional racism and that the poorer quality care afforded to them in the health care system is too. But what indicates the power of everyday acts of racial discrimination even more is the fact that the microcosmic manifestations of racism—the silent stares—are, cumulatively, *at least* as harmful to African Americans' health as poor dietary and exercise habits and racially discriminatory health care practices. This puts the issue of health disparity between blacks and whites in a different light, one that shows that it is not only the edifices of American society that weigh heavily upon the backs of blacks, but also the burdens of tiny, daily repudiations that tear African American bodies limb from limb.

Conclusion

Who cares? Really—why should African Americans worry if others have racist attitudes? If a person fails to recognize the sentience and humanity of someone just because they are black, it may be wrong but it is their right. It's no big deal, right?

It's a huge deal. Rights do not justify this phenomenon. One may have the legal right to discriminate in regard to, say, their social circle, but having such rights does not pardon their wrongful consequences. The matter of people hating or disliking African Americans is not simply some vain, cosmopolitan rendition of a high school popularity contest in which blacks have come out as the socially inept, shunned losers. Racial bias has veritable consequences which have significantly affected all of the societal structures thus far explored in *Last in Line*.

When a person can look into the bright eyes of a black child as they jump from a playground slide and see nothing, it disrupts the pulse of our society, palpitating our shared heart. When a person can watch this child leap onto the monkey bars, emitting jubilant laughter in propulsion, and not see or feel this joy, our country bleeds. When a person can see this beautiful young black child fall from these monkey bars, hitting hard ground, breaking soft, young bones, screaming, writhing in pain—and see absolutely nothing—it puts our country into a vegetative state from which we may never emerge.

Truth can be changed but not circumvented or refuted. Power is unequal in the United States—this is as modern a characterization as it is historical. But it is not to history that we must look for evidence of this truth. We must look to the faces of our leaders in government and society today. The judges resegregating our souls; the members of Congress fueling disparity with tainted, unjust substance; the policemen accosting the bodies and futures of young black men; the financial agents peddling onslaughts on the dollar; and the physicians dispensing terminal treatment are all agents and symbols of American racial inequality. It is they who defer our American destiny.

Until Americans change our truth to that of an equitable society in which power and wealth are proximate between all races, African Americans will have to be mindful of the dangerous racial attitudes that threaten their destiny. Their survival depends on it. As of this day their education, financial well-being, health, and freedom are not fully in their hands. Until that new day of declaration, in which America belongs to all, arrives—and first and foremost, in order to get to that destiny—we must closely monitor the abusive agents that hold in their hands the power to deny life to Americans, both those living and those yet to be conceived.

9

A National Salvation

Colorblindness is illusory. Skeptical eyes having seen this far can no further be shortsighted. I am critical of the term but I do not deride the vision that lies behind it. We should honor the image of an America in which race truly does not matter and men and women of all colors have equal opportunities and tones of wealth, resources, and freedom. But to illustrate the colorblind society before its arrival is to mock it. Ours is a caricature. It denies— America's galleries have separate, unequal standards of service. "Colorblindness" is a striking subject, but our awe of this ideal is deluded entertainment. We cannot toast to this exhibition, for America is not yet party to the society in which one's epidermal cover doesn't deny admittance. This land—this celebration—is far away.

Colorblindness is a curious condition. Whenever I hear the assurances of those who "don't see color," I react—purely on impulse—with boisterous laughter. Smirks go straight. "What's so funny?" Realizing my ableism, I echo Lincoln. "Nothing...but if I didn't laugh, I would most assuredly cry." What compels the declaration? Someone colorblind would lack the *perception* of color; the sight of a "colored" person would not compel disclosure. "Colorblind" is a pat on the back—not that of the "colored" or "dysgenic," thankfully. It's a high five to oneself. Unlike color vision deficiency, colorblindness resolves on its own—when someone of another color wants the same job, house, or opportunity. Studies show that the most effective cure for colorblindness is interior design. Children have the eye for introducing to hearth unfashionable yet therapeutic color and lighting schemes. Without aid of Lasik surgery, contact lenses, or any visual repair aids, colorblindness reverses. Somehow, after corneas are cleansed of foreign substance, the benign condition returns.

With the right policy changes, we can achieve an America in which racial equality exists. But America can never be colorblind. As long as humans' visual abilities don't devolve to outright blindness, we will continue to observe physical differences between people of different racial backgrounds. Some may criticize so literal a reading of the term, arguing that it's a shrewd misrepresentation of the idea. To those critics, I ask: why use the term "colorblind"? It doesn't remotely characterize America and still won't when we achieve racial equality. Colorblindness would not represent evolution, but atavism; an America in which race went unobserved would disallow the celebration of diversity. "Colorblind" is a term shrouded in corny, phony cuteness that is as inane as the paradigm of racial injustice it is artificially employed to defend.

Some will persist in their use of the term "colorblind." Others, like me, will opt for "racially egalitarian," "racially equitable," or any other combination of words representing the society in which racial equality is action and law. It is not language that matters, but matter itself. Not matter of machines or matter of men, but matter of souls. Race dialogue forms the soul substance which activism congeals into equality. Mechanics will save our

Constitution—they will arrange the disordered parts of the American soul into that fit for a nation committed to a just world not as a hypothesis or a theory, but a universal law. Although this America awaits our arrival, forgiving our disregard for its time, colorblind pretense delays our journey. It is the sole roadblock. Only with just public policy can that path be cleared and thus our journey to destiny steered. Absent this infrastructural reform, fantasy will never be brought to fruition. Without socks, shoes, or bootstraps, America will amble a dirt road toward a destination of eternal injustice.

Change is a compound formed not only of dialogue and action, but ideas. Throughout *Last in Line* I have touched on policy solutions, but in this chapter I provide an organized delineation of policy suggestions. I emphasize both government and social policy changes as means of mitigating America's racial disparity. ("Social policy," in this usage, refers to social movements driven by nongovernmental organizations and citizens). Both areas are critical, but the latter is chiefly a means toward realizing the former. Still, citizens and even noncitizens can act independent of government to effect change. With regard to government policy, I emphasize the need for bureaucratic oversight, mechanisms to promote pro-civil rights jurisprudence, and punitive measures to reduce racial disparity in America's justice, education, economic, and health care systems. In the realm of social policy, I emphasize the power of shaming, advocacy, protesting, and rejecting privilege, and how these things can both effect direct change and push our government toward change to liberate America.

Government Policy Suggestions

Bureaucratic oversight, pro-civil rights jurisprudence, and punitive measures are all necessary on the part of government to check and eliminate racial disparities. Although I emphasize the need for the use of oversight and punitive measures in the detection and eradication of racially discriminatory systems, agents, and operators, I do not advocate a far-reaching, *1984*-derived "Big Brother" system in which every action of every judge, police officer, or bank lender is monitored for signs of discrimination. Our legal system has a revered standard of innocence until proven guilt, one to which our courts today often seem oblivious. Only when reasonable suspicion exists will oversight investigations occur and only upon proven guilt will punitive measures be taken against institutionally racist offenders.

Similar to the lending oversight legislation promoted by former congressman Joseph Kennedy II, I promote policies establishing federal oversight systems in justice, education, economic, and health care systems, both internal and external, along with appropriate punitive measures. Judges, educators, banks, corporations, physicians, and health administrators are some of the actors who, based on extensive research confirming their racial biases in relation to petitioners, students, borrowers, employees, patients, and other clients, will in some cases likely require monitoring. Beyond oversight, policy measures like abolishing the death penalty and mandatory minimum sentences, repealing stop-and-frisk and stand-your-ground laws, federally mandating restitution for the wrongfully incarcerated, modifying education funding policy, adopting more uniform teacher pay standards, and other reforms are suggested. The electorate's responsibility in elevating the right agents within these systems is duly emphasized.

The Justice System

In chapter 5, I suggested abolishing both the death penalty and mandatory minimum sentencing policies, abandoning the "tough-on-crime" bravado that gives birth to draconian laws, and holding abusive judges accountable. I also mentioned the controversial idea of jury nullification, abrogating unconstitutional stop-and-frisk laws, and the necessity of instituting compensation programs for wrongly convicted individuals. The problems that stand-your-ground laws present and the need to repeal such laws are also discussed.

One of the biggest problems with the modern judiciary is its unchecked and unbridled power. In American politics, it is considered anathema to even entertain defrocking judges. During the debates for the 2012 Republican presidential primaries, one of the most criticized policy suggestions was that of removing federal judges. Former House Speaker Newt Gingrich's plan to send U.S. marshals to arrest judges and force them to explain controversial rulings was met with outrage by Republican voters and may have cost him his frontrunner status.[827] Despite the fact that the Founding Fathers envisioned the judiciary as the weakest of the three federal branches,[828] in modern times it has proved the most difficult branch to check. Whereas presidents, their bureaucrats, and members of Congress serve at the pleasure of the people, our judges serve at their own pleasure.

There are no real mechanisms for defrocking federal judges, which is problematic given that so many federal judges uphold and enforce legal standards in racially discriminatory fashions. A case can be made for judges violating the standard of "good behavior" *if* their rulings directly promote institutionally racist practices. Impeachment proceedings can occur for judges found to have track records of racially biased rulings in criminal cases. The oversight mechanism can be as simple as assessing a judge's compiled record of rulings and statistically analyzing them for clear trends of racial bias. If a statistically significant trend of racial bias is found, whether in favor of black, white, or any race, then grounds for impeachment are sufficiently established.

The area of civil lawsuits could prove more difficult to address. The only way to ensure that judges sitting on the bench are friendly to civil rights is to require stricter assessment of candidates for federal judgeships. The records of these candidates must be made open and clear during confirmation hearings. This can only apply to candidates with some prior legal or judicial record capable of exhibiting a pattern of racial bias, which virtually all candidates have. This mode of screening can apply to lower-level judges, district attorneys, prosecutors, and those in similar legal roles. If it can be shown that a candidate for a federal or Supreme Court judgeship has a history of ruling in favor of resegregation, for example, it would be the responsibility of the voting senators to represent the people fairly and reject such candidates. If the Senate still votes to approve them, then the senators voting in favor of discriminatory candidates must be identified and voted out of office in the next election.

This method is problematic because it depends on the will of the enfranchised. If the majority of voters are in favor of anti-civil rights judges, in part due to voter suppression, then the will of the greater electorate can remain unrepresented. But if the public has clearer knowledge of the racial biases held by judges and the senators who approve of them, this at least enables citizens to duly punish elected officials when they deviate from their duty of protecting civil rights. These methods can also apply to the evaluation of candidates at the state and local levels.

Both the death penalty and mandatory minimum sentencing policies must be abolished immediately. The Justice Department's 2013 move to draw back on mandatory minimum sentencing represented the first motion toward unweaving the draconian legislative fabric and altering the judiciary. But the policy's limited impact in its first few years shows that citizens must demand follow-through. Because it is applied in a racially discriminatory manner, the death penalty violates the Equal Protection Clause of the Fourteenth Amendment. Although the Supreme Court has recognized this before and ruled it unconstitutional, it regrettably moved to reinstate it after just four years. Thus, the phenomenon of judicially sponsored, racially biased killing in America continues.

Whether or not one concurs with the death penalty in principle, as long as it is applied in a fashion that is more lenient to white offenders and more stringent to black and Hispanic offenders, it is not constitutional and must therefore be repealed. Mandatory minimum sentencing must also be abolished, as such sentences affect blacks disproportionately and circumscribe the jurisprudence of judges who may otherwise acknowledge the pettiness of small possession crimes that blacks are disproportionately convicted of and offer appropriate sentences. Plea bargaining must also be called in for questioning and cross-examined as a valid prosecutorial method, given that it allows for the unjust imprisonment of hardworking, law-abiding Americans like Dorothy Gaines.

Jury nullification seems an abuse of our judicial system but has been applied extensively throughout the history of American justice, usually in ways that violated the civil rights of African Americans. If applied to protect civil rights, jury nullification could be valid and even necessary. If this seems extreme, one need only look at Dorothy Gaines and ask what's more extreme—the unconstitutional detention of innocent, respectable American citizens, or a legal practice that would free these wrongly convicted individuals from the jaws of a cruel justice system? It is also worth emphasizing that nullification is a right that juries are legally entitled to apply at their discretion.

Stop-and-frisk policies, which have proven unconstitutional and racially discriminatory in the most offensively apparent way, must be repealed. Whereas it is necessary that judges respect the U.S. Constitution and rule against such laws, it is of the utmost importance that our elected officials in both executive and legislative branches not pass legislation that conflicts with the Fourth and Fourteenth amendments of the Constitution. The franchise must be used to ensure that those who advocate such unconstitutional laws are kept from election or, if elected, unseated at the soonest opportunity possible.

Unless America wants to continue to produce further Trayvon Martin-like firestorms, stand-your-ground laws must be repealed. There is enough data showing the laws' applied antiblack racial bias to render them legally indefensible. Stand-your-ground laws protect racist killings, discriminating on account of the victim's race more so than the case's situational circumstances. Because such laws must be addressed on the state level, citizens of states with stand-your-ground laws must make it clear that such unjust legislation is intolerable and that elected officials who advocate and pass such laws will be voted out of office and, if necessary, impeached. When blatantly discriminatory laws are on the books—laws with ferocious, lethal teeth—citizens must bite back with valiant effort to dismantle such laws and remove the purveyors of injustice from positions meant for those who will rule on behalf of equity.

Judges cannot be forced to rule in the interest of civil rights, but those whose rulings clearly contribute to the disproportionate deaths and incarcerations of African Americans as well as undue sentences, even when factors are controlled for, must be held accountable. Arresting judges may be extreme, but defrocking judges whose rulings are biased is not. Bureaucratic infrastructure must be established to detect and eliminate racial bias in America's courts. The more effective measure is keeping racially biased judges from the bench, something that is largely contingent on the sorts of officials Americans elect to Congress.

We must also stop encouraging recidivism by disallowing felons' rights of voting, qualifying for public housing, qualifying for decent paying jobs, and doing the things that enable them to regain status as respectable members of society. The punitive measures of the justice system go too far, extending far beyond the jail cell. Formerly incarcerated Americans should not be required to indicate this on job applications. They should at least be allowed to get their feet in the door, demonstrate their job skills, and display their desire and humanity. After evaluating prospective candidates on the basis of merit and then looking at their criminal records, employers should be allowed to make a fair and comprehensive decision. It makes no sense to criticize prisoners who relapse into penitentiaries when we force them to do so by preventing them from finding jobs. In addition, ex-convicts must be made eligible for public housing, thus allowing them access to basic shelter after their sentences are served. Government is responsible for rehabilitating criminals, not recriminalizing them. It's the least that government can do, especially given that bad government policy is to blame for mass incarceration.

Lastly, when the system fails—and it's certainly a matter of when, not if—and innocent Americans slip through the justice system's wide and numerous cracks, it is government that must pay the price. Wrongfully convicted individuals must receive compensation in all U.S. states, not just the 24 that have statutes for this, and they must come without caveats and with appropriate support services.

The Education System

Civil rights policies in the education system largely depend on legal standards established by the courts. Without progressive rulings from the courts, it is difficult to check the discriminatory and segregative practices enforced in so many school districts in America. However, absent high-level judicial intervention, there are policy changes that can make for a more racially just education system.

State education departments must mandate the hiring of more African American teachers. Because much of the racial bias in the education system is related to the overwhelming racial homogeneity of school faculties, improving the racial balance of faculties may serve to mitigate racial bias. Unfortunately, race-conscious hiring policies will fail to directly counteract racial bias that teachers and administrators may express in the classroom. Daniel Moynihan made a similar suggestion, advocating that more black male teachers teach black male students. But because even blacks can exhibit antiblack bias, such measures cannot alone significantly mitigate racial bias in the education system.

Ideally, state education departments will mandate the monitoring of classroom racial bias. It would be the responsibility of education superintendents and school boards to monitor data on detentions, suspensions, expulsions, and other disciplinary actions to determine the incidence of racial bias. Students' voices must also be heard. Students who feel that they face racial discrimination must be allowed to air grievances without fear of minimization, dismissal, or reprisal. Teachers consistently reported for accusations of racial bias must be investigated by school districts to determine if they exhibit racial bias in instruction and discipline. This won't always work, given that much of the racial bias that affects minority students so badly is covert and difficult to detect. Still, minority students deserve a voice and a right to challenge instructors whom they feel may be discriminating against them.

If students believe school administrators are not hearing and addressing their complaints, they should be allowed to report directly to their school districts. If school districts are neglecting their claims, students should be allowed to report to their state departments of education. If students' complaints still aren't addressed at the state level, then students should be allowed to petition the federal Department of Education for intervention. Students must be properly informed of the availability of such avenues and their right to pursue them. Teachers, administrators, education superintendents, and others who abuse or neglect their entrusted duty of educating black and minority children must be duly punished.

Allocation of education funds should not be based on local property taxes, but must instead be drawn from a statewide or regional pool of taxpayer money and distributed based, in part, on the number of students attending a particular school. Schools in low-income areas should be afforded additional funding to negate the effects this disadvantage renders on students' ability to learn. It must be kept in mind that although addressing the plight of disadvantaged schools is paramount, lending it too much focus may take away from endeavors for school desegregation. In addition to erasing funding disparities, state education departments must also commit to desegregation. If they fail to do so, the executives, school board members, and superintendents of such districts must be accordingly voted out or otherwise removed from office to make room for those taking heed of the lessons of change.

State departments of education must guarantee uniform pay standards for instructors and administrators. Salary standards should be established so that earnings are determined and allocated directly and equitably by education departments instead of schools or school districts, thereby limiting the manifestation of income disparity between those teaching in poorer and those teaching in more affluent districts. As happens in the Corridor of Shame, many teachers leave impoverished, predominantly minority school districts for better salaries and benefits elsewhere. Low compensation should never frustrate career decisions that have such immense impact on the futures of young Americans.

If pay is administered from the hands of education departments and teachers are given financial incentive to teach in disadvantaged schools, the teacher competence problem affecting predominantly minority schools will be solved. Education departments must also require that AP, magnet, honors, and other programs be as available at predominantly black schools as they are at predominantly white or integrated schools. Although the separate but equal doctrine that America regresses toward is untenable and suggestions on improving mostly black schools may seem counterintuitive to the push for desegregation, until we enact more integrative policies we cannot spare any more time in addressing the educational needs of insulated minority students.

The Economic System

Representative Joseph Kennedy II was a trailblazer in promoting legislation tracking banks' racially discriminatory practices. This was paramount in detecting the prevalence of racial bias in lending, but stopped short of punishing banks participating in such activities. Thus, in the aftermath of the housing bubble's burst we found African Americans more heavily subjected to predatory lending practices than ever before. The Justice Department has sued banks found engaging in such practices, but the settlements originating from such lawsuits yield paltry sums to the injured parties and, from a punitive standpoint, are hardly significant enough to even register the sensation of a slap on the wrist.

Government must not only sue banks and lenders found engaging in such practices; it must impose regulatory measures on these banks that will make government oversight mandatory for a specified duration following their crimes. After witnessing a few examples made of discriminating competitors, banks will likely follow suit and act independently to reverse predatory lending and other discriminatory practices within their systems before government intervenes. If banks refuse to act on their own volition and are accused of discrimination, the Justice Department can conduct probes, file lawsuits, extract fair settlements on behalf of injured parties, and institute racially balancing regulatory measures.

This form of oversight must apply not only to banks, but also realtors found engaging in discriminatory selling practices. If certain real estate agencies are repeatedly accused of discrimination, the Justice Department will be advised to conduct probes. If evidence of discrimination arises, due lawsuits can be filed, fair settlements can be procured, and oversight measures can be enacted that will require these agencies to disclose their business practices with clients based on race, gender, sexual orientation, and other traits with regard to specific socioeconomic demographics. This form of oversight can even be extended to employment practices, tracking activities like hiring, firing, and promotion in relation to employees' race, gender, education, and other factors. Companies found engaged in biased practices can be sued, forced to fairly settle for discriminated-against parties, and compelled to adhere to standards that will make for racially balanced work environments. Nonprofit, nonpartisan research of corporate practices can be used by government in oversight reviews, as it can reveal biases and discrimination that often persist under the veneer of "diversity and inclusion" programs that often serve functions contrary to their stated missions. The same practices can apply to nonprofits.

These punitive measures are most convenient because they often won't need to go beyond the simple bearing of teeth by government. If these banks, realtors, businesses, and other entities are faced with the prospect of government intervening on behalf of racial equity, change will ensue. They will often act preemptively to subtly put a stop to incidences of racial bias within their practices before elements of public humiliation and government control bear down.

The Health Care System

Proposals dedicated to eliminating racial health disparities have already been introduced into U.S. health care policy. The Disparities Solutions Center was established at the Massachusetts General Hospital in 2005 with the goal of "developing and disseminating models for identifying and addressing racial and ethnic disparities in health care nationally, regionally, and locally."[829] The organization's goal is to work with hospitals, doctors, insurers, community health centers, and schools in Massachusetts and across the country to eliminate gaps in health care provision. Although the organization started out with around $3 million in funding, that's hardly far-reaching enough to make a significant impact on the problem of racial health care disparities.[830]

The DSC has been most effective in working directly with minority patients in offering counseling for conditions such as diabetes and examination for procedures such as colonoscopies. It has also developed the Disparities Dashboard, which monitors racial and ethnic disparities in quality of care. The DSC's commendable efforts are effecting change by making up for the negligent attitudes that private physicians often display toward their minority patients. Its program provides an unprecedented model that can be followed by hospitals nationwide, especially in predominantly minority demographics. But save for substantial budget increases, the DSC will be unable to address greater systemic needs. Therefore, government agencies must step in.

State health departments must develop their own "disparities dashboards" that monitor racially discriminatory practices in hospitals, health insurance companies, private practices, and among physicians. Given the particularly sensitive nature of human health, monitoring for racial discrimination must be ongoing for public hospitals and other public health care facilities. Doctors, nurses, and other health care administrators must be monitored for trends like rates of procedure recommendation—whether abnormally high or low—and readmission. Those definitively found engaging in racially discriminatory practices must be subjected to appropriate measures by state health and medical boards to delicense and remove them. Private hospitals and physician's clinics must be subjected to state justice department probes when reasonable suspicion of their discrimination arises. If found to be discriminating, lawsuits must be filed and, in addition to the issuance of fair settlements, direct government oversight must be introduced to ensure the elimination of organizational racial bias.

In patient interaction, state health departments must require doctors to adopt more uniform recommendation standards. Instead of brushing off a patient's chest pains as the effects of, say, a new workout regimen, doctors should be required to suggest that the patient undergo procedural examinations to determine the cause of the symptom. It has been found that the symptoms and health conditions of black patients are taken lightly by our medical professionals. If doctors are required to be more ethically judicious in the recommendation of EKGs for minority patients who report chest pains that could indicate heart disease or in suggesting X-rays for minority patients who report persistent migraine headaches that could indicate brain cancer, much of racial health care disparity can be eliminated. Although people may argue that such liberality in recommendation is not economically sustainable, the only thing truly unsustainable is discriminatory medical carelessness that results in the loss of so many American lives.

The federal government must be the last line of defense. If state health departments fail to address issues of racial discrimination in their health care systems, the U.S. Department of Health and Human Services must have power to investigate discriminatory health practices attributed to state policies and, where appropriate, use proper avenues to file lawsuits and institute necessary oversight measures.

Health insurance coverage must be made universally available. This is the quickest way to address disparities resulting from the wide lack of health care coverage in minority communities. Much is made of the fact that African Americans are widely uninsured; 17 percent lacked health insurance coverage in 2014.[831] The Affordable Care Act has performed tremendous work in lowering black uninsurance rates from 21 percent in 2011.[832] But obstructive efforts of Congress and state legislatures have kept this figure much higher than what it ought to be given America's adoption of universal health care under the Obama administration.

The greatest obstacle to detecting racial bias in health care is caused by patients' fears of racial discrimination. Although suggestions have been made for minority patients to more openly disclose their race, national origin, gender, and other personal details to providers and insurance companies, many are reluctant to do so for fear that such information will be used against them. A 2006 report from the Commonwealth Fund established the prevalence of this phenomenon.[833] Such consternation is well understood given the prevalence of medical and other forms of discrimination in American society. For minority patients to feel comfortable in disclosing such information, health care providers and other organizations collecting such data must allow for greater transparency in their data collection processes and, more importantly, establish—under threat of legal penalty—that patient data will only be used for specific goals of monitoring and reducing the prevalence of racial disparity in health care. It is tenable this policy could even go so far as to suggest that the protective transparency of such data collection practices be legally required for all heath care providers, but it would be more pragmatic to start by exclusively mandating this for public health care organizations.

Government Policy Wrap-Up

American policymakers on both sides of the aisle throw up arms, choreographing rigor mortis possessed by beasts of burden. These ghouls, these demons, these aliens, it is said, cannot escape a yet more chilling creature—pragmatism. Politicians exorcise cardial rhythm, grounding in killed corpses get-down souls strutting as slaves to the system; they shuck intrepid in the face of hell's hounds—only at the behest of a foul, green stench. This capitulatory brand of politics spurns soul-saving captivation for soul captivity to a sole root—the evil of the tiller. Jiving is the capital offense of American politicians, ever willing to liquidate at the wanton insistence of multimillion-dollar checks made out to the Capitol. Strangely, such profligate fluidity freezes at the sight of freedom—to them, funk masquerading as fragrant vision.

Pragmatism is the boon of the Super PAC and the bane of the subhuman. For one, it is crash, cash, and hanging chad. For the other, it is simply…hanging. No matter misdeeds ascribed to the donor class for whom it slavishly shuffles, American political pragmatism never lacks breathing room for its suffocating ideals. But no matter the statistics schedule demonstrating racial disparity's prevalence in the United States, America's pragmatic policymakers prove only capable of holding their breath and, to boot, covering their ears in an altogether puerile gesture. American cries for cake have called in coarse castigation. For many Americans, the suggestion that an affliction of racial disparity grips the soul inspires mutinous outrage—directed at the *subjects*. Their indignation exists not because American citizens endure such smug tyranny; their resistance is supported by the idea that it is *their* possession being mocked by the mere idea of policy reform. Harboring private prejudice cannot be prohibited. But when those prejudices extend, resulting in multitudes of injuries doled unto minorities, they become both illegal and indefensible. The racism of individuals cannot be tolerated when it infringes upon the rights of American citizens.

The government's power to effect change in our society cannot be understated. The government's power to *enforce* racial equality is undeniable, as it wasn't until the passage of the Civil Rights Act of 1964 and its inclusion of federally backed punitive measures that real and true change was effectuated in America. It has repeatedly been proven that asking nicely just doesn't work. Our laws and policies must endure painful teething so that they will act with more bite than bark to guarantee that our institutions will no more inflict undue suffering on our society.

Some may argue that because many of the agents of racial discrimination in our systems are implicitly biased and therefore do not know what they do, sacking them is unfair. After all, they don't *mean* to discriminate. Intent does not matter, only output. If people are denying quality health care, education, legal representation, and other unalienable rights to minorities, even unbeknownst to themselves, they must be removed from positions that will enable their continued unconscious discrimination. Is this suggestion really more extreme than allowing black infant mortality to remain double that of whites when we have empirically established that health care racism and other forms of racism effectuate this outcome? We must step back, assess, ask what's truly unfair, and answer that critical inquiry in the spirit of justice.

What of rehabilitating those harboring unconscious biases? The issue of calibrating the psychological and moral compasses of people so that they no longer register racial prejudice is an intricate one. A host of influences, practically from infancy, program the mind into a haven for biases both implicit and explicit. It would be no easy task to undo a lifetime of exposure to such influences. Enacting measures that reduce the ability of biased agents to harm minorities, intentionally or otherwise, is likely more efficacious in the greater scheme. Although it is worth addressing, the problem of unraveling or preventing biases within individuals is a complex subject that requires a commensurate magnitude of psychosocial analysis which cannot be offered here.

Social Policy Suggestions

High-level government policy reforms are prioritized because they wield the most power to effect change on a mass scale. But the power of the American citizenry, the true force behind government, can never be understated. We are the fabric from which our flag is woven and, as individual, unbreakable threads of this flag, must merge to cut a striking, enduring symbol of freedom. American citizens have a major role to play in reducing institutional racism, one which transcends petitioning government for social change.

Refraining from overt acts of racism is woefully insufficient to reduce racism's prevalence. The same goes for having a black friend, family member, favorite entertainer, or even spouse. Overt or terroristic acts of racism are only the tip of the proverbial iceberg. Instead of devoting sole media attention to horrors like the 2015 Charleston church shooting, we should devote at least as much media attention to the 100,000 African Americans who die at the hands of our health care system solely because of their race, or the Troy Davises of America who go to their deaths at the behest of our judges, even when their doubt is beyond unreasonable. America's social institutions are to blame; they inspire the spite that possesses men to drag a black man like James Byrd's body down the road while themselves dragging thousands down the system's roads every day.

Inclusion is not only important, but necessary to efforts to dismantle institutional racism. But having a "black friend" solely to prove one isn't racist is itself a racist act, one that dehumanizes the value of that person and reduces them to a utility; it belies friendship's promise of acknowledging the essence of heart and soul. (Interestingly, studies show many of these token black friends to be mythical.)[834] Similarly, black relatives—whose existence, except in the case of a child, one doesn't control—do absolutely nothing to prove one's commitment to deconstructing systemic racism. Talk of having black or nonwhite friends, relatives, and even lovers does nothing to enable those intimate associates to have a better chance in the world.

Americans can do numerous things, not only in our personal lives but also in shaping society, to reduce institutional racism's influence. Americans have the power to 1) shame society's racist institutions, 2) advocate through nonprofit civil rights organizations, and 3) protest and boycott America's institutional Goliaths. Litigation is particularly important. Americans can use the legal system to topple society's racist institutions, especially with the help of nonprofit civil rights organizations staffed with qualified, effective lawyers fitted out for such tasks. In turn, the airing out of institutions' soiled laundry in a heated atmosphere offers fodder for smoldering shaming campaigns. In addition, white Americans can, in particular, 4) reject their racial privilege.

Shaming

Businesses put profits first. Lawsuits and public humiliation both serve as major hindrances to profitability. Lawsuits impose the penalties of court settlements on companies and deal devastating blows to their public images. Both negatively affect profits. Abercrombie & Fitch is just one example of a company sued and shamed into jettisoning racially discriminatory hiring practices. In December 2005, the company settled a class action lawsuit for $50 million in response to allegations that it discriminated against African American, Asian American, and Hispanic employees and applicants.[835] They were additionally forced to institute policies and programs designed to promote diversity throughout all Abercrombie & Fitch-owned stores. Among other empty tokens of their newfound commitment to racial equality, Abercrombie & Fitch even moved to institute a diversity essay contest.[836]

Litigation isn't always the best way to shame a company, however. Many discrimination lawsuits filed against major business enterprises fly under the radar; few garner enough consistent and widespread media attention to significantly tarnish the images of discriminating companies. Short of lawsuits, how can we shame businesses into abandoning discriminatory practices? If media outlets fail to expose the discriminatory practices of businesses, Americans must take it upon themselves to publicly shame such businesses. This would require wealthy donors or efficient fundraising apparatuses to collect smaller donations from the masses. Similar to PACs, these proposed advocacy organizations can run effective "campaign ads" against discriminating businesses.

Such ads can, among other things, feature statistics affirming the discriminatory habits of targeted businesses, off-the-record quotations exposing overtly racist statements made by agents and administrators of such businesses, and personal accounts of employees and applicants claiming experiences of racial discrimination at the hands of these businesses. They can also publicize underreported discrimination lawsuits. These ads can take the form of television commercials, radio advertisements, websites, online advertising, targeted advertising social media campaigns, and even lawn signs. It's worth contemplating the possibility of—perhaps in return for funding donations—endorsing rival companies, but only if these companies commit themselves to eliminating any potential racially discriminatory practices within their own structures and fully devote themselves to maintaining racially equitable practices.

These ad campaigns would have tremendous potential to effect change not only by hitting the images of individual racially discriminatory companies hard, but also by forcing entire industries to commit themselves to racial equality. At the individual level, social media has proven an effective platform for highlighting instances of racial unfairness in America, railing against everything from police violence to Academy Award snubs. Throwing coordinated or organizational weight behind such tactics can prove tremendous for motivating businesses and other organs of society into racially just action.

Advocacy
Organizations such as the NAACP, ACLU, Southern Poverty Law Center, and the National Urban League advocate for civil rights and liberties. They don't just march, sing, host conferences, conduct research, and give out awards. In addition to those expressions of advocacy, they take the battle for racial equality into America's courtrooms, fighting on behalf of American citizens and noncitizens who, by themselves, often lack the financial means to take the system head-on. Instead of simmering over everyday experiences of institutional discrimination, Americans must utilize the assistance of advocacy groups; they can make a fundamental difference in our individual lives and the state of our communities. Civil rights advocacy groups often focus more on fighting overt forms of racism demonstrated by hate groups and private businesses, but their scope can and must be expanded to include implicit, surreptitious forms of racism that are so pervasive in America and that afflict us so much more.

These organizations are not only interested in fighting individual cases of racial discrimination. They also endeavor to set legal precedents that will prevent racially discriminatory practices from occurring in the future. Advocacy groups that already have tremendous clout and stature, such as the NAACP, are ideal vehicles through which Americans can wage new wars for desegregation, agitate for justice system reform, reduce the prevalence of job and housing discrimination, and improve America's health care systems for minorities.

These advocacy groups can and do play a fundamental role in the shaming process as well. Still, I propose *ad hoc* nonprofit shaming groups be formed so as to not take away from the organizational and legal focus established nonprofit groups devote toward addressing community problems. These advocacy groups can still play a fundamental role in assisting with funding for shaming campaigns, however.

For-profit legal avenues cannot be dismissed, as they too enable agitation against the system. The private firm Lieff, Cabraser, Heimann & Bernstein was responsible for carrying out the lawsuit filed against Abercrombie & Fitch and settling on behalf of the over 10,000 discriminated-against employees and job applicants.[837] A large number of discrimination lawsuits are spearheaded by private firms, which allow for litigation at a reduced cost, if not *pro bono*. Such firms are generally more affordable because they tend to favor class action lawsuits, which require several potential litigants with claims of racial discrimination against the same company or organization. Because of their outsized costs, corporate lawsuits often fail to allow for individualized discrimination suits to arise. Though their individual payouts are often meager, class action lawsuits enable citizens to challenge corporations through the courts, cost-free. We should not neglect the critical role that private firms play in the fight against discrimination, but people who lack access to pecuniary means or class action avenues must turn to advocacy groups for assistance.

Protest and Boycott

The Occupy Wall Street movement reminded us of the power of American protest, a spirit that dates to the time of the Revolution. Black Lives Matter has similarly embodied this tradition. We must continue to resurrect those traditions and march, protest, and occupy those businesses, courts, schools, and other societal structures that we find insensitive to minorities. Although the act of standing around or ambulating in masses may in some ways seem ineffectual, the amassing of so many individuals refusing to budge in the face of an imperious system displays the power of vast human networks and proves their potential to—when organized—effect change. Bank of America's quick repeal of proposed debit card fees in 2011 was largely tied to the efforts of Occupy protestors.[838] The Occupy movement has proven parochial, however, in that many protestors, black and white alike, emphasize the colorblind narrative of class marginalization to the exclusion of race. Since Occupy's peak, Black Lives Matter has given greater voice to problems of inequality often ignored by the far-left. The fictitious colorblind narrative so influential in modern public policy ignores the reality that, unlike poor whites, poor blacks must factor class and race as reasons for indigence. Hence, it is important that such vast networks be organized with appropriate, inclusive ideologies.

2013 brought the 50th Anniversary of the March on Washington and Martin Luther King, Jr.'s "I Have a Dream," with President Obama echoing King's call for "jobs and freedom." The anniversary march also paid tribute to the legacy and importance of mass organizing—one which must prevail in modern-day America with dogged determination. If massive numbers of

Last in Line: An American Destiny Deferred

Americans of all races not only march but also boycott businesses and institutions found to be racially discriminatory, change will ensue in rapid fashion. Imagine tens or hundreds of thousands of Americans boycotting businesses that engage in job discrimination, banks that engage in predatory lending practices, or health care providers that engage in racially discriminatory patient neglect. Once these businesses start losing millions, they will quickly detect, examine, and do away with discriminatory practices absent government intervention. We need only look at Rosa Parks and the bus boycotts of the 1950s to know that businesses will often do anything to regain lost profits, even if it involves doing away with racially discriminatory practices.

Given the ubiquity of discrimination in business, it seems a principle of boycott would effectively require us all to go on hunger strike. The simple solution to this dietary dilemma is to target only those businesses displaying the most egregious cases of discrimination and make examples of them, thereby motivating other companies to independently make changes before the courageous agents of social change are forced to intervene.

Imagine what would happen if American citizens occupied local, state, and federal courts—even the Supreme Court itself. The mass presence of Americans devoted to the cause of ensuring life, liberty, and happiness for all in our courts, legislatures, governor's mansions, and other houses of government will speak volumes. Imagine if we were to split institutional racism's atom, causing the act of fission that will render change of nuclear yet life-preserving proportions. If throngs can assert their will and demands for justice by effectively organizing themselves, as protestors in the nebulous Occupy and Black Lives Matter movements have been reluctant to do, the force produced by that fission will prove insurmountable. We will find their will unstoppable. If these amassed groups can commit themselves to appointing visionary leaders—who will *always* be necessary to make movements successful—and utilizing the ballot to get these leaders into our houses of government, their force will be perfected.

Rejecting Privilege

For white Americans seeking to undermine the structures of institutional racism, rejecting privilege is an absolute must.

Hold your horses, though.

This doesn't mean that you have to return your "A" paper to your professor for an egalitarian downgrade. It doesn't mean that you have to march into your principal or dean's office and command they immediately suspend or expel you from your mostly white high school or college and furnish a cheap bus ticket to the nearest school-to-prison pipeline academy. It doesn't mean that you should tell your bank to give you the subprime deal they would offer to the average African American of equal creditworthiness. It doesn't even mean that you need to walk into the nearest police station and demand that a cop unconstitutionally frisk you (although, by virtue of your asking, their subsequent search would respect your Fourth Amendment right). John "Osawatomie" Brown's spirit may smile upon such bold acts of defiance, but you don't have to go this far to work against institutional racism. As effectively as they may demonstrate one's commitment to the cause, such forms of protest are not the most effective means of challenging the system. Instead of asking for *less* for yourself, ask for *more* for your black fellow American.

Chapter 9: A National Salvation

Get involved with your neighborhood and community housing associations and lobby for community diversification. Go to school board meetings, write to your education administrators, and demand school diversification. Insist on your local schools increasing the number of African American and minority members on their faculties and staffs. Insist on schools introducing specialty programs for minorities that are committed to fostering inclusion while not emphasizing difference in a divisive fashion, as school diversity programs sometimes do. Lobby for changes in curricula that require balanced lesson plans that focus on African and black history not as phenomena insular and separate from the American and global narrative, but accounts directly and intimately linked with events of American and world history.

Refuse participation in school white flight. Instead, insist on your children going to racially mixed or even predominantly nonwhite schools and insist on administrators improving the quality of schools to obviate any potential need to place your children in parochial or private schools. If you insist upon your children attending such exclusive schools—hopefully with noble reason—insist on those schools reforming their policies to enable more underprivileged children from minority backgrounds to also have opportunities to receive the effective education these institutions have to offer.

If your African American colleague demonstrates similar job performance qualities and you are offered a promotion, insist that your higher-ups promote your qualified cohort as well. If you know your company is engaging in discriminatory practices, don't be disinclined to blow the whistle. There are even more seemingly small things that can make a big difference. Instead of laughing at or ignoring the utterance of a racial epithet or joke, rebuke the offender. Refuse to associate with people who use racist language and commentary. Such behavior inspires collective impassivity toward minorities and their continued plight. Make it a point to discourage such vile behavior at all costs.

The list goes on, but this enumeration offers a starting point for the multitude of ways we can fight institutional racism in our everyday lives.

Implementing these suggestions will in some cases prove challenging, as one cannot always clearly determine when racial discrimination plays a role and when it does not. Even though we cannot always pinpoint when it's happening, we must always know that it is—disparate impact analyses prove this. We know this just by looking at the circumstantial disparity between blacks and whites in America. We can either delude ourselves in the idea that in recognizing this apparent problem, we are "jumping to conclusions," or we can take the first step of admission so that we may close this description-experience gap. We all want to get ahead in our personal lives, reduce our financial struggles, and create stability for ourselves. But each time one accepts unjust and undue racial privileges, it takes a job from another hardworking mother, a bed from her child, a life from her ailing, elderly parent, and a future from America.

Social Policy Wrap-Up

We cannot count government's reckoning sufficient to remunerate the change society demands. It is up to everyday Americans to account for its neglected books, thus ensuring deliverance of our long deferred payment in full. We must both strike government for change and picket signs of the word to bring it about. Change comes from the ground up—this is no proverb.

Its consecration lies in deposits to be procured from Earth; that ground must be drilled by will and blessing of all Americans. Freedom's revival cannot be incarcerated in America's hotboxed wells, but must erupt into free soil tilled for bread broken by a Union—black, white, Hispanic, Asian, and beyond. Institutional racism may bear itself more heavily upon tarred, scabbed backs than those privileged from fate's tanning. But America's races share bloody communion at the behest of its snapping visitations. White Americans are not pardoned from scar treatment, either—they too suffer hell's scolds in unbridled deprivation of the beauty and possibility of divinity. All Americans suffer bondage to an increasingly unfree state. Escaping internecine bleeding consists in labor toward salvation of our national will.

By shaming, advocating, protesting, and shedding privilege we can together shape American institutions into racially sensitive and equitable spaces absent extensive "big government" intervention. Newly formed nonprofit advocacy organizations and existing civil rights advocacy organizations will prove indispensable to this cause. The movement to eradicate institutional racism starts here—in the hearts, minds, and actions of everyday Americans. Supreme Court cases and legislative bills often move at glacial paces, taking months, years, and even decades to render effect. But mass rapture is Godspeed; seven days part judgment and resurrection. On the seventh day, America's parted soul shall join so that the American people may carry a cross into a national salvation.

A National Salvation

I have proposed policy changes that will require the support and collaboration of all Americans. I have outlined the critical roles we all must play, both within our individual communities and together as a nation. Interracial solidarity is necessary to foster the perfect, thus far unrealized racial democracy that we must commandeer from tomorrow and own today. I have declared that solutions to our country's systemic problems will not stem from changes within the white community or changes within the black community, but changes in the American community.

This flies in the face of what many will think not only of the ideas presented in these pages but also of my articulation and presentation of those ideas. When these disillusioning yet incontrovertible facts are presented, many are quick to cast stones toward the messengers. They accuse ideas of freedom of being "divisive," "hatemongering," or even "antiwhite." The American spirit of cooperation gives way to one of division. Rather than consider ideas and facts, they go on the attack against well-proven information that tells us why black infant mortality is so high, why so many young black men are in prison, and why the prejudices of the past are as pernicious to progress as the prejudices of the present.

They reject their duties toward examination and solution, declaring loyalty to false and perfidious principles that pervert the work of our Constitution. The pillars of these structures support the institutions that are the true promoters of division in America. Beneath their foundations are the crushed, suffocating, breathless people of color who can rely on no medicine man or woman to elevate these pilasters from their chests. I could implore some Americans to put away the provincial scopes guarding their eyes from the threat before us. But I know it is more effective to administer the message—

and then sit in patience and allow fate and our God above to heal their precious souls.

That we live in a society in which speaking in opposition to flagrant human injustice merits the charge of divisiveness speaks volumes as to just how pressing our need is for national salvation.

Will some assert that works such as mine "upset" race relations? May they accuse me of employing "uncomfortable" tones and rhetoric? Is it possible that they will say that I am "setting us back" some arbitrary number of years over which little has changed and over which much has worsened? I cannot say with complete certitude, but given the ardor with which so many in the United States have, both past and present, resisted change, I surmise that my work will be ripped by the agents of stagnancy. They may rip—but they cannot tear it apart. It is a message both indelible and inevitable. It is the deferred dream of which Dr. King spoke with such great belief in the possibility of its fruition. They may wish for her to reside in the past, but America cannot be stagnated. Hardened hearts must not bog America down, for it is in American nature and it is in American destiny to move forward.

If this message does upset race relations, let us recognize that these flawed, unequal race relations are worth upsetting until America realizes social equilibrium. If my work makes some Americans "uncomfortable," let this be because they are so taken aback and outraged at the continued prevalence of racial injustice in the United States that our leaders have misled us into believing extinct, extirpated, extinguished. Discomfort must spring them into action and drive them to frontlines, alongside black Americans, in the battle against injustice. If my work "sets us back" some time, let it be so that we examine our past and better understand how these injustices permeate through time to our own day. If my work fulfills the accusations that democracy's opponents hurl in fury, let it not be because it confirms the erroneous, negative premises of their arguments, but because it harmonizes with some positive, optimistic truth their pitch betrays but their drum fails to beat.

An axiom insists "people are afraid of change." I do not believe this. I believe that when people understand the endless possibility that accompanies change, they embrace it. Without change, the human condition would be one of feral prowling instead of sinking into Shakespearean sonnets, composing symphonies that echo through history's annals, and unearthing groundbreaking scientific advances as gifts for posterity. We love change. We are change. We sometimes just don't realize it.

White Americans will understand that an affliction of disequilibrium does indeed grip the nation. They will understand that even though not all white Americans have slave owners in their family trees, the wealth generated by that institution accrues in a peculiar, asymmetric fashion, depriving its fruits to the descendants of America's slaves. They will realize that even if not all whites hold racial biases, a disturbing number do hold these beliefs which are often clandestine yet always conquerable. They will understand what racism means. They will come to understand its purveyors. And once they see how it conflicts with the principles of liberty upon which America was founded, all will come to despise it.

They will understand that senses of guilt, evil, or turpitude are feckless, as is denying the memory of those unpaid and unsung American heroes who built our Great Wall of wealth and prosperity. Seeing the portentous writing on that wall, they will understand that their role in reversing racism is valued and necessary to the end of eradicating it. They will understand the urgency of now, hearing the deafening call to action that together we will answer.

Black Americans will realize that there is no omnipotent "devil" with whom we must contend. They will realize that had history run a different course, our current roles in the system of inequality might very well be reversed. They will realize that not all of their neighbors are oblivious to the problems of systemic racism and that some of the most prominent and ardent activists are white Americans and that we *need* them as much as they *need* us. They will realize that America's journey to racial equality is one of black Americans and white Americans and Hispanic and Asian and Native Americans joining in hands of love to dismantle the edifices of hate.

We will realize that although each of our fateful journeys to this land has been marred by strokes of indigence and injustice, the beauty of America endures. We will understand that this beauty does not erode and that this brilliance does not fade because it is not America who is to blame for the injustices which gave birth to her, but the inauspicious souls who inherited her helm whom her children must never again allow to marshal her through the seas of fate.

Most paramount, however, are not the things that we will realize within the confines of our divided neighborhoods or the compartments of our American consciousness. They are the things that we will realize when our hearts and minds join together to form a more perfect union.

We will together understand that the price paid for spoiled fruits of racial injustice is, in the grand scheme, miniscule compared to the toll an ominous future will exact if we do not act now. We will together understand that debate does not suffice for change and that while we waste breath in dispute, the final, dying breath escapes the mouth of an American child who, in part because of his or her skin color, cannot afford the care of a doctor. We will together understand that, like other Americans, this child should not have to afford a doctor, that his or her right to live is unalienable, and that we must do all that we can to ensure that our children, black, white, Hispanic, Asian, Native American, and beyond are all allowed to inhale pristine American air through lungs nurtured by loving, impartial American givers of health.

We will together at last realize the power and truth of words we have uttered for many scores—that we are One Nation, Under God, with Liberty and Justice for All.

Conclusion

James Williams was born in 1870 to Americans whose fates contrasted as high noon does to twilight. His father came from a prominent South Carolina family, the Southern equivalent of a patrician *gens.* He was reared in an estate holding 150 tormented souls and many more acres fertilized by their blood and sweat. James' grandfather donned gray, fighting in valiant service to a disgraceful regime that guarded his mother's servile station. His father's life was one of possibility, affluence, and continual reminders of the power that he, a son of Europe, held over children of Africa.

Although James' father's family held humans as property, this did not stop him from creating a family with a woman whose station was arguably lower than that of even Rome's slaves. James' mother had no opulent, magnificent background, but only one of creating that reality for those who possessed her. Hers was a kismet of limitation and periodic reminders of powerlessness in the face of white American hegemony. In pains of bondage, she labored three beautiful children into the world, one of them my great-great grandfather James.

I sit before his image. He looks on his son with benevolence; it is expression of pacific bearing in the face of oppressed circumstance. I can only imagine how his mixed background compounded the confusion guaranteed by vice of his African descent. A pen does his image no justice, but only seizes. I search for a sliver of hope. It cannot lie in wrinkles—there are none. Perhaps Reconstruction seized it. If it lay in his eyes, a glimmer, it likely blinded him in the way it now did me.

I envision his parents' union a tale of triumph over the legally and socially codified traditions of their Southern day. I picture his father some iconoclastic, self-fancying agent of social change, committed to racial equality, the party of Lincoln, and his lady, a daughter of a far-away black land. I imagine his mother a rebel, one defiantly casting off chains, educating herself in defiance of social norms, and committing to effected change not by rejecting and hating the son of her former master, but by embracing him and trusting in his spiritual capacity to embrace her and her people.

This scenario is likely fantasy. There is little reason to believe their relationship was an improbable postbellum interracial love story fit for contemporary Hollywood. I do not know the nature of their union, but I do know that as far as white men's desires went in the South, "no" was absent from black women's lexicon. I cannot know if she willed this relationship or if it was forced upon her by a man exercising what he may have felt his social prerogative. That they together had three children and that he conferred on my grandfather James and his siblings some of the Williams family's fields of labor suggests some modicum of paternal obligation on his part. That he insisted upon his children bearing his surname and being educated also testifies to some semblance of courage on his part to defy mores of culture, class, and clan and embrace, rather than repudiate, flesh and blood.

Because such things are spoken of today only in faint whispers, I never knew the extent of this narrative until rummaging archival records to unearth the time capsules of my own legacy. It was not mere inquisitiveness that motivated me to excavate these relics of a largely forgotten America, but a burning desire to understand the specific ways that the prejudices of the past have affected my present. My mother often speaks of the tragic way that my grandfather James and his siblings lost the wholes of their property bequests as a result of the schemes and devices of sons more loyal to the lost Confederate cause than his father.

Wealth has not trickled down from this house; tears have. I testify to this as I try to fathom how a community could detest the perpetuation of its own flesh and blood. Even today when I mention the land dispossessions, my mother snaps, "I don't even want to *think* about it." It is hard for many to sometimes grasp the ways the injustices of the past permeate into our present. I am no exception. When I hear the pain and hurt in my mother's voice as she speaks of our stolen inheritance, it hits home. I imagine how my grandfather James felt—how the hurt and humiliation emanating from black chains characterized the whole of his existence. I only imagine.

To think that my beloved grandfather James' own grandfather did not think him worthy of post-church Sunday dinners, breezy carriage rides through Columbia, and gifts on Christmas day. To think that he thought his own grandchildren worthy of chains rather than classrooms, suffering rather than sweetness, labor rather than love. To think that he went to his grave without so much as ever seeing his black grandchildren, avoiding their sight for the sake of a cruel, selfish, segregated fantasy. To think that my great-great grandfather had cousins and second cousins who eschewed him, altogether denying his existence and rejecting his share of their dark familial legacy. To think that his own kinsmen might have lynched him at the slightest suggestion of their blood link. To think they may very well be the reason he and his siblings lost the land bestowed upon them and the opportunity and possibility that came with it. I can only think of how his blood link to a wealthy white family bequeathed not privilege, but misery and despair.

I can only imagine how these injustices have descended to my own day.

To think that I have cousins today, several generations removed, scattered between our ancestral lands in South Carolina and America's bustling metropolises, who would vomit at the idea of our relation. To think that they are both the beneficiaries and the agents of American racial oppression, adhering to the tradition of the ancestors we share and working against the descendants of the slaves of our forefathers. To think that they may scorn me, deny me a home, a job, and a chance at the American dream. To think that they may today work to deny me the freedom which our fathers denied my people.

It reminds me that racism is not some lost relic submerged in America's fecund soil. Today, we are not tied in chains, hung from trees, or burned on fiery stakes. We are not beaten with cats-o'-nine-tails, bred for riches, or castrated for actions, be they errors, courtesies, or nothings. These things no longer happen. Yet they do. Our children are lynched from trees meant to bear medicinal fruits. We are confined to chains clanked onto wrists by judges and politicians. We are burned in electric chairs reminiscent of the fiery crosses upon which our ancestors were crucified.

Malcolm X spoke of passionate hatred for his white grandfather. In his autobiography, he wrote, "I hated every drop of that rapist's blood in me..." Whether my own existence is attributed in part to the act of a man who coerced his desires or is indebted to a man who simply did not care about defending Dixie, opting to follow an unprejudiced heart, many would argue that I have the right to hate him. They would say that I have this right not only for the possibility of his having violated the will of my grandmother, but also because he was the child and beneficiary of the system that worked my great-great-great grandmother and her loved ones to death. They may also say that I could apply this hatred to my cousins who inherited the familial wealth and attendant opportunities for education, enterprise, and social advance not afforded to my own line.

They are right. I could hate them.

But I do not.

I do not hate James' father. I do not even hate his father's father, who may have held harsher views about my people and acted upon such beliefs with great cruelty. I could hate him for all he and his class inflicted on African Americans. But I know that such hatred is only bound to further aggravate wounds which time failed to heal—these wounds we continue to scrape in ignorance. They yearn for a poultice—that containing ingredients of love and acceptance. Not love and acceptance of an oppressed past and present, but love and acceptance of the sometimes hard to believe idea that even a slave owner such as James' grandfather had it within him to bear love and compassion for people of all races. It is love and acceptance of the idea that somewhere in his heart, he did love my grandfather James as well as James' beloved brother and James' beloved sister. It is love and acceptance of the idea that my white cousins can and quite possibly are working to deconstruct the institutions our and my ancestors fortified. It is love and acceptance of the idea that someday we will come together in love and honor of our American legacy, sharing the wealth, health, and opportunity our races have never before shared.

Although I might encounter them every day, I have never known these distant brothers and sisters of mine. They cannot be identified by resemblance—the features of our shared progenitor have long been wiped from the countenances of those in my bloodline and perhaps theirs as well. There is no inherited gait or idiosyncratic laugh I can pinpoint as a shared heirloom. For all I know we have shared classrooms, football fields, and even hearth. But I need not know. I need not see, I need not hear, I need not feel to trust in them.

I trust they can be unlike the many in America today who speak of race with hate. I trust they can look a brother in the eye and say with whole conviction, "I believe in you." I trust they can be unlike the many working against the salvation of our nation and on behalf of the edifices of oppression. I trust they can place a gentle hand on my shoulder and say, "Your life matters." I trust they can reject pseudoscience that finds the seed of racial hierarchy in enigmatic, microscopic double-helixes that are said to limit our humanity. I trust they can see black America's trials and tribulations not as a predetermined fate, but a manifestation of a house in disrepair. I trust that, rather than snicker with cruel expectance, they can volunteer a loving hand to rescue the fate of our great nation, the United States of America. And I know in my heart that in their heart—*our heart*—bodes stars and stripes comprising the image of our humanity.

Maybe they can embrace *us* in warmth and arms as fellow countrymen—as fellow Americans.

And just maybe—if he found it in himself not in this world but perhaps in a world beyond—our ancestor could smile upon this perfect union, embracing not only the image of his children united but America united.

183

Last in Line: An American Destiny Deferred

My family's story—the one flowing through my heart—is one of both fortifying and fighting oppression. But without the final chapter of triumph, it remains unfinished. This chapter cannot be written by a son or a family, but only a country.

Thus, truth is thicker than blood. It is not only truth of my relation to these children of white privilege or their relation to this child of black disadvantage, but truth of our relation to America. Although they may not realize, every white teacher in a racially mixed school has a racially mixed family. They have children of all colors, sharing playgrounds, cafeterias, proms, and dreams of college. They are all mothers and fathers and brothers and sisters. And their relation is biological.

It is biological in the sense that we are all members of the same race, the only verifiable race, the human race. And it is biological in the sense that we depend upon one another for survival. Lessons of lies divide our house against itself. They shake our foundations, portending tragic collapse unto America's children. In depriving them of holy models of humanism, our mismanagement of the spiritual molding of our nation traps our futures in rubble of oppression.

It is up to older generations to affirm equality to America's future generations. This is the first lesson for America's children. We are their shepherds. We cannot forsake our flock, being blind to the variant glow of varied coats. If we pass to our children the myth of the racial hierarchy, we will bequeath a debt to recycle into perpetuity. We will place the onus of resolution upon our posterity, who will bequeath this burden to the next generation, who will pass it to the next. It will recycle in perpetuity until at long last our nation—destitute—perishes, just as fate threatened a decade prior to James Williams' birth.

Endnotes

Introduction Endnotes

[1] Nietzsche, Friedrich Wilhelm, and Thomas Common. *The Gay Science*. Mineola, NY: Dover Publications, 2006. 90-91. Print.

[2] Berger, William. *Puccini Without Excuses: A Refreshing Reassessment of the World's Most Popular Composer*. New York: Vintage, 2005. 300. Print.

[3] Gane, Mike. *Auguste Comte*. London: Routledge, 2006. 21. Print.

[4] Ibid.

[5] Richardson, Alan, and John Bowden. *The Westminster Dictionary of Christian Theology*. Philadelphia: Westminster, 1983. 471. Print.

[6] Feldman, Burton, and Robert D. Richardson. *The Rise of Modern Mythology, 1680-1860*. Bloomington: Indiana University Press, 2000. 453. Print.

[7] Bergman, Jerry. *The Dark Side of Charles Darwin: A Critical Analysis of an Icon of Science*. Green Forest, AR: Master, 2011. 228-29. Print.

[8] Johnson, Paul E., James M. McPherson, Alice Fahs, and Gary Gerstle. *Liberty, Equality, Power: A History of the American People, Since 1863*. By John H. Murrin. Stamford, CT: Cengage Learning, 2007. 703. Print.

[9] Jackson, John P., and Nadine M. Weidman. *Race, Racism, and Science: Social Impact and Interaction*. Santa Barbara, CA: ABC-CLIO, 2004. 109-11. Print.

[10] Rucker, Walter C., and James N. Upton. *Encyclopedia of American Race Riots*. Westport, CT: Greenwood, 2007. 62. Print.

[11] Kelley, Robin D. G. *Into the Fire: African Americans Since 1970*. New York: Oxford University Press, 1996. 45. Print.

[12] Hackett, Conrad, Alan Cooperman, and Katherine Ritchey. *The Future of World Religions: Population Growth Projections, 2010-2050*. Rep. Washington: Pew Research Center, 2015. Print.

[13] Noll, Mark A. *The New Shape of World Christianity: How American Experience Reflects Global Faith*. Downers Grove, IL: IVP Academic, 2009. 41. Print.

[14] Bonner, William, Addison Wiggin, and Kate Incontrera. *Financial Reckoning Day Fallout: Surviving Today's Global Depression*. Hoboken, NJ: Wiley, 2009. 325. Print.

[15] Martin, Michael. *The Cambridge Companion to Atheism*. New York: Cambridge University Press, 2007. 50. Print.

[16] Coulter, Michael L. *Encyclopedia of Catholic Social Thought, Social Science, and Social Policy*. Lanham, MD: Scarecrow, 2007. 19. Print.

[17] O'Donnell, Victoria. *Propaganda & Persuasion*. By Garth S. Jowett. Thousand Oaks: SAGE, 2011. 69. Print.

[18] Vattimo, Gianni. *Dialogue with Nietzsche*. New York: Columbia University Press, 2006. 175. Print.

[19] Chen, Stephanie. "Growing Hate Groups Blame Obama, Economy." *CNN*. Cable News Network, 26 Feb. 2009. Web. 28 Aug. 2013.

[20] Golobay, Diana. "Housing Discrimination Complaints Top Record High." *Housing Wire RSS*. Housing Wire, 9 June 2009. Web.

[21] Forgas, Joseph P., Joel Cooper, and William D. Crano. *The Psychology of Attitudes and Attitude Change: An Introductory Overview*. Hove: Psychology, 2010. 96-97. Print.

[22] Parker, Laurence, Donna Deyhle, and Sofia A. Villenas. *Race Is—Race Isn't: Critical Race Theory and Qualitative Studies in Education*. Boulder, CO: Westview, 1999. Print.

[23] Cole, David. *No Equal Justice: Race and Class in the American Criminal Justice System*. New York: New, 1999. 4. Print.

[24] Kayyali, Randa A. *The Arab Americans*. Westport, CT: Greenwood, 2006. 145. Print.

[25] Arum, Richard, and Irenee R. Beattie. *The Structure of Schooling: Readings in the Sociology of Education*. Mountain View, CA: Mayfield Pub., 2000. 171. Print.

[26] Shelton, Maria M. *American K-12 Public Education: Its Imminent Demise*. New York: IUniverse, 2006. 5. Print.

[27] Glaser, James M. *Race, Campaign Politics, and the Realignment in the South*. New Haven: Yale University Press, 1996. 21. Print.

[28] "The Voting Rights Act: Hard-Won Gains, An Uncertain Future." *NPR*. 21 July 2013. Web. 28 Aug. 2013.

[29] Goulka, Jeremiah. "Are Voter ID Laws a Form of Racism?" *Mother Jones.* N.p., 15 Oct. 2012. Web. 28 Aug. 2013.

[30] McEnteer, James. *Shooting the Truth: The Rise of American Political Documentaries.* Westport, CT: Praeger, 2006. 121. Print.

[31] Miller, Mark Crispin. *Fooled Again: How the Right Stole the 2004 Election & Why They'll Steal the Next One Too (Unless We Stop Them).* New York: Basic, 2005. 214. Print.

[32] Pareene, Alex. "Texas Flier Tells Blacks Not to Vote for Democrats." *Salon.* Salon, 29 Oct. 2010. Web. 27 Dec. 2012.

[33] Ibid.

[34] Hartman, Chester W. *Poverty & Race in America: The Emerging Agendas.* Lanham, MD: Lexington, 2006. 402. Print.

[35] Emerick, Yahiya. *The Complete Idiot's Guide to Islam, 3rd Edition.* New York: Penguin Group (USA) Incorporated, 2011. 6. Print.

[36] Staples, Brent. "A History of Racism at the University of Missouri." *Taking Note.* New York Times, 10 Nov. 2015. Web. 05 Feb. 2016.

[37] Norton, Michael. *365 Ways to Change the World: How to Make a Difference —one Day at a Time.* New York: Free, 2007. 18. Print.

[38] Kaplan, H. Roy. *The Myth of Post-Racial America: Searching for Equality in the Age of Materialism.* Lanham, MD: Rowman & Littlefield Education, 2011. 111. Print.

[39] Ibid.

[40] Hughey, Matthew W., and Gregory Parks. *Black Greek-Letter Organizations 2.0: New Directions in the Study of African American Fraternities and Sororities.* Jackson: University of Mississippi, 2011. 165. Print.

[41] Akhtar, Salman. *The African American Experience: Psychoanalytic Perspectives.* Lanham, MD: Jason Aronson, 2012. 255-56. Print.

[42] Painter, Nell Irvin. *Creating Black Americans: African-American History and Its Meanings, 1619 to the Present.* New York: Oxford University Press, 2006. 346-47. Print.

[43] Lin, Ann Chih., and David R. Harris. *The Colors of Poverty: Why Racial and Ethnic Disparities Exist.* New York: Russell Sage Foundation, 2008. 264-66. Print.

44 Green, Jonathon. *The Macmillan Dictionary of Contemporary Quotations*. London: Macmillan, 1996. 336. Print.

45 Community Health Association of Mountain/Plains States. "Region VIII Demographics Data Summary". June 2012.

46 Desmond-Harris, Jenée. "The Myth That There Are More Black Men in Prison than in College, Debunked in One Chart." *Vox*. VoxMedia, 12 Feb. 2015. Web. 05 Feb. 2016.

47 Corlett, J. Angelo. *Heirs of Oppression Racism and Reparations*. Lanham, MD: Rowman & Littlefield Publishing, 2010. 268. Print.

48 Fluehr-Lobban, Carolyn. *Race and Racism: An Introduction*. Lanham, MD: AltaMira, 2006. 185. Print.

49 Bass, S. Jonathan., and Martin Luther King. *Blessed Are the Peacemakers: Martin Luther King, Jr., Eight White Religious Leaders, and the "Letter from Birmingham Jail"* Baton Rouge, LA: Louisiana State University Press, 2001. 235-36. Print.

50 Ibid.

51 Ramage, Craufurd Tait. *Great Thoughts from Classic Authors*. New York: John B. Alden, 1891. 583. Print.

Chapter 1 Endnotes

52 Cosby, William Henry, Jr. "Pound Cake Speech." NAACP 50th Anniversary Celebration of Brown V. Board. Constitution Hall, Washington, DC. May 2004. Speech.

53 "Welfare Queen' Becomes Issue in Reagan Campaign." *New York Times*. 15 Feb. 1976: 51. Print.

54 Dyson, Michael Eric. *Is Bill Cosby Right?: Or Has the Black Middle Class Lost Its Mind?* New York: Basic Civitas, 2005. 6. Print.

55 Ibid.

56 Harris, Hamil R., and Paul Fahri. "Debate Continues as Cosby Again Criticizes Black Youths."*Washington Post* [Washington, DC] 3 July 2004: A01. Print.

57 "Tough Talk: Bill Cosby." Interview by Ray Suarez. *Tough Talk*. Public Broadcasting Service. Washington, District of Columbia, 15 July 2004. Television.

58 Interview by William J. O'Reilly, Jr. *The O'Reilly Factor*. FOX News. New York, New York, 21 May 2004. Television. Transcript.

59 Wise, Tim J. *Colorblind: The Rise of Post-Racial Politics*. 68. Print.

Endnotes

[60] Peffley, Mark, Jon Hurwitz, and Paul M. Sniderman. "Racial Stereotypes and Whites' Political Views of Blacks in the Context of Welfare and Crime." *American Journal of Political Science* 41.1 (1997): 30-60. *JSTOR*. Web. 30 Dec. 2012.

[61] Ibid., 88.

[62] Ibid., 90.

[63] Ibid., 77.

[64] "Bill Cosby Fast Facts." *CNN*. Cable News Network, 24 June 2013. Web. 28 Aug. 2013.

[65] Skipper, John C. *Showdown at the 1964 Democratic Convention: Lyndon Johnson, Mississippi and Civil Rights*. Jefferson, NC: McFarland &, 2012. 67. Print.

[66] Kohel, Selena L. *The Role of Categorization and Goal Compatibility, Relative Power, and Relative Status on Intergroup Attitudes between Various Racial/ Ethnic Groups in the United States*. ProQuest, 2008. 5. Print.

[67] Ibid.

[68] Loury, Glenn C. *The Anatomy of Racial Inequality*. Cambridge, MA: Harvard University Press, 2002. 83. Print.

[69] Adams, John, and George A. Peek. *The Political Writings of John Adams: Representative Selections*. New York: Liberal Arts, 1954. 19. Print.

[70] Shepard, Christopher Michael. *The Civil War Income Tax and the Republican Party, 1861-1872*. New York: Algora Pub., 2010. 96. Print.

[71] Rosen, Hannah. *Terror in the Heart of Freedom: Citizenship, Sexual Violence, and the Meaning of Race in the Postemancipation South*. Chapel Hill: University of North Carolina, 2009. 179-80. Print.

[72] Henry, Mike. *Black History: More than Just a Month*. Lanham, MD: Rowman & Littlefield, 2012. Print.

[73] http://digitallibrary.hsp.org/index.php/Detail/Object/Show/object_id/49000.

[74] Trefousse, Hans L. *Andrew Johnson: A Biography*. New York: Norton, 1989. 58. Print.

[75] Johnson, Andrew, and Paul H. Bergeron. *The Papers of Andrew Johnson*. Knoxville: University of Tennessee, 1989. 77. Print.

[76] Nash, Howard P. *Andrew Johnson: Congress and Reconstruction*. Rutherford [N.J.]: Fairleigh Dickinson University Press, 1972. 35. Print.

[77] Morris, Roy. *Fraud of the Century: Rutherford B. Hayes, Samuel Tilden, and the Stolen Election of 1876.* New York: Simon & Schuster, 2003. Print.

[78] Wang, Xi. *The Trial of Democracy: Black Suffrage and Northern Republicans, 1860-1910.* Athens: University of Georgia, 1997. 260. Print.

[79] Ibid.

[80] Conley, Dalton. "The Cost of Slavery." *New York Times* [New York] 15 Feb. 2003: n. peg. Print.

[81] Blackmon, Douglas A. *Slavery by Another Name: The Re-Enslavement of Black People in America from the Civil War to World War II.* New York: Doubleday, 2008. Print.

[82] Jones, Jacqueline. *American Work: Four Centuries of Black and White Labor.* New York: W. W. Norton, 1998. 282. Print.

[83] Ibid.

[84] Anderson, Claud. *Black Labor, White Wealth: The Search for Power and Economic Justice.* [Edgewood, MD]: Duncan & Duncan, 1994. 13. Print.

[85] Ibid.

[86] Sullivan, Laura, et al. *The Racial Wealth Gap: Why Policy Matters.* Rep. New York: Demos/IASP, 2015. Print.

[87] Moore, Antonio. "America's Financial Divide: The Racial Breakdown of US Wealth in Black and White." *Black Voices.* Huffington Post, 13 Apr. 2015. Web. 06 Feb. 2016.

[88] Wise, Tim J. *Colorblind.* 67. Print.

[89] Ibid., 68.

[90] Anderson, Claud. *PowerNomics: The National Plan to Empower Black America.* Bethesda, MD: PowerNomics of America, 2001. 18. Print.

[91] Bradburd, Rus. *Forty Minutes of Hell: The Extraordinary Life of Nolan Richardson.* New York: Amistad, 2010. 72. Print.

[92] Rucker, Walter C., and James N. Upton. *Encyclopedia of American Race Riots.* Westport, CT: Greenwood, 2007. 260. Print.

[93] Shearer, Benjamin F. *The Uniting States: The Story of Statehood for the Fifty United States.* Westport, CT: Greenwood, 2004. 975. Print.

[94] Sykes, Lori Latrice. *Making the System Work for You: The Alexander Norton Story.* M&B Visionaries, 2008. 15. Print.

⁹⁵ Ibid.

⁹⁶ Cross, Theodore L. *The Black Power Imperative: Racial Inequality and the Politics of Nonviolence.* New York: Faulkner, 1984. 123. Print.

⁹⁷ Ogletree, Charles J., and Austin Sarat. *When Law Fails: Making Sense of Miscarriages of Justice.* New York: New York University Press, 2009. 52. Print.

⁹⁸ Butler, John S. *Entrepreneurship and Self-Help among Black Americans: A Reconsideration of Race and Economics.* Albany: State University of New York, 1991. 210. Print.

⁹⁹ Ibid., 211.

¹⁰⁰ Wall, Barbra Mann., and Arlene Wynbeek Keeling. *Nurses on the Front Line: When Disaster Strikes, 1878-2010.* New York: Springer Pub., 2011. 130. Print.

¹⁰¹ Ibid., 76.

¹⁰² Wang, Hongyu an Nadine Olson. *A Journey to Unlearn and Learn in Multicultural Education.* New York: Peter Lang, 2009. 64. Print.

¹⁰³ Henry, Mike. *Black History: More than Just a Month.* Lanham, MD: Rowman & Littlefield, 2012. 50. Print.

¹⁰⁴ Aptheker, Herbert. *A Documentary History of the Negro People in the United States. Volume 3.* Secaucus, NJ: Citadel, 1951. 332. Print.

¹⁰⁵ Wishart, David J. *Encyclopedia of the Great Plains: A Project of the Center for Great Plains.* Lincoln, NE: University of Nebraska, 2004. 240. Print.

¹⁰⁶ Wise, Tim J. *Colorblind.* 74. Print.

¹⁰⁷ Ibid.

¹⁰⁸ Ibid.

¹⁰⁹ Wilson, Amos N. *Blueprint for Black Power: A Moral, Political, and Economic Imperative for the Twenty-First Century.* New York: Afrikan World InfoSystems, 1998. Print.

¹¹⁰ Ibid.

¹¹¹ Ibid.

¹¹² Ibid.

¹¹³ Ibid.

[114] Ibid.

[115] Ibid.

[116] Ibid.

[117] Ibid.

[118] "Senate Panel Rejects Reagan Nominee for Federal Judgeship: Critics Accused Him of Racially Insensitive Talk." *Los Angeles Times.* 05 Jan. 1986: Print.

[119] Schroeder-Lein, Glenna R., and Richard Zuczek. *Andrew Johnson: A Biographical Companion.* Santa Barbara, CA: ABC-CLIO, 2001. 305. Print.

[120] Scher, Richard K. *Politics in the New South: Republicanism, Race, and Leadership in the.* Armonk, NY: M.E. Sharpe, 1997. 250. Print.

[121] Mjagkij, Nina. *Organizing Black America: An Encyclopedia of African American Associations.* New York: Garland, 2001. 194. Print.

[122] US Equal Employment Opportunity Commission. Newsroom. *EEOC Releases Fiscal Year 2014 Enforcement and Litigation Data.* 5 Feb. 2015. Web. 6 Feb. 2016.

[123] Nelson, William E. *Black Atlantic Politics: Dilemmas of Political Empowerment in Boston and Liverpool.* Albany: State University of New York, 2000. 115-16. Print.

[124] Ibid.

[125] Ibid.

[126] Mydians, Seth. "Woman Guiding Spirit in Boston School Fight." *Eugene-Register Guard* [Eugene, Oregon]. 7 Nov. 1974: 8. Print.

[127] *The Crisis.* Apr. 1984: 4. Print.

[128] *Editorials on File.* Vol. 15. New York: Facts on File, 1984. 99. Print. Part 1.

[129] Ibid., 110.

[130] Tucker, Ronnie Bernard. *Affirmative Action, the Supreme Court, and Political Power in the Old Confederacy.* Lanham, MD: University of America, 2000. 96-97. Print.

[131] Enchautegui, María E., Michael Fix, Pamela Loprest, Sarah C. Von Der Lippe, and Douglas Wissoker. *Do Minority Owned Businesses Get a Fair Share of Government Contracts?* Rep. Washington: Urban Institute, Dec. 1997. Print.

[132] Tucker, Ronnie Bernard. *Affirmative Action, the Supreme Court, and Political Power in the Old Confederacy*. Lanham, MD: University of America, 2000. 126. Print.

[133] Martin, Michael T., and Marilyn Yaquinto. *Redress for Historical Injustices in the United States: On Reparations for Slavery, Jim Crow, and Their Legacies*. Durham: Duke University Press, 2007. 331. Print.

[134] Ibid., 336.

[135] Downey, Dennis B., and Raymond M. Hyser. *Coatesville and the Lynching of Zachariah Walker: Death in a Pennsylvania Steel Town*. Charleston, SC: History, 2011. Print.

[136] Leslie, Naton. "What's It Worth? Or, Is It Just Trash?"*That Might Be Useful: Exploring America's Secondhand Culture*. Guilford, CT: Globe Pequot, 2005. 119. Print.

[137] *Lynching in America: Confronting the Legacy of Racial Terror*. Rep. Montgomery, Alabama: Equal Justice Initiative, 2015. Print.

[138]Hatch, John B. *Race and Reconciliation: Redressing Wounds of Injustice*. Lanham [etc.: Lexington]. 2008. 321-23. Print.

[139] Bickerstaff, Linda. *Modern-day Slavery*. New York: Rosen Publishing Group, 2010. 44. Print.

[140] Henneberg, Molly. "Reparations Disclaimer on Slavery Apology Stirs Backlash among House Dems." *FOX News*. 25 Apr. 2009. Web. 2 Apr. 2011.

[141] Greiff, Pablo De. *The Handbook of Reparations*. Oxford, England: Oxford University Press, 2006. Print.

Chapter 2 Endnotes

[142] McClain, Charles J. *Chinese Immigrants and American Law*. New York: Garland Pub., 1994. Print.

[143] Thornton, Jeremy. *The Gold Rush: Chinese Immigrants Come to America (1848-1882)*. New York: PowerKids, 2004. Print.

[144] Lai, H. Mark. *On Becoming Chinese American: A History of Communities and Institutions*. Walnut Creek, CA: Altamira, 2004. 207. Print.

[145] Gabbidon, Shaun L., and Helen Taylor Greene. *Race and Crime*. Thousand Oaks: Sage Publications, 2005. 36. Print.

[146] Zesch, Scott. *The Chinatown War: Chinese Los Angeles and the Massacre of 1871*. London: Oxford UP, 2012. Print.

[147] Cho, Jenny. *Chinatown in Los Angeles*. San Francisco, CA: Arcadia Pub., 2009. 19. Print.

[148] Ibid.

[149] Perlman, Selig. "The Anti-Chinese Agitation in California." *History of Labour in the United States.* By John R. Commons. New York: A. M. Kelley, 1966. 253. Print.

[150] Ethington, Philip J. *The Public City: The Political Construction of Urban Life in San Francisco, 1850-1900.* Cambridge [England: Cambridge UP, 1994. 32. Print.

[151] Soennichsen, John Robert. *The Chinese Exclusion Act of 1882.* Santa Barbara, CA: Greenwood, 2011. Print.

[152] Ibid.

[153] Ibid., 14

[154] Trinh-Shevrin, Chau, Nadia Shilpi Islam, and Mariano Jose Rey. *Asian American Communities and Health: Context, Research, Policy, and Action.* San Francisco: Jossey-Bass, 2009. 232-34. Print.

[155] Leon, Frederick T. L. *Asian American and Pacific Islander Children and Mental Health.* Santa Barbara, CA: Praeger, 2011. 152. Print.

[156] Ling, Huping. *Surviving on the Gold Mountain: A History of Chinese American Women and Their Lives.* Albany : SUNY Press, 1998. 169-72. Print.

[157] Fujiwara, Lynn. *Mothers without Citizenship: Asian Immigrant Families and the Consequences of Welfare Reform.* Minneapolis: U of Minnesota, 2008. Print.

[158] Wise, Tim J. *Colorblind: The Rise of Post-racial Politics and the Retreat from Racial Equity.* San Francisco: City Lights, 2010. 94. Print.

[159] Mann, Geoff. *Our Daily Bread: Wages, Workers, and the Political Economy of the American West.* Chapel Hill: U of North Carolina, 2007. 97-99. Print.

[160] Howard, Victor B. *Black Liberation in Kentucky: Emancipation and Freedom, 1862-1884.* Lexington, KY: U of Kentucky, 1983. 104-05. Print.

[161] Krenn, Michael L. *Race and U.S. Foreign Policy in the Ages of Territorial and Market Expansion.* New York: Garland Pub., 1998. 162-67. Print.

[162] Chang, Iris. *The Chinese in America: A Narrative History.* New York: Viking, 2003. Print.

[163] Cohen, Lucy M. *Chinese in the Post-Civil War South: A People without a History.* Baton Rouge: Louisiana State UP, 1984. Print.

[164] Lee, Jennifer, and Frank D. Bean. *The Diversity Paradox: Immigration and the Color Line in Twenty-first Century America.* New York: Russell Sage Foundation, 2010. 30-31. Print.

Endnotes

[165] Vera, Hernan, and Joe R. Feagin. *Handbook of the Sociology of Racial and Ethnic Relations.* New York: Springer, 2007. 131-33. Print.

[166] Wise, Tim J. *Colorblind: The Rise of Post-racial Politics and the Retreat from Racial Equity.* San Francisco: City Lights, 2010. 94. Print.

[167] Ibid., 94-5.

[168] Ogbaa, Kalu. *The Nigerian Americans.* Westport, CT: Greenwood, 2003. 69. Print.

[169] Saegert, Susan. *Community Development.* By James DeFilippis. New York: Routledge, 2013. 276. Print.

[170] Leonard, Thomas M. *Encyclopedia of the Developing World Index.* New York: Routledge, 2006. 1696. Print.

[171] Ibid.

[172] Jalloh, Alusine, and Toyin Falola. *The United States and West Africa: Interactions and Relations.* Rochester, NY: University of Rochester, 2008. 189. Print.

[173] Rodriguez, Junius P. *Slavery in the United States: A Social, Political, and Historical Encyclopedia.* Santa Barbara, CA: ABC-CLIO, 2007. 81. Print.

[174] Ibid., 230.

[175] Hornsby, Alton. *A Companion to African American History.* Malden, MA: Blackwell Pub., 2005. 9. Print.

[176] Gordon-Carter, Glynne. *An Amazing Journey: The Church of England's Response to Institutional Racism.* London: Church House, 2003. 3. Print.

[177] Neusner, Jacob. *World Religions in America: An Introduction.* Louisville: Westminster John Knox, 2009. 56-7. Print.

[178] Stampp, Kenneth M. *The Peculiar Institution: Slavery in the Ante-bellum South.* New York: Knopf, 1956. 157. Print.

[179] Ibid.

[180] Fulop, Timothy Earl., and Albert J. Raboteau. *African-American Religion: Interpretive Essays in History and Culture.* New York: Routledge, 1997. 123. Print.

[181] Ibid., 356.

[182] Fulop, Timothy Earl., and Albert J. Raboteau. *African-American Religion: Interpretive Essays in History and Culture.* New York: Routledge, 1997. 158. Print.

183 Ibid.

184 Durant, Thomas J., and J. David. Knottnerus. *Plantation Society and Race Relations: The Origins of Inequality.* Westport, CT: Praeger, 1999. 44-45. Print.

185 Farnam, Henry W., and Clive Day. *Chapters in the History of Social Legislation in the United States to 1860.* Washington: Carnegie Institution of Washington, 1938. 203. Print.

186 Haggard, Dixie Ray. *African Americans in the Nineteenth Century: People and Perspectives.* Santa Barbara, CA: ABC-CLIO, 2010. 23. Print.

187 Brown, William Wells. *Narrative of William W. Brown, a Fugitive Slave.* Boston: Anti-Slavery Office, 1847. 83-84. Print.

188 Wilson, Amos N. *Blueprint for Black Power: A Moral, Political, and Economic Imperative for the Twenty-first Century.* New York: Afrikan World InfoSystems, 1998. 58. Print.

189 Dunaway, Wilma A. *The African-American Family in Slavery and Emancipation.* New York: Cambridge UP, 2003. 64. Print.

190 Dunaway, Wilma A. *The African-American Family in Slavery and Emancipation.* New York: Cambridge UP, 2003. 64. Print.

191 Ibid., 74.

192 Marable, Manning, and Leith Mullings. *Let Nobody Turn Us Around: Voices of Resistance, Reform, and Renewal : An African American Anthology.* Lanham: Rowman & Littlefield, 2000. 48. Print.

193 Dunaway, Wilma A. *The African-American Family in Slavery and Emancipation.* New York: Cambridge UP, 2003. 56. Print.

194 Parish, Peter J. *Slavery: The Many Faces of a Southern Institution.* Edinburgh: Edinburgh UP, 1979. 50. Print.

195 Stampp, Kenneth M. *The Peculiar Institution: Slavery in the Ante-bellum South.* New York: Knopf, 1956. 346. Print.

196 Ibid.

197 Holland, Jearold Winston. *Black Recreation: A Historical Perspective.* Chicago: Burnham, 2002. 66-67. Print.

198 Savitt, Todd Lee. "Insanity." *Medicine and Slavery: The Diseases and Health Care of Blacks in Antebellum Virginia.* Urbana: University of Illinois, 1978. 247-80. Print.

Endnotes

[199] Schwalm, Leslie A. *A Hard Fight for We: Women's Transition from Slavery to Freedom in South Carolina.* Urbana: University of Illinois, 1997. 112-13. Print.

[200] James, Stanlie M., and Abena P. A. Busia. *Theorizing Black Feminisms: The Visionary Pragmatism of Black Women.* London: Routledge, 1993. Print.

[201] Schwartz, Marie Jenkins. *Born in Bondage: Growing up Enslaved in the Antebellum South.* Cambridge, MA: Harvard UP, 2000. 93. Print.

[202] Cottrol, Robert J. *The Long, Lingering Shadow: Slavery, Race, and Law in the American Hemisphere.* Athens, GA: University of Georgia, 2013. 45. Print.

[203] Phillips, William D. *Slavery from Roman times to the Early Transatlantic Trade.* Minneapolis: University of Minnesota, 1985. 37. Print.

[204] Perry, Marvin. *Western Civilization: Ideas, Politics and Society.* Boston: Houghton Mifflin, 2009. 120. Print.

[205] Perry, Marvin. *Western Civilization: Ideas, Politics and Society.* Boston: Houghton Mifflin, 2009. 120. Print.

[206] Patterson, Orlando. *Slavery and Social Death: A Comparative Study.* Cambridge, MA: Harvard UP, 1982. 126. Print.

[207] Bonacich, Edna. *Immigrant Entrepreneurs: Koreans in Los Angeles ; 1965-1982.* By Ivan H. Light. Berkeley: University of California, 1991. 19. Print.

[208] Center for American Progress. *Who Are Korean Americans?* Rep. Washington: Center for American Progress, 2015. Print.

[209] Jackson, Yo. *Encyclopedia of Multicultural Psychology.* Thousand Oaks, CA: SAGE Publications, 2006. 284. Print.

[210] Hurh, Won Moo. *The Korean Americans.* Westport, CT: Greenwood, 1998. 36-37. Print.

[211] Ibid.

[212] Cha, Marn J. "The Roles of the State, Social Capital, and Transnationalism." *Koreans in Central California (1903-1957): A Study of Settlement and Transnational Politics.* Lanham, MD: University of America, 2010. 188. Print.

[213] Lee, Jae-Hyup. *Dynamics of Ethnic Identity: Three Asian American Communities in Philadelphia.* London: Taylor & Francis, 1998. 40. Print.

[214] Hurh, Won Moo. *The Korean Americans.* Westport, CT: Greenwood, 1998. 39-40. Print.

[215] Ibid.

216 Lee, Essie E. *Nurturing Success: Successful Women of Color and Their Daughters*. Westport, CT: Praeger, 2000. 119. Print.

217 Pew Research Center. *The Rise of Asian Americans*. Rep. Washington, DC: Pew Research Center, 2012. Print.

218 Frazier, John W., Joe T. Darden, and Norah F. Henry. *The African Diaspora in the U.S. and Canada at the Dawn of the 21st Century*. Albany: State U of New York, 2010. 244. Print.

219 *World Migration 2008: Managing Labour Mobility in the Evolving Global Economy*. Geneva, Switzerland: International Organization for Migration, 2008. 108. Print.

220 Gambino, Christine P., Edward T. Trevelyan, and John T. Fitzwater. *The Foreign-Born Population From Africa: 2008–2012*. Rep. Washington, DC: US Census Bureau, 2014. Print.

221 Falola, Toyin, and Niyi Afolabi. *African Minorities in the New World*. New York: Routledge, 2008. 248. Print.

222 Okpewho, Isidore, and Nkiru Nzegwu. *The New African Diaspora*. Bloomington: Indiana UP, 2009. 116. Print.

223 Wiltz, Teresa. "Growing African Immigrant Population Is Highly Educated, Underemployed." Web log post. *Stateline*. Pew Charitable Trusts, 14 May 2015. Web.

224 Vakunta, Peter W. *A Nation at Risk: A Personal Narrative of the Cameroonian Crisis*. Bloomington, IN: Iuniverse, 2012. 41. Print.

225 Phillips, David A. *Development without Aid: The Decline of Development Aid and the Rise of the Diaspora*. London: ANTHEM, 2013. 133. Print.

226 Barkan, Elliott Robert. *Immigrants in American History: Arrival, Adaptation, and Integration*. Santa Barbara, CA: ABC-CLIO, 2013. 693. Print.

227 Aberjhani, and Sandra L. West. *Encyclopedia of the Harlem Renaissance*. New York: Facts On File, 2003. 2. Print.

228 Haines, David W. *Refugees in America in the 1950s: A Reference Handbook*. Westport, Conn. [u.a.: Greenwood, 1996. 147. Print.

229 "Median household income in the past 12 Months (in 2010 inflation-adjusted dollars)". *2006-2010 American Community Survey*. United States Census Bureau. 2010. Retrieved 22 April 2013.

230 Mohapatra, Sanket, and Dilip Ratha. *Remittance Markets in Africa*. Washington, D.C.: World Bank, 2011. 115. Print.

231 "FY 2008-11 USAID-State Foreign Assistance Appropriations." *USAID*. USAID, n.d. Web. 25 May 2013.

Endnotes

[232] Getahun, Solomon Addis. *The History of Ethiopian Immigrants and Refugees in America, 1900-2000: Patterns of Migration, Survival, and Adjustment.* New York: LFB Scholarly Pub., 2007. 197. Print.

[233] Ungar, Sanford J. *Fresh Blood: The New American Immigrants.* New York: Simon & Schuster, 1995. 263-64. Print.

[234] Cavalli-Sforza, L. L., Paolo Menozzi, and Alberto Piazza. *The History and Geography of Human Genes.* Princeton, NJ: Princeton UP, 1994. 175. Print.

[235] Cavalli-Sforza, L. L., and Francesco Cavalli-Sforza. *The Great Human Diasporas: The History of Diversity and Evolution.* Reading, MA: Addison-Wesley, 1995. 199. Print.

[236] Ungar, Sanford J. *Fresh Blood: The New American Immigrants.* New York: Simon & Schuster, 1995. 263-64. Print.

[237] Gnamo, Abbas H. *Conquest and Resistance in the Ethiopian Empire, 1880-1974: The Case of the Arsi Oromo.* Boston: BRILL, 2014. 126-27. Print.

[238] Hinks, Peter P., John R. McKivigan, and R. Owen. Williams. *Encyclopedia of Antislavery and Abolition.* Westport, CT: Greenwood, 2007. 248. Print.

[239] Migration Policy Institute. *The Nigerian Diaspora in the United States.* Rep. Washington: Migration Policy Institute, 2015. Print.

[240] Ogbaa, Kalu. *The Nigerian Americans.* Westport, CT: Greenwood, 2003. 30. Print.

[241] Marech, Rona. "Nigerian Immigrants Make a Home in Md." *Baltimore Sun.* N.p., 28 Nov. 2005. Web. 25 May 2013.

[242] Okpewho, Isidore, and Nkiru Nzegwu. *The New African Diaspora.* Bloomington: Indiana UP, 2009. 247. Print.

[243] Hayes, Patrick J. *The Making of Modern Immigration: An Encyclopedia of People and Ideas.* Santa Barbara, CA: ABC-CLIO, 2012. 150. Print.

[244] "Median household income in the past 12 Months (in 2010 inflation-adjusted dollars)". *2006-2010 American Community Survey.* United States Census Bureau. 2010. Retrieved 22 April 2013.

[245] Okafor Mpa, Tochukwu O. *Joy of Success: What It Means to Transform Success into Excellence.* By Tochukwu O. Okafor. [S.l.]: Iuniverse Com, 2013. 39. Print.

[246] Pellegrini, Giulia. *Knowledge, Productivity, and Innovation in Nigeria: Creating a New Economy.* By Ismail Radwan. Washington, D.C.: World Bank Publications, 2010. 98-99. Print.

[247] *World Economic Outlook Database.* International Monetary Fund, Apr. 2015. Web. 2 Jan. 2016.

248 "Central Intelligence Agency." *CIA*. CIA, n.d. Web. 25 May 2013. <https://www.cia.gov/library/publications/the-world-factbook/geos/ni.html>.

249 World Bank. GDP growth (annual %), Nigeria. Raw data. Washington http://data.worldbank.org/indicator/NY.GDP.MKTP.KD.ZG/countries/NG?display=graph.

250 "The Wealth Report 2012." *Rise Of The New Rich*. N.p., n.d. Web. 25 May 2013. <http://www.thewealthreport.net/economic-trends/rise-of-the-new-rich.aspx>.

251 Claydon, David. *A New Vision, a New Heart, a Renewed Call, Volume 1*. Pasadena: William Carey Library, 2005. 136. Print.

252 Ogbaa, Kalu. *The Nigerian Americans*. Westport, CT: Greenwood, 2003. 56. Print.

253 Burnett, John. "Nigerian Church Spreads African-Style Zeal Across North America." *Weekend Edition Sunday*. National Public Radio. Washington, DC, 18 May 2014. Radio. Transcript.

254 Hall, Gwendolyn Midlo. *Slavery and African Ethnicities in the Americas: Restoring the Links*. Chapel Hill: University of North Carolina, 2005. 130. Print.

255 Berlin, Ira. *The Making of African America: The Four Great Migrations*. New York: Viking, 2010. Print.

256 Moore, Darrell. "Epidermal Capital: Formations of (Black) Subjectivity in Political Philosophy and Culture." Diss. Northwestern U, 1997. Print.

257 Wise, Tim J. *Colorblind: The Rise of Post-racial Politics and the Retreat from Racial Equity*. San Francisco, CA: City Lights, 2010. Print.

Chapter 3 Endnotes

258 Hines, Gary. "The Anatomy of an Execution." *Lodi (Ca.) News Sentinel* [Lodi, California] 10 June 1987: 6. Print.

259 Mills, Steve, Maurice Possley, and Ken Armstrong. "3 Cases Weaken Under Scrutiny." *Chicago Tribune* [Chicago] 17 Dec. 2000. Web. 28 May 2013.

260 Ibid.

261 Ibid.

262 SPIN Media LLC. "Capital Punishment." *SPIN*. Nov. 1991. Print.

263 Spradley, Jermaine. "George Zimmerman Not Guilty: Jury Lets Trayvon Martin Killer Go." *The Huffington Post*. 13 July 2013. Web. 28 Aug. 2013.

[264] "George Zimmerman's Dad Says Travyon Told His Son, 'You're Gonna Die Now.'" *NBC News*. 29 Mar. 2012. Web. 28 Aug. 2013.

[265] Stutzman, Rene, and Jeff Weiner." Zimmerman Says Trayvon Circled His SUV, Frightened Him." *Orlando Sentinel*. 3 May 2012. Web. 28 Aug. 2013.

[266] "Transcript of George Zimmerman's Call to the Police." *Mother Jones*. n.p., n.d. Web. 28 Aug. 2013.

[267] Donaghue, Erin. "George Zimmerman Trial: Will Zimmerman's Call to Dispatchers Boost the Prosecution's Case?" *CBS News*. 04 June 2013. Web. 28 Aug. 2013.

[268] Stutzman, Rene. "Police: Zimmerman Says Trayvon Decked Him with One Blow Then Began Hammering His Head." *Orlando Sentinel*. 26 Mar. 2012. Web. 28 Aug. 2013.

[269] "Trayvon Martin Case Evidence: Weed Out, Fighting In, Texts Blocked, Gold Teeth Out." *Trayvon Martin Case: Weed Evidence Out, Fighting In, Gold Teeth Out*. n.p., 28 May 2013. Web. 28 Aug. 2013.

[270] Capehart, Jonathan. "George Zimmerman's Relevant Past." *Washington Post*. 28 May 2013. Web. 28 Aug. 2013.

[271] Vamburkar, Meenal. "Former George Zimmerman Co-Worker Describes Him As 'Jekyll And Hyde': 'When The Dude Snapped, He Snapped'." *Mediaite*. 30 Mar. 2012. Web. 28 Aug. 2013.

[272] Capehart, Jonathan. "George Zimmerman's Relevant Past." *Washington Post*. 28 May 2013. Web. 28 Aug. 2013.

[273] Ibid.

[274] Chappell, Bill. "Zimmerman Arrested on Murder Charge in Martin Case; Will Plead Not Guilty." *NPR*. 11 Apr. 2012. Web. 28 Aug. 2013.

[275] "45 Days After Killing Trayvon Martin & Sparking National Outcry, George Zimmerman Finally Charged." *Democracy Now!* 12 Apr. 2012. Web. 28 Aug. 2013.

[276] Lucas, Lisa, and Dareh Gregorian. "Trayvon Martin Murder Trial: Prosecution's Star Witness, Self-Described 'Good Friend,' Testifies He Thought Zimmerman 'Creepy'." *New York Daily News*. 26 June 2012. Web. 28 Aug. 2013.

[277] Lemieux, Scott. "The Zimmerman Acquittal Isn't about 'Stand Your Ground'." *The American Prospect*. n.p., 14 July 2013. Web. 28 Aug. 2013.

[278] Curry, Colleen, Matt Gutman, Seniboye Tienabseo, Miseon Lee, Josh Margolin, and Aaron Katersky. "George Zimmerman's Wife on 911 Tape: 'I Am Really, Really Scared'." *ABC News*. ABC News Network, 9 Sept. 2013. Web. 07 Feb. 2016.

279 "George Zimmerman's Girlfriend Showed Police a Photo of Marks on Her Neck after 'He Choked Her'." *Daily Mail Online*. Associated Newspapers, 26 Feb. 2014. Web. 07 Feb. 2016.

280 Thomas, Emily. "George Zimmerman's Controversial Celebrity Boxing Match Canceled." *Black Voices*. The Huffington Post, 8 Feb. 2014. Web. 07 Feb. 2016.

281 Goldman, Russell. "George Zimmerman Painting Sells for $100,000." *ABC News*. ABC News Network, 23 Dec. 2013. Web. 07 Feb. 2016.

282 Wagner, Pete, and Bernadette Rabuy. *Mass Incarceration: The Whole Pie 2015*. Rep. Easthampton, MA: Prison Policy Initiative, 2015. Print.

283 "International Centre for Prison Studies." *International Centre for Prison Studies*. n.p., n.d. Web. 28 May 2013. http://www.prisonstudies.org/info/worldbrief/wpb_stats.php?area=all

284 Ibid.

285 Ibid.

286 Bliss, William Dwight Porter. *The Encyclopedia of Social Reforms: Including Political Economy, Political Science, Sociology and Statistics ...* New York, NY: Funk & Wagnalls, 1897. 410. Print.

287 Roth, Mitchel P. *Crime and Punishment: A History of the Criminal Justice System*. Belmont, CA: Thomson Wadsworth, 2005. 151. Print.

288 Morris, Charles. *A New History of the United States: The Greater Republic: Embracing the Growth and Achievements of Our Country from the Earliest Days of Discovery and Settlement to the Present Eventful Year ...* New Haven, CT: Butler & Alger, 1899. 278. Print.

289 *US and World Population Clock*. Application. *US and World Population Clock*. US Census Bureau, 1 Jan. 2016. Web.

290 Cooper, William J., and John McCardell. *In the Cause of Liberty: How the Civil War Redefined American Ideals*. Baton Rouge: Louisiana State University Press, 2009. 137. Print.

291 Jones, Howard. *Blue & Gray Diplomacy: A History of Union and Confederate Foreign Relations*. Chapel Hill: University of North Carolina, 2010. 230. Print.

292 Alexander, Michelle. *The New Jim Crow: Mass Incarceration in the Age of Colorblindness*. New York: New, 2010. 28. Print.

293 Ibid.

294 Oshinsky, David M. *Worse than Slavery: Parchman Farm and the Ordeal of Jim Crow Justice*. New York: Free, 1996. 21. Print.

[295] Kennedy, Randall. *Race, Crime, and the Law*. New York: Pantheon, 1997. 86. Print.

[296] Alexander, Michelle. *The New Jim Crow: Mass Incarceration in the Age of Colorblindness*. New York: New, 2010. 31. Print.

[297] Welch, Susan. *Understanding American Government*. Minneapolis/St. Paul: West, 1997. 452. Print.

[298] Bessette, Joseph M. *American Justice*. Pasadena, CA: Salem, 1996. 817. Print.

[299] Szalavitz, Maia, and Maia Szalavitz." Study: Whites More Likely to Abuse Drugs than Blacks." *Time*. Time, n.d. Web. 28 May 2013. http://healthland.time.com/2011/11/07/study-whites-more-likely-to-abuse-drugs-than-blacks/

[300] *Constitution of the Confederate States of America: Adopted Unanimously by the Congress of the Confederate States of America [sic], March 11, 1861*. Milledgeville, GA: Boughton, Nisbet & Barnes, State Printers, 1861. 19. Print.

[301] Carrillo, Karen Juanita. *African American History Day by Day: A Reference Guide to Events*. Santa Barbara, CA: Greenwood, 2012. 152. Print.

[302] Smith, Jessie Carney. *Black Firsts: 4,000 Ground-Breaking and Pioneering Historical Events*. Detroit: Visible Ink, 2003. 317. Print.

[303] Lane, Charles. *The Day Freedom Died: The Colfax Massacre, the Supreme Court, and the Betrayal of Reconstruction*. New York: Henry Holt, 2008. 155. Print.

[304] Zuczek, Richard. *Encyclopedia of the Reconstruction Era*. Westport, CT: Greenwood, 2006. 376. Print.

[305] Coakley, Robert W. *The Role of Federal Military Forces in Domestic Disorders, 1789-1878*. Washington, D.C.: Center of Military History, US Army, 1989. 325. Print.

[306] Ibid.

[307] Wagner, Margaret E., Gary W. Gallagher, and Paul Finkelman. *The Library of Congress Civil War Desk Reference*. New York: Simon & Schuster, 2002. 787. Print.

[308] Beatty, Jack. *Age of Betrayal: The Triumph of Money in America, 1865-1900*. New York: Alfred A. Knopf, 2007. 114. Print.

[309] Fuchs, Richard L. *An Unerring Fire: The Massacre at Fort Pillow*. Rutherford, NJ: Fairleigh Dickinson University Press, 1994. 75. Print.

[310] Ibid.

[311] Sutherland, Jonathan. *African Americans at War: An Encyclopedia, Volume 1.* Santa Barbara: ABC-CLIO, 2004. 331-32. Print.

[312] Goldstone, Lawrence. *Inherently Unequal: The Betrayal of Equal Rights by the Supreme Court, 1865-1903.* New York: Walker &, 2011. 93. Print.

[313] Goldstone, Lawrence. *Inherently Unequal: The Betrayal of Equal Rights by the Supreme Court, 1865-1903.* New York: Walker &, 2011. 91. Print.

[314] Alexander, Michelle. *The New Jim Crow: Mass Incarceration in the Age of Colorblindness.* New York: New, 2010. Print.

[315] Baum, Dan. "Legalize It All: How to Win the War on Drugs." *Harper's Magazine.* Apr. 2016: 22-34. Print.

[316] Ladner, Joyce A., and Theresa Foy. DiGeronimo. *Launching Our Black Children for Success: A Guide for Parents of Kids from Three to Eighteen.* San Francisco: Jossey-Bass, 2003. 216. Print.

[317] McCollum, Walter R. *Strength of a Black Man: Destined for Self Empowerment.* Oak Harbor: Empty Canoe, LLC, 2004. 78. Print.

[318] National Institute on Drug Abuse. *Results from the 2013 National Survey on Drug Use and Health: Summary of National Findings.* Rep. Washington: US Department of Health and Human Services, 2014. Print.

[319] Wallace, Jr., John M., Tony N. Brown, Jerald G. Bachman, and Thomas A. LaVeist. *Religion, Race, and Abstinence from Drug Use among American Adolescents.* Rep. Ann Arbor: Institute for Social Research, University of Michigan, 2003. Print.

[320] *CDC-Youth Online-High School YRBS 2011 Results.* Rep. Centers for Disease Control, n.d. Web. 17 Aug. 2013.

[321] Centers for Disease Control and Prevention. *Youth Risk Behavior Surveillance — United States, 2013.* Rep. Washington: US Department of Health and Human Services, 2014. Print.

[322] *CDC-Youth Online-High School YRBS 2001 Results.* Rep. Centers for Disease Control, n.d. Web. 17 Aug. 2013.

[323] Arrests of Youth, by Race, from Crime in the United States, 2001. (2002). Washington, DC: Federal Bureau of Investigations; Population of Youth from Puzzanchera, C., Finnegan, T. and Kang, W. (2005). "Easy Access to Juvenile Populations" Online. Available: http://www.ojjdp.ncjrs.org/ojstatbb/ezapop/

[324] Federal Bureau of Investigations, Criminal Justice Information Services Division. *Crime in the United States.* Rep. Washington: US Department of Justice, 2012. Print.

[325] Sickmund, Melissa, Sladky, T.J., and Kang, Wei. (2004) "Census of Juveniles in Residential Placement Databook." Online. Available: http://www.ojjdp.ncjrs.org/ojstatbb/cjrp/

Endnotes

[326] *Justice on Trial: Racial Disparities in the American Criminal Justice System.* [Washington, D.C.]: Leadership Conference Education Fund, 2000. 7. Print.

[327] Welch, Kelly. "Black Criminal Stereotypes and Racial Profiling." *Journal of Contemporary Criminal Justice* 23.3 (2007): 278. *Sage Publications.* Web. 16 Aug. 2013.

[328] Wise, Tim J. *Colorblind.* 80. Print.

[329] Ibid., 84.

[330] Truly, Traci. *Teen Rights (and Responsibilities): A Legal Guide for Teens and the Adults in Their Lives.* Naperville, IL: Sphinx Publishing, 2005. 222. Print.

[331] Bratton, William J. *New York City Police Department Stop Question & Frisk Activity.* Rep. New York: New York City Police Department, 2015. Print.

[332] Ridgeway, Greg. *Analysis of Racial Disparities in the New York Police Department's Stop, Question, and Frisk Practices.* Rep. Santa Monica, CA: RAND Corporation, 2007. Print.

[333] Gelman, Andrew; Fagan, Jeffrey; Kiss, Alex (September 2007). "An Analysis of the New York City Police Department's 'Stop-and-Frisk' Policy in the Context of Claims of Racial Bias." *Journal of the American Statistical Association* 102 (479): 813–823.

[334] Flegenheimer, Matt. "New Message on Frisking from De Blasio's City Hall Amid Criticism." *NY Region.* The New York Times, 12 June 2015. Web. 07 Feb. 2016.

[335] Ridgeway, Greg. *Analysis of Racial Disparities in the New York Police Department's Stop, Question, and Frisk Practices.* Rep. Santa Monica, CA: RAND Corporation, 2007. Print.

[336] Ibid.

[337] Geigner, Timothy. "Federal Judge: NYC Stop And Frisk Violates The Fourth Amendment." *Techdirt.* 23 Aug. 2013. Web. 28 Aug. 2013.

[338] Bloomberg, Michael." Frisks Save Lives." *New York Post.* New York Post, 12 Aug. 2013. Web. 17 Aug. 2013. http://www.nypost.com/p/news/opinion/opedcolumnists/frisks_save_lives_EOW52JdKUpPUd91Rmv7W8M

[339] Peck, Adam. "Mayor Bloomberg: NYPD 'Stops Whites Too Much and Minorities Too Little'." *Think Progress.* Center for American Progress, 28 June 2013. Web. 17 Aug. 2013. http://thinkprogress.org/justice/2013/06/28/2231761/mayor-bloomberg-nypd-stop-whites-too-much-and-minorities-too-little/

[340] Adams, Nate. "Blacks 5X More Likely to be Arrested for Marijuana." *Haverford-Havertown Patch.* 11 June 2013. Web. 17 Aug. 2013. http://haverford.patch.com/groups/police-and-fire/p/blacks-5x-more-likely-to-be-arrested-for-marijuana

341 Dempsey, John S., and Linda S. Forst. *Police*. Clifton Park, NY: Delmar Cengage Learning, 2013. 185. Print.

342 Hemmens, Craig, and Cassia Sphon. *Courts: A Text/Reader*. Thousand Oaks, CA: SAGE Publications, 2011. 363. Print.

343 http://norml.org/pdf_files/state_penalties/NORML_SC_State_Penalties.pdf

344 Cole, David. *No Equal Justice: Race and Class in the American Criminal Justice System*. New York: New, 1999. Print.

345 Scraton, Phil, and Jude McCulloch. *The Violence of Incarceration*. New York: Routledge, 2009. 12-13. Print.

346 Ibid.

347 Ibid.

348 DeVeaux, Mika'il. *The Trauma of the Incarceration Experience*. Rep. Cambridge, MA: Harvard Civil Rights-Civil Liberties Law Review, 2013. Print.

349 Petersilia, Joan. *When Prisoners Come Home: Parole and Prisoner Reentry*. Oxford: Oxford University Press, 2003. 142. Print.

350 *No Second Chance People with Criminal Records Denied Access to Public Housing*. Rep. New York: Human Rights Watch, 2004. Print.

351 Mauer, Marc, and Virginia McCalmont. *A Lifetime of Punishment: The Impact of the Felony Drug Ban on Welfare Benefits*. Rep. Washington, DC: Sentencing Project, 2013. Print.

352 Noonan, Margaret E. *Mortality in Local Jails and State Prisons, 2000-2010 - Statistical Tables*. Rep. Washington, D.C.: US Department of Justice, Office of Justice Programs, Bureau of Justice Statistics, 2012. Print.

353 Maruschak, Laura M. *HIV in Prisons, 2001-2010*. Rep. Washington, D.C.: US Department of Justice, Office of Justice Programs, Bureau of Justice Statistics, 2012. Print.

354 Noonan, Margaret E. *Mortality in Local Jails and State Prisons, 2000-2010 - Statistical Tables*. Rep. Washington, DC: US Department of Justice, Office of Justice Programs, Bureau of Justice Statistics, 2012. Print.

355 "Dorothy Gaines, X-POWD." *Dorothy Gaines, X-POWD*. Web. 17 Aug. 2013. http://dorothygaines.org/about.htm

356 Ibid.

357 Gonzales, Doreen. *A Look at the Fourth Amendment: Against Unreasonable Searches and Seizures*. Berkeley Heights, NJ: Enslow, 2008. Print.

Endnotes

[358] Dennis J. Callahan, The Long Distance Remand: Florida v. Bostick and the Re-Awakened Bus Search Battlefront in the War on Drugs, 43 Wm. & Mary L. Rev. 365 (2001), http://scholarship.law.wm.edu/wmlr/vol43/iss1/10

[359] Cole, David. *No Equal Justice*. 17. Print.

[360] Ibid., 18-21.

[361] Ibid.

[362] Ibid., 47-8.

[363] *The Death Penalty: Beyond Abolition, Part 285*. Ed. Council of Europe. Strasbourg: Council of Europe, 2004. 207. Print.

[364] Cole, David. *No Equal Justice*. New York: New, 1999. 149-53. Print.

[365] Ibid, 132-4.

[366] Ibid, 134.

[367] Lau, Peter F. *From the Grassroots to the Supreme Court: Brown v. Board of Education and American Democracy*. Durham: Duke University Press, 2004. 350. Print.

[368] Mandery, Evan J. *Capital Punishment in America: A Balanced Examination*. Sudbury, MA: Jones & Bartlett Learning, 2011. 380. Print.

[369] Ibid.

[370] Margolick, David. "Rarity for US Executions: White Dies for Killing Black." *New York Times* [New York]. 7 Sept. 1991. Print.

[371] Ibid.

[372] Rudman, Laurie A. *Implicit Measures for Social and Personality Psychology*. Los Angeles: SAGE, 2011. 34. Print.

[373] Patterson, James T. *Brown v. Board of Education: A Civil Rights Milestone and Its Troubled Legacy*. New York: Oxford University Press, 2002. 87. Print.

[374] Ibid.

[375] Meierhoefer, B. S. *General Effect of Mandatory Minimum Prison Terms*. Rep. no. NCJ 137258. Washington, DC: Federal Judicial Center, 1992. Print.

[376] Merica, Dan, Carol Cratty, and Jessica Yellin." Eric Holder Seeks to Cut Mandatory Minimum Drug Sentences." *CNN*. Cable News Network, 12 Aug. 2013. Web. 28 Aug. 2013.

[377] The United States Department of Justice. Office of Public Affairs. *In Milestone for Sentencing Reform, Attorney General Holder Announces Record Reduction in Mandatory Minimums Against Nonviolent Drug Offenders*. Washington, DC: n.p., 2015. Print.

378 Neil, Martha. "Despite Holder's Call for Clemency to Free over 10,000, Actual Number so Far Is Much Lower." *ABA Journal.* American Bar Association, 9 Dec. 2015. Web. 09 Feb. 2016.

379 Safire, William." ON LANGUAGE; Drop That Card." *New York Times Magazine* [New York]. 18 Sept. 1988: n.p. Print.

380 Persily, Nathaniel, Jack Citrin, and Patrick J. Egan. *Public Opinion and Constitutional Controversy.* Oxford: Oxford University Press, 2008. 23-24. Print.

381 Brand-Ballard, Jeffrey. *Limits of Legality: The Ethics of Lawless Judging.* Oxford: Oxford University Press, 2010. 142. Print.

382 Timberg, Bernard, and Bob Erler. *Television Talk: A History of the TV Talk Show.* Austin, TX: University of Texas, 2002. 171. Print.

383 Roman, John. *Race, Justifiable Homicide, and Stand Your Ground Laws: Analysis of FBI Supplementary Homicide Report Data.* Rep. Washington: Urban Institute, July 2013. Print.

384 Allen, Freddie. "Whites Who Kill Blacks More Likely to Escape." *The Madison Times.* 27 Aug. 2013. Web. 28 Aug. 2013.

385 Innocence Project. "Wrongful Conviction Compensation Statutes." *CNN.* Cable News Network, Mar. 2012. Web. 28 Aug. 2013.

386 Ibid.

Chapter 4 Endnotes

387 Ross, Janell. "Antonin Scalia's Strange Idea That Blacks Might Do Better in 'less- Advanced Schools'." *The Fix.* The Washington Post, 10 Dec. 2015. Web.

388 Ibid.

389 Kohn, Sally." Affirmative Action Has Helped White Women More Than Anyone." *TIME.* Time Inc., 17 June 2013. Web. 17 Aug. 2013. <http://ideas.time.com/2013/06/17/affirmative-action-has-helped-white-women-more-than-anyone/>.

390 Goodwin, Michele. "The Death of Affirmative Action, Part 1." *Chronicle of Higher Education.* The Chronicle of Higher Education, Inc., 15 Mar. 2012. Web. 17 Aug. 2013.

391 Marable, Manning. *Beyond Black and White: Transforming African-American Politics.* London: Verso, 1995. 85. Print.

392 Wise, Tim J. "Is Sisterhood Conditional?: White Women and the Rollback of Affirmative Action." *National Women's Studies Association Journal* 10.3 (Fall 1998). Tim Wise, 23 Sept. 1998. Web. 17 Aug. 2013.

[393] Montoya, Arthur I. *America's Original Sin: Absolution & Penance.* Bloomington: Xlibris Corporation, 1997. 155-56. Print.

[394] Wise, Tim J. "Is Sisterhood Conditional?: White Women and the Rollback of Affirmative Action." *National Women's Studies Association Journal* 10.3 (Fall 1998): n. pag. Tim Wise, 23 Sept. 1998. Web. 17 Aug. 2013.

[395] Ibid.

[396] Ibid.

[397] "Graduation Rates of First-time Postsecondary Students..." *Digest of Education Statistics.* National Center for Education Statistics, Nov. 2011. Web. 17 Aug. 2013.

[398] Glazer-Raymo, Judith. *Unfinished Agendas: New and Continuing Gender Challenges in Higher Education.* Baltimore: Johns Hopkins UP, 2008. 15. Print.

[399] Wherry, Frederick F., and Juliet Schor. *The SAGE Encyclopedia of Economics and Society.* Los Angeles: SAGE Reference, 2015. 60. Print.

[400] Kohn, Sally. "Affirmative Action Has Helped White Women More Than Anyone." *TIME Ideas.* TIME, 17 June 2013. Web.

[401] Moore, Jamillah. *Race and College Admissions: A Case for Affirmative Action.* Jefferson, NC: McFarland, 2005. 146. Print.

[402] Ibid.

[403] Ibid.

[404] Swanson, Paul. *An Introduction to Capitalism.* n.p.: Routledge, 2012. 108. Print.

[405] Bolick, Clint. *The Affirmative Action Fraud: Can We Restore the American Civil Rights Vision?* Washington, DC: Cato Institute, 1996. 53. Print.

[406] Aniagolu, Emeka. *Co-whites: How and Why White Women" Betrayed" the Struggle for Racial Equality in the United States.* Lanham, MD: University of America, 2011. 199. Print.

[407] Moore, Jamillah. *Race and College Admissions: A Case for Affirmative Action.* Jefferson, NC: McFarland, 2005. 148. Print.

[408] McClam, Erin, and Pete Williams." Supreme Court Raises Bar for Affirmative Action in College Admissions." *NBC News.* 24 June 2013. Web. 30 Aug. 2013.

[409] Liptak, Adam. "Supreme Court Upholds Affirmative Action Program at University of Texas." *New York Times.* 23 June 2016. Web.

[410] Finkelman, Paul. *Encyclopedia of African American History, 1896 to the Present: From the Age of Segregation to the Twenty-First Century.* New York: Oxford University Press, 2009. 485. Print.

[411] "Homesteading By the Numbers." *National Parks Service.* US Department of the Interior, 12 Aug. 2013. Web. 17 Aug. 2013.

[412] "Presidential Quotes about the Homestead Act." *National Parks Service.* US Department of the Interior, 11 Aug. 2013. Web. 17 Aug. 2013.

[413] Williams, John Hoyt. *A Great & Shining Road: The Epic Story of the Transcontinental Railroad.* New York: Times, 1988. 152. Print.

[414] Hayes, Rutherford B. *Annual Message of the President of the United States to the Two Houses of Congress at the Commencement of the Second Session of the Forty-Fifth Congress.* Washington: G.P.O., 1877. Print.

[415] Wise, Tim J. *Colorblind.* 74. Print.

[416] Bradsher, Greg. "How the West Was Settled: The 150-Year-Old Homestead Act Lured Americans Looking for a New Life and New Opportunities." *Prologue Magazine.* Winter 2012: 26-35. *National Archives.* Web. 17 Aug. 2013.

[417] Jensen, Laura. *Patriots, Settlers, and the Origins of American Social Policy.* Cambridge, UK: Cambridge University Press, 2003. 231. Print.

[418] Ibid.

[419] Ridge, Martin. *Westward Expansion: A History of the American Frontier.* By Ray A. Billington. Albuquerque: University of New Mexico Press, 2001. 349. Print.

[420] Campbell, James M., and Rebecca J. Fraser. *Reconstruction: People and Perspectives.* Santa Barbara, CA: ABC-CLIO, 2008. 238. Print.

[421] Ibid.

[422] Katznelson, Ira. *When Affirmative Action Was White: An Untold History of Racial Inequality in Twentieth-Century America.* New York: W.W. Norton, 2005. Print.

[423] Ibid.

[424] Harrison, Charles H. *Tending the Garden State: Preserving New Jersey's Farming Legacy.* New Brunswick, NJ: Rivergate, 2007. 49-50. Print.

[425] Ibid.

[426] Ibid.

⁴²⁷ Kennedy, David M., Lizabeth Cohen, and Thomas Andrew Bailey. *The American Pageant: A History of the American People*. Boston: Wadsworth Cengage Learning, 2010. 911. Print.

⁴²⁸ Massey, Douglas S. *Categorically Unequal: The American Stratification System*. New York: Russell Sage Foundation, 2007. 63. Print.

⁴²⁹ Freeman, Joshua Benjamin. *American Empire: The Rise of a Global Power, the Democratic Revolution at Home, 1945-2000*. New York: Viking, 2012. 1933. Print.

⁴³⁰ Jones, Trina. *Law and Class in America: Trends Since the Cold War*. By Paul D. Carrington. New York: New York University Press, 2006. 343. Print.

⁴³¹ Loss, Christopher P. *Between Citizens and the State: The Politics of American Higher Education in the Twentieth Century*. Princeton: Princeton University Press, 2012. 116. Print.

⁴³² Edwards, Rebecca, James A. Henretta, and Robert O. Self. *America's History*. Vol. 2. London: Macmillan, 2011. 855. Print.

⁴³³ Mettler, Suzanne. *Soldiers to Citizens: The G.I. Bill and the Making of the Greatest Generation*. Oxford: Oxford University Press, 2005. 102. Print.

⁴³⁴ Ibid.

⁴³⁵ Massey, Douglas S. *Categorically Unequal: The American Stratification System*. New York: Russell Sage Foundation, 2007. 63. Print.

⁴³⁶ Gibson, Truman K., and Steve Huntley. *Knocking down Barriers: My Fight for Black America*. Evanston, IL: Northwestern University Press, 2005. 10. Print.

⁴³⁷ Roth, Dena. "It's Not Diversity, Stupid: The Case for Affirmative Action." *The Columbia Current*. Web. 18 Aug. 2013.

⁴³⁸ Ibid.

⁴³⁹ Ibid.

⁴⁴⁰ Ibid.

⁴⁴¹ Ibid.

⁴⁴² Ibid.

⁴⁴³ Katznelson, Ira. *When Affirmative Action Was White*. 2006. Print.

⁴⁴⁴ Ibid.

⁴⁴⁵ Ibid.

[446] Ibid.

[447] Ibid.

[448] Ibid.

[449] Ibid.

[450] Mettler, Suzanne. *Soldiers to Citizens: The G.I. Bill and the Making of the Greatest Generation.* Oxford: Oxford University Press, 2005. 80. Print.

[451] Nadasen, Premilla, Jennifer Mittelstadt, and Marisa Chappell. *Welfare in the United States: A History with Documents, 1935-1996.* New York: Routledge, 2013. Print.

[452] Lin, Ann Chih., and David R. Harris. *The Colors of Poverty: Why Racial and Ethnic Disparities Exist.* New York: Russell Sage Foundation, 2008. 55. Print.

[453] Gillespie, Andra. *The New Black Politician: Cory Booker, Newark, and Post-Racial America.* New York: New York University Press, 2012. 25. Print.

[454] Salinas, Moises F. *The Politics of Stereotype: Psychology and Affirmative Action.* Westport, CT: Praeger, 2003. 72. Print.

[455] Smelser, Neil J., William J. Wilson, and Faith Mitchell. *America Becoming: Racial Trends and Their Consequences.* Washington, D.C.: National Academy, 2001. 161. Print.

[456] Wilensky, Harold L. *Rich Democracies: Political Economy, Public Policy, and Performance.* Berkeley: University of California, 2002. 302. Print.

[457] Weiner, Rachel. "The Fight over Food Stamps Explained." *Washington Post.* 11 July 2013. Web. 18 Aug. 2013.

[458] Ibid.

[459] Ibid.

[460] "Grutter v. Bollinger." *Grutter v. Bolling.* n.p., 01 Apr. 2003. Web. 18 Aug. 2013.

[461] Ibid.

[462] Ibid.

[463] Jacobsohn, Gary J. *American Constitutional Law: Essays, Cases, and Comparative Notes.* By Donald P. Kommers and John E. Finn. Belmont, CA: Rowman & Littlefield, 2010. 669. Print.

[464] Lee, Francis Graham. *Equal Protection: Rights and Liberties under the Law.* Santa Barbara: ABC-CLIO, 2003. 319. Print.

[465] Harris, Richard A., and Daniel J. Tichenor. *A History of the US Political System*. 406. Print.

[466] Williams, Dr. Walter E. "Affirmative Action or Racism." *Affirmative Action or Racism*. n.p., 21 Jan. 2003. Web. 18 Aug. 2013.

[467] Ogletree, Charles J. *All Deliberate Speed: Reflections on the First Half-Century of Brown v. Board of Education*. New York: W.W. Norton, 2004. 244. Print.

[468] Wherry, Frederick F., and Juliet Schor. *The SAGE Encyclopedia of Economics and Society*. Los Angeles: SAGE Reference, 2015. 60. Print.

[469] Wise, Tim J. *White like Me: Reflections on Race from a Privileged Son: The Remix*. Berkeley, CA: Soft Skull, 2011. Print.

[470] Ibid.

[471] Harris, Richard A., and Daniel J. Tichenor. *A History of the US Political System*. Santa Barbara, CA: ABC-CLIO, 2010. 406. Print.

[472] Paige, Rod, and Elaine P. Witty. *The Black-White Achievement Gap: Why Closing It Is the Greatest Civil Rights Issue of Our Time*. New York, NY: AMACOM, American Management Association, 2010. 24-27. Print.

[473] Ibid., 70-113.

[474] *Corridor of Shame: The Neglect of South Carolina's Rural Schools*. Dir. Charles "Bud" T. Ferillo. Ferillo & Associates, Inc., 2005. DVD.

[475] Ibid.

[476] Ibid.

[477] Wise, Tim J. *White like Me*. Print.

[478] Ibid.

[479] Ibid.

[480] Ibid.

[481] Ibid.

[482] Ibid.

[483] Ibid.

[484] Sullivan, Laura, Tatjana Meschede, Lars Dietrich, Thomas Shapiro, Amy Traub, Catherine Ruetschlin, and Tamara Draut. *The Racial Wealth Gap: Why Policy Matters*. Rep. New York: Demos/IASP, 2015. Print.

[485] Grant-Thomas, Andrew, and Gary Orfield. *Twenty-First Century Color Lines: Multiracial Change in Contemporary America*. Philadelphia: Temple University Press, 2009. 4. Print.

Chapter 5 Endnotes

[486] *Corridor of Shame*. DVD.[487] Ibid.

[487] Ibid.

[488] Rosen, James. "Obama and Congress Collide on School Improvement Funds." *McClatchy DC*. n.p., 12 Feb. 2009. Web. 18 Aug. 2013.

[489] Ibbitson, John. "Obama Risks Votes by Proving He's Black Enough." *The Globe and Mail*. n.p., 26 Jan. 2008. Web. 18 Aug. 2013.

[490] "Teachers Miss out on $144 Million in Federal Funds - Wistv.com - Columbia, South Carolina I." *WIS-TV*. 15 Aug. 2011. Web. 19 Aug. 2013.

[491] Plumb, Terry. "Commentary: S.C. Congressmen Sure Showed Uncle Sam." *McClatchy Washington Bureau*. n.p., 26 Aug. 2011. Web. 18 Aug. 2013.

[492] Ibid.

[493] Sanderson, Jamie. "South Carolina's Mick Zais Intends to Keep Educational Opportunity Low." *Daily Kos*. n.p., 9 Sept. 2012. Web. 18 Aug. 2013.

[494] Plumb, Terry. "Commentary: S.C. Congressmen Sure Showed Uncle Sam."

[495] "Education Woes Concern Voters." *The State* [Columbia, SC] 6 Oct. 2002: D1. Print. 19 Aug. 2013.

[496] Adcox, Seanna. "Study Ranks SC 49th in School Dropouts." *Post and Courier* [Charleston] 17 Sept. 2003: 8. Print.

[497] Ladner, Matthew, Andrew T. LeFevre, and Dan Lips. *Report Card on American Education*. Rep. 16th ed. Washington: American Legislative Exchange Council, 2010. Print.

[498] "Teachers Miss out on $144 Million in Federal Funds." *WIS-TV*.

[499] Ladner, Matthew. *Report Card on American Education: State Education Rankings*. Rep. Washington, DC: American Legislative Exchange Council, 2015. Print.

[500] http://www.linkedin.com/pub/bud-ferillo/a/393/b98

[501] *Let's Talk with Bud Ferillo*. The State, 22 Sept. 2012. Web. 19 Aug. 2013.

[502] Ferillo, Charles "Bud." E-mail interview. 19 Jan. 2012.

[503] Ibid.

504 Ibid.

505 Rosen, James. "Finally, Obama Sends Funds to Replace Run-down School." *McClatchy Washington Bureau*. McClatchy, 26 Jan. 2010. Web. 19 Aug. 2013.

506 Ibid.

507 Ferillo, Charles "Bud." E-mail interview. 19 Jan. 2012.

508 Ibid.

509 Ibid.

510 Ibid.

511 Self, Jamie. "SC Supreme Court Sets February Deadline in School-Equity Lawsuit." *The Buzz*. The State Newspaper, 24 Sept. 2015. Web. 10 Feb. 2016.

512 Scaturro, Frank J. *The Supreme Court's Retreat from Reconstruction: A Distortion of Constitutional Jurisprudence*. Westport, CT: Greenwood, 2000. 15. Print.

513 Goldstone, Lawrence. *Inherently Unequal: The Betrayal of Equal Rights by the Supreme Court, 1865-1903*. New York: Walker, 2011. 129. Print.

514 Curry, James A., Richard B. Riley, and Richard M. Battistoni. *Constitutional Government: The American Experience*. Dubuque, IA: Kendall/Hunt Pub., 2009. 261. Print.

515 Graham, Barbara L. *The Supreme Court, Race, and Civil Rights: From Marshall to Rehnquist*. By Abraham L. Davis. Thousand Oaks: SAGE, 1995. 278. Print.

516 Tatum, Beverly Daniel. *Can We Talk about Race?: And Other Conversations in an Era of School Resegregation*. Boston, MA: Beacon, 2007. 10. Print.

517 Ibid.

518 Ibid.

519 Ibid.

520 "Parents Involved in Community Schools v. Seattle School Dist. No. 1." *Parents Involved in Community Schools v. Seattle School Dist. No. 1*. Cornell Law Review. 04 Dec. 2006. Web. 19 Aug. 2013.

521 Bean, Jonathan J. *Race and Liberty in America: The Essential Reader*. Lexington: University of Kentucky Press, Published in Association with the Independent Institute, 2009. 298. Print.

22 Wrightsman, Lawrence S., and Solomon M. Fulero. *Forensic Psychology*. Boston: Wadsworth Cengage Learning, 2008. 322. Print.

523 K'Meyer, Tracy Elaine. *From Brown to Meredith: The Long Struggle for School Desegregation in Louisville, Kentucky, 1954-2007*. Chapel Hill: University of North Carolina Press, 2013. 120. Print.

524 Lomotey, Kofi. *Encyclopedia of African American Education*. Los Angeles: SAGE, 2010. 502. Print.

525 Farley, Ollie Mae. *The Life He Chose, Biography of Pastor Tom Weeks, Jr.* n.p.: Xlibris, 2011. 230. Print.

526 Winders, Jamie. *Nashville in the New Millennium: Immigrant Settlement, Urban Transformation, and Social Belonging*. 82. Print.

527 *The Georgetown Journal of Gender and the Law* 8 (2007): 399. Print.

528 Hudson, David L. *The Handy Supreme Court Answer Book*. Canton, MI: Visible Ink, 2008. 333. Print.

529 Eaton, Susan E. *The Children in Room E4: American Education on Trial*. Chapel Hill, NC: Algonquin of Chapel Hill, 2007. 87. Print.

530 Gaillard, Frye. *The Dream Long Deferred: The Landmark Struggle for Desegregation in Charlotte, North Carolina*. Columbia, SC: University of South Carolina, 2006. 157. Print.

531 Ibid.

532 Ibid., 158.

533 Ibid.

534 Ibid., 160.

535 Ibid.

536 Ibid., 169.

537 Ibid., 178.

538 Richwine, Jason. "The Myth of Racial Disparities in Public School Funding." *Heritage Foundation*. Heritage Foundation, Apr. 2011. Web. 19 Aug. 2013.

539 Phillips, Meredith. *The Black-white Test Score Gap*. By Christopher Jencks. Washington: Brookings Institution, 1988. 465. Print.

540 Frierson, Henry T., James H. Wyche, and Willie Pearson. *Black American Males in Higher Education: Research, Programs and Academe*. Bingley: Emerald, 2009. 274-75. Print.

541 Shepard, Jon M. *Cengage Advantage, Sociology*. 11th ed. Belmont, CA: Wadsworth, Cengage Learning, 2011. 353. Print.

Endnotes

[542] Planty, Michael, William J. Hussar, and Thomas D. Snyder. *The Condition of Education 2009*. Washington D.C.: National Center for Education Statistics, Institute for Education Sciences, U.S. Dept. of Education, 2009. 52. Print.

[543] "Family Income Differences Explain Only a Small Part of the SAT Racial Scoring Gap." *JBHE: Weekly Bulletin*. Journal of Blacks in Higher Education, 12 Jan. 2009. Web. 10 Feb. 2016.

[544] Kaplan, Leslie S., and William A. Owings. *American Education: Building a Common Foundation*. Belmont, CA: Wadsworth, 2009. 360. Print.

[545] Schwartzman, David. *Black Unemployment: Part of Unskilled Unemployment*. Westport, Conn.: Greenwood, 1997. 163. Print.

[546] Ford, Donna Y. *Reversing Underachievement among Gifted Black Students: Promising Practices and Programs*. New York: Teachers College, 1996. 207. Print.

[547] Arrighi, Barbara A., and David J. Maume. *Child Poverty in America Today*. Vol. 4. Westport, CT: Praeger, 2007. 140. Print.

[548] Lin, Ann Chih., and David R. Harris. *The Colors of Poverty: Why Racial and Ethnic Disparities Exist*. New York: Russell Sage Foundation, 2008. 33. Print.

[549] Paige, Rod, and Elaine P. Witty. *The Black-White Achievement Gap: Why Closing It Is the Greatest Civil Rights Issue of Our Time*. New York, NY: AMACOM, American Management Association, 2010. Print.

[550] Ibid., 29.

[551] Gadsden, Vivian L., James Earl Davis, and Alfredo J. Artiles. *Risk, Schooling, and Equity*. Thousand Oaks: SAGE, 2009. 6. Print.

[552] Paige, Rod, and Elaine P. Witty. *The Black-white Achievement Gap: Why Closing It Is the Greatest Civil Rights Issue of Our Time*. New York, NY: AMACOM, American Management Association, 2010. 31. Print.

[553] Ibid., 41.

[554] Ibid.

[555] Ibid.

[556] Ibid.

[557] Ibid., 60.

[558] Ibid., 63.

[559] Ibid., 64.

[560] Ibid., 66.

[561] Ibid., 71.

[562] Ibid., 64.

[563] Ibid., 63.

[564] Ibid., 64.

[565] Ibid., 66.

[566] "Family Income Differences Explain Only a Small Part of the SAT Racial Scoring Gap." *JBHE: Weekly Bulletin*. Journal of Blacks in Higher Education, 12 Jan. 2016. Web. 10 Feb. 2016.

[567] Holmes, Jack. "White Kids Get Medicated When They Misbehave, Black Kids Get Suspended — or Arrested." *Science of Us*. New York Magazine, 6 Aug. 2015. Web.

[568] Ramey, David M. "The Social Structure of Criminalized and Medicalized School Discipline." *Sociology of Education* XX.X (2015): 1-21. *SAGE*. Web. 10 Feb. 2016.

[569] Khaing, Zaw, Darrick Hamilton, and William Darity. "Gender, Race Influences When Teens Start Drinking, Smoking and Doing Drugs." *Race and Social Problems* 8.1 (2016): 103-15. Web.

[570] Sanders, Nancy I. *America's Black Founders: Revolutionary Heroes and Early Leaders: With 21 Activities*. Chicago, IL: Chicago Review, 2010. 8. Print.

[571] Ibid.

[572] Lincoln, Abraham. *Lincoln: Political Writings and Speeches*. Cambridge [England]: Cambridge UP, 2012. 71. Print.

[573] Rodriguez, Junius P. *Slavery in the United States: A Social, Political, and Historical Encyclopedia*. Vol. 2. Santa Barbara, CA: ABC-CLIO, 2007. 172. Print.

[574] Rodriguez, Junius P. *Encyclopedia of Slave Resistance and Rebellion*. Westport, CT: Greenwood, 2007. 105. Print.

[575] Rodriguez, Junius P. *Slavery in the United States: A Social, Political, and Historical Encyclopedia*. Vol. 2. Santa Barbara, CA: ABC-CLIO, 2007. 616. Print.

[576] Reevy, Gretchen, Yvette Malamud. Ozer, and Yuri Ito. *Encyclopedia of Emotion*. Santa Barbara, CA: Greenwood, 2010. 440. Print.

[577] Ibid.

Endnotes

[578] Ibid.

[579] Lynn, Richard. *Race Differences in Intelligence: An Evolutionary Analysis.* N.p.: Washington Summit, 2006. Print.

[580] Murray, Charles. "Affirmative Action in the Workplace." *Bell Curve: Intelligence and Class Structure in American Life.* By Richard J. Herrnstein. New York: Simon and Schuster, 2010. N. pag. Print.

[581] Valencia, Richard R. *Dismantling Contemporary Deficit Thinking: Educational Thought and Practice.* New York: Routledge, 2010. 51. Print.

[582] Glauberman, Naomi and Russell Jacoby. *The Bell Curve Debate: History, Documents, Opinions.* New York: Random House Incorporated, 1995. 372. Print.

[583] Herrnstein, Richard J., and Charles A. Murray. *The Bell Curve: Intelligence and Class Structure in American Life.* New York: Free, 1994. 666. Print.

[584] Bohm, Robert M., and Brenda L. Vogel. *A Primer on Crime and Delinquency Theory.* Australia: Wadsworth, 2010. 53. Print.

[585] Shermer, Michael. *Why People Believe Weird Things: Pseudoscience, Superstition, and Other Confusions of Our Time.* New York: W.H. Freeman, 1997. 242. Print.

[586] Nelkin, Dorothy, and M. Susan. Lindee. *The DNA Mystique: The Gene as a Cultural Icon.* New York: Freeman, 1995. 113. Print.

[587] Tucker, William H. *The Funding of Scientific Racism: Wickliffe Draper and the Pioneer Fund.* Urbana: University of Illinois, 2002. 198. Print.

[588] Ibid.

[589] Ibid.

[590] Wahlsten, D. (1995) *Review of "Race, Evolution and Behavior"* by J. P. Rushton. Canadian Journal of Sociology, 20, 129-133.

[591] Ibid.

[592] Barash, D.P (1995) "Book review: Race, Evolution, and Behavior" by J.P. Rushton. *Animal Behaviour* 49: 1131–1133.

[593] Jackson, John P., and Nadine M. Weidman. *Race, Racism, and Science: Social Impact and Interaction.* Santa Barbara, CA: ABC-CLIO, 2004. 229. Print.

[594] Montagu, Ashley. *Race and IQ.* New York: Oxford UP, 1975. 398. Print.

[595] Walker, Samuel, Cassia Spohn, and Miriam DeLone. *The Color of Justice: Race, Ethnicity, and Crime in America*. Belmont: Wadsworth Pub., 1996. 11-12. Print.

[596] Shilgba, Leonard K. *From My Heart the Black Race: Myths, Realities, and Complexes*. N.p.: Strategic Book, 2011. 249. Print.

[597] Tucker, William H. *The Funding of Scientific Racism: Wickliffe Draper and the Pioneer Fund*. Urbana: University of Illinois, 2002. 5. Print.

[598] Chomsky, Aviva. *Linked Labor Histories: New England, Colombia, and the Making of a Global Working Class*. Durham: Duke UP, 2008. 21. Print.

[599] Garcia, Matt. *A World of Its Own: Race, Labor, and Citrus in the Making of Greater Los Angeles, 1900-1970*. Chapel Hill, NC: U of North Carolina, 2001. 91. Print.

[600] "Harry H. Laughlin, Superintendent of Eugenics Record Office, Cold Spring Harbor; President, American Eugenics Society 1928-29 :: DNA Learning Center." *DNALC Blogs*. Web. 20 Aug. 2013.

[601] Streissguth, Thomas. *Hate Crimes*. New York: Facts on File, 2003. 173. Print.

Chapter 6 Endnotes

[602] US Census Bureau. Average Earnings of Full-Time, Year-Round Workers by Educational Attainment in 2006, Constant Dollars. 2009. Raw data.

[603] Ibid.

[604] Ibid.

[605] Ibid.

[606] Bruenig, Matt. "The Top 10% of White Families Own Almost Everything." Web log post. *PolicyShop*. Demos, 5 Sept. 2014. Web. 11 Feb. 2016.

[607] Rushe, Dominic. "Revealed: Huge Increase in Executive Pay for America's Top Bosses." *The Guardian*. N.p., 14 Dec. 2011. Web. 20 Aug. 2013.

[608] Oliver, Melvin. "Sub-Prime as a Black Catastrophe." *The American Prospect*. N.p., 20 Sept. 2008. Web. 20 Aug. 2013.

[609] "The Employment Situation–December 2015." Bureau of Labor Statistics. 1 Jan. 2016.

[610] *Black Employment and Unemployment in December 2011*. Rep. Berkeley, CA: UC Berkeley Center for Labor Research and Education, 2012. Print.

[611] Censky, Annalyn. "Black Unemployment Rate: Highest since 1984." *CNNMoney*. Cable News Network, 02 Sept. 2011. Web. 20 Aug. 2013.

[612] Ibid.

[613] Mizrahi, Terry, and Larry E. Davis. *The Encyclopedia of Social Work.* Washington, DC: NASW, 2008. 81. Print.

[614] Ibid.

[615] "Wealth Gap Grows between Black and White Americans." *BBC News.* BBC, 18 May 2010. Web. 20 Aug. 2013.

[616] McEachern, William A. *Economics: A Contemporary Introduction.* Cincinnati: South-Western Pub., 1991. 409. Print.

[617] Galbraith, James K. *Created Unequal: The Crisis in American Pay.* New York: Free, 1998. 57. Print.

[618] Schmitt, John. *The Minimum Wage Is Too Damn Low.* Issue brief. Washington, D.C.: Center for Economic Policy and Research, March 2012. Print.

[619] Harrison, Bennett, and Barry Bluestone. *The Great U-turn: Corporate Restructuring and the Polarizing of America.* New York: Basic, 1988. 112-13. Print.

[620] Galbraith, James K. *Created Unequal: The Crisis in American Pay.* New York: Free, 1998. 56-7. Print.

[621] Goldfarg, Zachary A., Tom Hamburger, and Carol D. Leonnig. "Obama's Record on Outsourcing Draws Criticism from the Left." *Washington Post.* 09 July 2012. Web. 21 Aug. 2013.

[622] Lusane, Clarence. "Persisting Disparities: Globalization and the Economic Status of African Americans." *Howard Law Journal* (1999): 431-50. Web. 21 Aug. 2013. <http://academic.udayton.edu/race/04needs/economic06.htm>.

[623] Anderson, Carol. *Eyes off the Prize: The United Nations and the African American Struggle for Human Rights, 1944-1955.* Cambridge, UK: Cambridge UP, 2003. 272. Print.

[624] D'Souza, Dinesh. *The Virtue Of Prosperity: Finding Values In An Age Of Technoaffluence.* New York: Simon and Schuster, 2002. 12. Print.

[625] Noah, Timothy. "The United States of Inequality, Entry 1." *Slate Magazine.* Washington Post Company, 3 Sept. 2010. Web. 21 Aug. 2013.

[626] Ibid.

[627] Weisman, Steven R. *The Great Tax Wars: Lincoln - Teddy Roosevelt - Wilson : How the Income Tax Transformed America.* New York: Simon & Schuster, 2004. 200-02. Print.

628 Noah, Timothy. "The United States of Inequality, Entry 1." *Slate Magazine.* Washington Post Company, 3 Sept. 2010. Web. 21 Aug. 2013.

629 Ibid.

630 *Gross Domestic Product, 1 Decimal (GDP).* Rep. Washington, DC: US Department of Commerce: Bureau of Economic Analysis, 2012. Print.

631 *United States: Gross Domestic Product, Current Prices (U.S. Dollars).* Rep. Washington, DC: International Monetary Fund, 2015. Print.

632 *Gross Domestic Product in Current and Chained (2005) Dollars: 1970 to 2010.* Rep. Washington: US Census Bureau, 2012. Print.

633 Judd, Dennis R., and Todd Swanstrom. "The Urban Crisis of the Twentieth Century." *City Politics.* 9th ed. London: Routledge, 2015. 166. Print.

634 DeParle, Jason. "Harder for Americans to Rise From Lower Rungs." *New York Times.* Washington Post Company, 4 Jan. 2012. Web. 21 Aug. 2012.

635 Noah, Timothy. "The United States of Inequality, Entry 1." *Slate Magazine.* Washington Post Company, 3 Sept. 2010. Web. 21 Aug. 2013.

636 Ibid.

637 Wise, Tim. "Getting What We Deserve? Wealth, Race and Entitlement in America." Weblog post. 26 Sept. 2011. Web. 22 Aug. 2013. <http://www.timwise.org/2011/09/getting-what-we-deserve-wealth-race-and-entitlement-in-america/>.

638 Ibid.

639 Hinks, Peter P., John R. McKivigan, and R. Owen. Williams. *Encyclopedia of Antislavery and Abolition.* Westport, CT: Greenwood, 2007. 253. Print.

640 Ibid.

641 Ibid.

642 Havelin, Kate. *Andrew Johnson.* Minneapolis: Lerner Publications, 2005. 68. Print.

643 Suri, Jeremi. *Liberty's Surest Guardian: American Nation-building from the Founders to Obama.* New York: Free, 2011. 73. Print.

644 Clark, Clifford E., Jr., Joseph F. Kett, Neal Salisbury, Nancy Woloch, and Harvard Stikoff. *The Enduring Vision: A History of the American People, Volume I.* Stamford, CT: Cengage Learning, 2010. 498. Print.

645 Wilson, Carter A. *Racism: From Slavery to Advanced Capitalism.* Thousand Oaks, CA: Sage Publications, 1996. 144. Print.

Endnotes

[646] Pendall, Rolf, Lesley Freiman, Dowell Myers, and Selma Hepp. *Demographic Challenges and Opportunities for U.S. Housing Markets.* Rep. Washington, D.C.: Bipartisan Policy Center, 2012. Print.

[647] Schwartz, Alex F. *Housing Policy in the United States.* New York: Routledge, 2010. 52. Print.

[648] Ibid., 53.

[649] Oliver, Melvin L., and Thomas M. Shapiro. *Black Wealth/White Wealth: A New Perspective on Racial Inequality.* New York: Routledge, 1995. 17. Print.

[650] Schwartz, Alex F. *Housing Policy in the United States.* New York: Routledge, 2010. 53. Print.

[651] Grant, Gerald. *Hope and Despair in the American City: Why There Are No Bad Schools in Raleigh.* Cambridge, MA: Harvard UP, 2009. 17. Print.

[652] Ibid., 15-16.

[653] Oliver, Melvin L., and Thomas M. Shapiro. *Black Wealth/white Wealth: A New Perspective on Racial Inequality.* New York: Routledge, 1995. 17. Print.

[654] Midgley, James, Martin Tracy, and Michelle Livermore. *The Handbook of Social Policy.* Thousand Oaks: Sage Publications, 2000. 242. Print.

[655] Polikoff, Alexander. *Waiting for Gautreaux: A Story of Segregation, Housing, and the Black Ghetto.* Evanston, IL: Northwestern UP, 2005. 113. Print.

[656] Midgley, James, Martin Tracy, and Michelle Livermore. *The Handbook of Social Policy.* Thousand Oaks: Sage Publications, 2000. 242. Print.

[657] Murray, Pauli. *States' Laws on Race and Color.* Athens: University of Georgia, 1997. 11. Print.

[658] Wallenfeldt, Jeffrey H. *The Black Experience in America: From Civil Rights to the Present.* New York, NY: Britannica Educational Pub., in Association with Rosen Educational Services, 2011. 57. Print.

[659] Hansberry, Lorraine. *A Raisin in the Sun: A Drama in Three Acts.* New York: Random House, 1959. Print.

[660] Corley, Cheryl. *Morning Edition.* National Public Radio. Washington, DC, 11 Mar. 2002. Radio.

[661] "HOUSING: Ghetto Shakedown." *Time* 10 Apr. 1972: n. pag. Web. 22 Aug. 2013.

[662] Turner, Robert L. "Joe Kennedy: The Happy Warrior." *Boston Globe* [Boston] 2 June 1989: A45. Print.

[663] Ibid.

[664] Frank, Peter H. "Blacks Far Less Likely to Get Mortgages, Fed Reports." *The Baltimore Sun* 22 Oct. 1991. Print.

[665] Oliver, Melvin L., and Thomas M. Shapiro. *Black Wealth/White Wealth: A New Perspective on Racial Inequality.* New York: Routledge, 1995. 17. Print.

[666] Savage, Charlie. "Countrywide Will Settle a Bias Suit." *New York Times.* N.p., 21 Dec. 2011. Web. 22 Aug. 2013.

[667] "DOJ/Countrywide Settlement Information." *USDOJ: US Attorney's Office.* Web. 22 Aug. 2013. <http://www.justice.gov/usao/cac/countrywide.html>.

[668] Johnson, Ivory J. "Bank of America Discrimination Settlement: A Result of Subprime Swindle." *The Grio.* 22 Dec. 2011. Web. 22 Aug. 2013. <http://thegrio.com/2011/12/22/bank-of-america-discrimination-settlement-a-result-of-subprime-swindle/>.

[669] Lee, Mara. *Subprime Mortgages: A Primer.* National Public Radio. Washington, DC, 23 Mar. 2007. Radio.

[670] Bocian, Debbie G., Wei Li, Carolina Reid, and Roberto G. Quercia. *Lost Ground, 2011: Disparities in Mortgage Lending and Foreclosures.* Rep. Washington, DC: Center for Responsible Lending, Nov. 2011. Print.

[671] Beckert, Jens, and Patrik Aspers. *The worth of Goods: Valuation and Pricing in the Economy.* New York: Oxford UP, 2011. 237. Print.

[672] Johnson, Ivory J. "Bank of America Discrimination Settlement: A Result of Subprime Swindle." *The Grio.* 22 Dec. 2011. Web. 22 Aug. 2013. <http://thegrio.com/2011/12/22/bank-of-america-discrimination-settlement-a-result-of-subprime-swindle/>.

[673] Savage, Charlie. "Countrywide Will Settle a Bias Suit." *New York Times.* 21 Dec. 2011. Web. 22 Aug. 2013.

[674] Henry, David. "Justice Department Presses Wells Fargo on Loans: Source." *Reuters.* 27 July 2011. Web. 22 Aug. 2013.

[675] Savage, Charlie. "Wells Fargo Will Settle Mortgage Bias Charges." *New York Times.* N.p., 12 July 2012. Web. 22 Aug. 2013.

[676] Simon, Ruth, and Victoria McGrane. "Wells Draws $85 Million Penalty in Subprime Case." *Wall Street Journal.* 21 July 2010. Web. 22 Aug. 2013.

[677] "Judge Rules Landmark Lawsuit, First to Link Bundling of Mortgage-Backed Securities and Racial Discrimination, Can Proceed." *American Civil Liberties Union.* N.p., 25 July 2013. Web. 22 Aug. 2013.

[678] "SunTrust Bank, U.S. Reach Settlement in Discrimination Case." *Chicago Tribune.* N.p., 31 May 2012. Web. 22 Aug. 2013.

⁶⁷⁹ Spangler, Todd. "Michigan Bank Accused of Racial Discrimination Reaches Settlement with Justice Dept." *Detroit Free Press*. 15 Jan. 2013. Web. 22 Aug. 2013.

⁶⁸⁰ *A Report on U.S. Compliance with the International Covenant on Civil and Political Rights*. New York, NY: Human Rights Watch, 1993. 18. Print.

⁶⁸¹ Chen, Liyan, and Andrea Murphy. "Global 2000." *Forbes*. 6 May 2015. Web. 11 Feb. 2016.

⁶⁸² Forbes Staff. "Forbes Announces Inaugural List Of America's 50 Richest Self-Made Women." *Forbes*. Forbes Corporate Communications, 27 May 2015. Web. 11 Feb. 2016.

⁶⁸³ Lule, Jack. *Globalization and Media: Global Village of Babel*. Lanham, MD: Rowman & Littlefield, 2012. 3. Print.

⁶⁸⁴ "Luxury Store Apologizes to Oprah." *CNN*. Cable News Network, 22 June 2005. Web. 22 Aug. 2013. <http://www.cnn.com/2005/SHOWBIZ/TV/06/22/oprah.apology/>.

⁶⁸⁵ "The World's Billionaires." *Forbes*. Forbes Magazine, 11 Feb. 2016. Web. 11 Feb. 2016.

⁶⁸⁶ Wilson, Amos N. *Blueprint for Black Power: A Moral, Political, and Economic Imperative for the Twenty-first Century*. New York: Afrikan World InfoSystems, 1998. 5. Print.

⁶⁸⁷ Oliver, Melvin L., and Thomas M. Shapiro. *Black Wealth/White Wealth: A New Perspective on Racial Inequality*. New York: Routledge, 1995. 29. Print.

⁶⁸⁸ Ibid.

⁶⁸⁹ Ibid.

Chapter 7 Endnotes

⁶⁹⁰ Wilson, William J. *The Declining Significance of Race: Blacks and Changing American Institutions*. Chicago: University of Chicago, 1978. Print.

⁶⁹¹ Sandlin, Jennifer A., Brian D. Schultz, and Jake Burdick. *Handbook of Public Pedagogy: Education and Learning beyond Schooling*. New York: Routledge, 2010. 595. Print.

⁶⁹² Ibid.

⁶⁹³ Battistella, Edwin L. *Bad Language: Are Some Words Better than Others?* Oxford: Oxford UP, 2005. 145. Print.

⁶⁹⁴ Lewis, Neil A. "Black English Is Not a Second Language, Jackson Says." *The New York Times*. The New York Times, 23 Dec. 1996. Web. 22 Aug. 2013.

[695] Tanner, Dennis C. *Medical-legal and Forensic Aspects of Communication Disorders, Voice Prints, and Speaker Profiling*. Tucson, AZ: Lawyers & Judges Pub., 2007. 231. Print.

[696] Curran, Andrew S. *The Anatomy of Blackness: Science & Slavery in an Age of Enlightenment*. Baltimore: Johns Hopkins UP, 2011. 130. Print.

[697] Crooks, Robert, and Karla Baur. *Our Sexuality*. Redwood City, CA: Benjamin Cummings Pub., 1990. 14. Print.

[698] Gilens, Martin. *Why Americans Hate Welfare: Race, Media, and the Politics of Antipoverty Policy*. Chicago: University of Chicago, 1999. 155. Print.

[699] Dillard, Joey L. *Black English; Its History and Usage in the United States*. New York: Vintage, 1973. 74-77. Print.

[700] Au, Wayne. *Rethinking Multicultural Education: Teaching for Racial and Cultural Justice*. Milwaukee, WI: Rethinking Schools, 2009. 93. Print.

[701] Williams, Robert L. *Ebonics: The True Language of Black Folks*. St. Louis: Robert L. Williams and Assoc., 1975. Print.

[702] Hall, Lena E. *Dictionary of Multicultural Psychology: Issues, Terms, and Concepts*. Thousand Oaks, CA: Sage, 2005. 58. Print.

[703] Dunaway, Wilma A. *The African-American Family in Slavery and Emancipation*. New York: Maison Des Sciences De L'homme/Cambridge UP, 2003. 158-59. Print.

[704] Paige, Rod, and Elaine P. Witty. *The Black-white Achievement Gap: Why Closing It Is the Greatest Civil Rights Issue of Our Time*. New York, NY: AMACOM, American Management Association, 2010. 83. Print.

[705] Reese, William J. *America's Public Schools: From the Common School to "No Child Left Behind*. Baltimore: Johns Hopkins UP, 2011. 77. Print.

[706] Rich, Wilbur C. *The Post-racial Society Is Here: Recognition, Critics and the Nation-state*. New York, NY: Routledge, 2013. 51-52. Print.

[707] Gates, Henry Louis. *The Oxford Handbook of African American Citizenship, 1865-present*. New York: Oxford UP, 2012. 294. Print.

[708] McArthur, Tom. *The English Languages*. Cambridge, United Kingdom: Cambridge UP, 1998. 217. Print.

[709] Taylor, Joyce S., and Lynn Taylor. Clark. *Intervention with Infants and Toddlers: The Law, the Participants, and the Process*. Springfield, IL: Charles C. Thomas, 2004. 138-39. Print.

[710] Harris, Tami Winfrey. "What's So Wrong with Sounding Black?" *Psychology Today*. N.p., 17 Sept. 2010. Web. 23 Aug. 2013.

Endnotes

[711] Alim, H. Samy., and Geneva Smitherman. *Articulate While Black: Barack Obama, Language, and Race in the U.S.* Oxford: Oxford UP, 2012. 24. Print.

[712] Alatis, James E., and Ai-Hui Tan. *Georgetown University Round Table on Languages and Linguistics 1999: Language in Our Time : Bilingual Education and Official English, Ebonics and Standard English, Immigration and the Unz Initiative.* Baltimore, MD: Georgetown UP, 2001. 204. Print.

[713] Hoosain, R., and Farideh Salili. *Language in Multicultural Education.* Greenwich, CT: Information Age Pub., 2005. 103. Print.

[714] Dillard, J. L. *Perspectives on Black English.* The Hague: Mouton, 1975. 246. Print.

[715] Paige, Rod, and Elaine P. Witty. *The Black-white Achievement Gap: Why Closing It Is the Greatest Civil Rights Issue of Our Time.* New York, NY: AMACOM, American Management Association, 2010. 63. Print.

[716] Ibid.

[717] Moynihan, Daniel. *The Negro Family: The Case for National Action, Issues 31-33.* Washington, DC: United States. Dept. of Labor. Office of Policy Planning and Research, 1965. Print.

[718] Rucker, Walter C., and James N. Upton. *Encyclopedia of American Race Riots.* Westport, CT: Greenwood, 2007. 427. Print.

[719] Moynihan, Daniel. *The Negro Family: The Case for National Action, Issues 31-33.* Washington, DC: United States. Dept. of Labor. Office of Policy Planning and Research, 1965. 15. Print.

[720] Ibid., 19.

[721] Ryan, William. *Blaming the Victim.* New York: Pantheon, 1971. 25-26. Print.

[722] Ibid., 26.

[723] Williams, Walter E. *Liberty versus the Tyranny of Socialism: Controversial Essays.* Stanford, CA: Hoover Institution, 2008. 337. Print.

[724] Mac Donald, Heather L. "The Hispanic Family: The Case for National Action." *National Review Online.* 14 Apr. 2008. Web. 23 Aug. 2013.

[725] Meehan, Thomas. "Moynihan of the Moynihan Report." *The New York Times* 31 July 1966. Print.

[726] Ibid.

[727] Sarat, Austin. *New Perspectives on Crime and Criminal Justice: Special Issue.* Bingley: Emerald JAI, 2009. 182. Print.

728 Demers, David. *The Ivory Tower of Babel: Why the Social Sciences Are failing to Live up to Their Promises.* New York: Algora Pub., 2011. 62. Print.

729 Rucker, Walter C., and James N. Upton. *Encyclopedia of American Race Riots.* Westport, CT: Greenwood, 2007. 794. Print.

730 Bouie, Jamelle. "Why Black-on-Black Crime" Is a Dangerous Idea." *The American Prospect.* 17 July 2013. Web. 28 Aug. 2013.

731 Sugrue, Thomas J. *Not Even Past: Barack Obama and the Burden of Race.* Princeton, NJ: Princeton UP, 2010. 107. Print.

732 Gabbidon, Shaun L., and Helen Taylor Greene. *Race, Crime, and Justice: A Reader.* New York: Routledge, 2005. 252-53. Print.

733 Cookson, Jr., Peter, Alan Sadovnik and Susan Semel." Schools and Organizations and Teacher Professionalization. " *Exploring Education.* Boston: Allyn and Bacon, 1994. 243-261. Print.

Chapter 8 Endnotes

734 Marsh, Jason, Rodolfo Mendoza-Denton, and Jeremy Adam Smith." Are We Born Racist." *Are We Born Racist?: New Insights from Neuroscience and Positive Psychology.* Boston: Beacon, 2010. Print.

735 Anderson, Claud. *Black Labor, White Wealth: The Search for Power and Economic Justice.* [Edgewood, MD]: Duncan & Duncan, 1994. 121. Print.

736 Ibid.

737 Parks, Gregory, and Matthew W. Hughey. *The Obamas and a (post) Racial America?* Oxford: Oxford UP, 2011. 61. Print.

738 Gutsell, Jennifer N., and Michael Inzlicht. "Empathy Constrained: Prejudice Predicts Reduced Mental Simulation of Actions during Observation of Outgroups." *Journal of Experimental Social Psychology* 46.5 (2010): 841-45. Print.

739 Moraes, Lisa De. "Kanye West's Torrent of Criticism, Live on NBC." *Washington Post.* N.p., 03 Sept. 2005. Web. 23 Aug. 2013.

740 Johnson, Cedric. *The Neoliberal Deluge: Hurricane Katrina, Late Capitalism, and the Remaking of New Orleans.* Minneapolis: University of Minnesota, 2011. 272-73. Print.

741 Craig-Henderson, Kellina M. *Black Women in Interracial Relationships: In Search of Love and Solace.* New Brunswick, NJ: Transaction, 2011. 34. Print.

742 Wise, Tim J. *Colorblind: The Rise of Post Racial Politics and the Retreat from Racial Equity.* San Francisco, CA: City Lights, 2010. Print.

Endnotes

[743] Halwachs-Baumann, Gabriele. *Congenital Cytomegalovirus Infection: Epidemiology, Diagnosis, Therapy.* New York: Springer, 2011. 57. Print.

[744] Swain, Carol M. *Be the People: A Call to Reclaim America's Faith and Promise.* Nashville: Thomas Nelson, 2011. 63. Print.

[745] Conlin, Joseph R. *The American Past: A Survey of American History, Enhanced Edition.* Boston: Cengage Learning, 2008. 111. Print.

[746] Eblen, Jack E. "New Estimates of the Vital Rates of the United States Black Population during the Nineteenth Century." *Demography* 11.2 (May 1974): 301-19. Print.

[747] Sreenivasan, Jyotsna. *Poverty and the Government in America: A Historical Encyclopedia.* Santa Barbara, CA: ABC-CLIO, 2009. 241. Print.

[748] Byrd, W. Michael., and Linda A. Clayton. *An American Health Dilemma: A Medical History of African Americans and the Problem of Race.* New York: Routledge, 2000. 369. Print.

[749] Amenga-Etego, Rose Mary, and Rosetta E. Ross. *Unraveling and Reweaving Sacred Canon in Africana Womanhood.* New York: Rowman & Littlefield, 2015. 174. Print.

[750] Aggleton, Peter, and Richard G. Parker. *Routledge Handbook of Sexuality, Health and Rights.* London: Routledge, 2010. 16. Print.

[751] Peiss, Kathy Lee., Christina Simmons, and Robert A. Padgug. *Passion and Power: Sexuality in History.* Philadelphia: Temple UP, 1989. 145. Print.

[752] Engelman, Robert. *More: Population, Nature, and What Women Want.* Washington, D.C.: Island, 2008. 193. Print.

[753] Swain, Carol M. *Be the People: A Call to Reclaim America's Faith and Promise.* Nashville: Thomas Nelson, 2011. 67. Print.

[754] Peiss, Kathy Lee., Christina Simmons, and Robert A. Padgug. *Passion and Power: Sexuality in History.* Philadelphia: Temple UP, 1989. 145. Print.

[755] Sanger, Margaret. "Birth Control and Racial Betterment." *Birth Control Review* Feb. 1919: 11-12. Print.

[756] Ibid.

[757] Sanger, Margaret. *Margaret Sanger: An Autobiography.* New York: Dover Publications, 1971. 366-67. Print.

[758] *Opposition Claims About Margaret Sanger.* New York: Planned Parenthood Federation of America, n.d. Print.

[759] Sanger, Margaret. *The Meaning of Radio Birth Control.* WFAB, Syracuse, New York, 29 Feb. 1924. Radio. Transcript.

[760] Laughlin, Harry H. "Eugenical Aspects of Legal Sterilization." *Birth Control Review* Apr. 1933: 87. Print.

[761] Popenoe, Paul. "Eugenic Sterilization." *Birth Control Review* Apr. 1933. Print.

[762] Ellis, Havelock. "Birth Control in Relation to Morality and Eugenics." *Birth Control Review* Feb. 1919: 7-9. Print.

[763] Rüdin, Ernst. "Eugenic Sterilization: An Urgent Need." *Birth Control Review* Apr. 1933: 102-04. Print.

[764] Joseph, Jay. *Missing Gene: Psychiatry, Heredity, and the Fruitless Search for Genes*. New York: Algora, 2006. 148. Print.

[765] Boyle, Gertrude. "Superman Arises." *Birth Control Review* Jan. 1918: 11. Print.

[766] Engs, Ruth Clifford. *The Progressive Era's Health Reform Movement: A Historical Dictionary*. Westport, CT: Praeger, 2003. 296-97. Print.

[767] Franks, Angela. *Margaret Sanger's Eugenic Legacy: The Control of Female Fertility*. Jefferson, NC: McFarland, 2005. 11. Print.

[768] Craven, Erma C. *BlackGenocide.org | Abortion and the Black Community*. LEARN Northeast. Web. 24 Aug. 2013.

[769] Jones, Rachel K., Lawrence B. Finer, and Susheela Singh. *Characteristics of U.S. Abortion Patients, 2008*. Rep. New York: Guttmacher Institute, May 2010. Print.

[770] Vazquez, Carmen Inoa., and Dinelia Rosa. *Grief Therapy with Latinos: Integrating Culture for Clinicians*. New York: Springer Pub., 2011. 145. Print.

[771] *Claim That Most Abortion Clinics Are Located in Black or Hispanic Neighborhoods Is False*. New York: Guttmacher Institute, June 2014. Print.

[772] *Maafa 21*. Dir. Mark Crutcher. Life Dynamics, Inc., 2009. DVD.

[773] Sanger, Margaret. "A Plan for Peace*." *Birth Control Review* Apr. 1932: 107-08. Print.

[774] Ibid.

[775] Ibid.

[776] Kessel, Michelle, and Jessica Hopper. "Victims Speak out about North Carolina Sterilization Program, Which Targeted Women, Young Girls and Blacks." *Rock Center with Brian Williams*. NBC. New York, 7 Nov. 2011. Television.

Endnotes

[777] Rothman, Barbara Katz. *The Book of Life: A Personal and Ethical Guide to Race, Normality, and the Implications of the Human Genome Project.* Boston: Beacon, 2001. 58. Print.

[778] Silliman, Jael Miriam. *Undivided Rights: Women of Color Organize for Reproductive Justice.* Cambridge, MA: South End, 2004. 53-54. Print.

[779] Amenga-Etego, Rose Mary, and Rosetta E. Ross. *Unraveling and Reweaving Sacred Canon in Africana Womanhood.* New York: Rowman & Littlefield, 2015. 174. Print.

[780] Wise, Tim J. "Racism and Health." Boston Public Health Commission, Boston. 11 July 2011. Speech.

[781] Ibid.

[782] Ibid.

[783] "Minority Health: Black or African American Populations." Centers for Disease Control and Prevention. 02 July 2013. Web. 24 Aug. 2013.

[784] Covey, Herbert C., and Dwight Eisnach. *What the Slaves Ate: Recollections of African American Foods and Foodways from the Slave Narratives.* Santa Barbara, CA: Greenwood/ABC-CLIO, 2009. 213. Print.

[785] Banks-Wallace, JoAnne, and Vicki Conn. "Interventions to Promote Physical Activity Among African American Women." *Public Health Nursing* 19.5 (2002): 321-35. Print.

[786] Berning, Jacqueline R., and Suzanne Nelson. Steen. *Nutrition for Sport and Exercise.* Gaithersburg, MD: Aspen, 1998. 1. Print.

[787] Wise, Tim J. *Colorblind: The Rise of Post Racial Politics and the Retreat from Racial Equity.* San Francisco: City Lights, 2010. Print.

[788] Gourdine, Michelle A. *Reclaiming Our Health: A Guide to African American Wellness.* New Haven: Yale UP, 2011. Print.

[789] Watters, Joanne L., and Jessie A. Satia. "Psychosocial Correlates of Dietary Fat Intake in African-American Adults: A Cross-sectional Study." *Nutrition Journal* 8.15 (2009): n. pag. Print.

[790] Byers, KG, and DA Savaiano. "The Myth of Increased Lactose Intolerance in African-Americans." *Journal of the American College of Nutrition* 24.6 (Dec 2005): 569S-73S. Print.

[791] Caballero, Benjamin. *Guide to Nutritional Supplements.* Oxford, UK: Elsevier/Academic, 2009. 497. Print.

[792] Cook, Roberta. *Tracking Demographics and U.S. Fruit and Vegetable Consumption Patterns.* Rep. Davis, CA: Department of Agricultural and Resource Economics, University of California, Davis, Oct. 2011. Print.

[793] Schattner, Ami, and Hilla Knobler. *Metabolic Aspects of Chronic Liver Disease*. New York: Nova Biomedical, 2008. 39-40. Print.

[794] Deen, Darwin, and Lisa Hark. *The Complete Guide to Nutrition in Primary Care*. Malden, MA: Blackwell Pub., 2007. 347. Print.

[795] Ross, Janell. "As Black Unemployment Climbs, Healthy American Eating Declines." *Huffington Post*. 17 July 2011. Web. 24 Aug. 2013.

[796] Winne, Mark. *Closing the Food Gap: Resetting the Table in the Land of Plenty*. Boston: Beacon, 2008. Print.

[797] Bratskeir, Kate. "Fast Food's Immediate Damage To Your Health." *The Huffington Post*. 27 Nov. 2012. Web. 24 Aug. 2013.

[798] Dallas, Mary E. "Minorities Harmed Most By Fast-Food Outlets Near School: Study." HealthDay News, 4 June 2013. Web. 24 Aug. 2013.

[799] "Compared with Whites, Blacks Had 51% Higher and Hispanics Had 21% Higher Obesity Rates." Centers for Disease Control and Prevention, 05 Apr. 2010. Web. 24 Aug. 2013.

[800] Fryar, Cheryl D., MSPH, Margaret D. Carroll, MSPH, and Cynthia L. Ogden. *Prevalence of Obesity Among Children and Adolescents: United States, Trends 1963–1965 Through 2009–2010*. Rep. Washington: Centers for Disease Control, September 2012. Print.

[801] Smith, Andrew F. *Fast Food and Junk Food: An Encyclopedia of What We Love to Eat*. Vol. 2. Santa Barbara, CA: ABC-CLIO, 2011. 680-81. Print.

[802] *Health Status of Minorities & Low Income Groups*. Washington: US Department of Health and Human Services, 1991. 48. Print.

[803] Ver, Ploeg Michele., and Edward Perrin. *Eliminating Health Disparities: Measurement and Data Needs*. Washington, DC: National Academies, 2004. 15. Print.

[804] Yonas, Michael A., Nora Jones, Eugenia Eng, Anissa I. Vines, Robert Aronson, Derek M. Griffith, Brandolyn White, and Melvin DuBose. "The Art and Science of Integrating Undoing Racism with CBPR: Challenges of Pursuing NIH Funding to Investigate Cancer Care and Racial Equity." *Journal of Urban Health* 83.6 (2006): 1004-012. Print.

[805] Troisi, Rebecca, and Kathryn M. Rexrode. Introduction. *Women and Health*. By Marlene B. Goldman. Waltham, MA: Academic, 2012. Xxix. Print.

[806] Borkus, Ellyn R., Alwyn Cassil, and Ann S. O'Malley. *Data Bulletin No. 35: A Snapshot of U.S. Physicians: Key Findings from the 2008 Health Tracking Physician Survey*. Rep. Washington: Center for Studying Health System Change, September 2009. Print.

[807] Smedley, Brian D., Adrienne Y. Stith, and Alan R. Nelson. *Unequal Treatment: Confronting Racial and Ethnic Disparities in Health Care.* Washington, D.C.: National Academies, 2002. Print.

[808] Ibid.

[809] Ibid.

[810] Wise, Tim J. *Colorblind: The Rise of Post Racial Politics and the Retreat from Racial Equity.* San Francisco, CA: City Lights, 2010. 115. Print.

[811] Sabin, Janice A., and Anthony G. Greenwald. "The Influence of Implicit Bias on Treatment Recommendations for 4 Common Pediatric Conditions: Pain, Urinary Tract Infection, Attention Deficit Hyperactivity Disorder, and Asthma." *American Journal of Public Health* 102.5 (2012): 988-95. Print.

[812] Wise, Tim J. "Racism and Health." Boston Public Health Commission, Boston. 11 July 2011. Speech.

[813] Firestone, David. "Frist Points to Racial Inequities in Health Care." *The New York Times.* 9 Jan. 2003. Print.

[814] Ibid.

[815] Ibid.

[816] Mercurio, John. "Lott Apologizes for Thurmond Comment." *CNN.* 09 Dec. 2002. Web. 25 Aug. 2013.

[817] Firestone, David. "Frist Points to Racial Inequities in Health Care." *The New York Times.* 9 Jan. 2003. Print.

[818] Ibid.

[819] Minority Health Improvement and Health Disparity Elimination Act, S.4024, 109th Cong. (2006). Print.

[820] "S.4024 - Minority Health Improvement and Health Disparity Elimination Act." *Congress.gov.* Web. 25 Aug. 2013. <http://beta.congress.gov/bill/109th/senate-bill/4024>.

[821] Kim, Seung Min. "McConnell: I'll Repeal Obamacare as Majority Leader." *POLITICO.* 29 June 2012. Web. 25 Aug. 2013.

[822] Wise, Tim J. "Racism and Health." Boston Public Health Commission, Boston. 11 July 2011. Speech.

[823] Ibid.

[824] Ibid.

[825] Ibid.

[826] Ibid.

Chapter 9 Endnotes

[827] Stein, Sam. "Gingrich Says He Would Arrest Judges With Capitol Police Or U.S. Marshals." *The Huffington Post.* 18 Dec. 2011. Web. 25 Aug. 2013.

[828] Chrysochoos, John. *In Reason We Trust.* Pittsburgh, PA: RoseDog, 2009. 194. Print.

[829] *Disparities Solutions Center.* Massachusetts General Hospital. Web. 25 Aug. 2013.

[830] Massachusetts General Hospital. *MGH Creates National, Hospital-based Center to End Racial and Ethnic Disparities in Health Care.* 26 July 2005. Web. 25 Aug. 2013.

[831] Health Affairs. *Under The ACA, Uninsurance Disparities Narrow For Black And Hispanic Adults. PRNewswire.* Robert Wood Johnson Foundation, 16 Sept. 2015. Web.

[832] "Overview of the Uninsured in the United States: A Summary of the 2011 Current Population Survey." *U.S. Department of Health & Human Services.* Office of the Assistant Secretary for Planning and Evaluation, 13 Sept. 2011. Web. 11 Feb. 2016.

[833] Deal, Anne C., M.D. *Quality of Care for Underserved Populations.* Rep. New York: Commonwealth Fund, 2006. Print.

[834] Dunsmuir, Lindsay. "Many Americans Have No Friends of Another Race: Poll. "*Reuters.* Thomson Reuters, 08 Aug. 2013. Web. 28 Aug. 2013.

[835] "Abercrombie Discrimination Racism Lawsuit: Official Website for Class Action Suit Against Abercrombie." Lieff Cabraser Heimann & Bernstein, LLP, n.d. Web. 25 Aug. 2013.

[836] "A&F CARES." *Abercrombine & Fitch.* Web. 25 Aug. 2013. <http://www.anfcares.org/diversity/internal/jsp>.

[837] "Abercrombie & Fitch to Pay $40M to Settle Bias Case." *USATODAY.COM.* 16 Nov. 2004. Web. 25 Aug. 2013.

[838] "Bank of America Fee Retraction Shows Effect of Consumer Rage." *USATODAY.COM.* 1 Nov. 2011. Web. 25 Aug. 2013.